ON CRIMINALIZATION

Law and Philosophy Library

VOLUME 19

The titles published in this series are listed at the end of this volume.

JONATHAN SCHONSHECK
Le Moyne College, Syracuse, New York

ON CRIMINALIZATION

An Essay in the Philosophy of the Criminal Law

KLUWER ACADEMIC PUBLISHERS
DORDRECHT / BOSTON / LONDON

Library of Congress Cataloging-in-Publication Data

Schonsheck, Jonathan.
On criminalization : an essay in the philosophy of the criminal law / by Jonathan Schonsheck.
p. cm. -- (Law and philosophy library ; v. 19)
Includes bibliographical references and index.

1. Criminal law--Philosophy. I. Title. II. Series.
K5018.S36 1994
345'.001--dc20
[342.501] 93-44434

ISBN 978-90-481-4356-6

Published by Kluwer Academic Publishers,
P.O. Box 17, 3300 AA Dordrecht, The Netherlands.

Kluwer Academic Publishers incorporates
the publishing programmes of
D. Reidel, Martinus Nijhoff, Dr W. Junk and MTP Press.

Sold and distributed in the U.S.A. and Canada
by Kluwer Academic Publishers,
101 Philip Drive, Norwell, MA 02061, U.S.A.

In all other countries, sold and distributed
by Kluwer Academic Publishers Group,
P.O. Box 322, 3300 AH Dordrecht, The Netherlands.

Printed on acid-free paper

This book is dedicated to my wife, Janet A. Coy

without whose loving support it could not have been written,

and

to my son, Stefan Coy Schonsheck

whose arrival made its completion both impossible and necessary.

TABLE OF CONTENTS

Acknowledgments ix

Introduction & Preview 1

PART ONE

ON THE DECIDING WHETHER CRIMINALIZATION IS MORALLY JUSTIFIED

Preface 23

Chapter One: "Balancing" as a Decision-Procedure for Morally Justified Criminalization 29

Chapter Two: The Topography of Actions Relevant to Criminalization 39

Chapter Three: "Filtering" as a Decision-Procedure for Morally Justified Criminalization 63

PART TWO

FAILURES TO JUSTIFY COERCION

Preface 101

Chapter Four: Issues in Paternalism 107
Two Dogmas of Paternalism 107
Scoccia's Novel Condition for Justified Paternalistic Interference 142
Concerns about Feinberg's "Voluntariness Tribunal" 155
Present Selves, Future Selves, and Other Selves: Parfit on Paternalism 175
Some Hard Words about Soft Paternalism 179

Chapter Five: Oblique Attempts to Expand the Criminalizing Authority of the State 183
Concerns about Feinberg's "Garrison Situations" 183
Deconstructing Community Self-Paternalism 196
Of Sheep and Men: On the Criminalization of Bestiality and the "Assumption of Compliance" 215

Chapter Six: The War on "Drugs" 227
A General Philosophical Critique of the "War on Drugs" 233
More Internecine Warfare 290
On the Alleged Racism of "Drug" Decriminalization 294

Overview and Review 301

Index 311

ACKNOWLEDGMENTS

I am grateful for the nurturance, in my early years, of two philosophers and teachers: Kenneth H. Klein of Valparaiso University, and William Richards of the University of Dayton. My interest in the philosophical issues of the criminal law developed at The Ohio State University; I am particularly indebted to John Quigley, Wade Robison, Daniel M. Farrell, and James P. Scanlan. An appointment to the faculty of Williams College gave me the opportunity to discuss a number of problems, and some early attempts at their solution. Over the last fifteen years, Le Moyne College has given great support to my research programs. I am particularly grateful to the Faculty Senate Committee on Research and Development: for Research Grants, a Courseload Reduction for Research, and a Summer Research Stipend.

Conversations with colleagues have ranged from gratifying to invigorating to frustrating—but are, of course, the sustenance of intellectual life. Discussions with Susan Bordo were invariably helpful. And I owe a special debt to J. Barron Boyd, Jr., and Patrick J. Keane. The persistent, intermittently civil challenges of Barron and Pat have forced me to look longer and think harder that I might otherwise have done. These three are true friends.

I am grateful to Douglas N. Husak for a careful reading of the penultimate draft. His comments and criticisms have led to a number of improvements. In the near future, I hope to set aside our agreements, and to continue our quarrel about paternalism.

Gretchen Pearson, one of Le Moyne's professional librarians, has been of great assistance.

The manuscript has benefitted from the copy editing and word processing skills of Jennifer Stanley, Kathy Gervasi, Carol A. Miller, and especially Sharyn Knight.

I hope the dedication makes clear my indebtedness to my wife, Janet A. Coy.

An early version of the decision-procedure for morally justified criminalization which I (now) call "Filtering" appeared in "On Various Hypocrisies of the 'Drugs' in Sports Scandal," *The Philosophical Forum*, Vol. XX, No. 4, Summer 1989. Chapter Three is devoted to the most recent incarnation.

A very short version of my critique of Margie A. Murdock and Kenneth Waxman's argument for motorcycle helmet laws was published in *The Western Journal of Medicine*, March 1993, under the title "Riding, Colliding, Criminalizing."

In an early paper, I raised objections to the early version of Joel Feinberg's "Voluntariness Tribunal." ("On Feinberg's 'Voluntariness Tribunal'," *Proceedings of the Creighton Club* [New York State Philosophical Association], 1979.) Some of those arguments now appear in Chapter Four.

My criticisms of Joel Feinberg's claims about "Garrison Situations," found in Chapter Five, evolved from my paper "Concerns about Feinberg's 'Garrison Situations'," read to the American Philosophical Association - Central Division, 1988.

My critique of Sunstein, also now in Chapter Five, also began with a paper read to the American Philosophical Association (1990), "May the Majority Morally Bind Itself to the Mast?" A later draft was discussed at the 1990 meeting of AMINTAPHIL. That which appears in Chapter Five is a slight modification of my article "Deconstructing Community Self-Paternalism," *Law and Philosophy*, Vol. 10, No. 1, Spring 1991. "Of Sheep and Men" was read to the Creighton Club in the fall of 1990; an earlier version can be found in the Club's *Proceedings*.

Although Chapter Six borrows from "On Various Hypocrisies of the 'Drugs' in Sports Scandal," the argument has been restructured, and the evidence updated. Additionally, I have made use of arguments from my review of *Drug Legalization: For and Against*, ed. Rod L. Evans and Irwin M. Berent, which appeared in *Canadian Philosophical Reviews*, April 1993, and "Degradation, Predation, and Drugs," forthcoming in the *American Philosophical Association Newsletter on Law and Philosophy*. Finally, the Chapter includes two entirely new topics: a critique of an article despite its urging some "drug" decriminalization (as it showcases the superiority of Filtering over Balancing), and a rejoinder to the claim that "drug" decriminalization would be "racist."

Sources and References

Finally, a word about references. I make frequent reference to a limited number of works throughout the entirety of the book; footnoting all these direct quotations would clutter the manuscript. In such cases, I shall bracket a straightforward abbreviation of the work, followed by the page number(s) of the quotation.

Joel Feinberg, *The Moral Limits of the Criminal Law*

Harm to Others [HTO]

Offense to Others [OTO]

Harm to Self [HTS]

Harmless Wrongdoing [HW]

John Stuart Mill, *On Liberty* [OL][1]

And within the individual "topics" of the chapters of Part Two, I shall adopt the convention of bracketed or parenthetical page numbers for mere citations. Footnotes proper will be reserved for other works, and for substantive matters.

---

[1]Joel Feinberg, *The Moral Limits of the Criminal Law* (New York: Oxford University Press). *Harm to Others*, 1984; *Offense to Others*, 1985; *Harm to Self*, 1986; *Harmless Wrongdoing*, 1988. John Stuart Mill, *On Liberty*, ed. Currin V. Shields, (Indianapolis: Bobbs Merrill), 1956.

INTRODUCTION & PREVIEW

I. INTRODUCTION

I begin by introducing the main issues of the work, and inviting their consideration; as enticement, I offer a sketch of their practical importance, and of the philosophical challenge they present. And I provide a preview of the work's organization and central argument.

There is something so obvious that it is easily—and often—overlooked: the enforcing of criminal statutes is the most intrusive and coercive exercise of domestic power by a state. Forcibly preventing people from doing that which they wish to do, forcibly compelling people to do that which they do not wish to do—and wielding force merely *attempting* to compel or prevent—these state activities have extraordinarily serious ramifications. Indeed, no state institutions are likely to have more profound an impact on the lives of individual citizens than those of the criminal justice system. I endorse Herbert Packer's assessment:

> The criminal sanction is the law's ultimate threat. Being punished for a crime is different from being regulated in the public interest, or being forced to compensate another who has been injured by one's conduct, or being treated for a disease. The sanction is at once uniquely coercive and, in the broadest sense, uniquely expensive.[1]

As a consequence, these state activities are in special need of moral warrant. Given the great potential for doing grave injustice, the power of the state embodied in the criminal justice system ought not be exercised in the absence of a complete and compelling moral justification.

Let us dwell for a moment on the realities of an encounter with the criminal justice system. Nothing will establish more firmly the importance and urgency of the issues addressed in this work than a vivid image of just how disruptive it is to be entangled in these institutions. I sketch a "typical" criminal arrest, prosecution, and punishment. Although no case is precisely "typical," most cases will be sufficiently similar for this account to be instructive. These disruptions of one's life are grouped under four headings: the indignities of

---

[1]Herbert L. Packer, *The Limits of the Criminal Sanction* (Stanford: Stanford University Press, 1968), p. 250.

arrest, the expense of defense, the consequences of incarceration, and the encumbrances of a criminal conviction.

I. A. An Encounter with the Criminal Justice System

1. The Indignities of Arrest

An arrest begins with a physical confrontation between the suspect and the arresting officers. Regardless of where this occurs, it is intrusive; the mere arrival of the police is likely to cause a scene, and arouse the curiosity of those in the vicinity: family, friends, neighbors, co-workers, employers, employees, gawking passers-by. The scene may mushroom into a true spectacle; a crowd may gather. The suspect is informed that she or he is under arrest—and everyone within earshot is informed of it too. The arrestee is read one's *Miranda* rights;[2] from watching countless "cop shows" on television, everyone knows that this ceremony—"You have the right to remain silent . . ."—signals the start of serious events. In front of whomever, the arrestee is searched for weapons, and handcuffed, and taken into custody. (Surely the mere thought of being led away in handcuffs is sufficient to trigger anxiety in virtually everyone, and sheer terror in many.) Regardless of one's plans for the remainder of the day, things are going to be different. Obligations—to family and friends, to employees or employers, to students or deans—will go unfulfilled. Anticipated pleasures—watching or participating in sports, playing with one's children, a romantic evening, revising an article for a professional journal—will be postponed, or missed. You are going to jail.

(Perform this thought-experiment. Imagine what it would be like if you, the reader, were to be arrested right now, as you read this passage. Who is around? Are you at home—so your family and neighbors would witness the event? Are you at a college or university—so your colleagues, administrators, and students would see you read your rights, searched, handcuffed, and led away? And now also imagine: in what setting might you be reading this passage such that your arrest would be much worse, much more humiliating? Finally, in what setting would your arrest be the least bad: and wouldn't it still be dreadful?)

---

[2]*Miranda v. Arizona*, 384 U.S. 486.

The series of indignities continues after one reaches the county lock-up. The suspect is fingerprinted and photographed—with, of course, the case number. One's clothes are taken away, exchanged for a prison uniform—and thus one exchanges a part of one's individuality for conformity. This change of clothing is part of the practice of a "strip search," which includes "body cavity" searches. In a body cavity search, a prison official probes the suspect's body cavities—mouth, anus, vagina—for weapons and other contraband. Some prison officials take sadistic pleasures in body cavity searches; some officials find them disgusting, and make that clear through rough and rude treatment. Few arrestees find this a pleasant experience. While naked, the suspect may be showered and de-loused. The suspect is then taken to a "holding cell;" in all likelihood, this will be shared with other persons recently arrested. Very unpleasant things—assault, rape, even murder—can happen in a holding cell; it's smart to be vigilant.

John Irwin catalogues some of (what I am calling) the "indignities of arrest" as follows.

> When persons are arrested and jailed, they suffer more than the obvious forms of discomfort and deprivation: sudden interruption of their affairs; instant and total loss of mobility; abrupt initiation into the jail; a subsequent restriction of activities to a very small area; virtual absence of all opportunities for recreation and expression; unavoidable and constant close contact with strangers, many of whom are threatening or repulsive; and a reduced health regimen that can lead to physical deterioration and occasionally to serious illness. These discomforts and deprivations are generally well recognized, tolerated and often intended by jail administrators, other criminal justice decision makers, and most of the public. Officials and the public want prisoners to suffer and to be controlled. But prisoners are more than inconvenienced and deprived. They are extricated and held away from outside social positions and relationships.[3]

Irwin refers to these consequences collectively as "disintegration."

One may call one's family or attorney, in hopes of making bail. Routinely, the names and addresses of people arrested are published in local newspapers.

---

[3]John Irwin, *Jail: Managing the Underclass in American Society* (Berkeley: University of California Press, 1985), pp. 45-6.

Generally, the space and ink devoted to a person's arrest is roughly proportional to that individual's standing in the community.

2. The Expense of Defense

Mounting a defense against a criminal prosecution is expensive: one must pay for attorneys, investigators, expert witnesses, etc. For a person of means, "it's only money." For the person without adequate resources, one's fate rests in the hands of a public defender. Almost without exception, public defenders are overworked, and thus have limited time to spend on any particular defendant's case. Often they are inexperienced. And they are likely to lack the resources necessary for investigation, expert testimony, and so forth. In a significant percentage of cases, the result is a plea-bargain, a "bargain" which usually includes a plea of "guilty" to some charge, and thus a criminal record.

Thus, the "expense of defense" includes both cash expenditures, and the array of "psychic costs" one will be compelled to pay.

3. The Consequences of Incarceration

The consequences of incarceration divide into the intended, and the unintended yet known.

Of course the main intended consequence of incarceration is the loss of freedom of the individual.

Additional intended consequences might include general deterrence (inducement to others to not elect that criminal activity), specific deterrence (inducement to the individual to not again elect that criminal activity), rehabilitation (re-ordering the individual's preferences), retribution (infliction of suffering, with no further consequences intended, or justification needed), or custodianship (temporarily preventing further [extramural] criminal activity by that individual). All of these, of course, are based upon the individual's loss of freedom.

Additionally, there are many unintended, but perfectly well known, consequences of incarceration. The evidence is incontrovertible that inmates become embittered, and brutalized, by incarceration. Many receive tutoring in subsequent criminality, becoming far more dangerous after incarceration than before it.

Although imprisoned as the perpetrators of crimes, inmates very often become the victims of crimes. In some instances, inmates are subjected to the violence of prison guards and other prison officials. More often, inmates are subjected to the violence of another inmate, or other inmates: robbery, assault, battery, rape, and murder.[4]

4. The Encumbrances of a Criminal Conviction

The disruptions of one's life do not end with one's departure from prison; a criminal conviction will constitute an encumbrance throughout the remainder of one's life. According to Richard G. Singer,

> It is generally thought that when a person leaves prison, or is released from probation or parole, his punishment has ended. For many offenders, however, the most serious and long-lasting aspect of their punishment is only beginning, since every state, to a greater or lesser degree, prohibits the ex-felon from exercising some of the most basic rights of free citizens, ranging from the right to vote to the right to employment by the state. These barriers, called collateral consequences, are for many criminals—particularly for the 50 percent of convicted persons who are never imprisoned—anything but collateral; they are, in fact, the most persistent punishments that are inflicted for crime.[5]

The "civil disabilities" imposed on those convicted of a crime vary from jurisdiction to jurisdiction, and vary with the nature of the offense.[6] Singer's

---

[4]Cf. James A. Inciardi, *Criminal Justice*, Second Edition, (Orlando: Harcourt Brace Jovanovich, 1987), Chapter 15: "Penitentiaries, Prisons and Other Correctional Institutions: A Look Inside the Inmate World; Peter Kratcoski and Donald B. Walker, *Criminal Justice in America: Process and Issues* (New York: Random House, 1984), "Brutality in the Prison," pp. 377-80. More generally, cf. *Prison Violence in America*, ed. Michael Braswell, Steven Dillingham and Reid Montgomery, Jr. (Cincinnati: Anderson Publishing Co., 1985).

[5]"Conviction: Civil Disabilities," signed article in the *Encyclopedia of Crime and Justice*, ed. Sanford H. Kadish, Volume 1 (New York: The Free Press, A Division of Macmillan, Inc., 1983), p. 243.

[6]According to Singer, this variation defies rational defense; in some jurisdictions, seemingly minor offenses can trigger substantial civil disabilities. This strengthens my point. Enacting new criminal legislation can impose "encumbrances of criminal conviction" that are crushing—and may be well out of proportion to the social threat posed by the action made criminal.

list of the possibilities includes: loss of citizenship, loss of the right to vote, loss of the right to hold public office (both elective and appointive), loss of standing to sue, and loss of the right to serve on a jury.

Additionally, "private rights" may be revoked. Reflect on these consequences of a criminal conviction.

> . . . in many states conviction alone, or conviction and imprisonment, may provide the impetus to legal dissolution of family ties.
>
> . . . a conviction may be declared grounds for divorce . . . .
>
> Conviction or imprisonment may result in the forfeiture of parental rights as well. Indirectly, imprisonment may serve as a basis for a finding of abandonment; in dependency and neglect proceedings in two states, a parent's criminality is an express ground for terminating parental rights. In virtually every state, a conviction is evidence of unfitness in a custody proceeding.
>
> A criminal conviction may also prevent the offender from participating in insurance, pension and workmen's compensation programs.
>
> Certainly the most pervasive disqualification is the exclusion, by statute or by administrative decision, of the convicted felon from specific types of employment. Because it significantly reduces the convicted offender's ability to reenter society as a working citizen, this exclusion is thought by many to either restrict offenders to menial jobs, or to impel them to return to crime.[7]

In all these ways, an encounter with the criminal justice system profoundly disrupts an individual's life. Because of this, we, as a society, need to be particularly sure of our justification before subjecting fellow citizens to the indignities of arrest, the expense of defense, the consequences—both intended, and unintended, but known—of incarceration, and the encumbrances of conviction. I agree with Joel Feinberg's claim that, "Given the inherent costs of criminalization, when a particular legal prohibition oversteps the limit of moral legitimacy, it is itself a serious moral crime."[8]

---

[7]Singer, p. 245.

[8]Joel Feinberg, *Harm to Others*, Volume One of *The Moral Limits of the Criminal Law* (New York: Oxford University Press, 1984), p. 4.

I. B. Determining Whether Actions May Morally be Criminalized: Two Concerns

Are there grounds for confidence that the state does not now exceed its moral authority in operating the criminal justice system? I think not. There is no consensus, even among those professionally responsible—legislators, jurists, philosophers of the criminal law—on what constitutes a "complete and compelling moral justification" for making some action a criminal offense. One hears an incessant clamoring for lengthening the calendar of crimes; it arises from editorials and letters to the editor, from legislators and those actively campaigning to become legislators, from jurists and philosophers. And yet there is no generally accepted criterion for determining which actions may morally be criminalized.

1. The "Balancing" of Reasons

By default, implicitly or explicitly, legislators and jurists and philosophers have come to use a decision-procedure of "Balancing" to determine whether an action may morally be criminalized, whether a criminal prohibition is morally justified. We are to picture a chemistry lab beam balance, with a pan suspended from each end of the beam. The reasons *in favor of* criminalizing the action in question are placed on one pan; the reasons *against* criminalization are placed on the other pan; the "weightier" reasons are to prevail.

I believe that this decision-procedure—or, more accurately, this metaphor masquerading as a decision-procedure—is deeply flawed. The several chapters of Part One of this work are devoted to exposing those flaws, and to defending an alternative way of thinking about criminalization, an alternative way of determining whether the criminalization of some action is morally justified.

The complete critique of "Balancing" requires significant preliminary work, work that is done in Chapter Two. However, there is a mistake often made in arguments about criminalization which can be discussed without that preliminary work. And discussing it will, I think, whet the philosophical appetite for the issues which follow.

The metaphor of "Balancing" includes no specification of which "weights," which reasons are to be placed on the two pans. This facilitates the *neglect* of essentials, the neglect of reasons which must be "weighed" if one is to have any chance of arriving at a defensible decision. No jurist, no philosopher of the criminal law, would—upon reflection—deny the importance of the realities of law enforcement in determining the moral justifiability of criminalizing a particular action. Whether it is morally permissible to criminally prohibit a given action depends, in some way, in some measure, on the possibility, the practicability, and the various "costs" of enforcing, or attempting to enforce, that prohibition. But while no philosopher, no jurist, would deny this, many are prone to forgetting it. One often encounters arguments for criminalizing some action which make no mention of the pragmatic issues of enforcement, or which mention them only in passing. Only rarely does one encounter a serious attempt to "weigh" such reasons against a proposed statute. Despite the fact that the deleterious consequences of attempting to enforce some statute could be so serious that that statute is not morally justified—and no philosopher, no jurist would (upon reflection) deny this possibility—the pragmatics of enforcement regularly get short shrift, or no shrift at all.

2. The "Assumption of Compliance"

Philosophers and jurists are also prone to making (what I shall call) the "assumption of compliance," to implicitly assume that the reaction of citizens to new criminal legislation will be *compliance.* Of course no philosopher, no jurist would be so foolish as to *proclaim* compliance—among the most obvious truths about the criminal law is that not everyone will obey it. And yet one often encounters arguments that some action may morally be criminalized, that some criminal statute is justified, which presupposes universal, or nearly universal, compliance.

The "assumption of compliance" admits various degrees, and takes various forms.

The most obvious form, and greatest degree, is to wholly neglect all the pragmatics of law enforcement, to fail to consider *any* of the difficulties which might arise in the attempt to enforce a statute, whether extant or proposed. In making this sort of an "assumption of compliance," the various costs of law enforcement are ignored, or are assumed to be negligible, and then neglected. And the various "side-effects" of criminalization are ignored, or are assumed to be negligible, and then neglected. Of the same form, but to a lesser degree: underassessing the social costs of enforcement, costs which might—for all one has shown—exceed the anticipated benefits of the statute.

Another prominent way the "assumption of compliance" is made is to use "prohibit" and "prevent" interchangeably: "Law *L* will prevent ________," with the blank being filled by reference to some activity deemed (by the speaker) to be socially undesirable. In some cases, the word "prevention" even appears in the title of the statute. In some cases, other terms are used to collapse "prohibit" to "prevent": "We don't *permit* that sort of behavior;" "That is *not allowed* here." But of course the enactment of a criminal law does not, strictly speaking, "prevent" people from electing the proscribed activity. It merely establishes the conduct as criminal; whether the enactment has an impact on the incidence of the activity is an *empirical* issue. It might be the case that the incidence of the proscribed conduct declines precipitously. In such a case, we might (loosely) say that the law "prevented" the conduct. But such a claim could be proved—if it were indeed true—only by the facts concerning that law's *consequences*, and not the mere fact of its enactment. It might be the case, on the contrary, that the incidence of the proscribed conduct remained unchanged. In such a case—whether speaking strictly or loosely—it would be just false to say that the law "prevented" anything. Furthermore, an empirical investigation of the consequences of the statute might unearth a host of unpleasant surprises.[9]

The use of the term "prevent" can itself constitute the "assumption of compliance." Suppose a philosopher were to claim that "The state has a right to prevent action *a*." If incautious, we immediately begin to think about the characteristics of action *a*, and our own theory of the state's range of morally permissible action. If cautious, however, we admit the obvious: "preventing" is an *achievement*, not a task; whether a state can in fact "prevent" action *a*—or prevent anything at all—is an *empirical* issue. The right that the state has—if indeed it has the right—is to *attempt to* prevent action *a*. When stated this way, two important things happen. First, we are forced to confront the possibility of failure, the possibility that nothing the state can do would succeed, would in fact "prevent" action *a*. Second, we are forced to confront the issue of *alternatives*, the array of ways the state might attempt to prevent action *a*. And immediately we are led to issues of efficacy, of cost, of the moral permissibility of the attempts themselves, etc. In short: it is illicit to ask whether the state has a right to "prevent" actions, as that presupposes that the state can in fact succeed. When one asks whether the state has a right to *attempt to* prevent actions, one begins an investigation as to whether there are

---

[9]At numerous points in the text, I investigate the consequences of criminalization, unearthing an array of unpleasant surprises.

any measures the state may morally take which will in fact reduce the incidence of action *a*.

Yet another prominent way in which the "assumption of compliance" is made, is to envision a society in which the proscribed conduct simply doesn't occur. Philosophers of the criminal law ask whether that society would be better (on some criterion or another) were the citizens to not elect certain actions; upon answering in the affirmative, they rush to the conclusion that a criminal statute is thereby justified. Not factored into the argument is the possibility that the response of some citizens to the new statute will not be cheerful (or even grumbling) compliance, but rather will be furtive, resentful and alienated *non*compliance. The enactment of the criminal statute may well *not* result in a society free of the proscribed conduct, but rather a society in which the proscribed conduct persists, while scarce criminal justice resources are devoted to detecting violations, and to prosecuting, and incarcerating, any apprehended perpetrators. The claim that *that* society is "better" than the same society before the enactment of the new criminal statute may well be a matter of some controversy, and may be demonstrably false. In any event, only substantial argument could prove that that society is indeed superior.

Perhaps the most subtle way to make the "assumption of compliance" is to misdescribe the behavior of citizens in a way such that compliance with a prohibitory statute could reasonably be expected. However, when that behavior is accurately described, compliance with a prohibitory statute can*not* reasonably be expected.[10]

Philosophers of the criminal law—and jurists, and legislators, and ordinary citizens—are not entitled to make the "assumption of compliance," not entitled to assume that citizens will universally (or near universally, or even "for the most part") obey newly enacted criminal statutes. To make the "assumption of compliance" is to make a methodological mistake; any argument for morally justified criminalization which rests upon the "assumption of compliance" is flawed. Indeed, an essential task in justifying *any* criminal statute is an inquiry into the actual consequences of the enactment and enforcement of that statute. The proponent of criminalization must ask—and answer—myriad questions about the proposed statute. What "side-effects" will result from criminalization—and will the "costs" of these side-effects be so high that they exceed the expected "benefits" of criminalization? Will criminalization, for

---

[10]Chapter Five, Topic Three: "Of Sheep and Men."

example, create a "crime tariff" on a commodity for which there is an inelastic demand, thereby enriching those willing to break the law, and providing the funds to corrupt various public officials, and inducing consumers of that commodity to live a life of acquisitive crime in order to secure the money needed to meet the artificially high price of the commodity?[11] What social resources will be devoted to enforcement efforts—and will this be a wise expenditure of scarce criminal-justice dollars? And as regards the behavior which constitutes a violation of the statute—does it pose so serious a threat to the social order that imprisonment—at the cost of the individual's liberty, and significant resources of the state—is warranted? Could the incidence of the behavior be reduced to an acceptable level by means less coercive and costly than a criminal statute? And the list goes on. In sum: No argument for morally justified criminalization is sound unless it takes full consideration of the realities of law enforcement.

Of course, one could make the "assumption of compliance" without relying upon the metaphor of "Balancing" to guide one's thinking about criminalization. And one could rely upon Balancing without making the "assumption of compliance," without forgetting to investigate the pragmatics of state coercion. I think it more than coincidental, however, that those who rely upon Balancing are prone to making the assumption of compliance. Minimally this is true: if our thinking about criminalization were guided by a different metaphor, a metaphor which made it more difficult to neglect the issues of enforcement, then the prospects for correctly determining which actions may morally be criminalized would be greatly improved. Bearing in mind the transcending seriousness of an encounter with the criminal justice system, the importance of getting these matters right can hardly be overstated. To be subjected to the indignities of arrest, the expense of defense, the consequences of incarceration, and the encumbrances of conviction—all for electing an action which ought not be a criminal offense, an action whose criminalization is not morally justified—is to be the victim of egregious injustice.

My more general point is this: it is mistaken to maintain, or to be fairly committed to maintaining, positions like these:

---

[11]The term "crime tariff" is from Herbert Packer, *op.cit.*

> "Criminalizing action *a* is morally justified—although the side effects of enforcing a statute against action *a* are so serious that action *a* ought not be criminalized."
>
> "Criminalizing action *a* is morally justified—but it would be wrong to devote scarce resources to enforcing a statute prohibiting action *a*."
>
> "Criminalizing action *a* is morally justified—although the incidence of action *a* could be as effectively reduced by a program of public education."

And so on. Yet the philosophical literature is replete with such instances: the claim that some specified criminal prohibition is justified, or would be justified, without an adequate consideration of the array of consequences of the proposed criminalization. For all that has been shown, the statute under discussion might well be seriously counterproductive, or a waste of resources, or pointless, or excessively intrusive, etc.—and thus is *not* morally justified. Indeed, the greatest philosophical controversy swirls about actions that would be prohibited under the principle of Legal Paternalism, or the principle of Legal Moralism, or as instances of "harmless wrongdoing," or under various novel expansions of the state's moral authority to criminalize actions.[12]

It is a methodological mistake to assume compliance. Ironically, it is in precisely *these* cases that assuming compliance is clearly unwarranted. Citizens are very likely to view the state as "meddling" in their private lives, and are likely to ignore the statute.

A central thesis of this work is that there is a gap—indeed, a chasm—between (i) showing that an action is inconsiderate, or unhelpful, or even harmful, that it is "foolish, perverse or wrong,"[13] and (ii) showing that that action ought to be a criminal offense. There are many actions which it would be wrong for a person to do, but which it would be wrong for the state to criminalize. Let me illustrate this with a straightforward example, saving the controversial cases for later chapters.

---

[12]These principles are discussed at length in Chapter Three. For present purposes, it is enough to say that Legal Paternalism countenances the criminalization of an action solely because it harms the agent oneself; Legal Moralism countenances the criminalization of an action solely because it is immoral.

[13]John Stuart Mill, *On Liberty*, ed. Currin V. Shields, (Indianapolis: Bobbs Merrill, 1956), p. 16.

I. C. Wrongs and Crimes

There is conclusive evidence, according to a recent report of the Environmental Protection Agency, that so-called "second-hand smoke" is harmful to non-smokers.

> William K. Reilly, the E.P.A. Administrator, told a news briefing that the report supported a growing scientific consensus that smoking is not just a health risk to smokers but also a significant risk to nonsmokers, particularly spouses and children.[14]

Among the findings:

> Higher exposures to secondhand smoke, like that in enclosed homes, small rooms or automobiles, cause higher risks. The spouses of people who smoke at home face a high lung cancer risk of about 2 in 1,000, Mr. Reilly said.
>
> Health officials said the dangers to infants and children were particularly alarming. These were among the report's findings on the effects of second-hand smoke on children:
>
> It increases the frequency and severity of symptoms in 200,000 to 1 million children with asthma and also increases the risk of developing asthma.
>
> It causes 150,000 to 300,000 cases of respiratory infections like bronchitis and pneumonia each year in children up to 18 months of age.
>
> It also causes fluid buildup in the middle ear, a condition that can lead to ear infections common among children.[15]

Given the fact that secondhand smoke causes significant harms—especially in confined spaces like homes—it might be thought morally permissible to criminalize the action of forcing others to become "passive smokers" in their own homes.[16] But a moment's reflection on the pragmatics of enforcing such a statute is sufficient to reveal that the "costs" of such a statute would exceed the "benefits." Begin by asking: how would police come to know that the

---

[14]As reported in *The New York Times*, Friday, January 8, 1993, p. A14.

[15]*Ibid.*

[16]It should be noted that the E.P.A. does not make this recommendation.

statute had been violated? Either by surveillance, or by a complaint from an affected party. The sorts of surveillance techniques that would be required to determine that someone was smoking in the unwilling presence of another would make a mockery of the U.S. Constitution's protection against "unwarranted" searches.[17] And such surveillance would inevitably yield unrelated, sensitive information that could be put to nefarious purposes, like blackmail. Suppose, on the contrary, that arrests would be made only upon information supplied to authorities. How might this information be obtained? Might elementary schoolteachers ask their pupils whether Mommy or Daddy smokes in the home? Would the children's answers be reliable, or a way to win a favorite teacher's favor? Would parents counsel their children to lie about family practices, and threaten to punish truth-telling? Suppose that arrests would be made only upon a criminal complaint, sworn out by an adult. This would leave children, the most vulnerable, unprotected—unless an adult could file a complaint on their behalf. But this would open the floodgates; complaints would pour in from various members of nuclear and extended dysfunctional families: Dad has Mom arrested, Mom has Dad arrested, Mom and her Mother have Dad arrested, etc., etc.[18] And think of the social resources that could be expended on this. Claims and counterclaims would proliferate; trials would be chaotic. Unsuccessful prosecutions would result in bitterness and resentment; successful prosecutions would result in bitterness, resentment and incarceration. In most instances, I suspect, it is better—even for affected children—to have parents smoking at home, rather than smoking in jail.

Health and Human Services Secretary Dr. Louis W. Sullivan "said his department's Centers for Disease Control and Prevention would use the report's findings to begin a public information campaign on the dangers of secondhand smoke."[19] This, in my judgement, is an excellent idea; it is precisely what the government ought to be doing. And laws which prohibit

---

[17]See Amendment IV.

[18]Imagine the following scene.

Parent: "That was a *terrible* thing to do. You're grounded for two weeks."

Child: "If you ground me, I'll dial 911 and tell them you smoke in the house, and that it makes me sick." [coughs loudly]

Parent: "Well, OK, you're *not* grounded. But if you ever set the couch on fire again, you're in big trouble!"

[19]*The New York Times*, *op. cit.*

smoking in public places are likely justified. But smoking in one's home, in the unwilling presence of others, is a clear example of an action which is wrong, which harms others, but which ought not be a crime.

II. PREVIEW

This work is divided into two Parts. Part One, containing Chapters One through Three, is called "On the Deciding Whether Criminalization is Morally Justified." The slight awkwardness of the title is wholly intentional; my concern is not with the criminalization of any particular actions, but rather "on the deciding," on the determination of justifiability itself.

In Chapter One, I criticize "Balancing" as a decision-procedure for morally justified criminalization. Virtually every philosopher of the criminal law has employed "Balancing"—usually without comment, always without defense. I argue that this decision-procedure is deeply flawed. Reasons in favor of criminalizing particular actions are of many different sorts, arising from different philosophical positions as to the extent of the moral authority of the state. And reasons against criminalization are also of many different sorts, including the presumption in favor of liberty, and an array of pragmatic constraints on criminalization (for example, the difficulties of enforcement, and the unintended side-effects of criminal legislation). "Balancing" requires the precise assignment of "weight" to each of these different sorts of reasons; this "comparing of incomparables" is philosophically suspect. Worse, this decision-procedure includes no specification of the various *sorts* of items to be "weighed," the items to be placed on one pan of the balance or the other. This feature facilitates the omission of items which *must* be weighed if one is to obtain a justifiable determination. An additional consequence of using this decision-procedure is that, when it is decided that the deleterious pragmatic consequences of a criminal statute "outweigh" the reasons in favor of it, the supporters of that statute are likely to view the matter as their "principles" being outweighed by "practicalities." This gives rise to much of the controversy that surrounds various criminal laws, and proposed criminal laws.

In Chapter Two, I introduce the concept of a "topography of actions." I then review and modify the topography of actions discernible in John Stuart Mill's *On Liberty*, developing a perfectly neutral topography.

In his classic work, Mill argues for a "Sphere of Individual Liberty"—a set of actions over which each competent adult ought to be sovereign. Most of the subsequent controversy has focused on the "size" and the "contents" of that set of protected actions. In this chapter, I focus on a related but different matter. The vast majority of philosophers of the criminal law have implicitly assumed that proving some action does not fall within the "Sphere of Individual Liberty" is sufficient, or very nearly sufficient, to prove that that action is justifiably criminalized. I reject this inference; I argue that some actions are neither in the Sphere of Individual Liberty, nor are justifiably made criminal offenses. The proponent of criminalization, upon proving that some particular action ought not be left to individual choice (i.e., is not "protected" by arguments for respecting autonomy), must address a new set of issues. The proponent of criminalization (or other sorts of coercion) must show that there are specific measures the state (or private citizens) could take that both (i) are an effective remedy, and (ii) are not morally impermissible on other grounds, on grounds other than that the action is protected by respect for autonomy.

The relationships among the various sets of actions I discuss are most perspicuously shown when drawn as relations among sets; I use several diagrams—hence the term "topography." A derivative notion is the "topographic error;" this error is committed when one, for example, assumes that showing "action *a* is not in the Sphere of Individual Liberty" is indeed sufficient to prove "the state may criminalize (or private citizens interfere with) action *a*."

In Chapter Three, I reject the process of "Balancing" in favor of a quite different decision-procedure, what I call "Filtering." For an action to be justifiably criminalized, it must pass—successfully and successively—through three distinct Filters. The first filter is the Principles Filter; at this Filter one addresses the issues of the moral authority of the state. Located here are the battles among "Liberals" and the proponents of other principles: Legal Paternalism, Legal Moralism, etc. The second filter is the Presumptions Filter: once it has been determined that an action falls within the moral purview of the state, a determination must be made as to whether the incidence of the action could be sufficiently reduced by some state actions, by measures less coercive than a criminal statute—for example, a program of public education. The final filter is the Pragmatics Filter: if an action falls under the purview of the state, and cannot be sufficiently discouraged by non-criminal deterrents, one must ask: what will be the pragmatic consequences of the enactment and enforcement of such a statute—and what new moral issues arise from these consequences? At this Filter, one must perform a cost/benefit analysis of the statute's consequences. Only if the benefits exceed the costs does the action pass through the Pragmatics Filter.

Filtering provides a set of necessary and sufficient conditions for justified criminalization. If an action falls under the moral purview of the state, and it cannot be sufficiently discouraged by non-statute measures, and the enactment of a criminal statute would produce a net benefit, then such a statute is morally justified. Conversely: if an action is not of a *sort* with which the state may morally interfere, or if that action can be adequately discouraged by less coercive means, or if the enactment of a statute prohibiting that action would produce a net excess of cost over benefit, then such a statute is not justified. Finally, no purported justification for a criminal statute is complete unless it is persuasive at all three Filters.

Of course the issues addressed at each Filter will often be, and may remain, controversial. But it is a virtue of Filtering that these controversies are organized in a way conducive to philosophical progress.

The diagrams of Chapter Two, together with the arguments of Chapter Three, help highlight an important fact about criminalization: that there is a considerable difference between showing that an action ought not be elected, and showing that that action ought to be a *crime*.

The chapters of Part Two are devoted to a variety of "Failures to Justify Coercion." Each of the chapters is composed of several topics.

In Chapter Four, I use the decision-procedure I call Filtering, and the work I have done on the topography of actions, to reject the positions of some paternalists.

The first topic I address: laws requiring the use of seat belts in automobiles, and helmets on motorcycles. I have two goals here. I want to determine whether the state is morally justified in legally requiring the use of these devices, and I want to block the "slippery slope" argument of many Legal Paternalists: "If these laws are justified—and they are—then *other* paternalistic laws are justified, for example . . . ."

In the second portion of the chapter, I criticize a recent essay on "paternalism," Danny Scoccia's "Paternalism and Respect for Autonomy"[20] Scoccia's piece is a paradigmatic case of the "topographic error." Having successfully argued that desires and values, as well as choices, can fail to be

---

[20]Danny Scoccia, "Paternalism and Respect for Autonomy," *Ethics*, Vol. 100, No. 2, January 1990.

autonomous, he concludes that "forcible interference" with such is permissible—without adequately specifying the sorts of forcible interference he has in mind, much less arguing that that sort of interference isn't objectionable or prohibited on other moral grounds. Additionally, I argue that the criterion proposed by Scoccia is not helpful to a person contemplating paternalistic interference, is not helpful "prospectively." Thus, it is not "action-guiding." Yet it is precisely such guidance when contemplating paternalistic interference that would have practical, as well as philosophical, importance.

Specific sorts of interference *are* proposed by Joel Feinberg, first in "Legal Paternalism,"[21] and more recently in *Harm to Self*.[22] I argue that Feinberg too commits a "topographic error," moving immediately from the premise that certain actions are not protected by respect for autonomy, to the conclusion that state interference is justified. "Filtering" directs our attention to the issues of just how Feinberg's proposed "Voluntariness Tribunal" would operate in practice; careful investigation reveals significant moral objections to the proposed institution.

Derek Parfit, in *Reasons and Persons*,[23] claims that "We ought to prevent anyone from doing to his future self what it would be wrong to do to other people."[24] Even if one accepted the propriety of protecting future selves—actions which harm one's future self are not in the "Sphere of Individual Liberty"—precisely how would the state attempt to achieve this? To accept Parfit's position is to countenance state interference on a massive scale. Parfit's argument is another instance of the "topographic error." Furthermore, one must wonder about the strength of "We ought." In an era of scarce resources, how high a priority ought to be given to the task of protecting future selves from present selves? Most people, I suspect, would choose to devote these resources to protecting their present selves from *other* present selves.

Finally I have some "Hard Words for Soft Paternalism," arguing that the proponents of so-called "soft paternalism" are particularly prone to "topographic errors."

---

[21]Joel Feinberg, "Legal Paternalism," *Canadian Journal of Philosophy*, Vol. 1, No. 1.

[22]Volume 3 of *The Moral Limits of the Criminal Law* (Oxford University Press; 1984, 85, 86, 88).

[23]Derek Parfit, *Reasons and Persons* (Oxford: Clarendon Press, 1984). As I shall argue, the use of "prevent" here is an instance of the "assumption of compliance."

[24]Parfit, #107.

In Chapter Five, I use the decision-procedure I call Filtering, and the work I have done on the topography of actions, to reject three oblique attempts to expand the criminalizing authority of the state.

In *Harm to Self*, Feinberg claims that actions which are self-regarding in ordinary circumstances become "other-regarding" when society is in a situation analogous to a military garrison under siege. After attacking the plausibility of the analogy, I grant it *arguendo*, and investigate the implications. Even if, in garrison situations, various actions are no longer self-regarding, it remains to be shown that there is anything the state may morally do. As it turns out, the "remedy" proposed by Feinberg is the state's attempting to compel "specific performance" by the citizenry—and this is notoriously difficult. Thus, even if such actions are other-regarding and not self-regarding (and consequently are not in the "Sphere of Individual Liberty"), it may well be the case that *nothing* the state could do would be both effective and morally permissible.

Cass R. Sunstein, in "Legal Interference with Private Preferences,"[25] claims that citizens who constitute a majority may morally use criminal statutes to foreclose their own options. According to Sunstein, this would be a political analog of the story of Ulysses and the Sirens. Richard J. Arneson, in "Liberalism, Freedom and Community,"[26] endorses a similar position, calling it community "self-paternalism." While this proposed justification of criminal statutes has initial plausibility, close scrutiny reveals it to be morally reprehensible. At its core, this is the claim that it is permissible to threaten some individuals with criminal prosecution, and actually incarcerate them, in order to compensate for the weakness of will of other individuals. Despite its initial attractiveness, the proposed justification is shown to not be *self*-paternalism at all, but rather is shown to be a paradigmatic violation of the Kantian maxim prohibiting the treatment of other people as means merely.

Richard J. Arneson also argues, in "Liberalism, Freedom, and Community," that Joel Feinberg's liberalism ought to be rejected in favor of "utilitarian liberalism." Arneson claims that the criminalization of bestiality—an instance of "harmless wrongdoing"—shows that utilitarian liberalism is in-practice different from, and superior to, "Feinberg-style liberalism." I reject Arneson's

---

[25]Cass R. Sunstein, "Legal Interference with Private Preferences," 53 University of Chicago Law Review 4, 1986.

[26]Richard J. Arneson, "Liberalism, Freedom and Community," *Ethics*, Vol. 100, No. 2, January 1990.

"stylized" account of the practice of bestiality in favor of the account offered by sex researcher Alfred C. Kinsey. I then look to the consequences of criminalizing bestiality—our attention is directed there by "Filtering"—arguing that utility does *not* in fact favor criminalization. Thus, Arneson has not shown a practical difference between the two sorts of liberalism, much less the superiority of "utilitarian liberalism." Hidden in Arneson's "stylized" account of the practice of bestiality is a subtle instance of the "assumption of compliance."

Chapter Six is devoted to a critique of the "War on Drugs." Portions of it are based on my article "On Various Hypocrisies of the 'Drugs' in Sports Scandal."[27] Despite its title, this is an article in the philosophy of the criminal law. At the time it was written, there was minimal interest in the issues of "drug" laws; introducing those issues by reference to professional athletes was a "journalistic hook." It is an understatement to say that no "hook" is now needed when discussing proposals of "drug" decriminalization. I shall respond to an array of objections that has appeared in the philosophical literature, and in the mass media, to the decriminalization of various psychoactives. In particular, I shall argue against the claim that decriminalization is racist. I shall argue that, on the contrary, the burdens of criminalization itself weigh especially heavily on African Americans; decriminalization would lighten those burdens. Examining the impact of decriminalization reveals new and powerful arguments for a policy change.

I synopsize the work of the whole, providing an accessible account of the flow of the entire argument, in the "Overview and Review."

Just as the proof of the pudding is in the taste, the proof of a decision-procedure is in its applications. Filtering insists that, in morally assessing a criminal statute, we consider means of altering behavior less coercive (and costly) than a statute. And it insists that we consider actually attempting to enforce a proposed statute (without assuming compliance), assessing both its costs and benefits, before claiming that the statute is justified. Doing these things undermines the various claims about justifiable coercion made by Gerald Dworkin and Joel Feinberg (motorcycle helmet laws), Danny Scoccia (private interference with nonautonomous actions), Feinberg ("Voluntariness Tribunal"), Derek Parfit ("paternalism"), Feinberg

[27]Jonathan Schonsheck, "On Various Hypocrisies of the 'Drugs' in Sports Scandal," *The Philosophical Forum*, Vol. XX, No. 4, Summer 1989, pp. 247-85.

("garrison situations"), Richard J. Arneson and Cass R. Sunstein ("community self-paternalism"), and Arneson ("utilitarian liberalism"). As a decision-procedure for criminalization, Filtering points the way to arguing against these attempts to morally authorize the use of force. And if my arguments are sound, considerably less coercion is morally justified than is claimed to be justified by these philosophers.

PART ONE

ON THE DECIDING WHETHER CRIMINALIZATION IS MORALLY JUSTIFIED

PREFACE

One frequently encounters arguments—in contexts ranging from newspaper and television editorials, news magazines, and letters-to-the-editor; to the professional journals of philosophy, and law reviews—advocating the criminalization or decriminalization of various actions. Typically, these offer one or two (or more) reasons in support of the claim about criminalization; sometimes contrary arguments are raised and rebutted (in task, if not in achievement). Typically these have the structure of a grocery shopping list: here's a reason, here's another reason, here's yet another reason. Wholly absent is the specification of a criterion of *sufficiency*: what number of reasons, or what strength of reasons, are sufficient, are conclusive, do indeed secure the case for criminalization? (Typically, of course, the authors of these pieces are convinced that they *have* satisfied some sufficiency criterion, *have* made a conclusive case . . . .) Logically prior to such a criterion of sufficiency—but at least as elusive—is the *recipe* for constructing a conclusive case: how does one go about building an overarching argument that would satisfy a criterion of sufficiency, were such a criterion established? Or is there nothing more to be done than the enumerating of arguments?

The three chapters of Part One are devoted to various issues of the *deciding whether* the criminalization of actions is morally justified—i.e., to the matter of a *decision-procedure* for morally justified criminalization, and to a criterion of sufficiency. I mean nothing excessively technical by "decision-procedure," just the answer to the question "How ought one *go about deciding* which actions are justifiably criminalized, and which actions are not justifiably criminalized?" And I mean nothing excessively technical by "criterion of sufficiency," just the answer to the question "What does one have to show, if one is to show that an action is (or is not) justifiably criminalized?"

More than a century ago, John Stuart Mill lamented that

> There is, in fact, no recognized principle by which the propriety or impropriety of government interference is customarily tested. People decide according to their personal preferences. Some, whenever they

> see any good to be done, or evil to be remedied, would willingly instigate the government to undertake the business, while others prefer to bear almost any amount of social evil rather than add one to the departments of human interests amenable to government control. And men range themselves on one or the other side in any particular case, according to the degree of interest which they feel in the particular thing which it is proposed that the government should do, or according to the belief they entertain that the government would, or would not, do it in the manner they prefer; but very rarely on account of any opinion to which they consistently adhere, as to what things are fit to be done by a government. [OL 12]

What is wanted is a reasoned position to which one *could* "consistently adhere" as to "what things are fit to be done by a government"—in particular, with the coercive power of the institutions of the criminal justice system. Such a decision-procedure, properly employed, could be used to justify existing statutes—or, alternatively, to provide good grounds for revision or repeal. Additionally, it could be applied to proposed new statutes, providing structure and organization to the dispute, assisting in the construction of the most persuasive case in favor of, and against, the proposed statute.

Despite the obvious value of a decision-procedure for morally justified criminalization, philosophers of the criminal law have devoted very little attention to the matter. Indeed, quite recently Douglas N. Husak echoed Mill's lament:

> Surprisingly few legal philosophers have developed detailed views about the conditions that must be satisfied before conduct may be criminalized. Commentators either avoid this problem altogether, content themselves with platitudes, or admit it to be too difficult to tackle. The absence of a viable theory about this issue has had a devastating impact upon criminal practice.[1]

The central goal of Part One of this work is to fill that lacuna, to explain just how a person—the good jurist, the good legislator, the good philosopher of the criminal law—ought to *go about* deciding which actions, which classes of actions, are justifiably made criminal offenses, and which actions are not. My

---

[1]Douglas N. Husak, *Philosophy of Criminal Law* (Totowa: Rowman and Littlefield, 1987), p. 225. [internal cites omitted]

goal is to design a decision-procedure which provides a satisfying justification for various actions' being criminal, and that can be used in deciding whether the calendar of crimes ought to be contracted, by decriminalizing certain actions, or expanded, by criminalizing additional actions.

To achieve the goal of defending a new decision-procedure for criminalization, I shall argue for its superiority over the decision-procedure relied upon—implicitly or explicitly—by most jurists and philosophers of law: "Balancing." In Balancing, one is to "weigh" all the reasons in favor of criminalizing a particular action, and "weigh" all the reasons *against* criminalization; the "weightier" set of reasons is to prevail.

Figure 1

I shall advocate, in competition with this one-step procedure, a three-step procedure I call "Filtering." Actions are justifiably criminalized only if they pass, successively and successfully, through three distinct "Filters." At the Principles Filter, one determines whether the action in question falls within the moral authority of the state. At the Presumptions Filter, one determines whether the incidence of the action can be reduced to an acceptable level by means less coercive and intrusive than a criminal statute. At the Pragmatics Filter, one investigates the consequences of enacting and enforcing a prohibitory statute, and performs a cost/benefit analysis of those consequences.

In keeping with the chemistry lab motif, picture a funnel with these three filters.

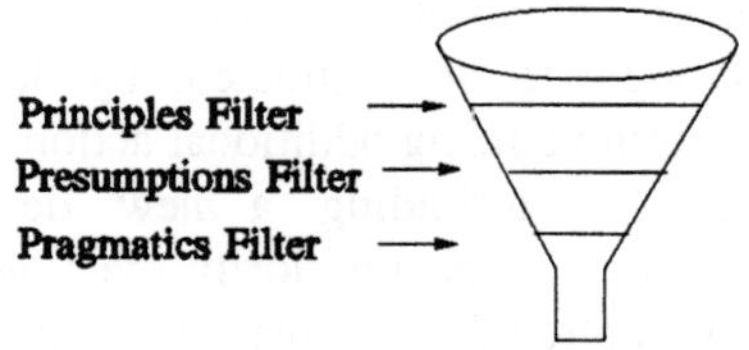

Figure 2

To show that some action may morally be criminalized, then, one must show that the action in question falls within the state's moral authority, that its incidence cannot be sufficiently reduced by means less intrusive and coercive than the criminal law, and that the social costs of enforcing the statute will not exceed the social benefits of that enforcement. If an action fails to pass through any Filter, then it ought not be criminalized. Conversely, if an action does fall within the state's moral authority, and its incidence cannot be reduced to an acceptable level by less coercive means, and the social benefits of enforcing the statute do exceed its costs, then criminalization *is* morally justified.

Thus, Filtering provides the "criterion of sufficiency" for morally justified criminalization; it specifies precisely what must be proved, if one is to prove that some action may morally be criminalized. Additionally, Filtering provides the "recipe" for constructing a conclusive case for morally justified criminalization: construct a persuasive argument at each Filter. An obvious but important implication: to fail to construct a persuasive argument at any Filter is to fail to justify criminalization.

More generally: I shall argue that Filtering better captures that which has occurred when criminalization is done best. I argue that, upon reflection, the criminalization which (albeit not consciously) satisfies this procedure is that about which we are, and ought to be, most confident.

Immediately we are confronted with a fundamental methodological issue: how ought one go about arguing that some decision-procedure is superior to another? One option would be to apply them both to actions we are all confident ought to be criminally prohibited—for example, murder, rape, assault, robbery, arson. But this will not do; no decision-procedure for criminalization could be correct if it didn't yield the result that *these* actions are justifiably criminalized. And it is unlikely that, in applying the competing procedures to such actions, the superiority of one over the other could be demonstrated. A second option would be to apply the two decision-procedures to matters of great controversy: prohibiting abortion, for example, or the use of psychoactive substances ("drugs"). Unhappily, this too is unlikely to succeed. First, the relative merits and demerits of the competing procedures will probably be swamped by the contentious considerations of the issues themselves. Second, if one of the competing decision-procedures yields a result with which one disagrees, it will be difficult to determine whether one should reject the outcome (the decision-procedure was misapplied), change one's mind about criminalization—or reject the decision-procedure itself.

The strategy I have selected is to first argue "contextlessly" for the superiority of Filtering over Balancing. I claim that, independent of the application of the two procedures to particular actions, there are strong reasons for choosing Filtering over Balancing. Afterwards, in the chapters of Part Two, I *apply* the two procedures to a variety of contentious issues in the philosophy of the criminal law. I argue that Filtering imposes a structure on these disputes, a structure which facilitates philosophical progress.

CHAPTER ONE

"BALANCING" AS A DECISION-PROCEDURE FOR MORALLY JUSTIFIED CRIMINALIZATION

I. ORDINARY-LIFE DECISION-MAKING & THE ISSUES OF THE CHAPTER

The language of ordinary-life decision-making is permeated with variations of the metaphor of "balancing." In deciding whether to do some particular thing, we "weigh" the "pros" and the "cons;" the "weightier" reasons prevail. We "weigh" the advantages of a given course of action against the disadvantages. Often we "weigh" the various alternatives available to us. And in some cases the benefits of a particular option are "outweighed" by, are "counterbalanced" by, the costs of electing that option. Etc., etc.

In the context of the law, we are all familiar with "Blind Justice." In one hand she holds a sword, and in the other: the "scales of justice," a simple beam balance. Given the ubiquity of "balancing" as a (primitive) decision procedure in everyday life, its presence in the philosophy of the criminal law ought not be surprising. In addition to being unsurprising, its presence in the philosophy of the criminal law is unfortunate. Or so I shall argue.

In Section II, I document the reliance on Balancing as a decision-procedure in the philosophy of the criminal law. In Section III, I offer a series of misgivings about Balancing as a decision-procedure for morally justified criminalization. I refer to these as "misgivings," and not "reasons for rejecting" Balancing as a decision-procedure, since it would be methodologically premature to urge the rejection of Balancing prior to offering an alternative decision-procedure. So as a matter of philosophical methodology, I postpone calling for the rejection of Balancing until the conclusion of Chapter Three—at which point I will have argued that "Filtering" is indeed a superior decision-procedure.

II. THE GENERAL RELIANCE ON "BALANCING"

The essence of the metaphor of Balancing is this: We are to picture a beam balance, with pans for weights at each end—just like the ones found in (outdated) high-school science laboratories. The arguments in favor of criminalization are placed on one pan; the arguments against criminalization are placed on the other pan. One then checks the "indicator" of the balance;

the "weightier" arguments prevail. The balance's indicator points in favor of criminalization, or against criminalization.

criminalize

not criminalize

Figure 1 — 1

What are these "considerations" which are placed on the balance's pans? Quite an array of things. The Harm Principle, and perhaps other such Principles: Legal Paternalism, Legal Moralism, etc. Additionally, concerns about the prospects for successful enforcement. Also, concerns about various "side effects" of criminalization. And issues of resource allocation. Etc.

Consider the following two passages; in each we find the explicit employment of "Balancing," and a (partial) list of the panoply of diverse "weights" to be placed on the pans of the Balance. The first is from Michael Bayles:

> Reasons for criminal legislation may be stated as principles. A principle for criminal legislation presents a characteristic of actions which constitutes a reason, but neither a necessary nor sufficient one, for legally prohibiting or requiring them. The characteristic presented in a principle does not constitute a necessary reason because that of another principle might by itself justify legislation. It does not constitute a sufficient reason because it might not outweigh the presumption against criminalization . . .. There are also principles which present reasons against criminalization, e.g., that a law cannot be effectively enforced. When conflicting principles apply to a proposed law, they must be balanced against one another. Collectively, all acceptable principles both for and against provide a standard of good criminal legislation.[1]

---

[1]"Criminal Paternalism," in *The Limits of Law: Nomos XV* (New York: Lieber-Atherton, Inc., 1974), p. 175. Internal cite omitted.

In a similar move, the early Joel Feinberg lists some principles in favor of criminal legislation (I do not discuss these principles here, as I shall later examine in detail his very recent formulations), and then writes:

> The liberty-limiting principles on this list are best understood as stating neither necessary nor sufficient conditions for justifying coercion, but rather specifications of the *kinds* of reasons that are always relevant or acceptable in support of proposed coercion, even though in a given case they may not be conclusive. Each principle states that interference might be permissible *if* (but not *only if*) a certain condition is satisfied. Hence, the principles are not mutually exclusive; it is possible to hold two or more of them at once, even all of them together, and it is possible to deny all of them. Moreover, the principles cannot be construed as stating sufficient conditions for legitimate interference with liberty, for even though the principle is satisfied in a given case, the general presumption against coercion might not be outweighed.[2]

Now in his four-volume series on *The Moral Limits of the Criminal Law*, Feinberg combines his concern about principles "outweighing" the presumption in favor of liberty, with the issues of enforcement raised by Bayles. Feinberg recounts the arguments of Mill (and others) supporting a presumption in favor of liberty, and notes that that presumption will ". . . transfer the burden of argument to the shoulders of the advocate of coercion who must, in particular instances, show that the standing case for liberty can be overridden by even weightier reason on the other side of the scales." [HTO 9] As I want to scrutinize a number of issues here, I offer a relatively long passage, this from the first volume of the series, *Harm to Others*.

> Thus, still another way of posing this work's basic question suggests itself: what kinds of reasons can have weight when balanced against the presumptive case for liberty? Answers to this question take the form of what I shall call "liberty-limiting principles" (or equivalently, "coercion-legitimizing principles"). A liberty-limiting principle is one which states that a given type of consideration is always a morally relevant reason in support of penal

---

[2]Joel Feinberg, *Social Philosophy* ("Foundations of Philosophy Series"; Englewood Cliffs, New Jersey: Prentice-Hall, Inc. 1973), pp. 33-4.

> legislation even if other reasons may in the circumstances outweigh it. So conceived, the diverse liberty-limiting principles proposed by various philosophers, while distinct and separate, are nonetheless not rivals. More than one, and even all of them, could be true. As formulated here they do not contradict one another.
>
> It is important to point out that these proposed coercion-legitimizing principles do not even purport to state necessary and sufficient conditions for justified state coercion. A liberty-limiting principle does not state a *sufficient condition* because in a given case its purportedly relevant reason might not weigh heavily enough on the scales to outbalance the standing presumption in favor of liberty. That presumption is not only supported by moral and utilitarian considerations of a general kind; it is also likely to be buttressed in particular cases by appeal to the practical costs, direct and collateral, of criminalization. A new crime on the books might put a strain on court facilities, divert police resources from more serious responsibilities, crowd prisons, and provide markets for the monopolistic and criminogenic enterprises of organized crime. . . . Moreover, no liberty-limiting principle claims to put forth a *necessary condition* for the justification of criminal statutes either. No one of them makes any claim about the truth or falsity of the other principles that have been proposed, and indeed there is nothing in a principle's formulation to preclude any or all of the others from being valid too. . . . In short, each liberty-limiting principle puts forth a kind of reason it claims always to be relevant—always to have some weight—in support of proposed legal coercion, even though in a given instance it might not weigh enough to be decisive . . . . [HTO 9-10; internal cites omitted]

Much—entirely *too* much—is going on here.[3]

---

[3]That "balancing" is the guiding metaphor of Feinberg's thinking can be seen in the following passages, gleaned from *Harmless Wrongdoing*—the fourth, final, and most recent volume of *The Moral Limits of the Criminal Law*.

"as reasons go, it is not much of one, typically putting only a modest weight on the balancing scales" (p. 5)

"harmless evils are 'as if weightless' on the scales when balanced against sovereignty" (p. 7)

"evils of the free-floating kind, the liberal insists, never have enough weight to counterbalance the standing case for liberty" (p. 20)

"How much weight, at a maximum, are non-grievance evils capable of putting on the scales to be weighed against liberty?" (p. 25)

III. PRELIMINARY MISGIVINGS ABOUT "BALANCING"

To make good on my claim that Filtering is a better decision-procedure for criminalization than Balancing, I need to show both procedures in operation, and show that Filtering is more successful in doing what we want done by a decision-procedure for criminalization. And that is a central task of the chapters of Part Two. What I want to do in this chapter is to raise, in a preliminary way, some misgivings about Balancing. My goal is to induce unease. By looking at some of the essential features of Balancing, I want to provide reasons for believing that Balancing is deeply flawed—even before its explicit competition with Filtering.

1. An Argument Has No "Objective" Weight

When working with a beam balance in a laboratory, the competent technician can determine which quantities of chemicals are more weighty, and which are less weighty. But there is something else the technician can do: put a quantity of chemical on one pan, and precisely calibrated weights on the other pan. In addition to comparing the weights of various quantities, the technician can determine the "objective" weight of any particular quantity of chemical.

We speak metaphorically of a particular argument as being "more weighty" than some other, or "less weighty" than some other. But it is just silly to ask of an argument, "objectively," how much it "weighs." Quantities of chemicals have "objective" weights; arguments do not. Strictly speaking—non-metaphorically speaking—we do not "determine" the "weight" of an argument, but *assign* a weight. And these assignments, far from being "objective," are intensely subjective and inherently controversial. (Competent chemists will agree on the weight of a quantity of chemical in a way that competent philosophers will not agree, on the "weight" on an argument.) Thus, "Balancing" the arguments for and against criminalization really isn't much like balancing quantities of chemicals at all. Any aura of scientific accuracy which might seem to surround "Balancing" is wholly undeserved.

"They have as much weight . . . in the legislative scales" (p. 32)

"I think it is even more like saying that human beings tend to weight more than mice, even though in an extremely rare case a given bloated mouse may weigh more than a premature human infant." (p. 67)

2. "*Balancing*" *is Simplistic*

The scales held by Blind Justice has two pans. When we think of the outcome of a criminal trial, this is perfectly appropriate: "guilty" or "not guilty." (A successful insanity defense results in a verdict that is a species of "not guilty.") But few decisions in ordinary life, and fewer still as regards criminalization, are so crisply disjunctive. While we sometimes have to decide between either "action *a*" or "not action *a*" [*a* v -*a*], much more often we have to decide among "action *a*" or "action *b*" or "action *c*" or "action *d*." And though it is possible—and even amusing—to imagine a multi-pan balance, a moment's reflection reveals the inadequacy of such a decision procedure. Two (or more) options might have the same advantages (or disadvantages); what constitutes a "pro" of one option might be a "con" of another. And so on. Additionally, there is the possibility of "conjunctive alternatives:" either "action *a* & action *c*," or "action *b*." No modified beam balance could be designed that would adequately "weigh" alternatives of these sorts.

Another way in which Balancing is too simplistic is that it does not provide a specification of the items to be weighed, does not provide any sort of a "checklist" of weights. As a consequence, it is easy to "overlook" weights, to fail to "weigh" considerations that are relevant to a statute's justification. Neglecting various "weights" might have no effect—either way, the statute is (or is not) justified. But the neglected weights might be *decisive*, might make the difference between a statute's being morally justified and its not being justifiable.

In the *final* analysis, as regards the criminal law, we do indeed arrive at a crisp disjunction: the action at issue is justifiably criminalized, or it is not. But there are many *other* things, important things, we may well wish to know. Suppose the conclusion is that some action is not justifiably criminalized. It might prove important to know the answers to a number of questions. Is the argument against justified criminalization based on the deleterious consequences of (attempting) enforcement? Is the argument against justified criminalization based on the fact that the behavior can be adequately discouraged in ways less coercive than a criminal statute? Is the argument against justified criminalization based on a persuasive case that the action is not of a *sort* with which the state may morally interfere? Still supposing that no criminal statute is justified: is some less coercive state action justified? And suppose that the conclusion is that the action is indeed justifiably criminalized. We might well want to know what precisely "weighed" in favor of criminalization, and what precisely was "outweighed."

3. The Weighing of Incommensurables

As Michael Bayles and Joel Feinberg indicated in the passages quoted above, *everything* that "weighs for" the enactment of a proposed criminal statute is placed on one pan; *everything* that "weighs against" the enactment of the statute is placed on the other pan. "Balancing" is a one-step procedure; once the "net weight" of each case has been "determined" (i.e., assigned), then (allegedly) the issue of justification has been determined. But how are we to determine the weights of the various entities plopped on the pans? How "weighty" is it that people are (to various degrees) *harmed* by the action at issue? How "weighty" is it that people are (to various degrees) *offended* by the action? How weighty is it that the action is *immoral*? How weighty is it that—were people to obey the law—they would do less harm to themselves? How "weighty" is it that—were people to obey the law—they would improve themselves? How "weighty" is it that some law would be difficult to enforce? How "weighty" is it that the law, in prohibiting commerce in a commodity for which there is an inelastic demand, would create enormous profits for those willing to violate the law? How "weighty" is it that those profits, made possible only by the law's enactment, would be a corrupting force in society—would induce police, prosecutors, judges, prison guards, bankers, etc. to violate the public trust? And so on. In Balancing, one must assign weights to the moral role of the state (the *sorts* of actions with which the state may morally interfere), the presumption in favor of liberty, the value of individual rights, the conduct of police and citizens, etc. Now there's no denying that we are called upon, in everyday life, to judge which set of reasons is the "weightier." But Balancing can operate only if "weights" can be assigned to quite an array of quite different considerations.

4. The Inherent Need for Precision

It's not just that, in Balancing, one must assess the weights of this large array of quite different considerations—though that is a serious problem. One must assess their weights *very accurately*. Inherent in the metaphor of "balancing" is the possibility that a very small difference in the weight on the two pans will be sufficient to "tip the balance," to be decisive in determining whether an action is justifiably criminalized. If the total weight of the various considerations on the pan favoring criminalization is, say, 100 pounds (or whatever), and the total weight of the various considerations on the pan opposing criminalization is, say, 100.4 pounds, then the criminal statute at issue is not justified. But it *would* be justified if only the considerations favoring criminalization weighed half a pound more—or if the considerations against criminalization weighed half a pound less. Or the former weighed a quarter-pound more and the latter weighed a quarter-pound less. So it's not just that "weights" have to be assessed—it's that the decision-procedure "Balancing" *can* work only if those weights are assessed (assigned) with great precision, for small inaccuracies can make all the difference. Slight overweights or underweights can make the difference between the statute's being justifiably enacted and not justifiably enacted. And that might well have a *profound* impact on the lives of many citizens; if the criminal statute is enacted, more things that people do will make them subject to the indignities of arrest, the expense of defense, the consequences—intended and unintended—of incarceration, and the encumbrances of criminal conviction.

Now it could be objected that there will be but a slight difference in weight between the case for criminalization and the case against criminalization only in rare cases. As regards many statutes—one prohibiting premeditated homicide, for example—the relative weights of the two cases will be quite different, *obviously* different. I agree. But this is of no help to the argument in favor of Balancing as a decision-procedure; indeed, it clarifies and sharpens this misgiving about Balancing. It is true that the case in favor of some criminal statutes is overwhelming. Some such statutes function as adequacy criteria: no decision-procedure for criminalization could be correct if it did not yield the result that the statute in question is justified. But this will not be the case as regards many criminal statutes—extant or proposed. As regards *these*, the matter will be close. But these are precisely the statutes of greatest philosophical interest; it is for *these* that a decision-procedure is so badly needed. The more controversial the statute, the closer in "weight" the case for and the case against, the greater the need for a decision-procedure. Yet the closer the issue, the more important that—in Balancing—each and every one of the diverse considerations favoring and disfavoring the statute be *precisely* weighed. Succinctly: the greater the need for a decision-procedure for criminalization, the greater this inherent problem of Balancing.

5. *A Curious Asymmetry*

There is a consensus among philosophers of law that "difficulty in enforcement" somehow "counts against" a proposed statute. Perhaps a criminal law could be enforced only if the police used intrusive detection techniques (e.g. wiretapping, informants, decoys), or detection would require an inordinate amount of police time, etc. Perhaps the enforcement of a statute would spawn other, and more serious criminality. And so forth. There is agreement that these facts in *some* way militate against the enactment of the proposed statute. These difficulties may count a little or a lot; they may be decisive in the final decision against enactment, or a mere regrettable consequence of the decision to enact the law. Regardless, difficulties in enforcement always matter, always count against enactment. Curiously, however, the converse is *not* true. That some proposed statute would be *easy* to enforce—violations would be public and obvious, for example—does not, *in and of itself*, count in favor of enacting the proposed statute. Why it is that, in Balancing, difficulty in enforcement "weighs against" a law, but ease of enforcement does not "weigh for" the enactment of a law. Why is it that matters of enforcement can put weight on one pan of the balance, but not on the other?

6. *Movement of the Balance's Indicator*

It is a characteristic of a beam balance that, whenever weight is added to one of the pans, the balance's "indicator" moves in the other direction. Thus, if one discovers some new argument that has the effect of increasing the load on one pan—e.g. novel reasons for believing that some action ought not be considered within a person's "Sphere of Individual Liberty"—then the indicator inevitably, by the design of the Balance, moves towards criminalization. In such a case, there will be a temptation to conclude from this movement of the indicator that the action in question has been determined to be justifiably criminalized. Yet it might well be the case that no such conclusion is warranted; justified criminalization requires not merely the movement of the indicator *towards* criminalization, but movement past the midpoint. The indicator must point to the reasons in favor of criminalization not merely as "weightier" than they had been acknowledged to be, but in fact "weightier" than the reasons against criminalization.[4]

IV. CONCLUSIONS

The metaphor of Balancing permeates the literature of the philosophy of the criminal law. By the end of this essay, I hope to have shown that it is as pernicious as it is ubiquitous. But I do not take myself to have shown that yet. My more modest goal in this chapter has been to induce unease about Balancing as a decision-procedure for morally justified criminalization, to expose inherent infirmities that should make the jurist, the legislator, the philosopher of the criminal law uncomfortable about employing "Balancing" in an enterprise as important as determining which actions may morally be criminalized.

I shall offer, at the end of Chapter Three, several arguments that Balancing ought to be abandoned in favor of Filtering. So let us now turn our attention to the materials from which those arguments will be constructed.

[4]This phenomenon is very like the one described by Plato, mistaking the mere cessation of pain, for positive pleasure. Cf. *The Republic*, Chapter XXXIII.

CHAPTER TWO

THE TOPOGRAPHY OF ACTIONS RELEVANT TO CRIMINALIZATION

I. INTRODUCTION TO THE CHAPTER

The contemporary debate about criminalization has as its origin John Stuart Mill's *On Liberty*. I open this chapter with an interpretation of the salient elements of that work, those portions of most relevance to the issues I examine in the remainder of this essay. In the course of relating Mill's theses, I shall pay particular attention to Mill's identification of various classes of actions—various sets into which actions can be sorted—and to important relationships among these classes. These sets and their relationships can be most perspicuously displayed by using a number of diagrams; various regions are marked off, and borders drawn between regions. Thus the vocabulary of maps and mapping is natural; I shall term this enterprise a "topography of actions."

The preliminary topography of actions discernible in Mill can be abstracted from Mill's substantive positions in the philosophy of the criminal law; with a few modifications, it can be made a perfectly *neutral* topography. By this I mean that the various sets of actions as identified by Mill and amended by me, and their relationships, will be acknowledged as veridical, regardless of one's substantive positions as regards criminalization. Legal Moralists, Legal Paternalists, etc. and Millean Liberals will disagree as regards which actions fall within which of the various classes specified by the topography. But there is compelling reason for all to agree that there *are* these distinct classes of actions, and that they are related in the ways indicated. Despite this neutrality, the topography has important implications for arguments about criminalization. Much of what has gone wrong in a number of arguments about coercion generally, and about criminalization in particular, can be traced to failures to respect this topography of actions. Or so I shall argue.

I provide an interpretation of Mill in Section II; I extract the imbedded topography, and amend it, in Section III. I argue, in Section IV, that this topography is indeed perfectly neutral among various substantive positions in the philosophy of the criminal law: the topography accommodates, and is presupposed by, Legal Paternalists, Legal Moralists, etc. Section V is devoted to (what I call) "topographic errors"—to the sorts of arguments for criminalization, or other sorts of coercion, which fail to respect this topography of actions. In Section VI, I take a closer look at one region of the topography, the "moral coercion of public opinion;" the persuasiveness of parts of my subsequent work depends upon showing the power of public opinion in encouraging and discouraging various actions which citizens might elect. I discuss *offensive* actions in Section VII. Mill clearly believed that offensive public conduct is justifiably prohibited; what is not clear is precisely how he defends that position. In Section VIII, I look at some of the shortcomings of Mill's decision-procedure for criminalization, noting Mill's reliance on some sort of "balancing." I conclude with a summary of the chapter in Section IX.

II. THE SALIENT ELEMENTS OF *ON LIBERTY*

Perhaps the best-known passage in the philosophy of criminal law is Mill's statement of the "Harm Principle:"

> The object of this essay is to assert one very simple principle, as entitled to govern absolutely the dealings of society with the individual in the way of compulsion and control, whether the means used be physical force in the form of legal penalties or the moral coercion of public opinion. That principle is that the sole end for which mankind are warranted, individually or collectively, in interfering with the liberty of action of any of their number, is self-protection. That the only purpose for which power can be rightfully exercised over any member of a civilized community, against his will, is to prevent harm to others. [OL 14]

Mill makes several important qualifications of the Harm Principle. First, the arguments concern the liberty of action of *competent adults*. He writes, "It is, perhaps, hardly necessary to say that this doctrine is meant to apply only to human beings in the maturity of their faculties." [OL 13] Thus, when he argues that there is a set of actions with respect to which people ought to be free to do or forebear, Mill must be understood as claiming that *competent adults* ought to be free to choose, and not that incompetent adults, or children, ought to be free to choose. (But he must *not* be read as claiming that "incompetent adults" ought *not* be free to choose—at least, in any simple way. But much more on this later.) Second, the "Harm Principle" places under society's jurisdiction not only actions which in fact harm others, but also those which pose (what we would today call) a "clear and present danger" of harm to others. In Mill's own words: "Whenever, in short, there is a definite damage, or *a definite risk of damage*, either to an individual or to the public, the case is taken out of the province of liberty and placed in that of morality or law." [OL 100; italics added]

The "object" of *On Liberty* is to defend the "Harm Principle"—but what is the object of defending the "Harm Principle?" Precisely what would a successful defense of the Harm Principle achieve? It would result in the specification of a set of actions over which each individual (competent adult) ought to be sovereign, a set of actions interference with which—*by the state or by private individuals*—would be morally wrong. We can call this set of actions the "Sphere of Individual Liberty" (often abbreviated as "SIL"); alternatively, we can call it simply "individual sovereignty."

Two questions immediately arise: what are the *contents* of the Sphere of Individual Liberty, and why does it contain precisely those actions?

According to Mill, the SIL contains "liberty of conscience in the most comprehensive sense, liberty of thought and feeling, absolute freedom of opinion and sentiment on all subjects" (including freedom of the expression of these), and "liberty of tastes and pursuits, of framing the plan of our life to suit our own character, of doing as we like, subject to such consequences as may follow, without impediment from our fellow creatures, so long as what we do does not harm them, even though they should think our conduct foolish, perverse or wrong." [OL 16] Why ought the state (and private individuals) respect every competent adult's "Sphere of Individual Liberty?" Ultimately, of course, Mill must hold that respecting SILs will maximize utility.[1] How is it that respecting SILs will maximize utility? We must imagine two cases: a *larger* SIL, and a *smaller* SIL.

Suppose that the Sphere of Individual Liberty were larger than specified by Mill, i.e., contained more actions than listed by Mill. Of necessity, the SIL would then contain actions which harm, or pose a clear and present danger of harm, to other people. Were people to have the right to elect such actions, the strong in society would prey upon the weak. But according to Mill, "All that makes existence valuable to anyone depends on the enforcement of restraints upon the actions of other people." [OL 8] Expanding the SIL to include actions which harm others (or pose a clear and present danger of such harm)

---

[1] "I regard utility as the ultimate appeal on all ethical questions; but it must be utility in the largest sense, grounded on the permanent interests of man as a progressive being." [*On Liberty*, 14]

would result in a net decrease of utility. Consequently, the SIL ought not be expanded.

Suppose, on the contrary, that the Sphere of Individual Liberty were *smaller* than specified by Mill, i.e., contained a proper subset of those actions which neither harm, nor pose a risk of harm, to others. Of necessity, society would have jurisdiction over some such actions. How would this lead to a net reduction in utility? Mill offers two arguments.

First, Mill notes that human beings have faculties and talents, and that these grow and improve when they are used, but atrophy when they are not used.

> The human faculties of perception, judgement, discriminative feeling, mental activity and even moral preference are exercised only in making a choice. He who does anything because it is the custom makes no choice. He gains no practice either in discerning or desiring what is best. The mental and moral, like the muscular, powers are improved only by being used. [OL 71]

How does one so use one's powers, one's faculties and talents? By designing, and living out, a "plan of life" that is one's own. For a person "who chooses his plan of life for himself employs all his faculties;" one "must use observation to see, reasoning and judgement to foresee, activity to gather materials for decision, discrimination to decide, and when he has decided, firmness and self-control to hold to his deliberate decision." [OL 71] Why ought human beings be encouraged to develop their faculties and talents (and thus society not limit liberty except to prevent harm to others)? Mill offers two sets of considerations. First, such individuals are better able to gain happiness for themselves—thereby increasing overall utility. Second, people who have developed their faculties and talents are better able to contribute to the overall happiness of society:

> . . . human life becomes rich, diversified, and animating, furnishing more abundant aliment to high thoughts and elevating feelings, and strengthening the tie which binds every individual to the race, by making the race infinitely better worth belonging to. In proportion to the development of his individuality, each person becomes more valuable to himself, and is, therefore, capable of being more valuable to others. [OL 76]

People with developed faculties and talents include athletes and actors, teachers and therapists and truckers, physicians and public servants, nurses and nannies, stock brokers and stock boys, musicians and writers, etc. People with developed faculties and talents constitute the economy, and enlighten and entertains us. By making life more valuable to others, such individuals increase the utility of others—thereby increasing overall utility.

Given Mill's heavy reliance on the use of one's critical, reflective faculties, it is perfectly appropriate to understand Mill as arguing, on utilitarian grounds, for the protection and enhancement of individual autonomy.

Mill's second argument is more compact, an analogical argument which refers immediately to the relative happiness of people if allowed to select from the largest possible array of plans of life—all plans which do not harm others—and the relative unhappiness of people if the array of available alternatives is truncated.

> But different persons also require different conditions for their spiritual development; and can no more exist healthily in the same moral than all the variety of plants can in the same physical, atmosphere and climate. The same things which are helps to one person toward the cultivation of his higher nature are hindrances to another. The same mode of life is a healthy excitement to one, keeping all his faculties of action and enjoyment in their best order, while to another it is a distracting burden which suspends or crushes all internal life. Such are the differences among human beings in their sources of pleasure, their susceptibilities of pain, and the operation on them of different physical and moral agencies that, unless there is a corresponding diversity in their modes of life, they neither obtain their fair share of happiness, nor grow up to the mental, moral and aesthetic stature of which their nature is capable. [OL 82-3]

Mill's position, then, is that some actions of competent adults fall within the "Sphere of Individual Liberty" (individual sovereignty); neither the state nor private individuals ought to interfere with those actions. For Mill, actions which do not harm others (or if they do, it is with the consent of the others) fall within the SIL. We can say of actions which *do* fall within the SIL, that it is respect for autonomy which places them there. In what follows, it will be helpful to think of actions in the SIL as thereby acquiring a "special immunity" from interference, a special immunity due to respect for autonomy.

III. THE TOPOGRAPHY OF ACTIONS

III. A. Mill's Topography

As I continue my interpretation of Mill's position in *On Liberty*, I shall rely more heavily on the language of topography—and shall begin to illustrate my exposition with diagrams.[2]

It would be easy to read Mill as subscribing to a two-region topography, based upon the dichotomy between individual sovereignty (the SIL) and Society's Jurisdiction (SJ); some passages of Mill seem to suggest such a simple dichotomy. Consider the opening paragraphs of Chapter IV:

> What, then, is the rightful limit to the sovereignty of the individual over himself? Where does the authority of society begin? How much of human life should be assigned to individuality, and how much to society?
>
> Each will receive its proper share if each has that which more particularly concerns it. To individuality should belong the part of life in which it is chiefly the individual that is interested; to society, the part which chiefly interests society. [OL 91]

The topography inspired by this could be diagramed in this way:

---

[2]Responding to two questions will help clarify matters. First: Is it action *types* or action *tokens* that fall into the various regions of the topography? The answer is: *both*. In some cases, the argument will focus on an action token: does some identifiable individual have a right to do some specifiable action at some particular point in time? In other cases, the argument will focus on action types: does the state have the moral authority to forcibly interfere with this *sort* of action? In what follows, I believe that the context will make clear whether it is an action type or an action token that is at issue.

This fluidity between type and token is a characteristic of ongoing disputes in the literature. It is quite common to find a philosopher of the criminal law arguing about a particular—often hypothetical—case (a token), and then generalizing the results to the rights of all individuals (a type), or the authority of the state (another type). Indeed, in the various topics of Part Two of this work, we shall encounter this argument strategy time and again.

Second: Are the diagrams of this chapter (and subsequent chapters) drawn "to scale?" Do the relative sizes of the various regions indicate the relative magnitude of their contents? The answer is: *no*. My concern here is to identify and distinguish various regions, and to discuss their relationships. I make no attempt to specify the relative sizes of the regions, e.g., to say what percentage of all actions, however individuated, fall within Society's Jurisdiction, and what percentage fall within the Sphere of Individual Liberty.

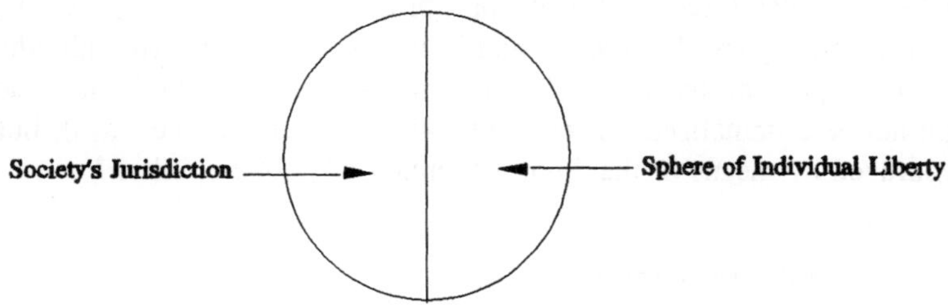

Figure 2 — 1

This simple dichotomy between society and individual is, however, *too* simple—and not supported by the remainder of the text. First, it fails to incorporate a distinction drawn by Mill in the statement of the Harm Principle itself: some actions in "Society's Jurisdiction" are appropriately subject to the "physical force of legal penalties," but other actions are appropriately subject only to the "moral coercion of public opinion." Now Mill offers little help in actually applying the distinction—but *that* he draws it is undeniable. In addition to its being marked off in the statement of the Harm Principle itself, the distinction is drawn in the following passage: "If anyone does an act hurtful to others, there is a *prima facie* case for punishing him by law or, *where legal penalties are not safely applicable*, by general disapprobation."[3] And additionally,

> The acts of an individual may be hurtful to others or wanting in due consideration for their welfare, without going to the length of violating any of their constituted rights. The offender may then be justly punished by opinion, though not by law. [OL 91-2]

Mill here makes it clear that the use of force—by the state or private individuals—is justified for *some*, but *not all* of the actions that fall within "Society's Jurisdiction." An action's falling within Society's Jurisdiction is a necessary condition, but by no means a sufficient condition, for the use of

---

[3]*On Liberty*, p. 14; second italics added.

force—whether "force" is the "physical force of legal penalties" administered by the state, or private forcible interference. (Hereafter, I shall often shorten this to "physical force." When appropriate, I shall explicitly distinguish "physical force *of legal penalties*" and "physical force of private individuals.") The topography can be amended to accommodate this—some harmful actions ought not be criminalized (or interfered with in other forcible ways), but only discouraged by means of the "moral coercion of public opinion."

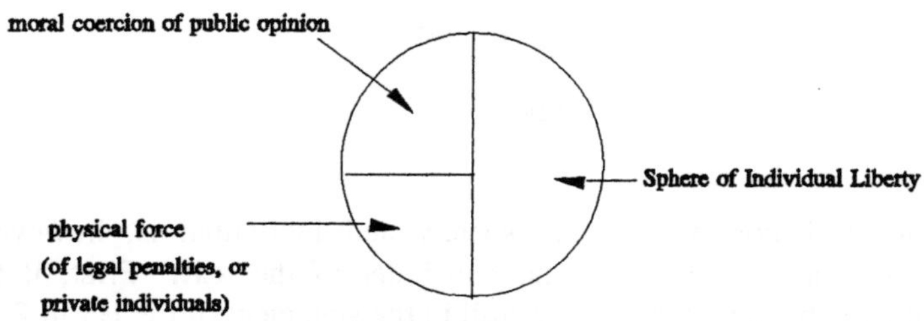

Figure 2 — 2

Thus, a careful reading of *On Liberty* reveals these sets of actions, and these relationships: some actions fall within a competent adult's Sphere of Individual Liberty, some actions fall within Society's Jurisdiction. The SIL and SJ are mutually exclusive. Within the SJ, some actions ought to be discouraged only by the "moral coercion of public opinion," while others ought to be subject to the "physical force of legal penalties."

III. B. Developing the Topography

This rudimentary topography of actions discernible in Mill's *On Liberty* can be developed to sort actions into classes that are more refined.

First, it would be quite bizarre to hold that some action *a* may morally be criminalized—it falls within the "pflp"—but may not morally be discouraged by the "moral coercion of public opinion." Of course discouraging that action through moral coercion might prove ineffective, or unwise—but that's quite another matter. Thus, the "pflp" ought to be represented as a *proper subset* of "mcpo."

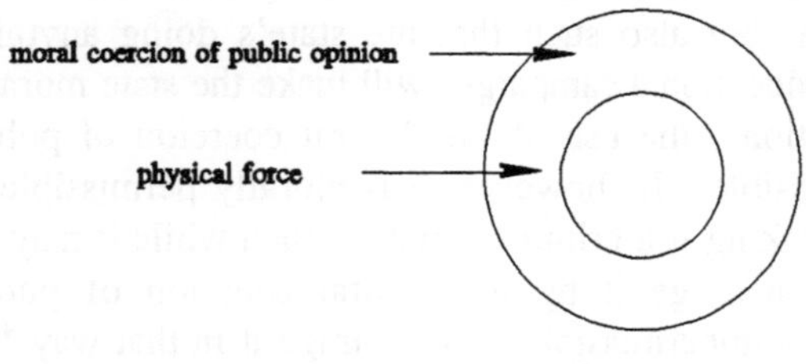

Figure 2 — 3

Second, it might be the case that some action *a* falls within Society's Jurisdiction—it is the sort of action with which a state is properly concerned—but which ought not be discouraged even by the "moral coercion of public opinion." Perhaps a program of public education would not reduce its incidence, but would instead increase its incidence, by "introducing" it to those ignorant of it. Perhaps it would inspire "copycats." Perhaps a program of public education would give it the aura of "forbidden fruit," thereby tempting the rebellious.

While I do not think this sort of action a central concern of the philosophy of the criminal law, an accurate topography will respect it. Thus, Society's Jurisdiction ought to be drawn as such:

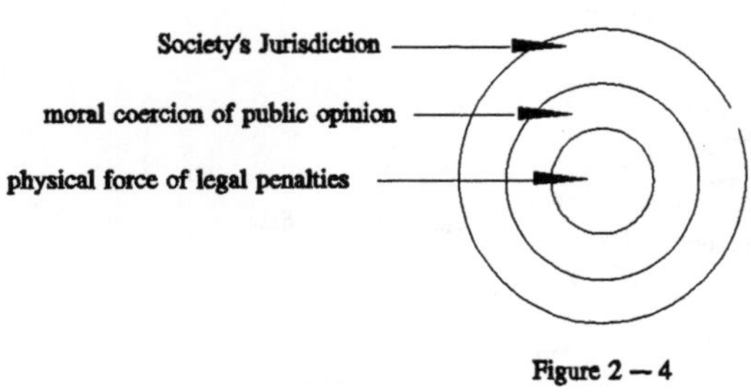

Figure 2 — 4

Three distinct regions are represented: some actions fall within Society's Jurisdiction *merely*; a proper subset of SJ is the "moral coercion of public opinion;" a proper subset of "mcpo" (and thus, of course, of SJ) is the "physical force of legal penalties."

It is important to distinguish this refinement from the previous one; what may appear to some as an inconsistency in fact is not. An action may be such that it is the *sort* of action with which a state is appropriately concerned—falls within Society's Jurisdiction—but also such that the state's doing anything about it, even launching an educational campaign, will make the state morally worse. As regards such actions, the use of the "moral coercion of public opinion" is *morally* impermissible. If, however, it is morally permissible to discourage some action by making it a criminal offense, then while it may be *imprudent* in practice to discourage it by the "moral coercion of public opinion," it cannot be *morally* impermissible to discourage it in that way.[4]

Finally, we must ask whether SJ and the SIL are, in addition to being mutually exclusive, also jointly exhaustive. Does every action of all adults fall into one or the other of these sets, or are there actions that are neither in the Sphere of Individual Liberty nor in Society's Jurisdiction? Might not there be actions which are in neither set? Mill does not explicitly address this issue. (His vacillation on pimping, and on running a gambling house, provide some reason to believe that *those* actions might fall in neither set.[5]) The topography ought not preclude this possibility; there is no inconsistency in holding that, as regards some actions, there is no compelling reason to think that they fall within the Sphere of Individual Liberty, but no compelling reason to think that they fall within Society's Jurisdiction either. So I accommodate this possibility in Figure 2 - 5; if it turns out that there are no such actions, then the space outside the circles representing Society's Jurisdiction and the Sphere of Individual Liberty—what I shall call the "interstice"—turns out to be empty.

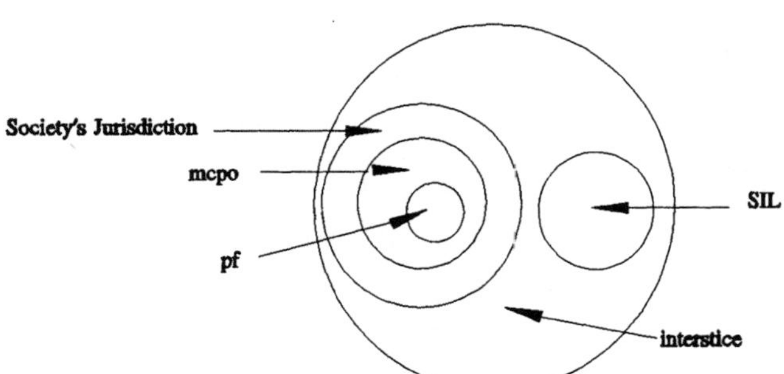

Figure 2 — 5

[4]Except, of course, in the sense that it is immoral for a state to do that which is counterproductive.

[5]*On Liberty*, p. 119-22.

Thus, if an action of a competent adult harms no one, or only the agent oneself, then that action falls within the "Sphere of Individual Liberty;" it has a special immunity from interference due to respect for autonomy. If an action does not fall within the SIL—well, arguments must be offered as to its precise location on the topography. It might fall in the interstice between the SIL and "Society's Jurisdiction." If it falls within Society's Jurisdiction, then further argument is required to determine whether it properly falls within "Society's Jurisdiction merely," the "moral coercion of public opinion," or "physical force," whether of legal penalties, or the private use of force.

IV. THE NEUTRAL TOPOGRAPHY OF ACTIONS

It was helpful (I trust), in relating Mill's substantive positions, to draw the diagrams and employ the language of topography. Now, however, I want to show that the topography of Figure 2 - 5 is a perfectly neutral topography of actions relevant to criminalization.

There are important disagreements between the Millean Liberal and, for example, the Legal Paternalist and the Legal Moralist. (And between the Millean Liberal and the proponents of yet other "liberty-limiting principles."[6] For ease and brevity of exposition, I shall use Legal Paternalism and Legal Moralism as exemplars; my arguments will apply to yet other positions *mutatis mutandis*.) The topography I have developed will *preserve* those disagreements—indeed, it will *clarify* those disagreements. The entire array of substantive positions—except for the endpoints of complete anarchy and complete totalitarianism—presuppose the various sets of the topography, and their relationships to one another. Let us see that this is so.

According to this topography, there is a set of actions which ought to be left to individual choice—the "Sphere of Individual Liberty"—and a set of actions that falls under Society's Jurisdiction. To deny that there is a SIL is to claim that all actions fall under Society's Jurisdiction; to claim this is to subscribe to an untenable totalitarianism. Neither Legal Paternalists nor Legal Moralists claim that there is no "Sphere of Individual Liberty." The Legal Paternalist claims that some actions which harm the agent oneself are not in the SIL; the Legal Moralist claims that some actions which are immoral are not in the SIL.

---

[6]Cf. Joel Feinberg, *HTO*, pp. 26-7.

But *both*—and everyone else, except the totalitarian—acknowledge a non-empty set of actions over which the individual ought to be sovereign. Even more clearly, everyone (except the anarchist) acknowledges a non-empty set of actions over which the state has jurisdiction. As noted above, Mill explicitly claims that some constraints on the actions of others are essential to civilized life. Legal Paternalists and Legal Moralists not only endorse a set of actions which constitute "Society's Jurisdiction," but hold that it contains even more actions than claimed by Mill: some self-harming actions (Legal Paternalists), or some immoral actions (Legal Moralists). The disagreement among Liberals, Paternalists and Moralists etc. center on the "size," the *contents*, of the SIL, and of Society's Jurisdiction; all acknowledge—indeed, insist upon—both as non-empty sets.

Consider now the set of actions called "Society's Jurisdiction." I have divided this into "Society's Jurisdiction" *merely*, its subset the "moral coercion of public opinion" and its proper subset, the "physical force of legal penalties." Would the Legal Paternalist, the Legal Moralist—or anyone else, for that matter—object to any of these sets, or dispute these subset and superset relationships? I think not. Millean Liberals believe that actions which harm others, or pose a clear and present danger of harm to others, fall within Society's Jurisdiction. Virtually all Legal Paternalists and Legal Moralists subscribe to the Harm Principle too, and would concur.[7] Lying to others, breaking promises to others, divulging the secrets of others—these can all cause harm to others, can result in an interest setback. In some cases—fraud, breach of contract, etc.—these are appropriately discouraged by the "physical force of legal penalties." But in most cases they are not. And it is most implausible to claim that all cases of lying, of promise-breaking, of breaking faith, ought to be discouraged by the "physical force of legal penalties." Nonetheless, we do believe it appropriate to teach our children to tell the truth, to keep their promises, etc. And in at least some instances, we think it right to publicly condemn lying, promise-breaking, and failing to keep faith. From this I conclude that "Society's Jurisdiction" has a proper subset, the "physical force of legal penalties," which in turn has the superset "moral coercion of public opinion." Put another way: some harms to others ought to be crimes, and some harms to others ought not be crimes—precisely the point I made in the Introduction, discussing the matter of "passive smoking."

---

[7]Joel Feinberg, *Harm to Others*, pp. 10-14.

While it is easy to cite examples of actions that are within Society's Jurisdiction, but not in the "physical force of legal penalties," it is less easy to cite examples of actions which fall within Society's Jurisdiction, but ought not be discouraged even by the "moral coercion of public opinion." Most of the difficulty, I believe, can be attributed to the controversies about precisely which actions are, and which actions are not, in Society's Jurisdiction at all. So I shall set aside this concern for now; in Chapter Five, I shall suggest bestiality as a possible example. But as I remarked earlier, the central issues of the philosophy of the criminal law concern the "moral coercion of public opinion" and the "physical force of legal penalties;" as will become clear, nothing in my argument requires "Society's Jurisdiction merely" to be an interesting set.

I do indeed believe that there is an non-empty interstice between the "Sphere of Individual Liberty" and "Society's Jurisdiction:" that with respect to some actions, there is no compelling argument for the action's falling within either the Sphere of Individual Liberty or Society's Jurisdiction. Furthermore, I can think of no reason for the Legal Paternalist, or the Legal Moralist—or anyone else, for that matter—to insist that the SIL and SJ be jointly exhaustive. Even the person who believes that an action falls within SJ if it harms others, or harms the agent, or is immoral, can believe that there is some action such that no plausible argument shows it to any of those, and no plausible argument shows it to fall within the SIL.

What emerges from this is the following topography:

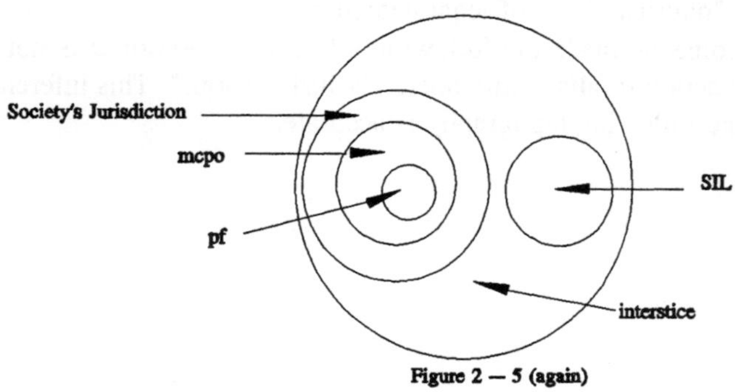

Figure 2 — 5 (again)

The disagreements among Millean Liberals, Legal Paternalists, Legal Moralists (and others) concern the *contents* of the various sets, the relative *size* of the various sets, and the criteria for determining which actions fall into which sets.

In no way do I wish to understate the importance of these disagreements; all the Chapters of Part Two of this work are devoted to these issues. However, this neutral topography, in and of itself, will prove of great help in understanding, and assessing, a number of arguments in the philosophy of the criminal law.[8]

V. "TOPOGRAPHIC ERRORS"

Let us take a close look as a couple of distinct (though clearly related) inferences. These inferences, when appearing in expository prose, may seem unobjectionable. When they appear as topographic claims, however, they are exposed as fallacious.

Suppose it has been shown that some action, call it action *a*, does not fall within a person's Sphere of Individual Liberty. Precisely where *does* it fall? An argument which shows only that it does not fall within the SIL—no matter how convincingly it shows it—does not and *can*not locate action *a* on the topography. Even though certain (*ex hypothesi*) that it is not within the SIL, we do not know whether it falls in Society's Jurisdiction or the interstice between the SIL and Society's Jurisdiction. An argument must be constructed, if one is to show that it falls within Society's Jurisdiction, an additional argument must be constructed if one is to show that it falls within the "moral coercion of public opinion;" yet an additional argument is needed to show that it falls within the "physical force of legal penalties."

Now suppose someone made the following inference: "Action *a* is not in the SIL, therefore action *a* falls within Society's Jurisdiction." This inference is sound only if the following topography is accurate.

[8]Still, it could be asked: is this the most perspicuous, the most helpful topography of actions relevant to criminalization? Or is there a superior topography (with more sets, or different sets, or different relationships)? I think this topography is very helpful, and it is the best I have been able to devise. I therefore commit it to the critical scrutiny of colleagues.

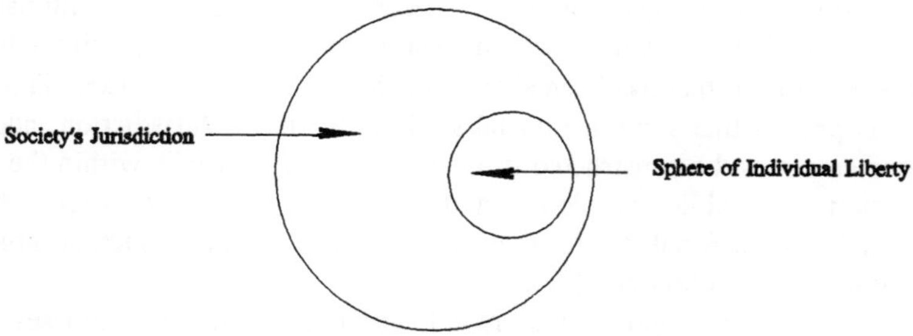

Figure 2 — 6 (Topographic Error)

But, as I have argued, this is not an accurate topography. Hence, the inference in flawed. It is an example of what I shall call a "topographic error." A "topographic error" is committed when one draws an inference which the accurate topography (Figure 2 - 5) shows is unwarranted. Put another way: an inference is a topographic error if its validity presupposes an inaccurate topography—for example, that represented by Figure 2 - 6.

Similarly, someone might make the following inference: "Action *a* is in Society's Jurisdiction, therefore it is permissible to prohibit action *a*, to make action *a* a crime." This inference is valid only if Society's Jurisdiction and the "physical force of legal penalties" are co-extensive, i.e., if the following topography were accurate:

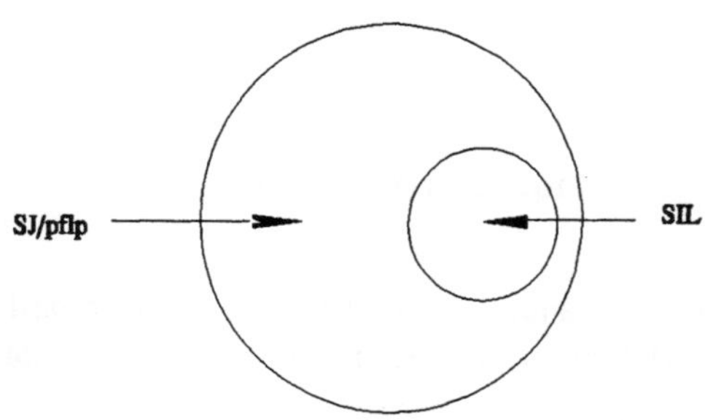

Figure 2 — 7 (Topographic Error)

But they are *not* co-extensive; the "pflp" is a proper subset of SJ; an action might fall within Society's Jurisdiction merely, and SJ also includes the "moral coercion of public opinion." There are some actions which fall within

Society's Jurisdiction which nonetheless ought not be made criminal: for any of a number of reasons, the "costs"—economic or moral—of criminalization exceed the benefits which would accrue to society from criminalization. Action *a*, for all that has been shown, could well be one of these. Thus, even if it is proved that some action falls within Society's Jurisdiction, additional arguments must be constructed if one is to show that it falls within the "moral coercion of public opinion," and then the "physical force of legal penalties"—that forcible interference is justified. Without such an argument, the inference is a topographic error.

A more blatant topographic error is committed when one crosses several borders in a single inferential leap: "Action *a* does not fall within an individual's SIL, therefore action *a* may justifiably be criminalized, is permissibly the subject of forcible interference." This inference ignores the possibility that action *a* is correctly placed in the interstice, and ignores the possibility that action *a* falls within Society's Jurisdiction merely, or within the "moral coercion of public opinion," but outside the "physical force of legal penalties." This inference presupposes the following, profoundly defective topography.

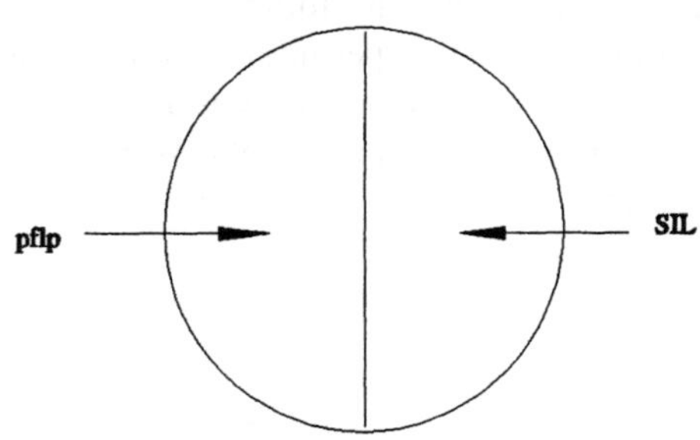

Figure 2 — 8 (Topographic Error)

All the previous instances have been straightforward examples of topographic errors. Before moving on, I want to discuss a more subtle sort of topographic error.

Recall Mill's position on these issues: actions which harm others, or pose a clear and present danger of harm to others, fall within Society's Jurisdiction; actions which harm no one, or only the agent, (or only those who have consented to the activity—they might be "damaged," but not, strictly speaking, "harmed," i.e., *wronged*), fall within the SIL. Recall as well Mill's two arguments for preserving a Sphere of Individual Liberty: that it helps the individual develop faculties and talents (thus maximizing utility), and that it creates an environment in which an individual may flourish (thus maximizing utility). There are some actions, I submit, such that (i) they neither harm, nor pose a clear and present danger of harm, to others, and (ii) they are not plausibly the subjects of Mill's two arguments. Consider, for example, a host of trivial and literally harm-less actions: scratching one's head, the hours one chooses to sleep, one's sleeping positions, etc., etc. As regards such actions, the claim that one is developing one's faculties and talents in a way that enriches one's life, and the lives of others, seems forced, strained, contrived. To a lesser extent perhaps, but nonetheless a significant extent, this is also true of claims that such actions are a part of an environment essential to one's flourishing. Nonetheless, in virtue of the fact that such actions do not harm, or pose a threat of harm to others, they are correctly placed in a person's Sphere of Individual Liberty. Thus, there is a set of actions properly placed in the SIL to which Mill's arguments do not apply. In consequence, a subtle topographic error can be committed: one might infer, from the fact that Mill's arguments do not apply to a particular action *a*, that action *a* does not fall within the SIL. But action *a* might nonetheless be one of these self-regarding "harm-less" actions. "Action *a* is not one of those actions to which Mill's arguments apply, therefore forcible interference with action *a* is morally permissible," commits a subtle topographic error. It presupposes this inaccurate topography:

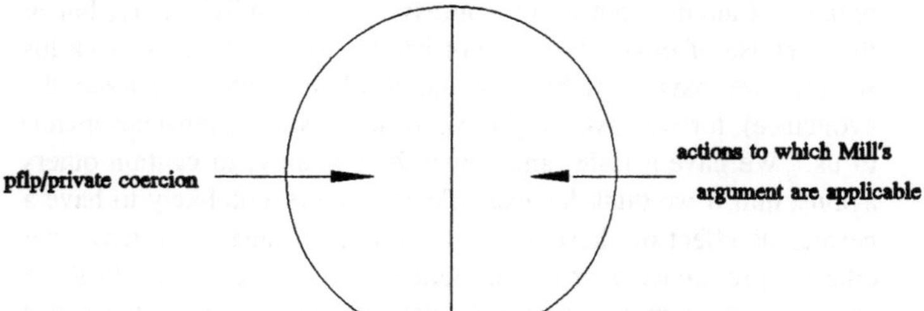

Figure 2 — 9 (Topographic Error)

This inference neglects the possibility that action *a* is indeed, after all, in the SIL—it is so not because of Mill's arguments for respecting autonomy, but by the "alternate route" of being literally "harm-less." This inference also, of course, commits the straightforward topographic errors of neglecting the possibilities of the action's being in the interstice, or in Society's Jurisdiction, but not in "pflp/private coercion." To show that Mill's arguments do not apply to some action is to take a step towards showing that it is eligible for forcible interference—but it is a step only; it is by no means to show that forcible interference is morally permissible.

VI. THE "MORAL COERCION OF PUBLIC OPINION"

I want to dwell for a moment on Mill's concept of the "moral coercion of public opinion." I want to clarify just what it is, and argue that it can be a powerful constraint on individual action. Because it *can* constrain, the "moral coercion of public opinion" is subject to the conditions specified by the Harm Principle: its use is morally justified only in an effort to discourage behavior which harms, or poses a clear and present danger of harm, to others.

The "moral coercion of public opinion" is, of course, distinct from the "physical force of legal penalties." It is also distinct from (what I shall call) the "social snub," and it can best be characterized by contrasting it with the social snub.

Mill claims that we are free to choose our friends—that prerogative is included in "individual sovereignty."

> We have a right, also, in various ways, to act upon our unfavorable opinion of anyone, not to the oppression of his individuality, but in the exercise of ours. We are not bound, for example, to seek his society; we have a right to avoid it (though not to parade the avoidance), for we have a right to choose the society most acceptable to us. We have a right, and it may be our duty, to caution others against him if we think his example or conversation likely to have a pernicious effect on those with whom he associates. We may give others a preference over him in optional good offices. . . . In these various modes a person may suffer very severe penalties at the hands of others for faults which directly concern only himself; but he suffers these penalties only in so far as they are the natural and, as it were, the spontaneous consequences of the faults themselves, not because they are purposely inflicted on him for the sake of punishment. [OL 94-5]

The parenthetical in this passage is crucial: to avoid a person's company is a "social snub;" to *parade* that avoidance is quite another matter. The former is an exercise of one's individuality; the latter is (an attempt to) motivate others to join in that avoidance—and thus an attempt to alter the behavior of that person. Parading avoidance—writing letters to the editors of newspapers, engaging in legal "informational" picketing (I set aside the difficulties of civil disobedience), etc., is an attempt to constrain conduct. And it is a matter of special concern when this sort of campaign is carried on, not by an individual, or a loose collection of individuals, but by the state, using the various institutions of the state. Educational campaigns by state agencies can have a powerful impact on people's conduct, despite the fact that that conduct is not being subjected to the "physical force of legal penalties." Directing public attention to behavior can indeed constrain that behavior.

Mill believed two things about the "moral coercion of public opinion:" that it was a powerful instrument of coercion, and that—as a consequence—it was subject to the constraints of the Harm Principle. And, according to the Harm Principle, it is justified only if directed at actions which harm, or pose a clear and present danger of harm, to others. Conversely: if a person's behavior neither harms others, nor poses a clear and present danger of harm to others, then it is permissible to avoid that person's company, but morally impermissible to *parade* that avoidance, to encourage others to avoid that person. (Though such a parading would be a moral wrong, it is unlikely that Mill would countenance its criminalization; Mill is a strong advocate of freedom of speech.)[9]

Mill's concern is clearly indicated in these two passages:

> The despotism of custom is everywhere the standing hindrance to human advancement, being in unceasing antagonism to that disposition to aim at something better than the customary . . . . [OL 85]

> Society can and does execute its own mandates; and if it issues wrong mandates instead of right, or any mandates at all in things with which it ought not to meddle, it practices a social tyranny more formidable than many kinds of political oppression, since, though not usually upheld by such extreme penalties it leaves fewer means of

[9]*On Liberty*, Chapter 2.

> escape, penetrating much more deeply in the details of life, and enslaving the soul itself. Protection, therefore, against the magistrate is not enough; there needs protection also against the tyranny of the prevailing opinion and feeling, against the tendency of society to impose, by other means than civil penalties, its own ideas and practices as rules of conduct . . . . [OL 7]

The "despotism of custom," this "social tyranny," was more potent a factor in Victorian England than, for example, contemporary United States—but the differences between the two societies is easy to exaggerate.[10] That it is operative in contemporary U.S. society is shown in the derailing of Gary Hart's campaign for the Democratic Party's nomination for President in 1988 (tales of "womanizing") and by Senator John Tower's (non)confirmation as Secretary of Defense (tales of womanizing and drinking). More generally: many "gays," many homosexuals of both genders, stay "in the closet," refusing to make public their sexual orientation, even in jurisdictions where homosexuality is not a criminal offense.

Mill continues,

> As soon as any part of a person's conduct affects prejudicially the interests of others, society has jurisdiction over it, and the question whether the general welfare will or will not be promoted by interfering with it becomes open to discussion. [OL 91-2]

This passage makes it very clear that an action's being in "Society's Jurisdiction," that an action's being "other-regarding," is *necessary* for criminalization—the question of interfering with the action cannot arise unless the action is in Society's Jurisdiction—but *not sufficient*: now it must be determined whether the general welfare will or will not be promoted by state interference.

Again, it is a shortcoming of *On Liberty* that no better criterion is offered. My point here is that the "moral coercion of public opinion" is a potent force in society, distinct from the "physical force of legal penalties;" it is appropriate that it is a distinct region in the topography of actions. And, as we shall see

---

[10]Joel Feinberg, *HTO*, pp. 3-4; C. L. Ten, *Mill On Liberty* (Oxford: Clarendon Press, 1980), as cited by Feinberg.

in subsequent chapters, it is a powerful weapon but an often neglected (and often misused) weapon in the arsenal of the state.

VII. OFFENDING OTHERS

Does Mill really hold that harm *per se* to others is a necessary condition for justified criminalization? In the following passage, he seems to hold otherwise:

> . . . there are many acts which, being directly injurious to only the agents themselves, ought not to be legally interdicted, but which, if done publicly, are a violation of good manners and, coming thus within the category of offenses against others, may rightly be prohibited. [OL 119]

Mill, his Victorian sensibilities brought to the fore, finishes the topic by saying only that "Of this kind are offenses against decency; on which it is unnecessary to dwell . . . ." [OL 119]

With this claim, Mill places himself in a dilemma. He believes that it is justifiable to make criminal the *public* performance of certain actions. Precisely *why* is this justified? If Mill is to remain consistent with his claim that "harm to others" is a *necessary* condition for justified criminalization, then he must hold that offending others in this way "harms" them. Now it is not implausible to claim that the concept of harm can be stretched to include the natural reaction to such displays—disgust, embarrassment, etc. This stretching of the concept of harm, however, is fraught with danger; "harm to others" is, for Mill, the criterion by which the actions of competent adults fall under Society's Jurisdiction (and thus are potentially eligible for restraint by either the "moral coercion of public opinion," or by "physical force"); enlarging the extension of "harm to others" is contrary to the central enterprise of *On Liberty*. Countenancing harms outside the intuitive core of the concept invites others to construct creative definitions of harm, legitimizing state prohibition of actions that Mill believes fall within individual sovereignty.[11] Conversely, Mill could argue that state prohibition of offensive public acts, even when they do not harm others, is justified. But in taking this stand, Mill would repudiate his claim that harm to others is a *necessary* condition for justified

[11]Feinberg, *Harm to Others*, Chapter Five; see also *Offense to Others*.

criminalization, that *only* harm to others justifies coercion—for he will have offered a non-harm, sufficient condition for legal prohibition. In point of fact Mill takes neither stand; he moves on to other topics.

VIII. MILL ON CRIMINALIZATION

Before moving on, I want to say what of Mill I accept, what I modify, and what I reject.

There is discernable in Mill a topography of actions relevant to coercion. More accurately, there are several different topographies of action suggested by different portions of the text. I have accepted from Mill the general approach of looking at actions which might be criminalized, rather than looking first to proposed criminal statutes. I have developed and modified and amended the various topographies, settling upon a single, neutral topography that I shall rely upon throughout the remainder of this work.

Mill makes clear that some actions ought not be criminalized despite their harming, or posing a clear and present danger of harm to others. This of course I accept—though it is overlooked, or its importance not realized, by many philosophers of the criminal law. Unfortunately Mill does not provide much help in determining just what actions those are; this is an issue I shall address at length in the next chapter.

Even if we accept the Harm Principle (duly qualified and modified) as correctly dividing Society's Jurisdiction from the Sphere of Individual Liberty, we are not given any criterion for dividing the actions which fall into Society's Jurisdiction into the three categories of Society's Jurisdiction merely, the "moral coercion of public opinion," and the "physical force of legal penalties." Without this, we lack some of the means necessary for determining which actions are justifiably criminalized, and which are not.

Additionally, there remains the problem of offensive public actions. Might something other than harm be sufficient for criminalization (contrary to the statement of the Harm Principle, that *only* harm to others can suffice), or are we to stretch the meaning of "harm to others" to include *offenses* (stepping onto a slippery slope, potentially countenancing the criminalization of many actions under the Harm Principle because of creative definitions of "harm to others")? When I shift from methodology to application—when I shift from Part One to Part Two—I shall take a stand on this issue.

To the extent that Mill relies upon a decision-procedure, it seems to be some sort of "balancing." In his discussion of gambling and prostitution, Mill agonizes; he is emphatic that people ought to be free to both gamble and to become or purchase the services of a prostitute. What is at issue: whether one ought to be free to encourage others to engage in such activities for one's own profit—to run a gambling house, or to pimp for prostitutes. Mill never answers the question; he merely concludes with a summary of the arguments "on both sides." [OL 120-22] In "weighing" the considerations which favor criminalization against considerations which oppose it, Mill seems to be engaged in a procedure of "balancing" of some sort.

IX. CHAPTER SUMMARY

A brief summary of the chapter is in order.

A careful reading of *On Liberty* reveals a variety of "topographic" claims; these form the basis of a complex, perfectly neutral topography of actions. According to Mill, if an action is that of a competent adult, and harms no one, or harms only that person oneself (or others who have given their consent), then the state ought not interfere with its performance—it falls within the Sphere of Individual Liberty. Actions which harm, or pose a clear and present danger of harm *to others*, fall within Society's Jurisdiction. Actions within Society's Jurisdiction might be tolerated (interference is likely to be ineffective, or even counterproductive), or discouraged by either the "moral coercion of public opinion" or by "physical force" in the form of legal penalties, or as exercised by private individuals. Although Mill clearly specifies the distinct categories of "moral coercion of public opinion" and "physical force of legal penalties," he says little of help in determining which actions fall into which category. While the "moral coercion of public opinion" was arguably a stronger force in Mill's time, its power today must not be neglected. The possibility exists that some actions fall neither into Society's Jurisdiction nor into the Sphere of Individual Liberty; if neither the argument for one nor the argument for the other is persuasive, then the action falls into the interstice.

A "topographic error" is committed by those whose claims presuppose a flawed topography. A topographic error is committed by those who believe that merely showing that an action does not fall into the Sphere of Individual Liberty is sufficient for showing that it is not in the interstice between the SIL and "Society's Jurisdiction," or (worse) that that is sufficient for showing that it is in Society's Jurisdiction, or (worse yet) that that is sufficient for showing that it is in the "moral coercion of public opinion, or (worst of all) that that is sufficient for showing that the use of force—of legal penalties, or by private individuals—is justified.

While it is clear that Mill believes that the public performance of offensive actions is justifiably prohibited, what is not clear is how he can defend that position in a way consistent with his claim that only the Harm Principle places an action within Society's Jurisdiction.

To the extent that Mill employs a "decision-procedure for morally justified criminalization," it seems to be some sort of "balancing" of the considerations in favor of, and opposing, criminalization. This is especially evident in his discussion of pimping, and keeping a gambling house.

How *ought* we determine which actions may morally be made crimes, and which not? What is it that must be shown—in addition to showing that an action *doesn't* fall within the Sphere of Individual Liberty—to show that it *does* fall within the "physical force of legal penalties?" Let us turn now to these issues.

CHAPTER THREE

"FILTERING" AS A DECISION-PROCEDURE FOR MORALLY JUSTIFIED CRIMINALIZATION

I. INTRODUCTION TO THE ISSUES OF THE CHAPTER

In this chapter I design a decision-procedure for morally justified criminalization which I call "Filtering," and argue that it is superior to "Balancing."

I endorse, in Section II, the presumption in favor of liberty accepted by most philosophers of the criminal law. Section III is devoted to an explanation of the decision-procedure itself; it includes a discussion of all three Filters, and a revision of the "liberty-limiting principles" formulated by Joel Feinberg—revisions made necessary by the pending rejection of Balancing. In Section IV, I look at the relationship between Filtering and its philosophical predecessors. The relationship between the topography of actions developed in Chapter Two, and Filtering, is the subject of Section V. In Section VI, I argue for the superiority of Filtering over Balancing; I begin by showing that Filtering respects the topography of actions developed in Chapter Three, while Balancing encourages the various "topographic errors" (as defined in Chapter Two), recount the "misgivings" about Balancing discussed in Chapter One (arguing that Filtering does not have the features which gave rise to those misgivings), and offer a final set of arguments against Balancing: a kind of case in which Balancing clearly is misguided. In Section VII, I discuss some "sources of frustration" in dealing with undesirable behavior. I ask whether Balancing could be salvaged, in Section VIII; I argue that it cannot be, and that there is no point to making the attempt. Section IX contains a "vocabulary of justification" for criminalization, a vocabulary that is based on Filtering. Finally, I summarize the Chapter's work in Section X.

II. THE BURDEN OF PROOF AS REGARDS CRIMINALIZATION

I agree with Joel Feinberg, and indeed most other philosophers of the criminal law, that there is, and ought to be, a presumption in favor of liberty: the burden of proof is on those who wish to criminalize actions, and not on those who wish to live free of such restrictions.

> . . . most writers on our subject have endorsed a kind of "presumption in favor of liberty" requiring that whenever a legislator is faced with a choice between imposing a legal duty on citizens or leaving them at liberty, other things being equal, he should leave individuals free to make their own choices. Liberty should be the norm; coercion always needs some special justification. [HTO 9]

The "special justification" that is required, as I see it, is defined by "Filtering."

III. FILTERING

I propose that we think about criminalization in this way: when it is suggested that some action be criminalized, we think of that action as having to pass, successfully and successively, through three distinct "Filters." Failure to pass through any Filter entails that the action cannot justifiably be criminalized; passing through all three Filters entails that the action is justifiably made criminal. My thesis is that successful Filtering is both necessary and sufficient for morally justified criminalization. Let us turn now to a discussion of each of these three Filters.

III. A. The Principles Filter

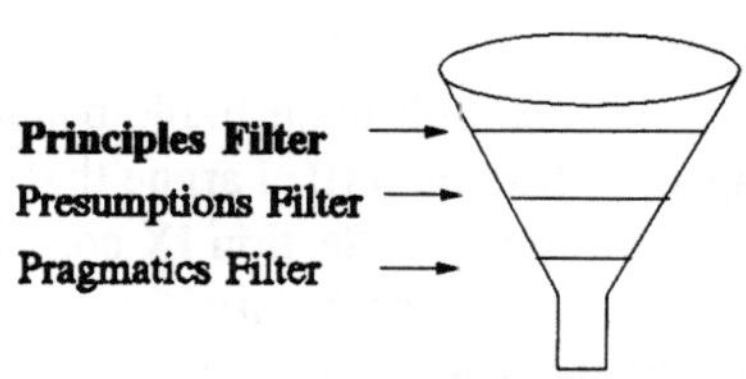

Morally Justified Criminalization
Figure 3 — 1

At the Principles Filter, one argues for one's set of Principles of State Authority, thereby specifying one's position as regards "things fit to be done by a government." What *are* these "Principles of State Authority?" The clearest way of answering this question is to contrast Principles of State Authority with Feinberg's "liberty-limiting principles."

As we saw in Chapter Two, Feinberg's "liberty-limiting principles" are quite lengthy and elaborate. In addition to addressing the issue of the moral authority of the state, they also raise the issues of "effectiveness," and also the issues of conflicts among values. My concern in Chapter Two was to show the heavy reliance of philosophers of the criminal law on a decision-procedure of "Balancing" (and, of course, to induce misgivings about it). Feinberg's formulations compel one to adopt Balancing as one's decision-procedure: to determine the "weight" of the presumption in favor of liberty, the "weight" of relevant liberty-limiting principles, the "weight" of various pragmatic consequences (issues of enforcement, unintended side-effects of criminalization, etc.) and then, in a single "weighing," determine the "weightier" set. This is clear from Feinberg's formulation of the Harm Principle:

> The Harm Principle: It is always a good reason in support of penal legislation that it would probably be effective in preventing (eliminating, reducing) harm to persons other than the actor (the one prohibited from acting) *and* there is probably no other means that is equally effective at no greater cost to other values. [HTO 26]

And Feinberg notes that that which follows the "and" is to be appended to all the other liberty-limiting principles he lists: "The clause following 'and' goes without saying in the subsequent definitions, but it is understood." [HTO 26, n. 2] Thus, the full statement of the Offense Principle is as follows:

> The Offense Principle: It is always a good reason in support of a proposed criminal prohibition that it is probably necessary to prevent serious offense to persons other than the actor and would probably be an effective means to that end if enacted—*and* there is probably no other means that is equally effective at no greater cost to other values. [HTO 26]

An so on for the other liberty-limiting principles Feinberg defines.

Of course I *do* believe that the issues of effectiveness, conflict with other values, etc. are important issues. Indeed, I think them so important that they deserve separate consideration; they ought not be jumbled together with the quite different issue of the state's moral authority.

In contrast with Feinberg, I offer the following list of "Principles of State Authority" (often "PSA"). They differ from Feinberg's "liberty-limiting principles" in two important ways. First, they are shorn of all "pragmatic" concerns; they focus exclusively on the moral role of the state. Second,

"Principles of State Authority" do not compel one to employ "Balancing" as one's decision-procedure for criminalization. Quite explicitly, there is no attempt to "weigh" other considerations relevant to an action's being justifiably criminalized—much less "weighing" them all at once.

Each Principle of State Authority is numbered and worded to correlate with Feinberg's "liberty-limiting principles."

1. The Harm Principle: An action is an appropriate concern of the state if that action causes harm to a person other than the actor.

2. The Offense Principle: An action is an appropriate concern of the state if it offends a person other than the actor.

3. The Liberal Position: The Harm Principle and the Offense Principle, duly clarified and qualified, between them exhaust the class of good reasons for an action's being an appropriate concern of the state.

4. Legal Paternalism: An action is an appropriate concern of the state if that action causes harm to the actor oneself.

5. Legal Moralism (narrow): An action is an appropriate concern of the state if it is inherently immoral, even though it causes neither harm nor offense to the actor or to others.

6. Moralistic Legal Paternalism: An action is an appropriate concern of the state if the action causes moral harm to the actor oneself.

7. Legal Moralism (broad): An action is an appropriate concern of the state if, while neither harming nor offending others, it constitutes or causes "free-floating" evils.

8. Benefit to Others: An action is an appropriate concern of the state if performing the action will produce benefit for persons other than the person oneself.

9. Benefit-Conferring Legal Paternalism: An action is an appropriate concern of the state if its performance will benefit that person.

10. Perfectionism: An action is an appropriate concern of the state if its performance will improve (a) other people, or (b) the individual oneself.

Again, I make no case here for which Principles of State Authority are *acceptable* PSAs; to do that would be the first step in *employing* the decision-procedure, and my goal here is to defend Filtering as a decision-procedure (or more precisely, to argue its superiority over Balancing). Thus my concern is not to resolve the competition among various PSAs, but rather to *locate* that argument within a decision-procedure for morally justified criminalization. The arguments of the Principles Filter are arguments about individual rights, and the appropriate role of the state. Thus, "Liberals" (in Feinberg's sense) offer arguments for individual sovereignty's having a large domain; Legal Paternalists argue that that domain should be smaller, that the state may require competent adults to perform, or refrain from, various acts—citing as the justification an agent's own good. This is the argument over the nature and extent of the moral authority of the state. In Filtering, all such arguments are arguments of the Principles Filter; this battle is waged in splendid isolation from issues of enforcement, and from the side-effects of criminalization. Whether the state has the *moral authority* to enact criminal laws on, for example, paternalistic grounds is an issue that ought to be decided independent of the issues of enforcement, and the other consequences of criminalization. Of course these matters are *crucial* in deciding whether such a criminal statute ought to be enacted. But that is a different matter, a matter of a different Filter. (In separating the issues of the moral authority of the state, of legitimate state function, from the practical concerns of law enforcement, Filtering ameliorates the "problem of incomparables" inherent in Balancing. That a law would be impossible for a state to enforce is a powerful reason for not enacting it—but no reason at all for believing that the action it would prohibit is not in Society's Jurisdiction. That's a separate matter: a matter that is handled separately in Filtering, but jumbled together with the others in Balancing.)

Thus, regardless of one's position as regards "things fit to be done by a government," under Filtering, the first step in arguing that some action ought to be criminalized is to show that that action falls under the purview of an acceptable Principle of State Authority. This itself requires two distinct achievements: (i) showing that some particular PSA is acceptable, and (ii) showing that the action in question falls under the purview of that particular Principle of State Authority.

III. B. The Presumptions Filter

Figure 3 — 2

The second Filter is the Presumptions Filter. Once the action has passed through the Principles Filter, the good legislator, the good philosopher of criminal law must ask: given that this is the *sort* of action with which the state is appropriately concerned, is there some technique of social control which will be successful in reducing the incidence of that action to an acceptable rate—but which is less intrusive, less coercive than a criminal statute? Alternatively: is there some action the state could take that, although not reducing the incidence of the conduct, would reduce the negative consequences of that conduct to an acceptable level?

If an investigation reveals the fact that *every* state action—even a "public awareness" campaign—would prove ineffective (a waste of resources) or counterproductive (would instigate a higher rather than a lower incidence)—then the action does not pass through the Presumptions Filter. If, however, there are state measures which would reduce the incidence, or the deleterious consequences, then the action does pass through the Presumptions Filter. However, one cannot have shown that the state is justified in criminalizing an action without investigating whether there are ways of successfully reducing the incidence of that action *without* engaging the machinery of the criminal justice system: police, prosecutors, courts, and the costly strictures of procedural due process. Now I am *not* arguing for reducing the strictures of due process in criminal prosecutions—far from it. My claim, rather, is that we ought to be more selective as regards precisely which actions will subject citizens to the machinery of the criminal justice system. Though I shall have (much) more to say about that machinery (in the context of the third Filter), I claim this here: there are many ways of discouraging behavior, and of reducing or eliminating the negative consequences of behavior; the good legislator, the good philosopher of the criminal law, ought to investigate very thoroughly just how those goals might be achieved in ways that allow for a freer society, ways which do not subject citizens to the indignities of arrest, the expense of defense, the consequences of incarceration, and the encumbrances of conviction—as detailed in the Introduction. The state, via education campaigns, has powerful instruments of persuasion at its disposal. So as regards particular actions, one must ask, "Might not a well-designed program of information about the deleterious consequences of this action reduce its incidence to a tolerable level—without involving police and prosecutors, courts and incarceration?" Additionally, taxation policies can be employed to alter behavior, or to indemnify the state if citizens elect especially risky behavior.[1] Additionally, the state might institute schemes of licensing, insurance, permits, etc. Regulation—even if the criminal law is used to enforce those regulations—might well prove effective, as well as less costly: both in terms of resources, and in terms of liberty.

The concern of this Filter is a companion of, but different from, the "presumption" in favor of liberty. That presumption holds that citizens ought to be free of restrictions unless it can be proved that they ought not; the Presumptions Filter holds that, as regards actions of the sort with which a state is appropriately concerned, *ceteris paribus* the less intrusive methods of discouraging that conduct are to be preferred over the more intrusive.

---

[1]Bear in mind I am speaking of actions that have already been shown within Society's Jurisdiction; Mill expresses concern about using taxation to discourage behavior that has not been shown to fall within Society's Jurisdiction. (*On Liberty*, pp. 122-3.)

III. C. The Pragmatics Filter

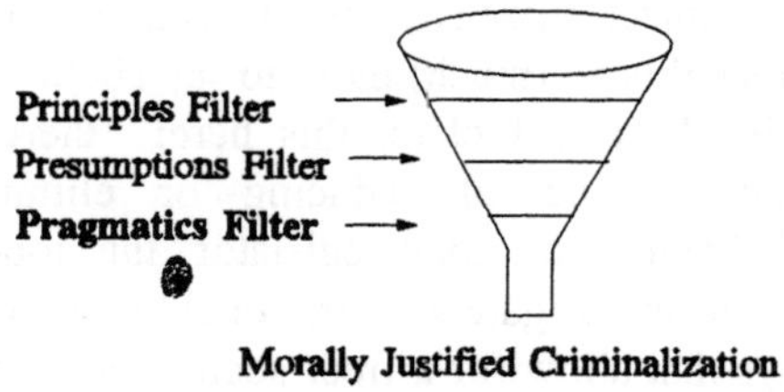

Figure 3 — 3

The third Filter is the Pragmatics Filter. At this Filter one investigates the *actual consequences* of criminalizing the action in question. The enactment and enforcement of criminal statutes have causal consequences: some will be immediate and obvious, some may be distant (in both time and space) and subtle, some may be quite surprising and very bizarre.[2] The good legislator, the good philosopher of the criminal law does one's best to anticipate these causal consequences, to envision the causal networks which will be created by a criminal statute prohibiting the action in question. And then a cost/benefit analysis must be performed; one must assess the social costs and benefits of enacting the proposed statute, and assess the costs and benefits of *not* enacting that statute. (As regards existing legislation: the social costs and benefits of that statute; the causal consequences of the repeal of that statute, and the costs and benefits of repeal.)

It is essential to note that there is a *moral* dimension to the issues of the Pragmatics Filter.

Let us say that the "primary" moral issues of criminalization are the issues of the Principles Filter: the arguments about the authority of the state. Then let us call the moral issues that arise in the context of the Pragmatics Filter "secondary" moral issues. What are these "secondary" moral issues? To enact a law that can be enforced only if the police use highly intrusive detection techniques (e.g. wiretapping) is to burden society with the moral debits of that practice. To enact a law that creates a "crime tariff" (discussed below) is to burden society with the evils associated with that tariff. And more generally,

[2]For example, see Chapter Six, "The War on Drugs," the arguments at the Pragmatics Filter.

all arguments of resource allocation raise the issue of the optimal plan for using those resources; devoting them to one task rather than to another task requires moral justification. If devoting police, prosecutorial, courtroom, and prison time to reducing the incidence of an activity is a gross misallocation of social resources—if it would be wrong to allocate resources in that way, since that allocation entails the neglect of other, more important law-enforcement efforts—then criminalization is not justified. Furthermore, criminalization is not justified on account of *moral* considerations. The arguments which arise from the "secondary" moral issues militate against the criminalization of actions if that criminalization will make the society *morally* worse off, given the pragmatics of enforcement.

Even though an action passes through the Principles Filter (is of a sort with which a state is properly concerned) and the Presumptions Filter (its incidence cannot be reduced to an acceptable level by means less intrusive than the criminal law), a prohibitory statute is not justified unless it can be shown that the benefits of such a statute will exceed its costs. Conversely: if criminalizing an action will make a society worse off, all things considered, than *not* prohibiting it, then the prohibiting law is not justified—even though the action in question is properly the concern of the state. Put even more starkly: there are actions which no one has a *right* to perform, but which the state cannot justifiably make criminal—because making it criminal would have worse consequences than not making it criminal. As Herbert Packer argues,

> There is always the alternative of doing nothing. After a careful appraisal of costs and benefits, we may conclude that it is better not to impose any sanction at all than to resort to one of the available ones. No lawmaker can say that he has thought the problem through until he has considered that possibility. It is only when we confront this "null hypothesis" that we can squarely confront the central issue of how high on our scale of values the suppression of a given form of conduct ranks.[3]

Thus, Filtering makes these claims. (1) Proving that some action is properly the concern of the state is necessary, but is not sufficient to prove that it is justifiably criminalized; one must also show that less coercive measures are

---

[3]Herbert L. Packer, *The Limits of the Criminal Sanction* (Stanford: Stanford University Press, 1968), p. 258.

unlikely to succeed, and that the statute will produce a net benefit over cost. (2) To prove that the benefits of a statute will outweigh the costs, one must show both that (i) there are measures the state *can* take, employing the machinery of the criminal justice system, which will be *effective* in reducing the incidence of the action in question, and (ii) (of course) that the costs of operating that machinery do not exceed its benefits. As I shall argue below, the first condition is often overlooked; independent of the issue of costs and benefits, in some cases the state cannot significantly reduce the incidence of the action, via the criminal law, *at all.* (3) The legislator, the philosopher of criminal law who fails to investigate the pragmatic consequences of enacting criminal statutes, and assess those consequences, has failed to justify coercion. And of course getting the consequences wrong, or assessing them incorrectly, is a failure too.

Obviously it would not be possible to list all the possible consequences of all possible criminal statutes. What I undertake now is a discussion of some of what Packer calls "limiting criteria"—the negative consequences of some statutes, some "costs" of criminalization, items which militate against certain criminal prohibitions. These are *illustrations*, not arguments; in providing these examples, I am not claiming that, as regards any particular criminal statute, these costs exceed any particular benefits. My goal simply is to identify some of the sorts of negative consequences which must be factored into the cost/benefit analysis that is the Pragmatics Filter.

1. The Crime Tariff

There is an "elastic" demand for a commodity if increases in price result in decreases in demand; the demand is "*in*elastic" if increases in price do *not* result in decreases in demand. If the state criminalizes the commerce in a commodity (either a "good" or a "service") for which there is an inelastic demand, it thereby creates a "crime tariff" on that commodity.[4] *Ex hypothesi* the demand is not reduced by price increases; consumers will pay whatever price is asked. The price of the commodity is driven up; for those willing to take the risks of commerce in illegal commodities, the profit potential is virtually unlimited.

---

[4]Of course "elastic" and "inelastic" are endpoints on a continuum; the demand for most commodities lies somewhere between. In general, the less elastic (more inelastic) the demand for a commodity, the higher the crime tariff. (I develop this point more fully in Chapter Six.)

The United States established a "crime tariff" on alcoholic beverages from 1920-33; the profits funded the establishment of "organized crime."[5] Various other commodities are currently subject to a crime tariff. Among the "goods" are some (but by no means all) psychoactive substances; among the "services" are prostitution, gambling and abortion.

Undeniably there is much evil "associated with" the commerce in illegal psychoactives—"drugs." In Chapter Six, I undertake a sustained investigation of the laws which establish a crime tariff on some psychoactive substances. Here, I simply offer some illustrations of the complex causal networks that are created by such legislation. Virtually all of the "evils" associated with the use of illegal "drugs" are *not* consequences of that use itself, but of the *criminalization* of "drugs"—principally from the crime tariff.

Consumers of illegal "drugs" are responsible for a substantial portion of the United States's acquisitive crime—things are stolen in order to pay the artificially high price of "drugs." With few exceptions, drug use *per se* does not cause anti-social behavior; crimes are committed to secure the resources needed to purchase the "drugs." And the purchase price is vastly higher than the production price, because commerce is risky—due to criminal statutes. The profits of this commerce are causally sufficient for a vast array of social ills. Rival businessmen fight—literally, and frequently, and sometimes with so-called "assault weapons"—for sales territory. The profits of the enterprise are used to bribe police officers, prosecutors, judges, members of juries, prison guards and officials, etc. And the protection of these enormous profits makes it worthwhile (in the eyes of some) to threaten, or to actually kill, police officers, justice department officials, jurors, etc. Profits make worthwhile the recruitment of new consumers—primarily young people. And the conspicuous consumption of those individuals profiting from this commerce guarantees that they will be taken as role models in their neighborhoods. And there are other negative consequences of establishing a crime tariff; some of these too will be discussed in Chapter Six.

I hope to have avoided becoming enmeshed in the controversies of "drug" laws themselves; my goal here is limited to displaying the operation of the Pragmatics Filter. I claim that criminal statutes are not justified unless they

---

[5]Cf. Herbert Packer, *The Limits of the Criminal Sanction*, p. 279; Humbert S. Nelli, *The Business of Crime* (New York: Oxford University Press, 1976), pp. 262ff.; *An Economic Analysis of Crime: Selected Readings*, ed. Lawrence J. Kaplan and Dennis Kessler (Springfield, Illinois: Charles C. Thomas, 1976), especially Chapters 8 and 9.

produce a balance of benefit over cost; to determine whether this is the case, one needs to get clear on the causal consequences of the statute. In some of the professional literature, and in almost all of the popular literature (and other media), however, causal connections are not accurately identified. This results in an incorrect "ledger entry:" deleterious consequences of the *statute* are entered as negative consequences of the actions made criminal—and thus as reasons in favor of criminalization, rather than as reasons against criminalization.

To criminalize commerce in a commodity is to create a crime tariff—whether on psychoactive substances, or ivory, or rhinoceros horn, or live birds of paradise, or the pelts of animals of endangered species. Or contract murders. Some such statutes are nonetheless justified (I suspect); some (I suspect) are not. My claim is this: in deciding whether to criminalize that commerce, one is negligent if one does not factor the consequences of creating a crime tariff into the decision whether to criminalize the action.

2. *Triviality of Intention*

It sometimes happens that laws are passed with no expectation that the police will arrest people for violating them, much less will prosecutors be prosecuting offenders, much less still will jail space be devoted to punishing offenders. The enactment is intended not so much as a serious addition to the calendar of crimes, but as a statement of disapproval. Sometimes the purported justification is that the law will serve to "educate" the citizenry. The criminal law is, however, a clumsy educator. Worse, the non-enforcement of criminal statutes fosters a generalized disrespect for the law. Additionally, it creates unsavory opportunities for the officials of the criminal justice system—the next concern.

3. *Capricious or Evil Enforcement*

When laws are passed without the intention that they be enforced, the opportunity for capricious or evil enforcement is created. As regards "serious" laws, the officials of the criminal justice system are subject to public criticism or removal from office if the laws are not vigorously enforced. But if there is no public outcry when certain laws are not vigorously enforced, problems can easily arise.

First, enforcement might be capricious: only a small percentage of violators are subjected to arrest and prosecution. As a consequence, those unlucky enough to be apprehended will believe that they have been treated unjustly. The one person in a crowd of jaywalkers to be charged with that "crime" is likely to feel unfairly "singled out."

Second, enforcement might be genuinely *evil*. Officers of the law can enforce the law in ways that advance some personal agenda: racist, sexist, ageist, etc. Police officers can selectively see or not see certain events; prosecutors can decide that a case is or is not strong enough to present to a grand jury, investigators can choose to be more or less diligent, etc. This is all obvious. But the abuse of discretion can also occur in circumstances which seem, at first blush, immune to abuse. I want to sketch one hypothetical of this sort.

Imagine that the officials of a toll road institute a program of checking entry and exit times printed on toll cards. They can be certain that any vehicle which has traversed a given distance in less than a specified time must have been speeding. If the automobile is occupied by only the driver, it must have been that individual who is guilty of speeding. (If the car contains multiple occupants, it will not be possible to determine which of the individuals committed the offense.)[6] Of course not all persons guilty of speeding can be caught in this way; one could speed, but not complete the entry/exit distance in too short an elapsed time, for having stopped for food or fuel. However, *everyone* ticketed under this program is indeed guilty of violating the speed law; *only* guilty parties are ticketed. Despite the fact that only the guilty are ticketed, this operation can be subverted by an abuse of discretion. Despite the fact that only the guilty are ticketed, tickets could be issued in a way that is evil: only to African Americans, or only to women, or only to men, or only to attractive women, or only to (those who appear to be) homosexuals, and so forth. My point: the operation of the criminal justice system can be strange and intricate, and injustices can appear in seemingly unlikely places. The good legislator, the good philosopher of the criminal law, will be alert to the possibilities of abuse of discretion, and will reflect on the complex causal nexuses that can be created by the enactment and enforcement of criminal laws.

---

[6]I set aside the possibility that a hitchhiker, dropped off before the car exited, was the guilty party.

4. Police as Intrusive

Some "crimes" are such that the police must intrude to determine *whether* a crime is being committed, and not merely to apprehend a person for a crime they know has been committed. These are particularly troublesome; the police are (correctly) seen as intrusive rather than protective. This perception leads to a spiraling deterioration of the relationship between the public and the police. The police will receive less cooperation from the citizenry, and that will hamper their protective activities. In consequence, they will (correctly) be viewed as ineffectual. And that perception will lead to even less cooperation . . . . Such a state of affairs is in no one's interests.

Overall, I agree with Herbert Packer's claim that

> In a sense, all limiting criteria reduce themselves to a simple prescription: first things first. The criminal sanction is the law's ultimate threat. Being punished for a crime is different from being regulated in the public interest, or being forced to compensate another who has been injured by one's conduct, or being treated for a disease. The sanction is at once uniquely coercive and, in the broadest sense, uniquely expensive. It should be reserved for what really matters.[7]

In expanding the calendar of crimes, one increases the burden on police, prosecutors, public defenders, courts, prisons, etc. On the perfectly safe assumption that resources for the criminal justice system are finite, there are important issues of precisely how to spend those dollars. How should police investigative time be spent? prosecutorial time? public defender time? Of all the things that people do, *which* are the most important to discourage—whether through deterrence (general or specific), rehabilitation, or custody? What is second most important? And what is *least* important?

> We cannot have all the things we want, crime prevention included. Every hour of police, prosecutorial, judicial, and correctional time that is spent on marginal uses of the criminal sanction is an hour lost to the prevention of serious crime. Conversely, every trivial, imaginary, or otherwise dubious crime that

---

[7]Herbert L. Packer, *The Limits of the Criminal Sanction* (Stanford: Stanford University Press, 1968), p. 250.

> is removed from the list of criminal offenses represents the freeing of substantial resources to deal more effectively with the high-priority needs of the criminal justice system. Whether our rational legislator is engaged in revising an existing criminal code or pondering a new proposal for invocation of the criminal sanction, he ought to remember that resources are limited, that every dollar and every man-hour is the object of competition among uses, and that (to end where we began) he should not only put first things first, but also, what is perhaps harder, put last things last.[8]

Of course, even though *finite*, resources need not be *static*: perhaps more should be devoted to the criminal justice system, either by a reallocation of existing resources, or by increasing revenues (raising taxes). But precisely the same sorts of issues must be addressed. Discouraging *which* sorts of behavior is worth how much money—taken from education, or welfare, or infrastructure maintenance, or debt reduction, etc.—or generated by new taxes?

5. *The Pragmatics Filter and the* Moral *Limits of the Criminal Law*

There is a mixture of pragmatic and secondary moral arguments at the Pragmatics Filter. When drawing the *moral* limits of the criminal sanction, we must consider both the "primary" moral issues of the Principles Filter, and also the "secondary" moral issues of the Pragmatics Filter. In an important way, this distinguishes my position from Joel Feinberg's. For Feinberg seeks to avoid the latter set of moral issues, the "secondary" moral issues, by separating the *moral* limits from other, "political" considerations.

> The book will not consider the further questions of cost-benefit analysis that must guide the legislator in his choice among those alternatives that do fall within the recommended moral limits. Within the proper limits a legislator must consider the social utility of his various options, their likely effects on various private and public interests, constituent desires and pressures, even the demands of "politics" in a narrow sense (log-rolling, compromising, political debt-paying, etc.) . . . I do not offer suggestions here about what it would be "a good idea" to legislate within the scope of what *may*

---

[8]Herbert L. Packer, *The Limits of the Criminal Sanction* (Stanford: Stanford University Press, 1968), p. 259-60.

> be legislated. This book is a quest not for useful policies but for valid principles. [HTO 4]

I agree fully that there are some "further questions" that are not within the domain of the philosophy of the criminal law. Suppose that Senator Alpha votes for S.B. 1, despite believing that it is not very good law, because Senator Beta has sponsored it, and Senator Alpha needs Beta's vote on S.B. 2, which Alpha believes of great importance. This sort of vote trading, though not immune from moral scrutiny, is not in the domain of the the philosophy of the criminal law.

In contrast, imagine that some criminal statute *S* is proposed. Suppose that the action which Statute *S* would prohibit is indeed an action appropriately the concern of the state. Suppose that the enactment and enforcement of *S* would create a crime tariff: *S* prohibits commerce in some commodity for which there is an inelastic demand. Suppose further that the profits from the crime tariff created by *S* would have far-reaching, deleterious effects on society: the corruption of police and prosecutors, judges and jailers; the spawning of acquisitive crime, etc. In sum, suppose that the society would be markedly worse off if it enacts *S* than if it does not. My claim is this: the *moral* limits of the criminal law are exceeded if statute *S* is enacted. In determining the moral limits of the criminal law, one must investigate the pragmatic consequences of there being such a law, and morally assess those consequences—one must take the measure of "secondary" moral issues. If one does not, one draws the moral limits of the criminal law at the wrong place; *moral* considerations which constrain the state are neglected.

More generally, if devoting criminal justice resources to enforcing a particular statute would require the diversion of resources from more important enforcement efforts, then this is a *moral* constraint on the state as regards criminalization. If one does not see the moral constraints on the state as including the moral issues of enforcement and resource allocation, then one gets the wrong result; one draws the moral limits of the criminal law too loosely. The state is *morally* constrained by the *moral* effects of the enforcement of statutes, and by the application of moral principles to the issues of resource allocation.

The "cost-benefit analysis" of the Pragmatics Filter is not, as it seems Feinberg would claim, a "further question" to be asked as regards "those alternatives that do fall within the recommended moral limits." [HTO 4]

Rather, the cost-benefit analysis is an essential component of the very *determination* of those "moral limits."

One could ask questions of this sort:

> "Which actions may morally be criminalized, if enforcement is free, if there are no "costs" of enforcement?"
>
> "Which actions may morally be criminalized, if resources for enforcement are infinite?"
>
> "Which actions may morally be criminalized, if prohibiting is preventing, if compliance can be assumed?"

Since there is no society in which enforcement if free, or the resources for enforcement are infinite, or the citizenry is fully compliant, I can see no value in asking these questions. Of less value still is spending time and energy attempting to answer them.

Thus, an action fails to pass through the third Filter, the Pragmatics Filter, if the social costs of such a statute exceed the social benefits. And those costs include issues of resource allocation, and "secondary" moral issues. An action might fail to pass through the Pragmatics Filter because no permissible state action would in fact prove effective in reducing the incidence of the action. It might fail to pass through the Pragmatics Filter because reducing the incidence of the action, with a criminal statute, isn't worth the moral worsening of the society that would be the consequence of enacting and enforcing such a statute. And it might fail to pass through the Pragmatics Filter because the enforcement of the relevant statute would be a misallocation of social resources.

IV. FILTERING AND PHILOSOPHICAL PREDECESSORS

I claim no originality as regards the specific issues addressed at each of the Filters; I make no claim to have discovered something that has eluded my philosophical predecessors. Quite to the contrary, my claim is that—upon reflection—all will assent to the central thesis at each Filter. If the action a statute would criminalize is not an action that is the proper concern of a state, then the statute is not justified. If the action a statute would criminalize is indeed of a sort with which the state is properly concerned, then (*ceteris paribus*) the less coercive measures for reducing its incidence (or its negative consequences) are to be preferred over the more coercive. If the costs of enforcing a criminal statute would exceed its benefits, then it ought not be enacted—even if the action it would prohibit is of the sort with which a state is properly concerned, and whose incidence cannot be effectively reduced in other ways. To make such actions *crimes*—to subject citizens to the indignities of arrest, the expenses of defense, the consequences of incarceration, and the encumbrances of conviction—for electing them, is morally wrong.

Conversely, if an action is appropriately the state's concern, and its incidence cannot be reduced by less coercive measures, and its prohibition would yield a net benefit, then its criminalization is justified. I submit that, upon reflection, these are the statutes that we are, and ought to be, most confident are justified. Consider: what *more* could one be asked to show?

Now it could be claimed that the issues of the three Filters are raised in Feinberg's formulations of "liberty-limiting principles." Consider the Harm Principle: "It is always a good reason in support of penal legislation that it would probably be effective in preventing (eliminating, reducing) harm to persons other than the actor (the one prohibited from acting) *and* there is probably no other means that is equally effective at no greater cost to other values." [HTO 26] The phrase "probably no other means" suggests the issues of the Presumptions Filter; the phrase "at no greater cost to other values" suggests some of the issues of the Pragmatics Filter. However—as I have shown—these "liberty-limiting principles are conjoined with Balancing, where the importance of these phrases fades. Indeed—and it is important to not make too much, or too little of this fact—these phrases are printed only with the Harm Principle and the Offense Principle. In a footnote to the latter, Feinberg writes "The clause following 'and' goes without saying in the subsequent definitions but is understood." [HTO 26, n. 2] Despite having four volumes of space, Feinberg did not think it important to print these phrases with the remaining principles. If one were to read any of the other principles on the list—including Legal Paternalism and Legal Moralism—one would not read the "complete" statement of the principle: unless one read the Harm or Offense Principle, and the accompanying footnotes.

I do not know whether Feinberg's "backgrounding" of these clauses is causally related to his "backgrounding" of these issues at points later in the text. What I shall argue, however, is that Feinberg has not taken the measure of these issues in some of his subsequent work—as regards the "Voluntariness Tribunal," and "garrison situations." As a consequence, he arrives at the wrong result—or so I shall argue in Chapters Four and Five.

Although claiming no originality for the issues addressed at each Filter, I do claim originality for divorcing them from the fatally flawed metaphor of Balancing, and assembling them in a way that captures what we, upon reflection, believe about criminalization. To make good on that claim, let us first turn to the relationship between Filtering and the topography of actions developed in Chapter Two.

V. FILTERING AND THE TOPOGRAPHY OF ACTIONS

In Chapter Two, I devised a neutral topography of actions relevant to criminalization. The arguments for the various regions of the topography, and the relations among the regions, were perfectly straightforward. Upon reflection, I believe, virtually everyone will assent to these regions, and their relationships. Only the anarchist would deny "Society's Jurisdiction," only the totalitarian would deny the "Sphere of Individual Liberty." Some actions that fall within Society's Jurisdiction ought to be ignored, some ought to be the subject of educational campaigns, some ought to be criminalized. The quarrels among proponents of various Principles of State Authority (for Feinberg, "liberty-limiting principles") are most clearly understood as disagreements about the *contents* of the various regions, and not disagreements about the regions themselves.

In the opening sections of this chapter, I have devised a decision-procedure for morally justified criminalization; I have argued that Filtering captures criminalization at its best.

In contrast with the dynamics of placing weights on the pans of a beam balance, I have pictured an action passing, or not passing, through three filters in a funnel. And when illustrating this, I have provided a side view of the funnel. Were that funnel viewed from the top, the filters would appear as concentric circles.

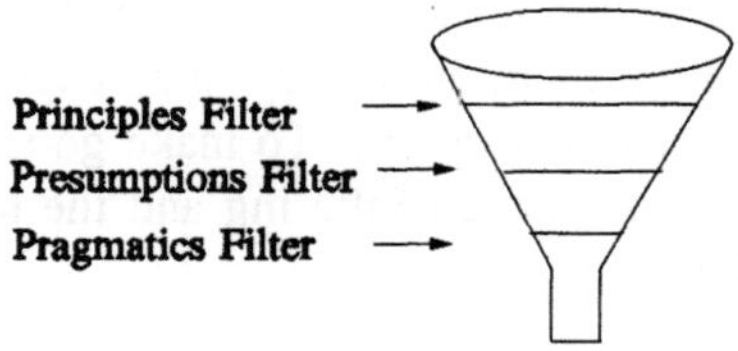

Morally Justified Criminalization

Figure 3 — 4

The topography of actions identified three regions within Society's Jurisdiction: Society's Jurisdiction merely, the "moral coercion of public opinion," and the "physical force of legal penalties." Filtering features three Filters: Principles, Presumptions, Pragmatics.

The Filters constitute the boundaries between the regions of the topography. If an action falls under the purview of an acceptable[9] Principle of State Authority, it passes through the Principles Filter: and lands in Society's Jurisdiction (merely). If the incidence of that action, or its deleterious consequences, can be reduced through measures less coercive and intrusive than a criminal statute, it passes through the Presumptions Filter: and lands in the "moral coercion of public opinion." If less coercive measures will prove ineffective, and if the benefits of a criminal statute exceed its costs, the action passes through the Pragmatics Filter: and lands in the "physical force of legal penalties" (or alternatively, "physical force" wielded by private citizens). Thus, the topography displays the regions; Filtering sorts actions into these regions.

If all is well, Filtering and the topography are not merely complementary, but synergistic. Confidence in Filtering gives added reason to subscribe to the topography's regions; confidence in the topography's regions gives added reason to adopt Filtering.

As this essay continues, the language of Filtering and the language of the topography will mesh. In contexts where it is clearer to speak of

---

[9]Filtering is a methodology; it is not a substantive position. It is intended as the superior decision-procedure for morally justified criminalization, superior to Balancing, regardless of one's substantive position. Hence, I take no position (at this point) on which Principles of State Authority are "acceptable" Principles of State Authority.

"boundaries," I will use the vocabulary of Filtering. In contexts where it is clearer to speak of "regions," I will use the vocabulary of the topography.

VI. THE SUPERIORITY OF FILTERING

The ultimate test of a decision-procedure for morally justified criminalization is its persuasive application to recalcitrant issues in the philosophy of the criminal law—precisely the task I undertake in the chapters of Part Two of this essay. However, as a result of my work on the topography of actions, and the explanation of Filtering itself, I can make the penultimate case for its superiority over Balancing.

The arguments come in three waves. In the first, I argue that Balancing accommodates, or even fosters, "topographic errors." In the second, I review the "misgivings" about Balancing raised in Chapter One, showing that Filtering does not suffer from the infirmities that gave rise to those misgivings.[10] In the third wave, I consider problems which occur when arguments for criminalization arise from more than one Principle of State Authority. The "natural" way of handling this in Balancing is misconceived; Filtering, I shall argue, handles this correctly.

VI. A. Topographic Errors

As we have seen, Filtering is an integral element of the neutral topography of actions, as developed in Chapter Two. In sharp contrast, Balancing suggests a much simpler, and deeply flawed, topography.

---

[10]Or if it does suffer from such an infirmity, it has a less serious case.

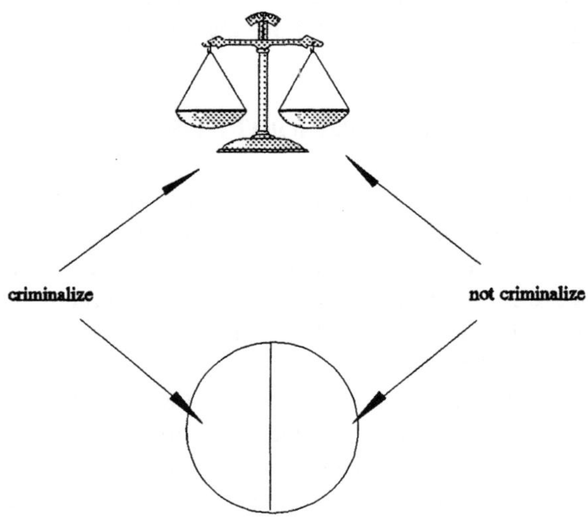

Figure 3 - 5

The result of "weighing" the various considerations in favor of criminalization, and "weighing" the various considerations against criminalization, is (ideally) a decision as to whether the action at issue is justifiably criminalized. Of course that's what's wanted as the final outcome of a decision-procedure for morally justified criminalization. But is that *all* that's wanted? I think not. While we *do* want to know whether an action is justifiably criminalized or not, we might well want to know much more about it than that—especially if the Balance tips *against* criminalization. If some action *a* ought not be criminalized, is it because it falls within the Sphere of Individual Liberty, or because it falls in the "interstice" between the Sphere of Individual Liberty and "Society's Jurisdiction?" Or does it fall in "Society's Jurisdiction" merely. Or may it be discouraged, but only by the "moral coercion of public opinion," and not by "physical force"—either privately exercised, or the "physical force of legal penalties?" The topography to which Balancing naturally gives rise does not distinguish among these crucially important classes.

We could devise a better topography for Balancing. Consider the following, which does include all the regions of the correct topography.

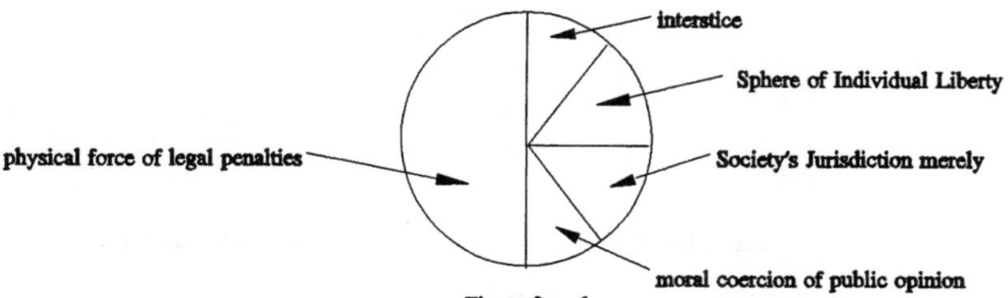

Figure 3 — 6

However, if the Balance tips *away* from criminalization, Balancing offers no technique for determining into *which* of the remaining "slices of the pie" an action falls. Furthermore, the relationships among the interstice, Society's Jurisdiction merely, and the "moral coercion of public opinion" are not perspicuously displayed.

The second defect can be remedied.

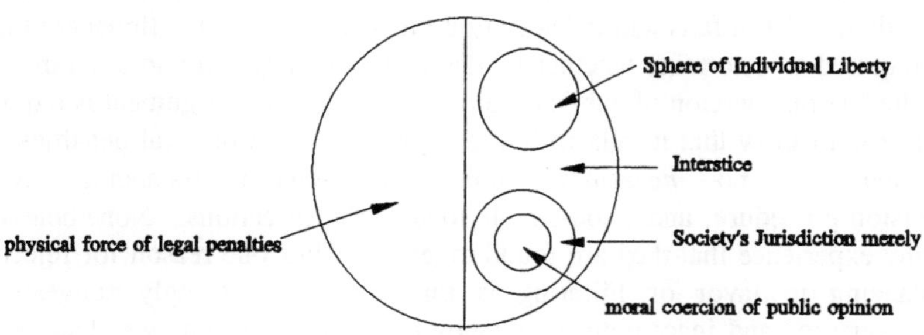

Figure 3 — 7

But once again, Balancing is silent on determining just where, on the regions on the right, a particular action is to be placed.[11]

Alternatively, one might believe that Balancing gives rise to these topographical regions:

---

[11]Of course, one could ask the sorts of questions one asks when Filtering. But that is not so much a modification of Balancing, as the adoption of Filtering. See Section VIII, "Can Balancing Be Saved? The Procrustean Impulse."

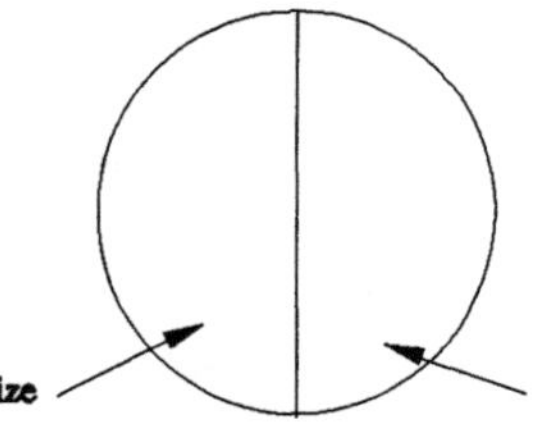

Figure 3 — 8

Under this topography, every action of competent adults either is a matter of individual sovereignty, or else is justifiably criminalized. An implication of this is that to show that an action is *not* in individual sovereignty is, *ipso facto*, to show that it is justifiably criminalized. But this is a species of the "topographic error." As I have argued, after one has successfully shown that some action is not in the "Sphere of Individual Liberty," *additional* argument is required: to determine whether it falls into the interstice, or in "Society's Jurisdiction;" if it falls within "Society's Jurisdiction," yet additional argument is required to determine whether it falls within Society's Jurisdiction merely, or the "moral coercion of public opinion." Yet additional argument is required if one is to show that it falls within the "physical force of legal penalties."

There is no *necessary* connection between Balancing as a decision-procedure, and a too-simple topography of actions. Nonetheless, it is my experience that they are found together. Thus one reason for rejecting Balancing in favor of Filtering is that Balancing strongly suggests an impoverished and inaccurate topography of actions. And as we shall see in Part Two, that inaccurate topography leads to a variety of mistakes in the philosophy of criminal law.

VI. B. The Misgivings of Chapter One

And now to the misgivings enumerated in Chapter One.

1. Arguments Have No Objective Weight

As we saw in Chapter One, the analogy between weighing chemicals and "weighing" arguments is tenuous right from the start: a given quantity of a chemical has an objective weight, while arguments do not. Although this disanalogy immediately raises concerns about Balancing, Filtering does not depend upon determining objective "weights" of arguments.

2. Balancing is Simplistic

Balancing has intuitive appeal when choosing between two mutually exclusive and jointly exhaustive alternatives. When selecting among three or more alternatives, or when the advantages and disadvantages of the alternatives are awkwardly distributed, the intuitive appeal of Balancing evaporates. Filtering does not suffer these defects. Alternative proposals can be Filtered individually. At each Filter, the arguments as regards some action can be applied, *mutatis mutandis*, to similar actions. If the case for criminalizing a particular action fails at any Filter, the reason(s) for failure are clear. Rather than the vague verdict of "outweighed" (in Balancing), Filtering more precisely specifies the failure: the action is not of a sort with which the state may morally interfere (Principles Filter), reducing the incidence of the action (or the deleterious consequences of the action) can be achieved by less coercive means (Presumptions Filter), or the net costs of criminalization are higher than the net benefits of the statute (Pragmatics Filter). This is of help to both the proponent and the opponent of criminalization, as it *focuses* the debate.

There is another way in which Balancing is too simple, and Filtering the necessary corrective. Balancing, in not specifying the sorts of concerns to be placed on the two pans of the balance, accommodates overlooking important considerations: that less coercive measures could suffice, or that deleterious consequences would result from criminalization. Thus Balancing accommodates, or even encourages, making the unwarranted "assumption of compliance," as discussed in the Introduction. In devoting a separate Filter to less coercive measures, and yet another Filter to the pragmatics of criminalization, Filtering makes it more difficult to neglect these essential considerations.

Of course Filtering cannot *prevent* one's making the "assumption of compliance;" *no* criterion is self-applying. The superiority of Filtering is to be found in its making more difficult the neglect of these essential considerations.

3. *The Weighing of Incommensurables*

Using Balancing, one has to assign precise "weights" to quite an array of profoundly different items: the "weightiness" of the moral authority of the state, the presumption in favor of liberty, the costs and benefits of criminalization, etc. In Filtering, these issues are handled in a cleaner, easier way.

4. *The Inherent Need for Precision*

Balancing requires the precise assignment of weights to the various considerations. And the "closer" an issue, the more important is the precision of that weight assignment. Filtering does not require the assignment of weights.

This does not mean that there will be no "close" issues when Filtering—indeed, the matter might be "close" at three different points, i.e. three different Filters. *Whether* an action falls within the scope of a particular Principle of State Authority (and whether that PSA is an "acceptable" PSA) may be controversial. *Whether* the incidence of an action can be sufficiently reduced by means less intrusive than a criminal statute may be controversial. *Whether* the social costs of enforcing a statute exceed the benefits of enforcement may be controversial. However, in sorting out the issues this way, in structuring the controversies, Filtering fosters philosophical progress. It will prove easier to address these clusters of arguments individually, rather than collectively at one grand "weighing."

5. *The Curious Asymmetry*

The curious asymmetry of Balancing is explained by Filtering. The practical difficulties of enforcement do count against enactment—but at the Pragmatics Filter. Ease of enforcement counts in favor of a statute *at that Filter*—i.e., after it has already been determined that the action is in Society's Jurisdiction, and that less coercive means will not suffice. At this point, the issues of enforcement difficulty are indeed symmetrical—which is precisely the correct result.

6. Movement of the Balance's Indicator

When employing Balancing, one could be misled by movement of the Balance's "indicator." As weight is added to, or subtracted from, one pan or the other, the indicator moves; it is possible to mistake movement *towards* criminalization for movement *to* criminalization (and conversely). Filtering incorporates no analogous source of deception.

No action may morally be criminalized unless it passes, successively, through all three Filters. This does not entail, however, that one may not "peek" at the argument at lower Filters. If the issues of criminalization is decisively resolved at a lower Filter—if it is persuasively shown that an action does not pass through a lower Filter—then the controversy at a higher Filter is thereby made moot. If it is clear that the costs of enforcing a criminal statute exceed the benefits which that enforcement would produce, then a prohibitory statute is not justified; opponents of the statute need not be concerned with the issue of whether the action does or does not pass through the Principles Filter or the Presumptions Filter.

Of course, if someone where opposed to *all* state initiatives as regards that action—even the "moral coercion of the public opinion"—then that person would still be concerned with the arguments at the Presumptions and Principles Filters. If the action does not pass through the Principles Filter, it is not the sort of action with which a state is properly concerned; if it does not pass through the Presumptions Filter, then even if the action is of a sort with which a state is properly concerned, even state action less coercive than a criminal statute will be counterproductive, and thus not justified.

VI. C. Arguments from Multiple Principles

It might happen that some action *a* falls under the purview of more than one Principle of State Authority (or for Feinberg, "liberty-limiting principle"). How is this to be handled? There are powerful reasons for believing that the way this is handled by Balancing is misconceived, and will—in at least some cases—yield the wrong result. For the purposes of discussion, we can focus on just two PSAs; the Harm Principle and Legal Paternalism will demonstrate the difficulty nicely. The argument I construct here will apply *mutatis mutandis* to the other PSAs; they will be applicable, but even stronger, if an action falls under the purview of three (or more) Principles of State Authority.

According to Michael Bayles (as cited in Chapter One), "When conflicting principles apply to a proposed law, they must be balanced against one another. Collectively, all acceptable principles both for and against provide a standard of good criminal legislation."[12] If a person accepts both the Harm Principle and Legal Paternalism, and if an action falls under the purview of both, then there are two kinds of reasons for criminalization. In Balancing, the "weight" that comes from an action's harming others, and the "weight" that comes from an action's harming the agent oneself, are *combined*. This suggests that which is surely natural, the "two scoops" solution: a "scoop" of weight from the Harm Principle, and a "scoop" of weight from Legal Paternalism, are placed on the "criminalize" pan.

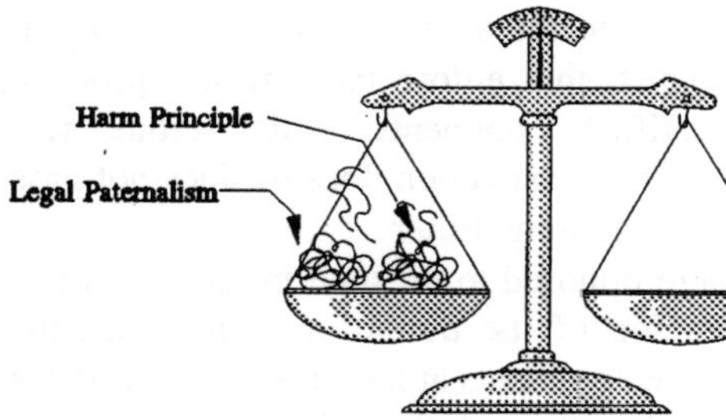

Figure 3 — 9

The result is greater weight for a single social response: criminalization.

But wait: solely from the fact that these two different Principles of State Authority are relevant, it follows that two quite different sorts of actions are of concern: people harming *others*, and people harming *themselves*. For all we know at this point, there could well be ways of reducing the incidence of each sort of action—varieties of the "moral coercion of public opinion"—less coercive, less intrusive than a criminal statute. Programs of public education might prove sufficient to reduce the incidence of people's harming themselves; programs of public condemnation might prove sufficient to reduce the incidence of people's harming others. (The public campaign against smoking, and against exposing others to second-hand smoke, seems a clear example of this.) Provided only that one believes that, of equally efficacious means, the

---

[12]"Criminal Paternalism," in *The Limits of Law: Nomos XV* (New York: Lieber-Atherton, Inc., 1974), p. 175. Internal cite omitted.

less coercive is to be preferred over the more coercive, the "two scoops" solution of Balancing is misconceived. The correct social response in such cases is to devise two distinct programs, aimed at two distinct actions to be discouraged. The correct social response is not to enact one program—a criminal statute—to discourage both sorts of actions. Thus the "two scoops" solution is wrong in principle, even if the combined "weights" of the two scoops is insufficient to "tip the balance" in favor of criminalization. And (of course) if the "weight" of the two scoops *is* indeed sufficient to tip the balance in favor of criminalization, then Balancing yields the wrong result.

In Filtering, the matter of an action's falling under the purview of two different Principles of State Authority is handled correctly. Again on the assumption that the Harm Principle and Legal Paternalism are acceptable, the action passes through the Principles Filter at two different points.

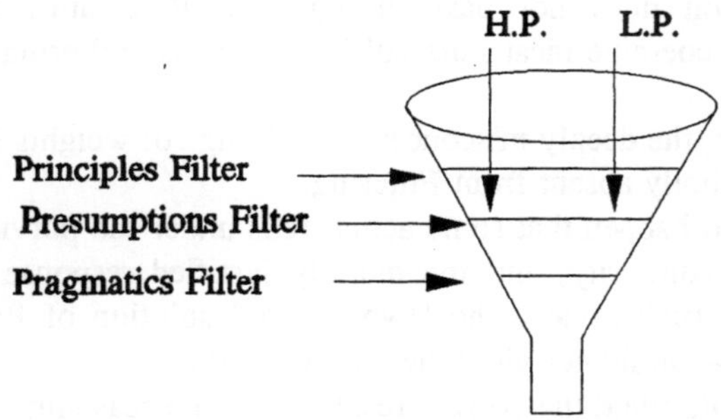

Figure 3 — 10

In each case, one is directed to ask: is there a means of social coercion that will reduce the incidence of the malady cited by the PSA by means of which the action passes through the Principles Filter? Thus, Filtering directs two distinct investigations; in such cases, the action passes through the Presumptions Filter at two points, showing the justifiability of two distinct social programs.

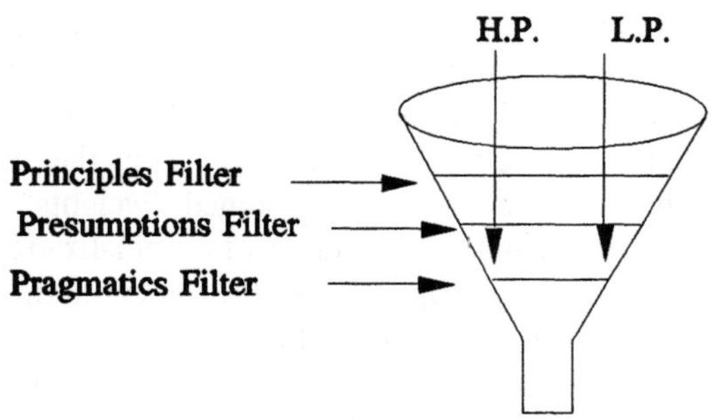

Figure 3 — 11

However, the action does not pass through the Pragmatics Filter; by hypothesis, the less coercive means are sufficient. Thus, Filtering yields the right result.

Just as important: the deeply misconceived "adding" of weights in favor of criminalization is wholly absent from Filtering.

Of course it could happen that some action falls under the purview of two Principles of State Authority, and the morally justified response is indeed criminalization. In such a case, the "two scoops" solution of Balancing—although misguided—would not yield the wrong result.

But Filtering would yield the correct result too. The reasoning for this is straightforward. As the action passes through the Principles Filter (by hypothesis, at two different points), it is the sort of action appropriate for state concern. Since it passes through the Presumptions Filter, less coercive state action is morally permissible; by hypothesis, less coercive measures will not suffice. At the Pragmatics Filter, we are to investigate the particulars of enforcement, and assess the costs and benefits. The benefits that accrue to the statute will be of two distinct sorts, correlated with the two Principles of State Authority in virtue of which the action passed through the Principles Filter—in the context of this illustration, reducing harms to self (Legal Paternalism) and harms to others (Harm Principle). At *this* point—having in fact made a determination that less coercive and intrusive measures will not suffice, the "benefits" of the statute do properly include two sources of benefits. But note how different this is from the "two scoops" solution of Balancing. Adding two "weights" at the outset, immediately "tips the scales" towards—and perhaps to—criminalization. There is no query, in Balancing, as to less coercive means which might remedy the different maladies.

Consider now a more subtle, but nonetheless powerful objection to the "two scoops" solution. As noted above, Filtering requires an inquiry into the remedies available for the maladies cited by the PSA by means of which an action passes through the Principles Filter. If an action falls under the purview of two (acceptable) PSAs, two distinct inquiries are required. And what these inquiries might reveal is that the social response most effective in reducing the incidence of one of those maladies will itself *exacerbate* the other malady. The most effective way—and perhaps the only way—to reduce harms to others, might increase the incidence of harms to self. The most effective way—and perhaps the only way—to reduce the incidence of harms to self might increase the incidence of harms to others. In short: the two Principles of State Authority might aim at mutually exclusive social goals. In such a case, the society will have to decide which of the goals it will seek to secure, and which it will abandon.[13]

There is no device within Balancing for identifying mutually exclusive goals. Quite to the contrary, the "two scoops" solution presupposes that a criminal statute is the remedy to all the maladies cited by multiple Principles of State Authority. By directing distinct investigations, Filtering facilitates the discovery of mutually exclusive goals.

I am not unaware of the fact that these two objections to Balancing are abstract. Of all actions which fall under the purview of two different Principles of State Authority, one might wonder whether there are any which have two less coercive remedies rather than one more coercive remedy. And one might wonder whether such an action could ever give rise to mutually exclusive social goals.

I make the abstract concrete in the chapters of Part Two.

Some people, in arguing for laws mandating the use of seat belts in cars, and helmets on motorcycles, offer a "two-scoops" argument: a scoop of financial harm to others, added to a scoop of concern about drivers and riders, is "weighty" enough to justify the law under discussion. I shall show that the purported justification fails, and that the decision-procedure it presupposes—Balancing—is inferior to Filtering.

---

[13]Perhaps it will abandon that goal with great regret. But attempting to simultaneously secure mutually exclusive goals will prove profoundly frustrating—and costly.

Some people, in arguing for laws prohibiting the use of various psychoactive substances—"drugs"—offer a "two-scoops" argument: a scoop of harm to others (predation), added to a scoop of concern for users themselves (degradation), is "weighty" enough to justify the legal prohibition. I shall show that the purported justification fails: the most effective means for reducing harms to self will themselves exacerbate harms to others; the most effective means for reducing harms to others will increase the incidence of harms to self. The social goal of the Harm Principle and the social goal of Legal Paternalism, it will be revealed, are mutually exclusive.

VII. SOME SOURCES OF FRUSTRATION

Let us pause for a moment, and reflect on the phenomenon of an action's failing to pass through a Filter. As it is the most perspicuous, consider first an action's failing to pass through the Pragmatics Filter; what we learn from that will be readily applicable to the other Filters.

Suppose some action *a* passes through the Principles and Presumptions Filter, but fails to pass through the Pragmatics Filter. It is, as it were, "trapped" in the zone between the Presumptions and Pragmatics Filters.

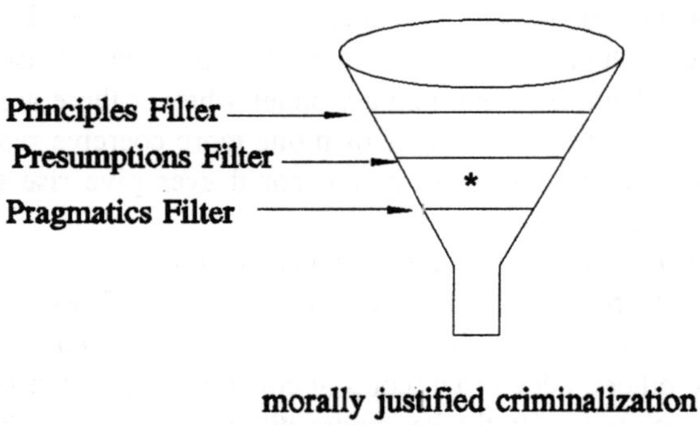

Figure 3 — 12

What do we know about action *a*? Since it has passed through the Principles Filter, action *a* is the *sort* of action with which the state is appropriately concerned. Since action *a* passed through the Presumptions Filter, measures less coercive and intrusive than a criminal statute will not reduce the incidence of action *a* to an acceptable level (or alternatively, will not reduce the deleterious consequences of action *a* to an acceptable level. However, since action *a* does not pass through the Pragmatics Filter, the benefits of a criminal statute would not exceed its costs—the criminal prohibition of action *a* is not justified. Thus, the measures the state may morally take regarding action *a* will not be effective; measures which might be effective (but might not; cases will have to be assessed individually), the state may not morally take. This will be a source of great frustration for those concerned about action *a*. But this possibility, I submit, must be accepted as one of the parameters of our moral lives. Some bad things will happen, about which nothing effective may morally be done. This is true of our individual moral lives, and, alas, it is true of our social moral lives. And it is a mark of moral maturity to transcend this frustration, to not allow that frustration to become debilitating.

Suppose some action *a* passes through the Principles Filter, but not the Presumptions Filter.

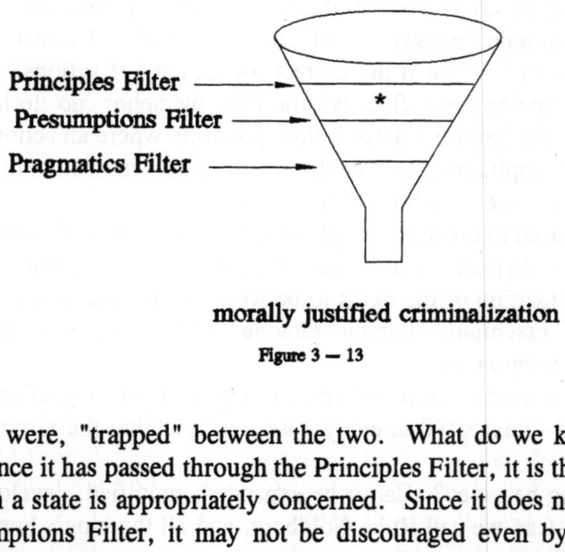

Figure 3 — 13

It is, as it were, "trapped" between the two. What do we know about that action? Since it has passed through the Principles Filter, it is the sort of action with which a state is appropriately concerned. Since it does not pass through the Presumptions Filter, it may not be discouraged even by measures less coercive than a criminal statute. Perhaps an educational campaign would be more likely to inspire experimentation than persuade people to abstain. This will be a source of great frustration for people concerned about the incidence of action *a*. No one has a *right* to do action *a* (having passed through the Principles Filter, the action is in Society's Jurisdiction, and not the Sphere of

Individual Liberty), yet measures taken to discourage it will prove counterproductive. Some bad things that happen must be simply ignored. Transcending this frustration is another mark of moral maturity.

Some actions will not pass through the Principles Filter—they are not the *sorts* of actions about which the state is appropriately concerned. This too will be a source of frustration for some people, but it is a frustration of a different kind. In the previous two cases, it was assumed that the action in question *was* properly the state's concern; frustration arose from the fact that morality and practicality precluded state activity. This is a more fundamental matter: disagreement about the state's moral authority. But this sort of disagreement surely is an inescapable fact about political life.

VIII. CAN BALANCING BE SAVED? THE PROCRUSTEAN IMPULSE

Can Balancing be saved from all these objections? I think not. Balancing suggests a too-simple topography of actions, thereby facilitating various "topographic errors." Even if the correct topography of actions is somehow attached to Balancing, we find within that metaphor no technique for determining, on the "not criminalize" side, precisely where an action falls. To appropriate is to capitulate; to take the set of questions from Filtering is to abandon Balancing and to subscribe to Filtering.

The inherent need to precisely weigh things which have no objective weight, and are also quite disparate a collection of entities, is inescapable, And since there is no specification of the items to be weighed, Balancing accommodates the neglect of essentials—thereby (among other failures)—fostering the "assumption of compliance."

When arguments arise from different principles, Balancing offers the "two scoops" solution—misguided in every case, and yielding the wrong result in some cases.

Can Balancing be saved? Can it be expanded, modified, developed? Can pans be added? Can we call Rube Goldberg, and all the king's horses and all the king's men?

One wonders: why bother? The central task of the philosophy of the criminal law is to determine which actions may morally be criminalized. If a metaphor is helpful, if a metaphor guides and structures our thinking in ways conducive to philosophical progress, we ought to use it. If a superior metaphor is developed, we ought to adopt it, and we ought to abandon the old metaphor. The central task of the philosophy of the criminal law is *not* to save the metaphor of Balancing.

Every guest of Procrustes neatly fit his iron bed. If they did not fit it when they arrived, no matter: those who were too short were stretched; those who were too long were chopped down to size.[14]

Can Balancing be saved? Perhaps, if we stretch and chop enough. But again—why bother?

IX. THE VOCABULARY OF JUSTIFICATION: CHALLENGES AND COUNTEREXAMPLES

I want now to introduce a vocabulary for determining whether actions may morally be criminalized.

I have argued that an action is justifiably criminalized if and only if it passes through all three Filters: Principles, Presumptions, Pragmatics. Consequently, a criminal statute is *justified* if and only if the action prohibited passes through the Principles Filter, the Presumptions Filter, and the Pragmatics Filter. A criminal statute is justified if and only if it prohibits an action which is in Society's Jurisdiction, the incidence of that action (or its deleterious effects) cannot be adequately reduced by less coercive and intrusive means, and the consequences of enacting and enforcing the statute—pragmatic and moral—yield a net benefit to society.

A *complete, adequate justification* of a criminal statute, then, is a justification which addresses the issues of all three Filters, and shows that the prohibited action passes successfully through the Principles Filter, the Presumptions Filter, and the Pragmatics Filter. Of course there will be controversy whether particular proposed justifications are indeed "complete, adequate justifications." My goal is not to specify in advance which proposed justifications succeed, but what it *means* for a justification to succeed, i.e., to provide *adequacy conditions* for justifications.

A justification for a statute is a *prima facie complete* justification if it addresses the issues of all three Filters.

---

[14]Edith Hamilton, *Mythology: Timeless Tales of Gods and Heroes* (New York and Toronto: The New American Library, Inc.), 1942, p. 150.

More importantly: A purported justification for a statute is not even a *prima facie* justification unless the issues of all three Filters are addressed. A purported justification cannot be an *adequate* justification without addressing those issues; at best it will be a *partial justification*.

A *partial justification* of a criminal statute is any chunk of argument addressed to the issues of any of the Filters.

Most of what one finds in the literature are partial justifications.

Now there's no shame in offering partial justifications; that is all one can do if one is limited to a few journal pages. But it is important to realize that that is *all* that one is doing: taking up a *portion* of the issues that must be addressed. This might seem too obvious to mention, were it not for the fact that so many partial justifications seem to be offered as complete, adequate justifications.

In some cases, a quick sketch of the argument at a particular Filter might be sufficient. What is absolutely vital in arguing issues of criminalization, however, is cognizance that the issues of each Filter *must* be addressed. The claim that some statute is justified—especially the claim that the calendar of crimes ought to be expanded by the addition of new crimes—*cannot* be persuasive unless it is persuasive as regards all three sets of issues. An argument which fails to be persuasive at any Filter, or which fails to address the issues of some Filter, is a failure to justify coercion.

To reject Filtering as the optimal decision-procedure, one would have to correctly employ it, and get the demonstrably wrong result. If one can show that an action passes through all three Filters, yet a statute prohibiting it is not justified, then one has an argument against Filtering as a decision-procedure. Alternatively, if one can show that some action does *not* pass through the three Filters, yet is justifiably criminalized, then one has an argument against Filtering.

If an action is such that it falls under the purview of an acceptable Principle of State Authority, and the incidence of it cannot be satisfactorily reduced by less intrusive and expensive a means of social coercion than the criminal law, and the effort to enforce such a statute will not have overriding deleterious effects on society, then such a criminal law is justified. If the action cannot pass through all three Filters, then criminalizing it is not justified. If it is not of the *sort* with which the state ought interfere, or if acceptable means less intrusive than the criminal law would prove effective, or if society would be worse off, all things considered, for *having* such a statute than not having it, then the criminal statute is not morally justified.

An important consequence of Filtering is that there will be some actions such that (1) they are within Society's Jurisdiction, (2) their incidence cannot be successfully eliminated or reduced by means less coercive than a criminal statute, and yet (3) they ought not be made criminal, for the consequences of enacting such a statute, including resource allocation and other secondary moral arguments, would prove so deleterious that the society would be worse off for having such a statute than it would be without the statute. Some actions just "fall between the stools;" society would be better off were the action not performed, yet also better off not criminally prohibiting the action. (Recall the example, in the Introduction, of prohibiting cigarette smoking in one's home, exposing others to second-hand smoke.) For "can do" Americans, this admission does not come easily. Yet it is nonetheless *true*, and the failure to realize this, and the failure to constrain legislation in the light of its truth, has led to an array of egregious ills within—and caused by—the criminal justice system. This is the subject of the chapters of Part Two of this work: Failures to Justify Coercion..

X. A BRIEF CHAPTER SUMMARY

What I call for, in this chapter, is a dramatic re-orientation in how we—philosophers of the criminal law, legislators, jurists, citizens—approach the justifying of coercion. I urge the rejection of the intuitively appealing but fatally flawed metaphor of "Balancing," and the adoption of the superior metaphor, the superior decision-procedure of Filtering. Filtering does not suffer the many afflictions suffered by Balancing. Filtering respects the correct topography of actions relevant to criminalization. And Filtering generates adequacy criteria for the justified use of "physical force," whether the private exercise of coercion, or the "physical force of legal penalties."

Why ought we be concerned about *justification*? Because the criminal justice system embodies the domestic power of the state. Because what is at stake here is subjecting citizens to the indignities of arrest, the expense of defense, the consequences of incarceration, and the encumbrances of conviction. Before doing this, we as a society must be *very* sure of ourselves.

PART TWO

FAILURES TO JUSTIFY COERCION

PREFACE

I am a Liberal.

I believe that the Harm Principle and the Offense Principle, duly modified and qualified, are the only acceptable Principles of State Authority.[1]

This position is, of course, analogous to Joel Feinberg's position. There is this crucial difference, however. For Feinberg, the Harm Principle and the Offense Principle are "liberty-limiting principles," and their use incorporates *all* the various items relevant to the deciding whether the criminalization of actions is morally justified. For that fact, among others, Feinberg adopts Balancing as his decision-procedure for criminalization. For me, the Harm Principle and the Offense Principle are Principles of State Authority. As such, their function is merely (merely?) to identify the extent of the state's moral authority. They play a role—an *important* role, to be sure, but *only* a role—in deciding whether actions may morally be criminalized. Additionally, they play that role in a superior decision-procedure for criminalization, Filtering. And Filtering encourages respect for, rather than violation of, the correct topography of actions. Furthermore, Filtering precludes—or at least makes more difficult—the "assumption of compliance."

In the chapters of Part Two, the correct topography of actions relevant to criminalization, and Filtering, are put to use. I take up a number of substantive matters in the philosophy of the criminal law, showing how the methodological work of Part One can contribute to philosophical progress on an array of recalcitrant issues. In each case, I construct (what I take to be) the correct Liberal position, and then reject the attempt of some philosopher or philosophers—liberals and illiberals alike—to expand the scope of morally permissible coercion. Significant space is devoted to criticizing various positions taken by Joel Feinberg. But then, internecine warfare is always the

[1]As we saw in Chapter Two, Mill says quite inconsistent things about offensive actions: that some may morally be prohibited, but *harm* to others is a necessary condition for prohibition. I am more concerned about creative definitions of "harm" than fidelity to Mill's claim that *only* harm to others can justify coercion. Thus, I am persuaded that Feinberg's resolution is correct: the Liberal accepts both the Harm Principle and the Offense Principle.

bloodiest.[2] Each philosopher I critique makes an attempt to justify additional private coercion, or makes an attempt to justify additional state criminalization. If these arguments were to prevail, more actions which might be elected by individuals would subject those individuals to the private exercise of force, or to criminal sanctions: to the indignities of arrest, the expense of defense, the consequences of incarceration, and the encumbrances of a criminal conviction.

I join a number of philosophical conversations "already in progress." In becoming oriented, I set aside the language of topography and the mechanics of Filtering. Once oriented to each controversy, however, I *re-structure* its various elements. I distinguish the issues of the Principles Filter from the issues of the Presumptions Filter from the issues of the Pragmatics Filter. And I impose on each controversy the criterion of success from Filtering: coercion is justifiable if and only if the action (type or token) under discussion passes through the succession of Filters.

Significant stretches of text will be devoted to arguments *at* one Filter or another. Since I am entering an ongoing dialogue, one which was initiated and has been carried on in the absence of Filtering, this ought not be a surprise. That does not mean, however, that Filtering is not at work in my argument. For Filtering is at work in the re-structuring of the dispute, and in establishing necessary and sufficient conditions for justified coercion. Conversely, the test of Filtering as a decision-procedure is its *successful* re-structuring of controversies: does it indeed organize issues in a way conducive to philosophical progress?

Part Two is divided into three chapters; each chapter is divided into several "topics." I want to say a bit about the nature of these topics, and then offer a preview of them.

In some of the topics I take up in the chapters of Part Two, I apply the methodology of Filtering immediately to policy issues. I assess laws that would require wearing a seatbelt when driving or riding in an automobile, laws that would require wearing a helmet when driving or riding on a motorcycle, laws prohibiting the use of various "psychoactive substances"—what we typically call "drugs."

---

[2]As Aristotle says, ". . . still, it presumably seems better, indeed only right, to destroy even what is close to us if that is the way to preserve the truth. And we must especially do this when we are philosophers; for though we love both the truth and our friends, piety requires us to honor the truth first." *Nicomachean Ethics*, trans. Terence Irwin (Indianapolis: Hackett Publishing Company, 1985), pp. 8-9.

In addition to these very specific applications, I apply the methodology of Filtering to more "theoretical proposals" in the philosophy of the criminal law. These "theoretical proposals," made by a number of different philosophers, are not arguments that some particular action—like failing to wear a seatbelt, or ingesting psychoactives—be made criminal. In contrast, they are proposals which—if accepted—would permit state (or private) coercion over a broad spectrum of actions, would make morally permissible state (or private) interference with numerous actions which people might elect. For example, were we to accept Joel Feinberg's argument about "garrison situations" (introduced below, and discussed in Chapter Five), a large number of particular actions would, in certain situations, be subject to state interference. For another example, were we to accept the arguments of Richard J. Arneson and Cass R. Sunstein regarding "community self-paternalism," it would be morally permissible for the state to criminalize a wide array of individual actions.

Thus, the chapters of Part Two contain applications of the methodology developed in the chapters of Part One. At some points, the application is immediately to issues of public policy; at other points, the application is mediately to issues of public policy, but immediately to creative, and seemingly attractive, theoretical proposals in the philosophical literature. My hope, of course, is that this mixture of issues will be found interesting and appealing.

I address five topics in Chapter Four, "Issues of Paternalism."

"Two Dogmas of Paternalism" is a consideration of laws which mandate the wearing of automobile seat belts, and motorcycle helmets. Although I am mildly concerned with those laws themselves—and especially with the suggestion that the failure to use these devices should be *criminalized*—I am more concerned with the function of these laws in advancing the legislative agenda of the Legal Paternalist. These laws are justified, argues many a Legal Paternalist, and furthermore they are *paternalistic* laws. Since some paternalistic laws are justified, the argument continues, perhaps some others are as well . . . . I challenge the justifiability of these laws, specify the conditions under which restrictions of this sort are indeed "paternalistic," and thwart the legislative strategy of the Legal Paternalist.

In "Scoccia's Novel Condition for Paternalistic Interference," I examine a quite recent argument that "more paternalism" is justified than is believed justified even by most paternalists. Danny Scoccia claims to have devised a new, multi-clause condition under which forcible paternalistic interference is warranted. According to that condition, if an action arises from desires or values which are not autonomously selected, then the actions themselves are not autonomous; this (together with some additional factors) is sufficient to justify forcible paternalistic interference. I argue that it is not; Scoccia commits a topographic error or two, and fails to consider just what it would be like to exercise force in this way. That is, he fails to undertake the sort of investigation mandated by the Pragmatics Filter.

Joel Feinberg, in an early article and in a recent book, proposes a state institution for dealing with suspected nonvoluntary actions. That institution, he concludes, would be acceptable even to liberals like Mill. I don't think so; I argue my case in "Concerns about Feinberg's 'Voluntariness Tribunal'." Feinberg too is guilty of topographic errors; from the fact that an action is nonvoluntary (or merely suspected of being nonvoluntary), he quickly concludes that state interference is justified. It isn't—or at least Feinberg's arguments do not show that it is. Worse, Feinberg has not given sufficient thought to the operation of his proposed institution. Once again, the kind of investigation required at the Pragmatics Filter has not been undertaken.

Derek Parfit, on the basis of his work on personal identity, claims to have created a new justification for paternalism: the protection of future selves from present selves. I argue that this ought to be rejected in "Present Selves, Future Selves and Other Selves." I think Parfit's novel justification is more ingenious than persuasive; additionally, as he devotes little space to the matter, many issues are left unaddressed. Also important is the issue of state priorities: most people, I suspect, would prefer to have scarce resources devoted not to protecting their future selves from their present selves, but rather to protecting their present selves from *other* present selves.

Finally, I have some "Hard Words for Soft Paternalism." The proponents of so-called "soft paternalism" are prone to a particular topographic error. They argue—in some cases persuasively—that a particular action does not fall within a person's Sphere of Individual Liberty. They seem to believe, however, that that fact alone is sufficient, or very nearly sufficient, to justify interference. What is *missing* from their arguments is a moral assessment of the proposed interference itself.

I address three topics in Chapter Five, which has the title "Oblique Attempts to Expand the Criminalizing Authority of the State." In each case, an attempt is made to enlarge the scope of the state's criminalizing authority. The attempts are "oblique" in that they are not arguments for the acceptability of some Principle of State Authority (or "liberty-limiting principle") in addition to the Harm and Offense Principles. Rather, each seeks to justify coercion by an alternate route, by a different sort of argument.

Feinberg claims that, when society resembles a garrison under siege, actions which would otherwise be self-regarding become other-regarding. From this alone, Feinberg concludes that they may be "emphatically prohibited." In "Concerns about Feinberg's 'Garrison Situations'," I argue that this inference is a topographic error: even if certain actions *do* become other-regarding in such situations, *much* more must be argued if one is to show that coercion is warranted. It is unlikely, I claim, that coercion *could* be successful—even in a garrison itself. Less persuasive still is the extension of this argument to society generally.

Richard J. Arneson and Cass R. Sunstein have endorsed a different oblique approach to expanding the state's criminalizing authority. Attempting to draw a political analogy with the legend of Ulysses and the Sirens, they believe that a majority is justified in advancing its second-order preferences (preferences about preferences) by making criminal those actions for which they do, or might come to have, a first-order preference—a first-order preference they do not wish to have. "Deconstructing Community Self-Paternalism" is a rejection of this strategy. Philosophical scrutiny reveals that this is *not* a sort of paternalism at all—hence the "deconstruction," and hence its placement in this chapter, and not the previous chapter. Their proposal is really a program of coercion of the political minority by the political majority. And all that can be offered by way of "justification" is the weakness of will of those in the majority. Thus, this is a paradigmatic case of treating others as means merely, and not as ends in themselves.

Arneson also argues that Feinberg's liberalism ought to be rejected in favor of "utilitarian liberalism." What Arneson needs to do to show this is to (i) show that the two species of liberalism are different, and (ii) that utilitarian liberalism is superior. To accomplish these tasks, Arneson must find some action on which the two sorts of liberalism differ (one would criminalize it, and the other would not), and then prove that "utilitarian liberalism" gets the matter right. The action Arneson selects is bestiality. Its criminalization is justified, claims Arneson, and that conclusion is reached by utilitarian liberalism and not by Feinberg's liberalism. "Of Sheep and Men" is devoted to defending Feinberg's position against Arneson. I argue that Arneson's "stylized" account of the practice of bestiality is not credible, and that his utility calculations are based upon this subtle and (of course) unwarranted "assumption of compliance." When one adopts an accurate account of the practice of bestiality, and does not assume compliance with a prohibitory statute, utility does *not* in fact favor said statute. Having failed to show an in-practice difference between the two species of liberalism, Arneson has also failed to show the superiority of utilitarian liberalism.

Chapter Six is devoted to a sustained critique of the inaptly-named "War on Drugs." In a literature that has grown explosively in recent years, one finds a great many arguments that the use of some psychoactive substances ought to be decriminalized, and a great many arguments that the use of currently illegal psychoactives ought to remain criminal offenses. Desperately needed in this dispute is some *structure*, some way of organizing these disparate arguments. I believe that Filtering provides such a structure. I ask whether the use of certain psychoactives will pass through the Principles, Presumptions and Pragmatics Filters—and ultimately answer that it does not. On the basis of that conclusion, I offer a series of proposals for "drug" decriminalization.

Two other topics are addressed in this chapter. I consider an unsigned article that appeared in *QQ: Report from the Center for Philosophy and Public Affairs*, an article which advocates limited decriminalization. Unfortunately, it contains some serious confusions about the appropriate role of "liberty-limiting principles" in arguments about criminalization; the application of Filtering clears up these confusions. Finally, I consider the claim that "drug" decriminalization is "racist"—that it would visit deleterious consequences on African-Americans. I argue that this is mistaken. Indeed, African-Americans bear a disproportionate share of the burdens of extant arrangements; it is far more plausible to hold that declaring "War on Drugs" is *itself* racist.

CHAPTER FOUR

ISSUES IN PATERNALISM

Topic One
TWO DOGMAS OF PATERNALISM

I. INTRODUCTION TO THE ISSUES

No small amount of philosophical ink has been devoted to the matter of laws which mandate the wearing of a seat belt while driving or riding in an automobile, and laws which mandate the wearing of a protective helmet when driving or riding on a motorcycle.

Of course what is at issue is *adults* riding helmetless or driving beltless; this essay is concerned with the Sphere of Individual Liberty of competent adults, and not the appropriate regulations concerning minors. Thus I am not denying the propriety of, for example, the legal requirement that infants be transported in child-restraint seats.

These two sets of legal restrictions could fairly be termed "two dogmas of paternalism." They are featured in arguments by Legal Paternalists that go something like this: "Laws which mandate the use of motorcycle helmets and seat belts are justified. Furthermore, these laws are *paternalistic* laws. So some paternalistic laws are justified. *A fortiori*, Legal Paternalism is an acceptable "liberty-limiting principle" ("Principle of State Authority"), and pure Liberalism—defined as acceptance of the Harm Principle and the Offense Principle only—is untenable." Any Liberal of intelligence and good character, the argument continues, must countenance *some* paternalistic laws. And once *some* paternalistic laws are acknowledged as justified, why not some *others*: why not ___________, and __________, and also _______? Once the dam against paternalism has been breached, it becomes ever more difficult to staunch the flow of yet more paternalism.

I come to these dogmas not to praise them, but to bury them.

But first, we need to gain perspective on the "liberty" imperiled, and the penalties exacted.

Upon reflection, it must be acknowledged that fundamental freedoms are not imperiled by these laws. Oh, I know that some motorcyclists like the feeling of wind in their hair (if not the taste of bugs in their teeth), and that some automobile drivers feel confined by seat belts (unable to slam into the instrument panel in case of impact). But after giving road romanticism its due, it must be acknowledged that the liberties that such laws restrict are peripheral at best. Compare them, for perspective, with the liberties protected by the U.S. Constitution's Bill of Rights. Or think of it in this way: if there were a state whose most serious violations of the rights of its citizens were laws mandating the use of motorcycle helmets and automobile seat belts—wouldn't you want to emigrate?

Reflect now on penalties. Failure to wear a seat belt or helmet is, generally, a "violation" and not a "crime." The violator is ticketed, and not "arrested;" appearance in court is an option, not a legal requirement—one may pay the small fine by mailing a check. No police record, no "rap sheet" is begun (or extended). Given these facts, what is at issue is the moral authority of the police to *pester* individuals.

It is, however, quite easy to imagine circumstances under which these matters could become considerably more serious. A hyperkinetic state legislator, deeply concerned about re-election, and armed with the mighty maxim "If it saves even a single life . . .," succeeds in having legislation enacted which makes helmetless biking and beltless motoring a misdemeanor. Transgressors are arrested, and subjected to criminal prosecution. (It would not be legitimate, of course, to assume compliance with this new statute.) I think that the laws requiring the use of seat belts and helmets, when merely an issue of the state's pestering citizens, are so inconsequential as to merit little philosophical time and energy. Additionally, when the stakes are so low, it is difficult to discern the essences of the issues. However, when such laws are criminal statues, when the prohibited activity is a crime (albeit a minor crime) and not a mere violation, the issues both become clearer, and worth worrying about. In the discussion that follows, then, I shall treat these restrictions as if they were misdemeanor statutes. What I shall be arguing is that such statutes are not justified, that the state ought not make helmetless cycling and beltless driving *crimes*. Then, having clarified the issues and marshalled the arguments, I shall extend my position: the state is also not justified in pestering citizens; the state exceeds its moral authority even in making these actions mere *violations*.

II. THE LEGAL PATERNALIST'S SYLLOGISM

The first thing to note about the "paternalist's syllogism" is that it is deeply flawed—indeed, it commits the fallacy of "affirming the consequent."

Loosely speaking, "paternalistic" can be a predicate of many different things: of actions, of interferences, of attitudes, of people—and, of course, of laws. Strictly speaking, however, "paternalistic" is a predicate of *justifications*. Citing the welfare of the person interfered with is what one does in justifying, in attempting to justify, an interference, an action, or a law. (People are paternalistic, or have paternalistic attitudes, when they cite the welfare of the "interferee" in justifying, in attempting to justify, their actions.) No law is paternalistic *per se*. Some laws have paternalistic justifications—or more accurately, *purported* justifications.[1] Thus, the paternalist's syllogism must be reconstructed as this:

> Seat belt and helmet laws are justified
> If Legal Paternalism were an acceptable "liberty-limiting principle,"
> then seat belt and helmet laws would be justified
> Therefore, Legal Paternalism is an acceptable "liberty-limiting principle"

And this is clearly fallacious.

Now this can be transformed into a valid argument, an instance of modus ponens, by altering the second premise: "Only if Legal Paternalism is an acceptable 'liberty-limiting principle' can seat belt and helmet laws be justified." Now the argument is this:

> Seat belt and helmet laws are justified
> If seat belt and helmet laws are justified, then Legal Paternalism is
> an acceptable "liberty-limiting principle"
> Legal Paternalism is an acceptable "liberty-limiting principle"

---

[1]Cf. Michael D. Bayles, "Criminal Paternalism," *The Limits of Law:* NOMOS XV, ed. J. Roland Pennock and John W. Chapman, (New York: Lieber-Atherton, 1974), pp. 174-88; Gerald Dworkin, "Paternalism," *Paternalism*,, ed. Rolf Sartorius (Minneapolis: University of Minnesota Press, 1983), pp. 19-34.

The price of validity, I shall argue, is soundness. For this formulation makes clear two lines of critique. The Liberal can reject the first premise, arguing that these laws are *not* justified, all things considered. Alternatively, the Liberal can reject the second premise, arguing that these laws are indeed justified, but that one need not accept Legal Paternalism in order to prove them so: a sufficient justification can be constructed which invokes only the Harm Principle or the Offense Principle.

In a sense, I shall take both tacks—despite their apparent inconsistency. More precisely, I shall argue that *some* state action may be permissible—but that the state action which might be permissible is not a criminal prohibition. Furthermore, the justification of that state action—if that state action is indeed justified—is not a paternalistic justification, but a Harm Principle justification, a justification appropriately invoked by the Liberal.

The philosophical literature devoted to motorcycle helmet laws is considerably larger than that devoted to automobile seat belts. So let us consider first the matter of a criminal statute requiring the use of automobile seat belts, with the intention of getting clear on precisely what state action is justified, and precisely why. Following that, attention can be turned more productively to the issue of a criminal statute mandating the wearing of a protective helmet when operating a motorcycle. Some of the arguments developed as regards seat belts will be readily applicable to helmets—but some will not. As we shall see, there are some interesting—and philosophically relevant—differences between the two matters.

III. SEAT BELT LAWS

Let us take up the issues of a legal requirement to wear a seat belt. And let us treat the matter as a disagreement between the Liberal and the Legal Paternalist. I shall simultaneously be arguing for two theses. First, I shall argue that the Liberal position—as I shall develop it—is the correct position on this matter. Second, I shall argue that Filtering, in organizing and clarifying the various considerations, is shown to be superior to Balancing as a decision-procedure for morally justified criminalization.

First, the facts. Seat belts save lives. And they prevent some injuries, and they lessen the seriousness of other injuries. They also take some lives, and exacerbate some injuries: when cars become submerged, or catch fire. And it sometimes happens that people are safely ejected from cars. But fires and submersions are relatively rare; safe ejections rarer still. All things considered, the safety evidence overwhelmingly favors the using of seat belts: fewer deaths, less serious injuries, fewer injuries at all. Conversely: *not* wearing a seat belt increases the risk of death or serious injury, or injury at all.

Those who are injured or killed while sitting on their seat belts are, undeniably, harmed.[2] They are harmed as a consequence of their own actions, the refusal to buckle up. The Legal Paternalist seeks to reduce this harm to self by enacting and enforcing a criminal statute. The Liberal denies the propriety of citing the welfare of the competent adult coerced (or otherwise interfered with) in justifying that coercion.

Arguably, the non-use of seat belts causes other harms—in particular, financial harms to all other citizens. Those who do not use seat belts are either insured, or they are not insured. If they are insured, then their conduct has the consequence of raising insurance premiums, for the insurer must pay a death benefit, or the increased medical costs of exacerbated injuries. If they are *un*insured, then (unless they are wealthy) the medical expenses of those injured are taken from social resources. Thus whether insured or not, those injured or killed while driving beltless inflict a financial harm on others. Their conduct results in an interest set-back to others: increased insurance rates, *and* increased taxes.[3]

Thus the Liberal has available a Harm Principle justification for the statute requiring the use of seat belts. (Whether that justification is, all things considered, a *sufficient* justification, has yet to be determined.)

Legal Paternalists, it can be assumed, also subscribe to the Harm Principle, i.e., consider it an acceptable "liberty-limiting principle." (It would be bizarre, and perhaps nonsensical, to claim that an action's harming the agent oneself is a good reason for criminalization, but an action's harming other people is not.) Thus the Legal Paternalist has two different justifications for the statute mandating the use of seat belts.

---

[2]Their interests are set back. They are not, however, *wronged*. See Joel Feinberg, *Harm to Others*, pp. 31-64.

[3]It might be argued that the amount of money involved is too small to constitute a genuine set-back of interests. As will become clear, I would welcome that conclusion. In the interests of philosophical progress, however, I shall assume that the sum is indeed sufficient to be a set-back—arguing that even if it is, it does not justify the criminalization of the refusal to wear a seat belt.

Imagine now that both the Liberal and the Legal Paternalist employ Balancing as their decision-procedure for morally justified criminalization. Recall that in using Balancing, we are to envision a beam balance with two pans; the arguments in favor of criminalization are placed on one pan, the arguments opposing criminalization are placed on the other pan. The indicator shows which pan contains the weightier arguments.

The Legal Paternalist and the Liberal may well quarrel about the relative "weights" of various considerations. However, the central dispute between the Liberal and the Legal Paternalist, when "Balancing," is the quarrel about precisely *which* "weights" it is appropriate to put on the two pans of the balance. The Legal Paternalist believes that "weights" representing harm to the agent oneself ought to be placed on the pan favoring criminalization; the Liberal thinks they ought not. The Legal Paternalist, when using Balancing, will adopt the "two scoops" solution (as discussed in Chapter Three): a scoop of Harm Principle, and a scoop of Legal Paternalism, are plopped on the "for criminalization" pan.

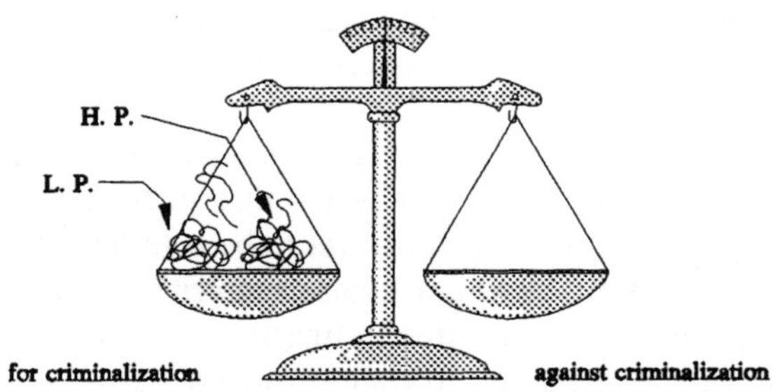

Figure 4 — 1

And recall that precise "weights" must be assigned to multitudinous considerations: the presumption in favor of liberty, the odds of being in an accident, the chances that one's automobile will catch fire, or become submerged, etc.

The Legal Paternalist, it is fair to surmise, will find that the combined weight of the harm to self, and the financial harm to others, tips the scales in favor of criminalization. The Liberal will not have placed on the scale any weights at all for the action's harming the individual oneself, but will have placed weight on the pan favoring criminalization for the action's causing financial harm to others. Will that be the heavier pan? Perhaps; it depends upon just how "weighty" the Liberal considers the presumption in favor of liberty. In other words, the Liberal could consistently hold either that the financial harm to others was sufficiently weighty to "counterbalance" the presumption in favor of allowing competent adults to live their lives free of state interference, or that the financial harm inflicted on others (higher insurance premiums and care for those who become wards of the state) was not so serious that it outweighed the presumption in favor of liberty.

Let us suppose now that the disputants used Filtering instead of Balancing as a decision-procedure for criminalization. And recall that within Filtering, one does not use the "liberty-limiting principles" as formulated by Feinberg, but rather the Principles of State Authority as formulated in Chapter Three of this work. (Briefly: Feinberg's "liberty-limiting principles" direct one to "weigh," all at once, all of the considerations relevant to criminalization. In contrast, Principles of State Authority focus exclusively on the appropriate role of the state; state actions other than criminalization *per se*, and the pragmatic consequences of criminalization, are postponed to subsequent Filters.)

The Legal Paternalist would see "beltless driving" as passing through the Principles Filter in two distinct ways: given that the action harms the agent oneself, it passes through that Filter due to Legal Paternalism; given that the action causes (financial) harm to others, is passes through the Principles Filter due to the Harm Principle. The Liberal sees the action pass through the Principles Filter due to the Harm Principle alone. But both do indeed see the action pass through the Principles Filter.

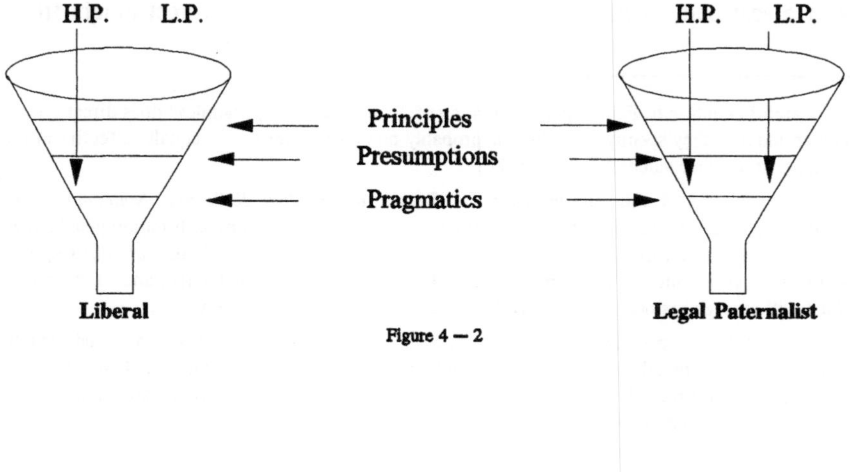

Figure 4 — 2

Having passed through the Principles Filter, "beltless driving" arrives at the Presumptions Filter. At this Filter one is directed to ask: can one find a less intrusive, a less coercive, way of reducing the incidence of the action, or reducing the deleterious consequences of that action?

It is important to note that no such inquiry is prompted by Balancing.[4] Typically the two pans of the Balance represent "criminalize" and "not criminalize;" the metaphor makes no provision for investigating alternative state actions. It is a virtue of Filtering, I submit, that it directs just such a search.

So: *is* there a less coercive, less intrusive alternative? For the Liberal, the answer clearly is "yes." The concern of the Liberal is the financial harm to others by the worsened injuries (including fatal injuries), or the injuries at all, that result from people's failure to use seat belts. This financial harm, as we have seen, is inflicted in two distinct ways: through higher insurance premiums (as a result of more claims, and higher claims), and through increased taxes (as a result of caring for the uninsured). There is, I submit, a perfectly straightforward way to indemnify others, both as citizens and as insurance premium payers: yet additional insurance.[5] Those who wish to drive or ride without wearing a safety belt would be permitted to do so—provided that they had secured "special" insurance to protect others from the financial loss resulting from worsened injuries in the event of a collision. Special license plates could be issued—the extra cost being borne by these individuals—indicating that they had indeed purchased the "special," additional insurance coverage.[6]

Under such a program, the legal requirement would be disjunctive: either wear a seat belt, or have in force "special" insurance to protect others from

---

[4]Careful attention to Feinberg's formulation of "liberty-limiting principles" does direct one to such an inquiry; they specify "and there is probably no other means that is equally effective at no greater cost to other values." [HTO, p. 26]

[5]I first suggested this alternative in *A Theory of Justified Reflective Noncompliance*, unpublished Ph.D. dissertation, 1979. A similar suggestion is made, as regards motorcycle helmet laws, by Gerald Dworkin in "Paternalism: Some Second Thoughts," in *Paternalism*, ed. Sartorius, p. 109. But it is made in passing, lacks the refinements I shall make, and—for reasons which will emerge—is not seen by Dworkin as a "solution" to the problem.

[6]Alternatively, a special registration card could be issued, listing the names of those individuals who carry the additional insurance, and thus who may legally drive without a seatbelt. The car might be stopped if the driver were beltless—but upon showing the special registration and proper identification, no citation would be issued.

preventable financial loss. No one would be legally required to wear a seat belt—but everyone would be required to either wear the belt or buy the insurance. All that would be prohibited is the conjunction of not wearing the seat belt and not having the insurance. This arrangement would enhance liberty while financially protecting others from the harmful consequences of the exercise of that liberty.

It is likely, however, that some persons would "cheat"—they would neither wear their seat belts, nor purchase the additional insurance. How could society be protected from financial loss resulting from injuries to "un-special-insured" motorists?

This is not a new problem, but a variation of an existing problem; it does not require a new solution, but a variation of an existing solution. Some states currently require citizens to carry liability insurance protection on their automobiles; one cannot register an automobile without proof that one has indeed secured that insurance. But people sometimes fail to pay their premiums. For that, and for other reasons, policies lapse. And people sometimes forge the relevant documents. Thus it sometimes happens, despite the legal requirement, that people drive—and are involved in collisions—while uninsured. So every insurance policy includes a special provision—additional insurance—for just such a contingency: "uninsured motorist insurance." If a policyholder suffers a loss in a collision with a person who is not insured, then one's own insurance carrier pays the claim.

Now it would be quite simple a thing to expand this sort of additional insurance to cover the losses of those who are more severely injured as a consequence of not wearing seat belts—whether they carried insurance, but not the "special" coverage, or whether they were wholly uninsured. My proposal (for the moment) is this.

Special Insurance Program - Seatbelts ("SIP-S")

> No automobile may be registered without proof of insurance. (Of course it is a crime to drive an unregistered automobile.) Every insurance policy will include an "uninsured motorist" provision, to cover losses that result from accidents involving uninsured motorists.
>
> No one is legally required to wear a seatbelt. However, everyone is legally required to either (i) wear a seatbelt, or (ii) purchase a "beltless driving" provision. Every insurance policy will include an "uninsured beltless driver" provision, to cover the "extra" losses that

> result from beltless driving by individuals who have not purchased the "beltless driver" provision.[7]

The correct Liberal position, then, is that "SIP-S" is justifiable on Harm Principle grounds. (In what follows, I shall offer reasons for questioning whether even this state action—though exceedingly mild—is justified.) However, a criminal statute mandating the wearing of a seatbelt is not justifiable on Harm Principle grounds.

Two objections might be raised against this position. First, all drivers would be required to pay the higher premiums of the additional coverage—and this is unfair. Second, it might be difficult, as a matter of fact, to determine just how much additional coverage is indeed needed to protect against losses of this sort. These can be rebutted in turn.

Suppose it were objected that compelling drivers to pay additional "uninsured beltless motorist" protection is unjustified—it is an extra expense for the imprudence of others. (It might even be objected that "uninsured motorist" insurance itself is an unfair burden.) I'm willing to concede that there's something to this objection—but that is a small concession indeed. At issue is a very small amount of money, a small percentage of an automobile insurance policy premium. Yet that small amount of money purchases increased liberty for others, and is part of a program that makes increased liberty (beltless driving) available to everyone (albeit at a small cost). Feinberg invokes the legal maxim "*De minimus non curat lex.*" ("The law does not concern itself with trifles"). [HTO 189] I think it appropriate to devise a corollary: *De minimis non curat philosophia*: "Philosophy does not concern itself with trifles." It is difficult to see this, even if a genuine "injustice," as an injustice worth worrying about. Once again, perspective is essential. If the most serious injustice of a regime were that it required people, for the privilege of driving an automobile, to purchase both liability insurance and "uninsured motorist" insurance (for both sorts of failure to insure)—wouldn't you be anxious to live there?

Second, suppose it were objected that it is too difficult to determine the "extra" injuries and deaths and medical costs that result from beltless driving and riding. Well, this objection plays right into the Liberal's argument. If it is not possible to determine the additional cost (when enough is known about

---

[7]Technically, these provisions are called "riders," but the term "beltless driver rider" is likely to be as confusing as it is amusing.

risk and probability to successfully operate existing programs of liability and collision insurance), then surely the potential loss is negligible. And if it is indeed negligible, then it is surely insufficient to justify a criminal statute mandating the use of seat belts. If the financial harm to others is indeed negligible, then it would be morally outrageous to subject people to the indignities of arrest, the expense of defense, the consequences of incarceration, and the encumbrances of a conviction (as these are detailed in the Introduction) to protect others from that negligible harm.[8]

Consider now the Legal Paternalist using Filtering, rather than Balancing. The Harm Principle concerns of the Legal Paternalist have been assuaged by the Special Insurance Program - Seatbelts. But this does not address the matter of harm to the agent oneself, the particularly paternalistic concern of the Legal Paternalist. But at the Presumptions Filter, the Legal Paternalist too is asked: is there a less coercive, less intrusive way of reducing the incidence of the conduct, i.e., driving and riding without the use of a seat belt? Continuing (and indeed expanding) educational campaigns, which graphically portray the consequences of non-use, seem ideally suited to reducing the incidence of beltless driving. This is especially true when made a part of driver education courses. Additionally, the extra insurance premium of the "special" insurance for beltless driving will serve as a (mild) monetary deterrent. Finally, as remarked above, the Liberal does not object to requiring children to be appropriately restrained; once the use of restraints becomes habitual, it is likely to remain so into adulthood. In sum: there are many reasons to believe that beltless driving will not pass through the Presumptions Filter, even when the Filtering is being done by a Legal Paternalist.

But suppose it *does* pass, suppose beltless driving arrives at the Pragmatics Filter. Now we are to envision the actual operation of a criminal statute: how it will be enforced, the consequences of enforcement—and the costs and benefits to society of all that. Recall the discussion, in the Introduction and in Chapter Three, of the "assumption of compliance." We are not entitled to assume that, upon enactment, everyone will comply with this statute. Some people surely won't—and surely some of those who don't comply will believe that the statute violates their rights, prohibits their doing something—beltless driving—which they ought to be free to do, especially since their conduct (in the context of "SIP-S") neither harms others, nor poses a clear and present

[8]Incarceration not inevitable for a misdemeanor conviction—but is possible.

danger of harm to others. What follows from this is that there will be miscreants, people who violate the statute. Recall also that, for the purposes of argument to this point, we are considering a statute that makes beltless driving a misdemeanor (and recall that later, the arguments will be extended to laws that make it a mere violation). This means that transgressors—those apprehended driving without a seat belt—will be subject to arrest and criminal prosecution. They will suffer the indignities of arrest: search, handcuffing, reading of rights, transportation to a lock-up, photographing, fingerprinting, strip search (including body cavity search), imprisonment until preliminary hearing. They will have to bear the expense of defense: the cost of a private attorney, or the costs of the uncertain quality of a public defender; the notoriety of arrest and prosecution. If convicted, they will suffer the consequences of incarceration: the intended consequence (loss of freedom), and the unintended but known consequences: brutalization, and the possibility of assault (or worse). And they will be encumbered by that conviction, in various ways, throughout the remainder of their lives. All this the Legal Paternalist must "justify" solely by citing the welfare of the person coerced, the person arrested for not wearing a seat belt. Is it at all plausible that this is *really* in a person's interests, even bearing in mind the increased safety of seat belt use? And there's more, of course. Enforcing the statute will consume scarce social resources: police time, public defender time, district attorney time, prison warden time. And in all these cases, time surely is money. When all things are considered, it just isn't credible to maintain that the seat belt statute would indeed pass through the Pragmatics Filter; the costs of attempting to enforce the statute (including the "secondary moral costs" of devoting scarce resources to attempting enforcement) exceed its benefits. This is especially obvious when one remembers two features of the overall argument: first, that the state is free to discourage beltless driving in the various non-statute ways identified at the Presumptions Filter; second, that the public treasury will be protected by the Special Insurance Program - Seatbelts.

That the public treasury can be protected by the "SIP - S" has special philosophical importance. It has been my experience[9] that those arguing in favor of seat belt laws are prone to mixing harm-to-others arguments with paternalistic arguments. If one is using Balancing as one's decision-procedure

[9]Thus what follows is anecdotal. But that means merely that I am citing experience and not the literature; it doesn't mean that it is false.

for morally justified criminalization, then this is not only legitimate, but virtually required by the metaphor. Every consideration that "weighs" in favor of the criminalization of some action is placed on the "pro-criminalization" pan of the Balance. In this case, a scoop of financial harm to others and a scoop of harm to self may well seem sufficient to tip the Balance in favor of criminalization. However, the foregoing argument makes clear just why this tactic is illegitimate. And in so doing, it makes clear the superiority of Filtering over Balancing. (Near the end of Chapter Three I offered, in abstraction, a critique of Balancing's "two scoops" solution to the matter of arguments arising from two different Principles of State Authority, promising to make that abstraction concrete later in the text. I have now kept that promise.)

Failing to use a seatbelt while driving or riding in an automobile does pose a harm to others: beltless people are more likely to be injured, and likely to be more seriously injured, in the event of an accident. The increased medical expenses or death benefit will result in higher insurance premiums (if the victims are insured) or will result in a drain on social resources (if the victims are not insured). Both would constitute financial harms to others. However, the Special Insurance Program - Seatbelts, including the "uninsured beltless motorist provision," provides complete protection from this financial harm, and is far less coercive than a criminal statute requiring the use of seatbelts.

This leads to three important conclusions. First, if a person cites both financial harm to others, and also harm to drivers and riders themselves, in arguing for seatbelt laws, then it is no longer accurate to call the law, strictly speaking, a "paternalistic law." It is illicit for a Legal Paternalist to surreptitiously invoke Harm Principle arguments to support a statute, then call that statute a "paternalistic law," and then argue that the Liberal (any Liberal who endorses seatbelt laws) must therefore accept some "paternalistic" laws, so Legal Paternalism must be an acceptable "liberty-limiting principle," or Principle of State Authority. Thus, this is not a breach in the dam against paternalism. Second, it is not legitimate to *combine* financial harms to others, and harm to self, in attempting to justify seatbelt laws, as the former "ill" has a "cure" less coercive than a criminal statute. Third, Balancing directs us to place both financial harm to others, and harm to self, on the pan favoring criminalization—and then yields the wrong result. Filtering directs us to consider financial harms to others, and harm to self, independently. And then Filtering directs us to search for less coercive measures. Filtering yields the right result—and this militates powerfully for its superiority as a decision-procedure for morally justified criminalization.

Thus the proponent of a statute mandating the use of seat belts, if a Liberal, must discover some novel harms to others, harms which cannot be prevented by the Special Insurance Program - Seatbelts (or some straightforward modification of it). The proponent of a statute mandating the use of seat belts, if a Legal Paternalist, must persuade us that the non-statute techniques of the Presumptions Filter are inadequate, and that—contrary to the arguments considered above—the benefits of the statute really do exceed the costs. The prospects of succeeding at either are not good. Alternatively, the proponent could search for a different Principle of State Authority by which beltless driving passes through the Principles Filter. But then one still confronts the difficulties of passing through the Presumptions Filter and the Pragmatics Filter.[10]

IV. MOTORCYCLE HELMET LAWS

Let us now take up the matter of a statute which would mandate the wearing of a helmet while driving, or riding on, a motorcycle. My discussion will engage Joel Feinberg's as found in *Harm to Self*, and will be informed by some of the arguments I constructed regarding automobile seat belts. It would be misleading to say, however, that all the arguments apply *mutatis mutandis*. For as will become clear, there are some very important differences between the two cases.

Feinberg's discussion begins with the hypothetical case of Victor Vroom, who wears a helmet initially only because it is required by law, and he wishes to avoid a fifty-dollar fine. Then one day he is involved in a collision. Victor is thrown from his motorcycle, landing on his head. Taken to the hospital, Victor is

> . . . treated for cuts and a minor concussion. Without the helmet, he was told, he would have been killed or severely brain-damaged.

[10]Finally, one may try an oblique approach, try to circumvent these procedures. I consider oblique approaches to expanding the criminalizing authority of the state, as regards other actions, in Chapter Five.

> Ever since the accident Victor has worn his helmet faithfully not only because the law requires it, but because he wishes to be protected from other unforeseeable accidents. But in the first instance, he would never have worn the helmet but for the fear of legal penalties. [HTS 135]

Feinberg relates some of the gruesome statistics of motorcycle accidents, including expert testimony that in many cases the wearing of a helmet prevented injury, or lessened the seriousness of a sustained injury. Based on these facts, Feinberg claims that "[c]ompulsory helmet legislation then surely has a point, and because of that, it is an embarrassment to the liberal and makes the strongest of the arguments for hard paternalism." [HTS 135] What's the Liberal to do? Feinberg relates a "trilemma" he attributes to Gerald Dworkin, then adds two other alternatives.

> (1) He can argue that helmetless motorcycle riding is typically (if not "necessarily") nonvoluntary by the appropriate standards; (2) he can argue that helmetless motorcycle riding, though typically voluntary (or voluntary enough) should be banned, but on grounds other than hard paternalism, for example in terms of the interest of third parties who are affected in ways they have a right to be protected against; (3) he can argue that despite the self-harm prevented by prohibitory legislation, the restrictive statutes are morally unjustified because they infringe personal sovereignty, and that noncoercive measures should be adopted to increase safety. We have already dismissed (see Chapter 19, #8), albeit respectfully, a fourth alternative, namely, that to restrict the domain boundaries of personal sovereignty to more fundamental interests or "significant projects" (Kleinig's phrase). A fifth possibility is to concede the game to the hard paternalist, thereby giving him encouragement to use his principle to justify criminal penalties for other forms of self-regarding risk-taking, from cigarette smoking to surfing. [HTS 135-6]

Avoiding the fifth alternative is precisely the point of the arguments of "Two Dogmas of Paternalism." I want to concede nothing to the Legal Paternalist; I want to show that there are in fact no breaches in the dam against paternalism. Feinberg rejects the first option; I endorse that rejection with little comment. It just isn't credible to claim that a person could not voluntarily choose to not wear a helmet. (And even if it were, that alone would not be sufficient to justify a prohibitory statute; to think that it is, is to commit a "topographic error.") As regards the fourth alternative: I want to agree with Feinberg and Kleinig that helmetless biking is not a central liberty—the point of my comments about maintaining perspective on these issues. As an empirical matter, however, it is generally the case that helmetlessness is more important to the biker plan of life than beltlessness is to the motorist plan of life. Nonetheless, I do not wish to concede this territory to the Legal Paternalist—and I believe that there are sound reasons for this refusal. I have, in a way, accepted the second and third options as regards automobile seat belt laws: I have argued that an outright prohibition of beltless driving violates rights and thus is not justified, and that legitimate third-party interests can be protected in ways that do not require a prohibition, i.e., by a Special Insurance Program.

In the end, Feinberg thinks a prohibition of helmetless riding is not justified, while Gerald Dworkin thinks that it is. The argument that Dworkin finds persuasive—an argument centering on "psychic costs," which will be discussed below—Feinberg finds *nearly* persuasive. In the end, I shall argue that Dworkin is wrong—a prohibition of helmetless riding is not justified. And I shall argue that Feinberg is wrong in thinking that the "psychic cost" argument is a powerful argument; it is not.

Let us watch the argument evolve—and then watch support for the statute dissolve.

Feinberg (rightly) dismisses a nonpaternalistic (Harm to Others) argument according to which helmetless riders are more prone to lose control of their bikes on account of being hit in the eye by a foreign object. And an out-of-control motorcycle, the argument continues, poses a clear and present danger of harm to others. Feinberg (rightly) calls these concerns "forced and contrived;" there is little evidence that this happens very often, and there are alternative ways of preventing, or at least reducing the danger. [HTS 138]

Feinberg then considers the following argument:

> A rather more persuasive nonpaternalistic argument for mandatory helmet statutes appeals to the great public costs (in dollars and cents) of accidents. Salaries must be paid to policemen, paramedics, ambulance drivers, and nurses. Hospital rooms, operating rooms, physicians, medication, and medical machinery are very expensive. Many of these costs are paid from general tax revenues, others from higher insurance premiums. Indirect costs, like lost productivity and lost tax payments from injured workers, and welfare payments to their dependents, further raise the price. Mandatory helmet laws

> could reduce this great public expense and that is their true rationale—or so the liberal might argue. [HTS 138]

As a Liberal, I too acknowledge these financial harms to others as serious. However—like the financial harms which arise from the failure to use automobile seat belts—I believe that they are not sufficient to justify a statute which prohibits helmetless riding. At most, these harms justify compulsory insurance, not compulsory helmet-wearing. So: consider a special insurance program analogous to the "Special Insurance Program - Seatbelts."

> Special Insurance Program - Helmets ("SIP-H")
>
> No motorcycle may be registered without proof of insurance. (Of course it is a crime to drive an unregistered motorcycle.) Every insurance policy will include an "uninsured motorcyclist" provision, to cover losses that result from accidents involving uninsured motorcyclists.
>
> No one is legally required to wear a helmet. However, everyone is legally required to either (i) wear a helmet, or (ii) purchase a "helmetless biking" provision. Every insurance policy will include an "uninsured helmetless biker" provision, to cover the "extra" losses that result from helmetless biking by individuals who have not purchased the "helmetless biker" provision.

The Liberal, in virtue of subscribing to the Harm Principle, can subscribe to the "Special Insurance Program - Helmets."

In "Paternalism: Some Second Thoughts," Gerald Dworkin mentions the possibility of an insurance program to protect against financial harm:

> The argument in the "safety" cases is that persons who are injured or killed because of their risky behavior impose costs on the rest of us. When the costs are economic, such as the costs of medical care, the obvious reply is that this might show we can require such individuals to purchase medical insurance, but it does not show that we can require them to actually wear safety helmets.[11]

[11]"Paternalism: Some Second Thoughts," *Paternalism*, ed. Sartorius, p. 109.

Feinberg, in relating Dworkin's suggestion, makes the program more elaborate. I supply the text from *Harm to Self*, and then turn to Feinberg's surprising—but quite accurate—introduction of the passage.

> If the reduction of publicly shared economic costs is the main part of our reason for passing compulsory helmet laws, then we can achieve that goal equally well without criminal prohibitions, simply by requiring the risk-takers to purchase extra medical insurance as a condition of their licensing. Perhaps a supplementary scheme would be to require a contribution to a state-operated fund which would pay the full social costs of motorcycle accidents, just as users pay fees to get on bridges or turnpikes out of which maintenance costs are paid. The supplementary scheme would not be fair, however, to the prudent cyclists who drive cautiously and wear helmets, for they would pay the same fees as their more reckless colleagues whose more serious subsequent injuries are greater drains on the fund. The compulsory medical insurance system would be more equitable in that respect, by and large, since insurance companies could selectively raise the premiums of drivers who don't take elementary precautions. Perhaps the two plans could be combined into one which would require self-insurance not only for medical costs of accidents but for other costs (road maintenance, police time, etc.) as well. Compulsion would still be involved indirectly, but no longer through the mechanism of criminal statutes justified on paternalistic grounds. Now punishment would be reserved as a backup threat against those who drive without a license and thus violate a quite unpaternalistic law. [HTS 139]

Feinberg's program is quite similar to the program I devised above, the "Special Insurance Program - Helmets." That in turn is based on a program I sketched many years ago.[12] However, Feinberg's proposal does *not* include an "uninsured helmetless cyclist" provision. This omission—as we shall see—results in some philosophical contortions which are completely obviated by such a codicil. But first, let us return to the argument between Feinberg and Dworkin.

Feinberg introduces the paragraph just quoted in the following way: "Gerald Dworkin, however, has a paternalistic rejoinder of some

---

[12] *A Theory of Justified Reflective Noncompliance*, unpublished Ph.D. dissertation.

strength." [HTS 139] Now in devising the insurance program as regards beltless motoring above, I did not consider my work a "paternalistic rejoinder"—far from it. I was arguing as a Liberal, claiming that there is a Liberal (in this instance, a Harm Principle) justification for some state actions—although not the enforcement of a statute requiring the use of seat belts. How can it be that Dworkin, in proposing a similar sort of insurance program, can be offering a "paternalistic rejoinder"?

When thinking in the terms of Balancing, this claim is indeed perplexing. It might seem that Dworkin urges that the "weight" of an insurance program ought to be placed on one pan, while I claim that it ought to be placed on the other pan. But that's not accurate. Indeed, placing this dispute in the context of Balancing does not help to clarify it. But it can be clarified, I maintain, if we think in the terms of Filtering.

For further clarification, let us return to the issue of seatbelt laws. The Liberal sees beltless driving pass through the Principles Filter only if it causes harm to others; the only plausible harm caused to others is the financial harm discussed. At the Presumptions Filter, the Liberal finds a way of preventing that financial harm in a way less coercive than a criminal statute, the Special Insurance Program - Seatbelts. The Legal Paternalist sees beltless driving pass through the Principles Filter in two quite different ways: as an instance of financial harm to others, and as an instance of harm to self. The Special Insurance Program - Seatbelts, while preventing harm to others, does not address the issue of harm to self: and that can be addressed only by a prohibitory statute. Now the Legal Paternalist who wishes to remain true to principle wants to argue that (i) Legal Paternalism is an acceptable "liberty-limiting principle" (or alternatively, an acceptable "Principle of State Authority"), *and* that (ii) beltless laws are justified, *and* that (iii) only by accepting Legal Paternalism can one arrive at the (correct) conclusion that beltless laws are indeed justified. (The Legal Paternalist wants to use the valid version of the "paternalist's syllogism" I discussed in Section II, and furthermore wants to argue that it is sound.) The Legal Paternalist must make sure, in arguing for (i) - (iii) above, that the case for the justifiability of the prohibition of beltless driving is *purely* paternalistic, is not "sullied" by factors which are really harms to others. In other words: if the case in favor of the statute contains any element of harm to others, any non-paternalistic factors, then the Legal Paternalist fails to show that *only* paternalism secures the justifiability of the statute.

This argument concerning seat belt laws (although not some others) is relevant, *mutatis mutandis*, to motorcycle helmet laws. If Dworkin is to show that mandatory *helmet* laws are justified, and that they are justified only if one accepts Legal Paternalism, then he must "purify" the argument, must expunge all concern about harm to others. He must show that protecting others from harm can be done in ways other than a prohibitory statute, so that if we are convinced that a prohibitory statute is indeed justified, we are compelled to accept Legal Paternalism. Thus the insurance program is correctly characterized as a "paternalistic rejoinder," for it precludes claiming that a statute mandating the use of a helmet is justified, but is justified on non-paternalistic grounds—namely, financial harm to others.

Filtering organizes this controversy; it requires that we ask precisely why each (Liberal and Legal Paternalist) believes that the action in question passes through the Principles Filter, and precisely what it is that requires a remedy at the Presumptions Filter. In so doing, it makes clear just what constitutes a "paternalistic" argument—and also the burden of proof that must be borne by the Legal Paternalist.

It is difficult to translate this explanation into the language of Balancing. The Legal Paternalist wants to put weight on the "pro-criminalization" pan because the action causes harm to the agent oneself; the Liberal claims that that is not a sufficient reason for putting any weight at all on that pan. Financial harm to others, the Liberal agrees, is some (but how much?) weight to be placed on the "for-criminalization" pan. Although the Legal Paternalist wants more weights on that pan, it's not *that sort* of weight that's wanted. So the Legal Paternalist, in proposing an insurance scheme, is arguing that *counterbalancing* weight be placed on the "against-criminalization" pan—that way, if the indicator finally moves to favor criminalization, it will not be as a result of the weight of harm to others placed on the "for-criminalization" pan. So both Dworkin and I would place the weight of the insurance program on the pan against criminalization—albeit for quite different reasons. I would do it because it weighs against criminalization; Dworkin would do it to purify the paternalistic argument.

But of course placing that counterbalancing weight on the "against-criminalization" pan moves the indicator *away from* justified criminalization. And this delights the Liberal, who hopes to see the indicator move away from justified criminalization. It is ironic, is it not, to see the Liberal's delight with this weight-placing of the Legal Paternalist . . . ?

There is more to be said against Balancing: one important issue is left on the periphery of the metaphor, while another is left completely outside the metaphor. On the periphery: should the weight of "harm to self" be placed on the "for-criminalization" pan or not? Outside the metaphor: suppose that financial harm to others is not sufficiently weighty to tip the balance in favor of criminalization—what then? Is that the end of the matter, or should one look for alternative state action to prevent that harm? The metaphor of Balancing, I submit, is too impoverished to accommodate suggesting a search for alternative actions. (Now one could add to Balancing something like "if there is harm on the 'for-criminalization' pan, but insufficient harm to warrant criminalization, then open an inquiry into the prospect . . . ." But of course this sacrifices the intuitive appeal of the simplicity of Balancing, without addressing the other misgivings about Balancing raised in Chapter One. And it makes for one ugly metaphor!)

Feinberg notes that the insurance scheme improves the Liberal position—and of course I agree. But there is one more consideration with which to deal.

> There may still be other grounds for the helmet requirement that can justify it, though not on obviously paternalistic grounds. I refer to what Gerald Dworkin calls "psychic costs," and what Kleinig calls "the public charge argument." [HTS 139]

According to Feinberg,

> *This* is the argument that justifies compulsory helmet laws if any argument does. The main question it raises is whether or not it is, at least in part, a paternalistic argument. [HTS 139]

Feinberg imagines that an insurance scheme has indeed been implemented.

> Now we must consider the problem raised by the small but inevitable number of cheaters who intentionally fail to insure themselves and are not in a position to pay their own costs in case of an accident. [HTS 139-40]

Feinberg notes Dworkin's claim that we ought *not* refuse to aid these people, and strongly endorses it; I too concur: we ought not refuse aid. But Feinberg has no proposal for paying for this aid. Feinberg writes,

> Dworkin's understated point is certainly correct. It is *unthinkable* that we leave the reckless, bareheaded young motorcyclist to die in his own pool of blood because he has not contributed to the costs of his own care. One way to try to escape this dilemma is to pass helmet statutes with criminal sanctions. Another way is to adopt the humanitarian policy of rescue for those who are injured while violating the statute against driving without a license, and then prosecute them for violating *that* law (though punishment may seem somewhat redundant if the victim is permanently paralyzed in the hospital). I see no clear advantage in the former method. [HTS 140]

There is no clear advantage in the former method, I agree—but there is none in the latter method either.

At issue here is just how to pay for the medical treatment of the individual who has not secured insurance coverage for that treatment (or alternatively, how to justify refusing treatment).

To even suggest that enacting a criminal statute requiring the wearing of a helmet is a potential solution is quite strange, for its presupposition is most implausible. The problem we confront is this: what to do about a biker who is lying in his "own pool of blood"—the result of an injury caused by, or exacerbated by, the refusal to wear a helmet—who has also refused to purchase insurance which would cover the costs of his care. To suggest a helmet law as a solution is to presuppose that there are bikers who (i) would prefer to ride without a helmet, (ii) will disobey a law requiring that they carry insurance, but (iii) would not disobey a law requiring the use of a helmet. Unless there are such people, this is no solution at all; unless (ii) and (iii) are true of most bikers who wish to ride without a helmet, it isn't very much of a solution. But surely it is more important to such bikers to ride without a helmet than to evade insurance premiums.

We need not rely upon a "humanitarian policy" either. The "uninsured helmetless biker" provision, included in every policy of the "Special Insurance Program - Helmets," will be quite sufficient. Every motorcyclist will be required to purchase general insurance; every policy will include "uninsured cyclist" coverage, and "uninsured helmetless biker" coverage. Some helmetless bikers will fail to purchase insurance; if injured, their medical costs will be paid from the "uninsured helmetless biker" funds. (Perhaps they would be prosecuted for failing to purchase the insurance; perhaps, as Feinberg claims, that would be redundant.) But no one is left on the road in a pool of one's own blood. The public treasury is protected. And there is *no* justification for helmet laws to be found in this argument.

It might well be unfair to responsible motorcyclists to be forced to purchase "uninsured cyclist" insurance, as Feinberg claims. But once again, maintaining perspective is essential. If proof of insurance is legally required for registration of a motorcycle, and if failing to register a motorcycle is a crime, then the "uninsured" will be limited to those who ride unregistered bikes, or who have forged their proof of insurance. As this is likely to be a small number, the extra premium charged for "uninsured motorcyclists," and "uninsured helmetless motorcyclists" will be quite small. Extra liberty is purchased very cheaply. *De minimis non curat philosophia.*

Feinberg considers yet one more argument in favor of helmet laws; though he finds this too insufficient, he does find it powerful. I too find it insufficient—but I find it power*less*.

> The argument from psychic costs, however, can apply altogether independently of the problem of economic costs and insurance schemes, and it is all the more forceful when it is more direct. If we permit a number of youths to be reckless with their own safety, the first dreadful consequence (cost) will be the damage to the unlucky victims themselves. [HTS 140][13]

But there are other victims.

> We suffer broken hearts as witnesses to, or participants in, violent accidents causing injuries aggravated by unprotected vulnerabilities, and our own liberal ideals seem to require us to shrug our shoulders and say "Well, he asked for it," or some such icy banality. Imagine the state of the motorist at fault in the Vroom collision if Victor Vroom had been killed or seriously brain-damaged. *He* needs protection too. And Victor's parents. And Victor's dependents. And attending medical workers. And traumatized witnesses. But *mainly* the other motorist. That appeal to psychic costs to others is the strongest nonpaternalistic argument for an effectively deterrent statute. It is not paternalistic . . .. [HTS 140-41]

---

[13]Note Feinberg's claim "If we *permit* . . .." This is a subtle form of the "assumption of compliance." We can *prohibit* recklessness, but not *per se* prevent it. Youths can, as a matter of fact, be reckless despite various prohibitions, despite our refusal to "permit" it.

Is Feinberg right in claiming that "our own liberal ideals seem to require us to shrug our shoulders and say 'Well, he asked for it', or some such icy banality"? No, Feinberg is wrong. *Nothing* in Liberalism requires that attitude, or that sort of utterance; "compassionate Liberal" is not self-contradictory, oxymoronic. It is perfectly consistent to be deeply sympathetic towards those who suffer as a result of their own risky conduct, and to be deeply empathetic with those who suffer as a consequence of the risky activity of loved ones—and yet be deeply persuaded that laws which might have reduced that particular injury (but might *not* have) are morally unjustified. The compassionate Liberal is free to subscribe to the "Special Insurance Program - Helmets," including the provision for "uninsured helmetless bikers;" Victor Vroom receives the medical care he requires. Such a Liberal thinks it appropriate that Victor was free to choose whether to wear a helmet, and that Victor either had obtained special insurance to pay for his medical care, or else that care will be funded by "uninsured helmetless biker" insurance (obtained by Victor as an element of general insurance—or, failing that, obtained by other bikers). The position of the "compassionate Liberal" is more defensible, and thus far more attractive, than that of Feinberg's "icy" Liberal. And the "psychic cost" argument for helmet laws is weakened; the "psychic costs" do not include the costs of ignoring Victor.

Despite the (incorrect) belief that the Liberal cannot come to the aid of Victor Vroom, Feinberg continues to pledge allegiance to Liberalism. His characterization of his own position, as well as of Dworkin's position, is quite wonderful.

> Dworkin is so convinced of the antecedent reasonableness of the coercive statutes, however, that he is prepared candidly to defend them on paternalist grounds, if other ways fail. I am less sure that the appeal to psychic costs won't suffice, but if it doesn't, I am so impressed, antecedently, with the claims of personal autonomy, that I would have no criminally sanctioned regulation at all, restricting the state to its still quite substantial role in educating, testing, licensing, taxing and insuring autonomous bikers, all in the pubic interest. [HTS 141]

So something remains of the "psychic cost" argument: the costs imposed by mangled Victor on medical personnel, on Victor's parents, and "*mainly* on the other motorist," the other person involved in the collision. These psychic costs are indeed harms to others. The question that remains: are these harms sufficient to justify a statute requiring helmet-wearing?

The main strength of (what remains of) the argument from "psychic cost," I believe, depends upon the presupposition that the voice of safety speaks univocally in favor of wearing a helmet. So long as we think that helmet-wearing either prevents injuries or reduces their seriousness—and could neither cause a collision, nor exacerbate an injury—then a psychic cost will be exacted whenever we view, or envision, a person injured while not wearing a helmet. This surely is Feinberg's presupposition. He cites statistics about the injuries sustained by helmetless riders, together with the professional judgement (of orthopedic surgeons) that certain injuries would have been worse had a helmet not been worn, and that certain injuries could have been prevented (or lessened) if only a helmet had been worn. And when speculating as to the reasons one might decide against wearing a helmet, he lists only the following: "mere convenience?, comfort?, a sense of freedom?, romantic symbolism?, adventurous life style?" [HTS 141] Were it true, on the contrary, that helmet-wearing *causes* some accidents, resulting in injuries that would otherwise not have occurred, the argument would lose strength. If some safety considerations speak loudly for helmetless riding, they sap virtually all the strength from the argument based on "psychic costs."

It is beyond question that, in collisions, motorcycle riders are more vulnerable than the occupants of automobiles. Those in cars are protected by many feet, many pounds, of sheet steel; motorcyclists are not. It is also beyond question—and not unrelated to the differential in sheet metal—that motorcycles are more agile than automobiles. In an emergency, a skilled motorcyclist is able to take evasive actions, to perform maneuvers impossible for cars to perform. But a prerequisite of evasive action when endangered is awareness of danger. Sometimes it is the faculty of sight that is essential: the biker sees the danger, and evades it. Other times, however, it is the faculty of hearing that is essential: the screech of tires, the blaring of a horn, the wail of a siren, even human shouts. Motorcycle helmets block some sounds, and they distort sounds. Helmets make it difficult to determine the direction of the source of a sound, and also its relative motion. Indeed, some bikers, in lobbying against helmet laws, would have legislators don motorcycle helmets, and then ask them to locate loud noises. The legislators couldn't.[14]

---

[14]Alex Heard, "Hogrolling," *The New Republic*, November 20, 1989.

Thus, we must add to Feinberg's list of reasons that some cyclists decline to wear a helmet; we must add *safety*. Since helmets impair hearing, they make it more likely that a biker will become involved in a collision.

The mistaken presupposition that safety speaks univocally in favor of helmet-wearing is found not only in the philosophical literature, but in the medical literature. Margie A. Murdock and Kenneth Waxman gathered data from individuals admitted to a Level I trauma center; they found that "when riders not wearing helmets were brought to our trauma center after accidents, they had increased risks of serious head and facial injuries, prolonged hospital stays requiring ventilatory support, and either died of head injuries or were discharged with neurologic deficit."[15] These data show, they claim, "the need for . . . mandatory helmet use legislation."[16] However, the only individuals investigated by Murdock and Waxman were those transported to their trauma center, were those who had in fact been involved in motorcycle collisions. What their data show is that *if* one is, in fact involved in an accident, then one is less likely to be injured, or likely to be less seriously injured, if one is wearing a helmet. But that is the very *most* their data can show. They show that it is safer to wear a helmet when *colliding*; the data do not, and cannot show that it is safer to wear a helmet when *riding*—given that helmetlessness raises the probability of avoiding collisions.[17] Indeed, no amount of data gathered at a trauma center, no amount of data gathered solely from collision victims, could show that it is safer to wear a helmet when riding a motorcycle. To show that, one would need to collect data on collisions *avoided* by helmetless riding. However, it is notoriously difficult to determine precisely how often events don't happen. It might be thought sufficient to compare the number of accidents per mile in states that do not require the wearing of a helmet with the number of accidents per mile in states that do require the wearing of a helmet. Unfortunately, this would not be sufficient; one must control for a number of other variables. Some bikers will wear a helmet even though it is not legally required; some bikers will not wear a helmet even though it is legally required. And one will have to control for varying levels

---

[15]Margie A. Murdock and Kenneth Waxman, "Helmet Use Improves Outcomes After Motorcycle Accidents," *Western Journal of Medicine*, October 1991, pp. 370-72.

[16]Murdock and Waxman, p. 372.

[17]I first argued this position in "Riding, Colliding, Criminalizing—Safety and Motorcycle Helmet Laws," *The Western Journal of Medicine*, Vol. 158, No. 3, March 1993, p. 310.

of experience and skill, licensing requirements, road conditions, traffic conditions, weather conditions, etc. In the absence of such data, however, no one is in a position to say whether safety in riding, in addition to safety in colliding, is promoted by the wearing of a helmet.[18]

Let us suppose, however, that extensive research—of necessity, carried out beyond the confines of the emergency room—yielded solid data that, all things considered, it is safer to wear a helmet when riding, and not just when colliding. (Perhaps motorists, like airline pilots, would be legally required to report "near misses.") Wouldn't this be sufficient to justify a mandatory helmet law? No, it would not. All that *these* data could show is that, in aggregate, more deaths and injuries were avoided by wearing a helmet in the collisions that did in fact occur, than were avoided by avoiding collisions. But this general claim is not easily applied to particular individuals. Skill levels vary among motorcyclists; even if in general it is safer to ride with a helmet, especially skilled bikers might well be safer riding helmetless. Conversely, it might be the case that the sounds of danger are most beneficial to novices.

Thus, the cyclist is confronted with two different sets of risks: (1) wearing a helmet, and increasing the probability of becoming involved in an accident, but also decreasing the probability of death or the seriousness of injury in the event of an accident; (2) not wearing a helmet, decreasing the probability of becoming involved in an accident, but increasing the probability of death or more serious injury in the event of an accident.

Choosing between sets of risks is precisely the sort of action that ought to be left to competent adults—including Victor Vroom. On this matter, I side with Mill: ". . . when there is not a certainty, but only a danger of mischief, no one but the person himself can judge of the sufficiency of the motive which may prompt him to incur the risk . . .." [OL 117]

I do not deny the claim that there are psychic costs, to passers-by, etc., but *mainly* to the other involved motorist, of witnessing the injuries suffered by a helmetless rider. But what must be factored into the argument about criminalizing the failure to wear a helmet are the accidents which that biker, and other bikers, were able to *avoid*, due in some measure to their enhanced

[18]Precisely the same must be said about comparing the accident rate before and after the enactment of legislation: unless one controls for these variables, one may not infer from the fact that the rate of accidents doesn't increase, that helmet wearing doesn't cause accidents. Cf. Waxman's response to my critique, *The Western Journal of Medicine*, Vol. 158, No. 3, March 1993, pp. 310-11.

ability to locate the source and direction of sounds—precisely because they were riding without a helmet. Of course the injury which prompts the sympathy and empathy is present, and perhaps gruesome; avoided accidents are, as it were, nonexistent. However, the fact that accidents were avoided is crucial to determining whether a statute is morally justified. Furthermore, the erosions of autonomy prevented by not enacting a statute are scattered in space and time. In the final analysis, however, focusing on the immediate and dramatic at the expense of the less dramatic and scattered is hardly an acceptable philosophical methodology.[19]

The best way to confront—and in my judgement *defeat*—the argument from psychic costs, is to imagine the collision between the "bare-headed young motorcyclist" and the "other motorist" occurring in a society which had adopted my proposal for a "Special Insurance Program - Helmets," and in which it was known that motorcycle helmets, by muffling and distorting warning sounds, *caused* some collisions. At the scene of the accident, the "other motorist" is likely to lapse into shock, or at least be overwhelmed by a mixture of compassion, sympathy, concern and horror. But later, upon reflection, the "other motorist" might well—and really should—say to himself the following.

[19]Motorcycle helmets prevent some head injuries, and reduce the seriousness of others. They interpose, between the head of the biker and various obstacles, a hard shell and some softer padding—similar in function to the sheet metal of automobiles. And like that sheet metal, helmets have weight. Wearing a helmet unavoidably has the effect of increasing the weight of the *head* of its wearer. And this is a crucial factor as regards *inertia*. The effects of inertia at rest are seen when, upon fast acceleration from a stoplight, the helmeted head of the cyclist snaps backwards. But so what—they should take it easy. The effects of inertia in motion are seen when, upon collision, the head of the cyclists snaps violently, in odd and contorted ways. The violence of the snap is, of course, increased due to the additional weight of the helmet. And this "snap" can cause injuries to the spinal cord, resulting in various degrees of paralysis. Murdock and Waxman cite studies purporting to prove that helmet-wearing does not exacerbate spinal cord injuries ("Helmet Use Improves Outcomes After Motorcycle Accidents," *The Western Journal of Medicine*, Vol. 155, October 1991, pp 370-372); anecdotal evidence from physical therapists suggests otherwise. Given this uncertainty, I do not rest any part of my argument upon it. If, however, it were to prove true that helmet-wearing causes or exacerbates spinal cord injuries in the event of an accident, then the voice of safety is even more equivocal. As a result, the argument in favor of helmet laws is even weaker: the state would be requiring bikers to accept both a higher risk of becoming involved in a collision, and a higher risk of one sort of injury—paralysis—than another sort of injury.

"I feel terrible about being involved in this collision. And the bareheaded biker was a gruesome sight. Part of me wishes that he had been wearing a helmet; that would have reduced the gore at the crash site.

"But I must acknowledge that reducing the messiness at the scene, merely to spare my sensibilities, isn't much of a reason for legally requiring a motorcyclist to wear a helmet.

"I know, and presumably the biker knew, that there are risks associated with wearing a helmet, and risks associated with *not* wearing a helmet. Today, it would have been better for him to have had a helmet. But I must remember: he himself may well have been able to avoid a number of collisions in the past, accurately locating the sounds of danger—precisely because he had chosen to ride without a helmet. On those occasions, had he been helmeted, he would have been hit—and someone else would be feeling the emotions that I now feel. Perhaps that accident would have been less gruesome, on account of the helmet—but that is a minor matter. And even if he himself has not evaded collisions in the past, surely other bikers, legally free to ride without a helmet, have avoided accidents.

"Suppose we had enacted a law requiring helmet-wearing. Perhaps this bare-headed young motorcyclist would have complied; perhaps not. If he had not, we would have fined him, and perhaps jailed him. Why? Because he wanted to run one set of risks rather than another; he wanted to rely upon the maneuverability of his motorcycle, and his own skill, seeking to avoid collisions, rather than run the increased risk of a collision, conjoined with better protection in case of collision. No, that's no reason for jailing, or even fining, a fellow citizen. Individuals *have* to be free to make choices like that.

"I am comforted by the fact that the costs of his care will be covered. If I am found at fault, my insurance company will pay; if he is at fault, his insurance company will pay. If he is at fault, and is uninsured—he forged his certificate of insurance, or let his policy lapse—then the special fund for uninsured bikers, created by the Special Insurance Program - Helmets, and funded by bikers, will provide for his care.

"I wish this hadn't happened to me; it's imposing a psychic cost. But it's just selfishness to wish that the motorcyclist has collided with someone else, on some other occasion, for having been legally required to wear a helmet. That doesn't reduce, much less eliminate, the psychic costs—it just changes the payer. *All* things considered, ours is a better society for allowing motorcyclists to select the risks they run (while protecting ourselves from financial harm by the SIP-H), rather than legally requiring them to run one particular set of risks, and prosecuting them if they prefer to run the other set of risks."[20]

There are no "icy banalities" in this soliloquy. Rather, it embodies the best Liberal position on these issues.

My rejection of the argument from psychic costs, my replies to Murdock and Waxman, and to Feinberg, depend crucially on the fact that safety does not speak univocally for wearing a helmet. Let us imagine that it *did*—and then assess the argument for a law requiring cyclists to wear this "hypothetical helmet."

Suppose that advances in materials technology make possible the construction of a motorcycle helmet that is comfortable (avoids the distractions of discomfort), light enough that it does not impede head movement, or exacerbate spinal cord injuries in the event of a collision, strong enough to reduce head injuries, and is "acoustically transparent"—it does not muffle or distort sounds. Safety would speak univocally for wearing such a helmet; unlike current helmets, there would be no safety concerns speaking against its use. Would a law mandating the use of this hypothetical helmet be justified?

The context of our discussion continues to be a society which has implemented the Special Insurance Program - Helmets. In consequence, there are no Harm Principle arguments in favor of the law; the SIP-H protects the society from financial harms. One would have to accept Legal Paternalism if one is to justify requiring the use of such a helmet.

Why would a biker decline to use the hypothetical helmet? Some of Feinberg's suggestions, made regarding extant helmets, are apt: convenience, a sense of freedom, romantic symbolism, adventurous life style. [HTS 141] Broader, but including the last two: image, and self-image. For any given individual, personal safety may or may not be the decisive consideration. For any given individual, appearance or pleasure may take precedence over safety. I do not believe the state is justified in compelling competent adults to exalt one value over all others, to exalt safety over the values of pleasure, image and self-image. It is wrong for the state to legally require people to choose safety over other values, and to subject them to arrest, prosecution and prison if they do not act in accord with the state's values. Even if the hypothetical helmet

[20]To make my argument more general, I have left open the matter of fault. In Feinberg's scenario, however, it is the "other motorist" that is at fault. This specification further weakens the argument; now the claim is that what justifies jailing helmetless bikers is protecting the sensibilities of motorists who have driven in an illegal manner. I don't think so.

could be constructed, the state would exceed its moral authority if it required the helmet's use, on pain of criminal prosecution.

Were the hypothetical helmet developed, the argument from psychic costs would gain strength—but it would still fail. The "other motorist," in thinking about the collision, would note that the biker was bare-headed not because he chose to run one set of risks rather than another (as with extant helmets), but because he valued something (which required bare-headed riding) more than he valued safety. Of course the "other motorist" would wish that the biker had valued safety more. But the "other motorist's" squeamishness is hardly a compelling reason for the state to override the expressed preferences of the motorcyclist.

However, the hypothetical helmet is merely hypothetical at this point. In deciding whether to wear an extant helmet, a motorcyclist is choosing between two bundles of risks: increased probability of becoming involved in a collision, but increased protection in the event of a collision; decreased probability of becoming involved in a collision, but decreased protection in the event of a collision. Choosing between bundles of risks such as these is a matter which ought to be left to competent adults, not imposed by the state.

Let us reflect a moment longer on these two bundles of risks; there is an additional, important conclusion to be noted about the Special Insurance Program - Helmets. And, as it turns out, it is applicable to the Special Insurance Program - Seatbelts, as well.

Suppose that solid evidence shows that one bundle of risks—those of helmet-wearing, for instance—was substantially smaller than the bundle of risks of riding helmetless. (I speak here of "objective" risks, not including individual skill, or individual aversions to particular kinds of injuries.) Suppose that the disparity is quite large; suppose it is roughly equivalent to the disparity between automobile driving with, and without, a seatbelt. (Recall that beltlessness is safer when one's automobile becomes submerged or catches fire; sometimes people are safely thrown clear of collisions.) Were this to prove true, the matter of helmets and the matter of seatbelts should be treated the same.

But how is *that*? One alternative is to treat seatbelts like helmets: emphasize the role of individual aversions. Just as some bikers would prefer a greater risk of death to a lesser risk of becoming involved in a collision at all, some motorists would prefer a greater risk of collision-injury, over a lesser risk of being burned, or of drowning.[21] On this alternative, there is insufficient justification for a law requiring the use of seatbelts. Indeed, there is insufficient justification for forcing people to choose between wearing a seatbelt and purchasing special insurance for beltless driving. Thus, on this alternative, not even the Special Insurance Program - Seatbelts is justified. The costs of this "extra" liberty will have to be borne by all motorists, in the form of (slightly) higher *standard* insurance premiums for all.

The second alternative is to treat helmets like seatbelts: emphasize the role of "objective" safety considerations. On this alternative, the state would permit motorcyclists to ride helmetless, and motorists to drive beltless—provided that they had obtained "special" insurance to indemnify the state for their especially risky activity. On this alternative, both the "Special Insurance Program - Seatbelts" and the "Special Insurance Program - Helmets" would be justified.

Note, however, this important point. The two "Special Insurance Programs" are the *most* coercive state measures that are justified. The arguments do not secure a criminal statute mandating the use of a seatbelt; the arguments do not secure a criminal statute mandating the use of a motorcycle helmet.

Although the state lacks the moral authority to make beltless driving and helmetless riding a crime, does it have the right to make them mere *violations*, to pester citizens about these activities? For all the reasons marshalled above, I think not. So long as they are mere violations, however, I am not particularly concerned about them. This is not because I think liberty is a matter of essential projects; I think this pestering does indeed infringe on liberty. However, there are (so) many more important infringements of liberty to worry about; these are not worth my philosophical time. Philosoph*ers*, like philosophy, ought not be concerned with trifles.

V. LEGISLATIVE AND PHILOSOPHICAL CONCLUSIONS

Let us review the legislative conclusions, and the philosophical conclusions, of these arguments concerning automobile seatbelt laws, and motorcycle helmet laws.

---

[21]But there is this disanalogy: although wearing a motorcycle helmet can make more probable one's involvement in a collision, I know of no evidence that wearing a seat belt can make one more likely to be involved in a collision.

I find it difficult to be very concerned about extant laws, valid in many jurisdictions, which make helmetless cycling and beltless driving a mere violation, not a *crime*. What my arguments show, however, is that pestering the citizens with tickets for said "violations" is not justified.

I find it easy to imagine scenarios under which these actions could be made misdemeanors, subjecting citizens to the indignities of arrest, the expense of defense, the consequences of incarceration, and the encumbrances of conviction. And as I think these state actions are very serious matters indeed, the issues become philosophically significant.

As regards seatbelts: the only plausible Harm Principle justification that can be offered, I believe, is the financial harm to others in the way of higher insurance premiums and state medical expenditures for the uninsured. But all that these justify is requiring motorists to *either* "buckle up," or "pay up"—to purchase special insurance to indemnify others (both as insurance purchasers and as tax payers) for the risk of additional expenses. No state action more coercive than the "Special Insurance Program - Seatbelts" is justified. And even *that* might not be justified. If we focus on subjective fears (e.g: burning and drowning), we might conclude that citizens ought to be free to choose risking greater impact injuries (or death) rather than risking those injuries (or death). The state could be protected from loss by a combination of (required) standard insurance and (required) uninsured motorist provisions. Although this would result in somewhat higher insurance premiums for all drivers, the additional cost for the privilege of driving would be a small price to pay for the additional freedom.

The issue of motorcycle helmets is more subtle, more complex, and more interesting. While it is difficult to imagine statistically significant ways in which the wearing of a seatbelt would contribute causally to collisions, the same cannot be said regarding the use of a motorcycle helmet. By making it difficult for a cyclist to locate sounds, helmets make it more difficult for cyclists to evade dangers. The motorcyclist confronts two bundles of risks. Choosing between the two bundles of risks ought to be both the right and the responsibility of the cyclist, and not the state. The state could be protected from loss by a combination of (required) standard insurance policies, which include (required) uninsured helmetless cyclist provisions. If subsequent research shows that there is in fact a great disparity between the two bundles of risks, the state could require cyclists to either ride the safer way (whichever it is), or purchase special insurance if electing to ride the less safe way. Once again, no state action more coercive than a Special Insurance Program is justified.

Viewed simply as proposed laws, the strongest case for both helmet and seatbelt statutes is a mixture of paternalistic considerations with financial harm-to-others considerations: proponents can appear both compassionate and acceptably self-interested. As my arguments show, however, preventing financial harm to others can be achieved in ways less coercive—more respectful of liberty—than a criminal statute. The purely paternalistic case—deprived of its illicit inclusion of harms to others—is quite weak. We are asked to believe that the Legal Paternalist cares very, very much for others' welfare—more than the affected individuals themselves care for their own welfare. The Legal Paternalist is prepared to override the judgement of competent adults, and "for their own good," subject them to the indignities of arrest, the expenses of defense, the consequences of incarceration (intended and unintended), and the encumbrances of conviction, in the effort to alter their behavior. And it is so important to do this that the Legal Paternalist is willing to devote scarce social resources to the enterprise. I am not persuaded.

Consider now the philosophical consequences.

The main philosophical interest in seat belt laws and motorcycle helmet laws—besides the prospect of the actions' being made crimes rather than mere violations—is the role they play in the Legal Paternalist's enterprise. As we have seen, however, such laws tend to get *called* "paternalistic" (and there is some plausibility to the claim that they advance the interests of the individual coerced), but the more persuasive elements of their justifications cite harms to others. And these harms to others can be reduced, or prevented, by means less coercive than criminal statutes.

This discussion showcases the virtues of Filtering and the vices of Balancing. If one employs Balancing as one's decision-procedure for criminalization, all the arguments for criminalization are placed on one pan, and all the arguments against criminalization are placed on the other pan, in one grand weigh-in. This facilitates the illicit adding of Harm Principle arguments and Legal Paternalism arguments—the "two scoops" solution—which in turn illicitly advances the Legal Paternalist's enterprise. In contrast, Filtering helps purify the arguments. If the Legal Paternalist claims that, for example, helmet laws pass through the Principles Filter since Legal Paternalism is an acceptable Principle of State Authority, the Paternalist cannot subsequently cite harms to others in support of the statute. Furthermore, Filtering compels both the Liberal and the Legal Paternalist to search for remedies less coercive than a criminal statute. The reasonably creative Liberal devises a Special Insurance Program, including the appropriate provisions. The argument from "psychic costs"—the strongest of the other Harm Principle arguments—is shown weak in two ways. First, since helmets contribute to collisions as well as protect bikers from some injuries, it is not at all clear that a law mandating the use of helmets will reduce the total psychic costs imposed on others. Furthermore, it is just a philosophical blunder to just presume that the "costs" of the gore of actual accidents *must* be greater than the "benefits" of accidents evaded, and the liberty available to all. Recall too that Liberalism is perfectly consistent with compassion. The Liberal is not compelled by consistency to abandon victims in the street. The Liberal can wholeheartedly support the care of victims; insurance programs can be implemented to indemnify other motorists, and the state.

The Legal Paternalist, blocked from illegitimate reliance on harm to others, comes off as a meddlesome busybody.

Topic Two
SCOCCIA'S NOVEL CONDITION FOR JUSTIFIED PATERNALISTIC INTERFERENCE

I. INTRODUCTION TO THE ISSUES

Why is it that philosophers are concerned about "paternalistic interference?" I believe it is due to a deeply felt tension. We have an abiding faith that, on *some* occasions at least, interfering with the self-regarding conduct of others can be crucial in promoting their interests, or preventing a setback of their interests. And yet we are keenly aware of the fact that interfering is fraught with danger. The paternalistic interference may fail to advance the interests of the person subjected to the interference; it may even set back those interests. More subtle—but no less important—the interference *itself* may be judged by that person as an unwarranted intrusion, whatever the other consequences of the interference.

In a recent article, Danny Scoccia[22] claims that even more "paternalism" is justified than is believed justified by an array of his paternalistic predecessors. Given the amount of philosophical attention that has been devoted to the various issues of paternalism, this claim is surprising and bold. If I am right, it is also false; Scoccia's position is another failure to justify coercion.

Scoccia begins by distinguishing two different views on "respecting autonomy;" it is respect for autonomy, he believes, that morally precludes much paternalistic interference. The first view, associated with Joel Feinberg and Jonathan Glover (among others)[23] considers respecting autonomy "a side constraint which forbids paternalistically motivated interference with any self-regarding, voluntary choice." (318) The second view also considers the respect of autonomy a "side constraint," "but one which permits interference if and only if a choice is irrational and the chooser would consent to the interference if he were fully rational and well informed;" (318) Scoccia

[22]Danny Scoccia, "Paternalism and Respect for Autonomy," *Ethics*, Volume 100, No. 2, January 1990, pp. 318-334.

[23]Also Donald VanDeVeer and Richard Arneson; Scoccia, p. 318.

believes this view held by Gerald Dworkin and John Rawls.[24] Scoccia hopes to persuade us that "the second view, far from tolerating too much paternalism, in fact does not tolerate enough." (319) I take this to mean that Scoccia's position is that more instances of actual paternalistic interference are justified than is thought justified by any of these philosophers.

Scoccia believes—and so do I—that not only choices, but "preferences or values themselves may be less than fully autonomous." (327) By way of characterization, Scoccia writes that "Fully autonomous desires will have at least two features: they will have survived some process of critical scrutiny, and they will mesh with their possessor's temperament, character, talents, and proclivities." (328) According to Scoccia, choices which arise from nonautonomous preferences or values are themselves not autonomous (327-8)—and once again, I concur. However, Scoccia further believes that respecting autonomy does not preclude interfering with choices (actions) which are nonautonomous for having arisen from nonautonomous values or preferences, provided that the interference meets his new criterion, the novel "condition (*c*). I no longer concur.

In Section II, I explain Scoccia's position, relating the thought experiment that motivates condition (*c*). I make a preliminary observation in Section III: Scoccia's topic is, and must be, *forcible* interference. In Section IV, a number of scenarios are sketched; I ask whether they satisfy condition (*c*). One sort of concern is raised if they do; another sort of concern is raised if they do not. I argue that condition (*c*) is more plausibly applied retrospectively than prospectively in Section V. Actions that would be eligible for interference under condition (*c*) are Filtered, and located on the topography of actions developed in Chapter Two, in Section VI. And I review my conclusions in Section VII.

II. SCOCCIA'S POSITION

Scoccia believes that his paternalistic predecessors hold the position that

> . . . interfering with a person's choices for his own good does not violate his autonomy if: (*a*) the person has highly autonomous

---

[24]Also "perhaps" Dan Brock; Scoccia, p. 318.

> desires, but the choice made does not accurately express those desires, and the person would consent to the interference if he were fully rational, or (*b*) the person has low autonomy desires, he lacks the capacity to form highly autonomous desires, and the interference is necessary to preserve his potential to develop it later. (330)

Scoccia's thesis is that there is an *additional* "occasion when thwarting a rational but nonautonomous choice is consistent with respect for autonomy" (330), namely condition (*c*).

Let us consider Scoccia's novel criterion for non-violation of autonomy as Scoccia does: in the context of a particular application.

Scoccia tells the story of Alex, who "was raised by fanatically religious parents who punished him in sadistic ways for the slightest transgressions against their puritanical standards of behavior." (330) As a consequence, the "demands of his super-ego—to be prim, chaste, etc.—are harsh, and he is eager to comply." (330)

> He is not wholly successful, though, because of "repressed desires" which surface every so often. His occasional thoughts about sex produce in him strong and unremitting feelings of worthlessness, guilt and shame. (330)

With the addition of one more supposition, we arrive at Scoccia's claim about Alex, and condition (*c*).

> But suppose that if he had high autonomy desires about sex they would figure prominently in his life plan and that their satisfaction would matter even more to him than his being able to make all of his own self-regarding decisions, free of outside interference. Then it seems clear to me that if forcing the help of a competent therapist on Alex is the only way to remove the neurosis, it is no violation of his autonomy. I think we should add to *a* and *b*: (*c*) the person has low autonomy desires, the interference would increase the autonomy of his desires (e.g. by removing an obstacle like neurosis or false consciousness to autonomous desire formation), and the person would not object to the interference if he were rational and had high autonomy desires. (331)

III. A PRELIMINARY OBSERVATION

A preliminary observation is in order. The topic of Scoccia's article is, and must be, *forcible* interference. Forcible interference *is* the topic, because "force" is the term Scoccia uses.[25] Forcible interference *must be* the topic, or else Scoccia has no thesis. A whole panoply of efforts to get Alex to a therapist—other than the exercise of force—is uncontroversial, is perfectly acceptable to Liberals. Indeed, in the very statement of the Harm Principle, Mill writes

> He cannot rightfully be compelled to do or forbear because it will make him happier, because, in the opinions of others, to do so would be wise or even right. These are good reasons for *remonstrating* with him, or *reasoning* with him, or *persuading* him, or *entreating* him, but not for compelling him . . .. [OL 13; emphasis added]

Scoccia has a quarrel with Liberals, champions a paternalistic position against Liberalism, only if he means—as he indeed says—that his arguments show the justifiable use of *force*.

IV. A SCENARIO OF SUCCESS, AND SEVERAL OTHER SCENARIOS

Now it is certainly possible to imagine a scenario that fits condition (c), and seems unobjectionable. Imagine that Alex goes away to college; as luck would have it, his assigned roommate is an upperclassman, an honors student majoring in clinical psychology. The roommate is able to identify Alex's sexual attitudes as neurotic; further, he is well acquainted with the faculty of the college, and their respective clinical practices. (Imagine further that this roommate has no *personal* stake in Alex's recovery.) Motivated by a concern for Alex's well-being (the sort of compassion that led him into clinical psychology to begin with), Alex's roommate overrides Alex's objections, and forces Alex to undergo therapy. Alex—though *forced* (regrettably) to attend

---

[25]In writing about Alex, Scoccia claims that "it seems clear to me that if *forcing* the help of a competent therapist on Alex . . .." (331; emphasis added). Additionally, in discussing the positions of others, Scoccia uses that term. (325, 326)

his first session of psychotherapy, goes willing and then gladly to subsequent sessions. His neurosis is lifted; he lives a full and rich and guilt-free sexual life. He makes a special point of expressing to his roommate his deep and heartfelt gratitude for the initial interference.

Although possible to imagine this successful scenario, it is much easier to imagine less successful, or even disastrous scenarios. Consider the following.

Alternative Scenario 1. Suppose the interferer is a knowledgeable and well-intentioned roommate as before, but Alex must be forced to attend thrice-weekly sessions for an entire semester. The therapy is partially successful; Alex is able to live a moderately satisfying sexual life, though sometimes he feels deep guilt. He has mixed emotions about his roommate's interference; at times he is grateful, at other times he believes his roommate was "way out of line."

Alternative Scenario 2. Suppose the interferer is a knowledgeable and well-intentioned roommate as above, and that Alex must be forced to attend each and every session. The therapy ends in failure. Alex is outraged at the actions of his roommate, and their budding friendship is destroyed. Alex emerges from the experience with a deep suspicion of psychotherapy; his neurosis is more firmly entrenched.

Alternative Scenario 3. Suppose Alex's roommate—the interferer—is just beginning his study of psychology. Suppose also that his motives are mixed: he would like to see Alex cured (enough to qualify the interference as, loosely speaking,[26] "paternalistic"), but in the meantime he enjoys taunting Alex about Alex's "hang-ups," and takes a perverse pleasure in the use of force against Alex. (He does believe that the taunting will motivate Alex to go to the sessions, and to rid himself of the neuroses.) The therapy fails, Alex's neurosis is more deeply entrenched, etc.

Alternative Scenario 4. Alex's roommate exercises great force: he binds and gags Alex, and quite openly carts him off to therapy. (He believes that the shame experienced by Alex will "help" in the therapeutic process, but also receives deep pleasure from humiliating Alex.) The therapy fails, Alex's neurosis is more deeply entrenched, etc.

Alternative Scenario 5. The person interfering with Alex—a heterosexual female, or a homosexual male—is motivated by an interest in having a sexual

---

[26]Recall that, strictly speaking, "paternalism" is a predicate of justifications, not of actions—for example, "interferences."

relationship with Alex (which, of course, is believed to be in Alex's best interest too, so the interference is still, loosely speaking, "paternalistic.") Great force is exercised, the therapy fails, etc., etc.

I trust that I do not have to *argue* that the interferences towards the end of the list, as least, are immoral; doing these things to Alex cannot be morally acceptable. At issue, then, is whether the interferences of the several Alternative Scenarios satisfy condition (*c*).

Condition (*c*) has three distinct clauses. First, "the person has low autonomy desires." I have accepted Alex as imagined by Scoccia, so there is no problem here. The second and third clauses are these, though the emphasis is mine: "the interference *would* increase the autonomy of his desires" and "the person *would* not object to the interference if he were rational and had high autonomy desires." (331) Each clause contains a crucial *counterfactual*. What we need from Scoccia—but do not get—are some criteria for determining the truth value of these counterfactuals. The roommate of Alternative Scenarios 1 - 3 can surely make the argument that *if* Alex *really were* rational, and *if* Alex *really did* have high autonomy desires, then he would not object to the interference. He isn't rational, and he doesn't have high autonomy desires, so he *does* object. But that's quite beside the point. (If he were rational, if he did have high autonomy desires, then he wouldn't need therapy, wouldn't be a candidate for paternalistic interference.)

We also need—and also do not get—a criterion for the truth of the counterfactual that is the second clause of condition (*c*): "the interference *would* increase the autonomy of his desires." (331; emphasis added) Scoccia must take great care that the criterion be neither too strict nor too lax. It would be too strict if it can be satisfied only by *successful* therapy: for then it could never be satisfied. We can have reasons for believing that the therapy will succeed. We can even have overwhelmingly good reasons for believing that it will succeed. But we cannot *know* that it will succeed; we cannot "know" future events, the truth or falsity of statements about future events. So if the criterion for satisfying "the interference would increase the autonomy of his desires" is knowing that it will, and we cannot "know" that it will, then condition (*c*) cannot be satisfied—and Scoccia's position is vacuous.

So let us relax our standards to something within the realm of the possible—that way, the position won't be vacuous. But how much should we relax our standards? If they are *too* lax, Scoccia's position won't be vacuous, but it will be wrong. Surely we cannot morally countenance paternalistic interference—*forcible* interference, remember—on the "vague hope" that "it would increase the autonomy of his desires." More than a "hunch" should be required. Is a "professional judgement" enough—or should we require more, before agreeing that forcible interference with one of our number—not because he is harming or offending others, but for his own good—is morally justified?

Scoccia is in an epistemic dilemma here. If the criteria for "would increase the autonomy of his desires" are too strict, if they are impossible to satisfy, then his position is vacuous. If the criteria are too lax, then his position lacks moral plausibility. What Scoccia needs to persuade us is that it is possible to satisfy the second clause of condition (*c*), that there is indeed a criterion lax enough to be satisfiable, but strict enough to have moral credibility. I do not see how this could be done.

A similar criterion is needed for both of the counterfactuals which constitute the third clause of condition (*c*). Precisely what does it take to show that Alex "would *not*" object to the interference, if he were rational, and if he had high autonomy desires—given the facts that he does not have high autonomy desires, that he is not rational, and that he *does* object to the interference? (On what grounds could we say what a person *would* agree to, if that person were profoundly different than she or he in fact is?) Once again, the criteria must be lax enough to be meet-able, but strict enough to preclude the morally offensive. I do not see how this could be done either.[27]

V. WHAT'S GONE WRONG? RETROSPECTIVE VERSUS PROSPECTIVE

The successful scenario sounded so good. What went wrong? I believe it is this. The successful scenario did not really rely upon counterfactual claims about the future, but upon facts of the past. The interference of the successful scenario had already taken place. The interference did indeed increase the autonomy of Alex's desires; he is now rational, he does now have high autonomy desires, and he doesn't object to the interference—indeed, he is grateful for it. If condition (*c*) contained the past tense, instead of counterfactuals, it would be very plausible. When applied *retro*spectively, it seems to capture the factors of interference in virtue of which they are regarded as morally acceptable, and perhaps even admirable.

[27]It would seem that Scoccia leans towards more strict criteria; see pp. 332-3.

Identifying the features which justify a past interference is no mean feat—but it is more modest a feat than Scoccia had intended to achieve. Scoccia intended to apply condition (*c*) *pro*spectively, to *contemplated* interferences. And as I said in beginning this Topic, it is the prospect of beneficial interferences that explains much of the philosophical interest in paternalism. When, however, we attempt to apply condition (*c*) to prospective interferences, we find ourselves in the epistemic dilemma: if our standards for satisfying the counterfactuals are not sufficiently lax, no prospective interference can satisfy them; if our standards are not sufficiently strict, they permit interferences that are immoral. It became clear that there is an epistemic dilemma when we thought about alternative scenarios with unhappy results, and inquired as to whether they satisfied condition (*c*). If they (at least the last several) cannot be excluded, then condition (*c*) must be rejected. But *some* scenarios which do not succeed do have to satisfy (*c*), for if none do, then it is vacuous (and must be rejected).

VI. TOPOGRAPHY AND FILTERING

My disagreement with Scoccia can be clarified and developed by casting it as a topographic argument, considering the reasons for placing actions in the various regions, and the reasons for an action's passing through Filters.

For ease of reference, let us call the class of actions with which an interferer may interfere, under condition (*c*), "(*c*)-eligible actions." Where do "(*c*)-eligible actions" fall on the topography of actions designed in Chapter Two? Scoccia claims, of course, that they fall within "physical force"—not the "physical force of legal penalties;" he does not speak of criminal statutes. But he does, and must, speak of "forcible interference" all the same.

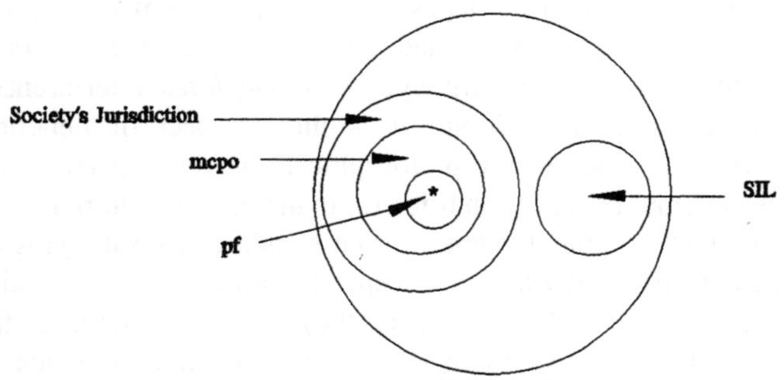

Figure 4 — 3

I disagree. In order to fall within "physical force," an action has to pass through the Pragmatics Filter; at the Pragmatics Filter, we are to envision the actual use of force. To dramatize my objections, the reasons for believing that (*c*)-eligible actions do not pass through the Pragmatics Filter, let us continue with the case of Alex. When we do envision forcible interference with Alex, a number of concerns come to mind—some of which have been anticipated in the "Alternative Scenarios" discussed above.

First: precisely what kinds, and what degrees, of force may permissibly be wielded? May Alex be threatened with bodily harm if he does not keep his appointments? May Alex be shackled and manacled, and deposited on the therapist's couch? According to condition (*c*), the interferer is permitted to interfere in whatever ways Alex would not object to, if Alex were rational and if Alex had high-autonomy desires. But these two counterfactuals provide very little guidance to a well-intentioned interferer, and precious little restraint on an ill-intentioned interferer.

Second: precisely *who is* this interferer? I have two sorts of concerns here: that there won't be anyone situated to interfere, and that there will be someone situated to interfere. In the former instance, no good can be produced; in the latter, there is the potential for a great deal of harm. What individual, what state agency, is envisioned as undertaking the interference? Who will wield this power, overriding Alex's objections? This has got to be a pretty distasteful task, compelling Alex to undergo therapy against his will. Who is going to accept this mission—and why? Perhaps someone who deeply cares about, who loves Alex. But this is problematical. Successful therapy will profoundly change Alex. How could someone who truly loves pre-therapy Alex, want Alex to undergo such a change? And it is certainly possible that the coercion itself would destroy the relationship; it is certainly possible that successful therapy would so deeply change Alex that the relationship would not survive. Thus an interferer, in addition to possessing a vast amount of counterfactual knowledge about Alex, must also be *motivated* to help Alex.

Perhaps the state could undertake the task. Is it believable that any state official would have the requisite motivation and knowledge?[28] Further reflect: in an era of dwindling social resources, how high a priority can this have?

Third: note the circumstances of the interference. Although Alex would not object to the (some) interference *if* he were rational, and *if* he had high autonomy desires, in fact he is *neither* rational *nor* in possession of high autonomy desires. Consequently, Alex *does* object to the interference. The interference, of whatever sort, will be against Alex's will; of necessity, it overrides his objections. How serious are these objections? A curious (and ironic) correlation: if the objections are mild, then the neurosis is probably not pernicious—but then the potential autonomy-enhancement is relatively small. On the contrary, if the neurosis or other obstacle to autonomous desire formation is a significant impediment, a consequence of its operation is likely to be *strenuous* objection. This raises the stakes of interference: the more damaging the neurosis (and thus the greater the potential gain in autonomy), the greater the objections to interference that will have to be forcibly overridden.

Fourth: what is offered as a justification for this interference with Alex, forcible interference contrary to his will, overriding his objections? More autonomous desires, and the fruits thereof. To secure these, one must possess counterfactual knowledge of three very personal, quite intimate facts about Alex: (i) that *if* he had high autonomy desires about sex, they would be an important part of his life plan, (ii) that *if* he had high autonomy desires about sex, satisfying those desires would be more important to him than making decisions free of outside interference, and (iii) that only treatment by a therapist will increase the autonomy of Alex's desires. How plausible is it that a potential interferer will have this knowledge about Alex?

---

[28]Joel Feinberg proposes a legal institution to undertake interference with self-regarding actions in "Legal Paternalism," *Canadian Journal of Philosophy*, Vol. 1, No. 1; a modified version of the proposal appears in *Harm to Self*, pp. 124-27. I have argued against the former incarnation in "On Feinberg's 'Voluntariness Tribunal'," *Proceedings of the Creighton Club*, Spring 1979; I urge the rejection of both incarnations in the next Topic of this Chapter.

Finally, there's this: would a competent therapist who is also *ethical* agree to treat Alex? And what is Alex's prognosis, given that he is being *forced*, over his objections, to undergo therapy?

Precisely what is peculiar about "(*c*)-eligible" actions? Principally, that they are the product of neurosis, or of false consciousness; they are not the product of one's critical, reflective faculties. So let us grant to Scoccia the fact that these are not the *sorts* of actions philosophers have in mind when urging the protection and enhancement of autonomy. More specifically, Mill's arguments for actions' falling within the Sphere of Individual Liberty, discussed in Chapter Two, are not applicable to (*c*)-eligible actions: there's no good reason to believe that acting on neurotic impulses, for example, will help develop and strengthen one's faculties and talents. So: (*c*)-eligible actions do not have that "special immunity from interference," since Mill's arguments about faculties and talents do not apply to them. That they lack that immunity, however, is not sufficient for claiming that they are not in the Sphere of Individual Liberty. For as we saw in Chapter Two, there is an "alternate argument" for an action's falling within the SIL. If an action is self-regarding, and literally "harm-less," then it falls within the SIL—even though the action does not develop one's faculties or talents. Although it may be peculiar to hold that individuals have a *right* to their neuroses, a *right* to perform neurotic actions, those actions may nonetheless fall within that person's Sphere of Individual Liberty. Even when we grant that Mill's arguments do not apply to these, agree that they do not contribute to developing faculties and talents, it does not follow without argument that these actions do not fall within an individual's SIL. If such actions do not harm others, nor pose a clear and present danger of harm to others, they might be in the SIL by this "alternate argument." And if they do indeed fall within a person's Sphere of Individual Liberty, then forcible interference with them does indeed violate that person's autonomy.

It could be argued, in response to this, that (*c*)-eligible actions are *not* literally harm-less: to suffer from a neurosis such as Alex's is to have one's interests set back. This sort of neurosis is sufficiently debilitating that the actions to which it gives rise are indeed harmful to the agent.

Suppose that this response is persuasive; suppose that (*c*)-eligible actions do *not* fall within a person's Sphere of Individual Liberty. The question remains: where *do* they fall? It is a topographic error to infer, solely from the fact that (*c*)-eligible actions do not fall within the SIL, that they fall within "physical force." They do not fall within "physical force" unless they pass through the Pragmatics Filter; as I have argued, they do not. Forcible interference with (*c*)-eligible actions is unlikely to be successful in enhancing autonomy, and practically begs for abuse.

In focusing on neuroses, I have argued against the more defensible incarnation of Scoccia's argument. Recall that a choice can fail to be autonomous if it arises from "false consciousness." Now I do not deny the phenomenon of false consciousness—indeed, I invoke it in Chapter Six. But what counts as false consciousness is very much a matter of interpretation. The claim that false consciousness is sufficient to justify forcible interference, constrained only by the amorphous counterfactuals of condition (*c*), is both implausible and frightening.

Looking back, one can discern the deep topographic error in Scoccia's thinking. At the outset of the article, Scoccia claims that more paternalism is in fact justified than is believed justified even by other paternalists. Scoccia intends to show this by persuading us to accept condition (*c*) (in addition to conditions (*a*) and (*b*), which are accepted by his paternalistic predecessors). However, forcible interference that satisfies condition (*c*)—according to the text—merely "does not violate [the interferee's] autonomy." Consequently, satisfying condition (*c*) constitutes a justification for paternalistic interference *only if* not violating the interferee's autonomy is *sufficient* for its being *justified* interference—i.e., if the *only* moral constraint on paternalistic interference is that it not violate the autonomy of the interferee. He cannot have shown that such interferences are morally justified (i.e., that "more paternalism" is justified) without showing that there *can be* no other sorts of moral objections to forcible interference. And this Scoccia has not done. Indeed, as I have shown, there are moral constraints on forcible interference other than, in addition to, concern for the interferee's autonomy. The interference *itself* must be subjected to close moral scrutiny, a moral assessment that is far more rigorous than the counterfactuals of condition (*c*).

VII. CONCLUSIONS

As philosophers, we are interested in paternalistic interference because we can imagine cases in which timely interference, against a person's stated preferences, will advance that person's interests. Scoccia's condition (*c*) does, I believe, identify features of past interferences in virtue of which we are likely to judge those interferences justified. But the several clauses of condition (*c*) are not readily applicable *prospectively*. If our criteria for satisfying the counterfactuals are not lax enough, no interference is authorized; if they are not strict enough they authorize immoral interference. It is not at all clear that there is a specification of these criteria which, like Baby Bear's porridge, is "just right."

Even if we *could* specify these criteria, it is not at all clear that the interference itself would not be morally worse than the effects of the actions that result from choices and values that are not themselves fully autonomous. We can agree that a world in which more actions arise from values autonomously acquired is morally superior to the actual world. Yet to be shown, however, is the moral superiority of a world in which actions that do not arise from values autonomously acquired, actions which neither harm nor offend other people, are subject to forcible interference. Scoccia's arguments fail to justify coercion.

Topic Three
CONCERNS ABOUT FEINBERG'S "VOLUNTARINESS TRIBUNAL"

I. THE PROPOSED TRIBUNAL

We found in Scoccia's position no significant discussion of the *modes* of forcible paternalistic interference. In contrast, Joel Feinberg has proposed a *state institution* for forcible paternalistic interference. So let us now turn our attention to the "Voluntariness Tribunal."

Feinberg proposed the Voluntariness Tribunal in 1971.[29] *Harm to Self*, published in 1986, incorporates portions of that earlier paper, including a somewhat "milder" version of the proposal. I consider first the bolder proposal; my objections to that version are more clear. Although this may seem unfair, it is not—for as I shall show, most of these objections are telling against *any* institution which *could* succeed in solving the problem Feinberg intends to solve with the bolder version of the Voluntariness Tribunal—they are, for example, telling against the milder version found in *Harm To Self* as well.

Feinberg's argument for the proposed Voluntariness Tribunal begins with a discussion of Mill's famous "unsafe bridge" case. The text of that case is as follows:

> If either a public officer or anyone else saw a person attempting to cross a bridge which had been ascertained to be unsafe, and there were no time to warn him of his danger, they might seize him and turn him back, without any real infringement of his liberty; for liberty consists in doing what one desires, and he does not desire to fall into the river. [OL 117]

Of course none of us can know all of the consequences of all our actions. But some of the consequences of at least some of our actions are sufficiently probable as to merit the label "foreseeable consequence." Now if a person engages in some action, and yet is ignorant of the foreseeable consequences,

[29]Joel Feinberg, "Legal Paternalism," Canadian Journal of Philosophy, Volume 1, No. 1, September 1971. Reprinted in *Paternalism*, ed. Rolf Sartorius (Minneapolis: University of Minnesota Press, 1983), pp. 3-18.

it is fair to say that one's so acting is not wholly *voluntary*—for it is not clear that one would so engage, were one to learn that which one does not know. In the case at hand, a foreseeable consequence of crossing an unsafe bridge is injury or death—or at least a thorough dunking. Given the attitude of most people toward these outcomes, at least most of the time, preventing the crossing until the person's ignorance is erased, seems warranted. In most cases, information *enhances*, rather that detracts from, liberty. The more we know of the probable consequences of various courses of action open to us, the better able we become to construct and live out a plan of life.

Suppose the person about to cross the unsafe bridge, having been given the warning, replies (with a devil-may-care smile) "I know that the bridge is unsafe. Isn't it a *rush* to risk life and limb this way?" Upon discovering that his plan of life included the taking of risks of this sort, permitting the person to continue is the morally correct course of action. As Mill writes, "no one but the person himself can judge of the sufficiency of the motive which may prompt him to incur the risk," and, provided he is not "delirious, or in some state of excitement or absorption incompatible with the full use of the reflecting faculty," the person ought "to be only warned of the danger; not forcibly prevented from exposing himself to it." [OL 117]

The fundamental issue of this Topic concerns an alternative that Mill did *not* consider. Suppose we come upon a person about to cross an unsafe bridge and, after a brief seizing to issue a warning, believe that the person's "choice" to continue with the crossing (at least, the *attempt* to cross) is not voluntary. Suppose we believe the person in a "state of excitement or absorption incompatible with the full use of [one's] reflecting faculty?" Ought the person be forcibly detained for an extended period of time, or not? While Mill does not address this issue, Feinberg does.

The position Feinberg takes is that (1) a *presumption* of nonvoluntariness warrants interference with liberty, and (2) a *finding* of nonvoluntariness warrants *preventing* the attempted course of conduct. This position is adopted while discussing another example, and proposing a new legal institution for dealing with such cases.

> It may be that there is no kind of action of which it can be said "No mentally competent adult in a calm, attentive mood, fully informed, etc., would *ever* choose (or consent to) *that*." Nevertheless, there are actions of a kind that create a powerful *presumption* that any given actor, if he were in his right mind, would not choose them. The point of calling this hypothesis a "presumption" is to require that

> it be completely overridden before legal permission be given to a person, who has already been interfered with, to go on as before. So, for example, if a policeman (or anyone else) sees John Doe about to chop off his hand with an ax, he is perfectly justified in using force to prevent him, because of the presumption that no one could voluntarily choose to do such a thing. The presumption, however, should always be taken as rebuttable in principle; and now it will be up to Doe to prove before an official tribunal that he is calm, competent, and free, and that he still wishes to chop off his hand. Perhaps this is too great a burden to expect Doe himself to "prove," but the tribunal should require that the presumption against voluntariness be overturned by evidence from some source or other. The existence of the presumption should require that an objective determination be made, whether by the usual adversary procedures of law courts or simply by a collective investigation by the tribunal into the available facts. The greater the presumption to be overridden, the more elaborate and fastidious should be the legal paraphernalia required, and the stricter the standards of evidence. (The law of wills might prove a model for this.) The point of the procedure would not be to evaluate the wisdom or worthiness of a person's choice, but rather to determine whether the choice really is his.[30]

Finally, Feinberg offers this assessment of his proposal:

> This seems to lead us to a form of paternalism that is so weak and innocuous that it could be accepted even by Mill, namely, that the state has the right to prevent self-regarding harmful conduct only when it is substantially nonvoluntary or when temporary intervention is necessary to establish whether it is voluntary or not. When there is a strong presumption that no normal person would voluntarily choose or consent to the kind of conduct in question, that should be a proper ground for detaining the person until the voluntary character of his choice can be *established*.[31]

What this proposal amounts to is this: If a police officer happens upon a person(s) engaged in conduct he believes no normal person(s) would engage

[30]Feinberg, "Legal Paternalism," p. 113.

[31]Feinberg, "Legal Paternalism," pp. 113-4; emphasis added.

in or consent to, the officer is entitled to interfere with that conduct, and warn the person(s) of the dangers of that conduct. If the officer is convinced that the participant(s) have chosen to participate voluntarily, they are to be left alone. If, however, that officer believes that they have *not* chosen voluntarily (they are ignorant, in an agitated state, etc.—they are "not capable of full use of the reflecting faculty") the police officer may seize them, and cause them to appear before a tribunal—a "Voluntariness Tribunal." The standard of proof is established by the Tribunal, i.e., it is the Tribunal which establishes the criteria of success for the person detained (e.g., preponderance of evidence, beyond reasonable doubt, to a moral certainty). Furthermore, the standard is "sliding;" the greater the presumption that the choice is nonvoluntary (i.e., the less inclined the Tribunal is to believe that a "normal" person would choose the course of action in question), the higher the standard of proof. Finally, there are two features of he proposal not explicitly mentioned by Feinberg, but necessary if the proposal is to have *any* chance of success in preventing non-voluntary, self-inflicted harm. First, if the Voluntariness Tribunal is to determine whether the person seized is to be permitted to do action *a*, the person must be prevented from *a*-ing prior to the "hearing." And second, if the Tribunal's decision is that the seized person's choice is not voluntary, then the tribunal must *prevent* the person from *a*-ing henceforth, or at least until such time as the person satisfies the Tribunal that the choice is voluntary.

II. TOPOGRAPHY, FILTERING, AND THE VOLUNTARINESS TRIBUNAL

II. A. Topography

Strictly speaking, Feinberg does not propose that we *criminalize* behavior that is, or is suspected of being, an instance of non-voluntary self-harming.[32] He is, however, proposing the use of coercion, of "physical force," by the state. As a matter of topography, Feinberg's position is that these actions are properly placed in this region:

[32]As we shall see, however, enforcing the judgements of the Tribunal may well require criminal sanctions.

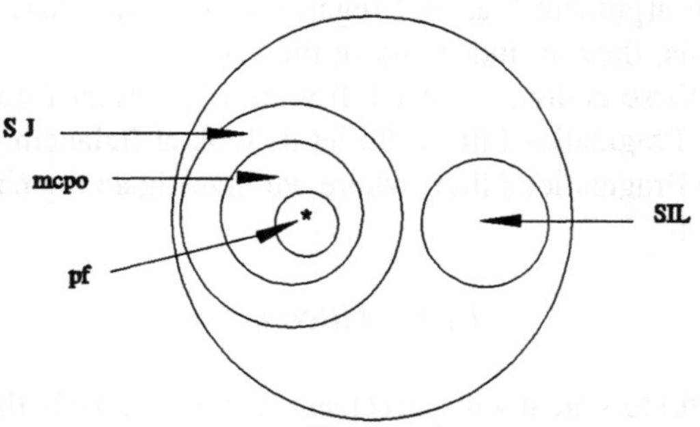

Figure 4 — 4

Our goal is to see whether this is so.

There is good reason to believe that these actions do not fall within a person's Sphere of Individual Liberty. As Feinberg notes, the case of a person about to cross an unsafe bridge, and the case of John Doe about to chop off his hand with an ax, are not the sorts of cases to which "Mill's arguments," as I called them in Chapter Two, are readily applicable. Even if we are generally loath to interfere with the *choices* of competent adults (because it is the constructing and living out of a plan of life that helps one develop one's faculties and talents), *these* cases are not of that sort. These are not cases of individuals living out a plan of life, exercising faculties and determining the consequences of choices. *Ex hypothesi* these are cases of persons engaged in risky, potentially self-destructive behavior, and it is not at all clear that these are genuine *choices*. As Feinberg rightly claims

> Nor should we *expect* anti-paternalistic individualism to deny protection to a person from his own nonvoluntary choices, for insofar as the choices are not voluntary they are just as alien to him as the choices of someone else.[33]

These "actions," then, do not (on *these* grounds anyway) merit immunity from interference; they are not the sorts of things that make individual sovereignty so valuable. Nor do these actions fall within the Sphere of Individual Liberty

[33]Feinberg, "Legal Paternalism," p. 112.

by the "alternate argument," as self-regarding, literally "harm-less" actions: also by hypothesis, they do indeed harm the agent.

Nonetheless, these actions do not fall within "physical force" unless they pass through the Pragmatics Filter. So let us look at Balancing and Filtering, and focus on the Pragmatics Filter, where we investigate the particulars of the proposed coercion.

II. B. Filtering

It will be helpful to state my disagreement with Feinberg in the metaphorical language of our competing decision-procedures. Feinberg's insight is that in cases of self-regarding harmful actions, the weight *against* coercive interference is less substantial than has been thought; when that is acknowledged, the Balance's indicator moves *towards* justified forcible interference. I agree that, in the terms of Balancing, the indicator moves *towards*; my claim is that it does not move *to* justified forcible interference.

But rather than quarrel about the relative "weights" of various and sundry considerations, I employ Filtering. Whether actions of this sort fall within Society's Jurisdiction or not is debatable; recall that the Sphere of Individual Liberty and Society's Jurisdiction do not together exhaust the possibilities; perhaps these actions fall within the "interstice." But let me grant *arguendo* that these actions do in fact pass through the Principles Filter. Additionally, I'll not pause at the Presumptions Filter—it is doubtful that e.g. an education campaign warning of the dangers of nonvoluntary choices makes much sense. But let us take a very careful look at the third filter, the Pragmatics Filter. Let's ask what it would be like to have the Voluntariness Tribunal operating in society. What are the potential benefits, and what are the potential costs? Do the benefits exceed the costs?

My overall strategy in this critique is to argue that the social benefits created by Feinberg's proposed Voluntariness Tribunal would be quite meager, while the social costs of such an institution would be quite high. Underlying the various individual objections is this claim: while it can be agreed that there will be cases in which paternalistic intervention would be, at least in the short run, utility-wise preferable to nonintervention, *which* cases are those cases cannot be determined *before* the intervention takes place. Intervention will be hit-or-miss—and the benefits realized from the "hits" will be overwhelmed by the costs of the "misses," combined with the inherent costs of the successes themselves.

The benefit to be realized from having a Voluntariness Tribunal is preventing people from harming themselves as a consequence of their nonvoluntary choices. Undeniably this is a noble goal. However, this benefit is not realized unless *all* of the following conditions are met: (i) the person is *detected* about to harm oneself, (ii) the person is *prevented* from harming oneself, and (iii) the person subsequently *regains* the use of the "reflective faculties," and does not choose to engage in the activity attempted before the intervention took place. If any of these conditions is not met—the person is not detected, or not prevented from self-harm, or not dissuaded (will attempt the action again, once not constrained)—*no* good is produced. Nonetheless, there are *costs* of having an institution like the Voluntariness Tribunal. And even in those cases where benefit is produced, there are significant costs which must not be neglected. Let us examine these problems in detail.

1. The Problem of Detection

In police-oriented television shows and movies, the starring officers regularly arrive at the scene of about-to-be-committed crimes: the stage is set for a crime, but it can be prevented. Or it is in progress, but the fast-acting police can interrupt the perpetrators, and prevent the intended evil. A common criticism of such plots by actual police officers is that they misrepresent the work of the police: rarely are the police able to intervene to prevent a crime, rarely do they happen upon a crime in progress. Most of their work (besides, of course, traffic accident investigation and public intoxication arrests) is the investigation of crimes that have already been committed, and have been reported to them. This compels one to ask: how often will the police happen upon a person about to injure oneself as a consequence of a nonvoluntary choice? There is good reason to believe that it will be *even less* often than the polices' arriving at the scene of a crime. In the case of an attempted crime, the potential victim is sometimes able to forestall the act, and call for the aid of the police. This just does not occur in cases of a person's harming oneself; only if the police genuinely "happen upon" the about-to-be-committed action will they even be in a position to interfere. Consequently, it is not credible that the police could very often successfully interfere; it is unrealistic to believe that very many nonvoluntary harms *could* be prevented by the proposed institution of the Voluntariness Tribunal.

2. *The Problem of "Arrest"*

Suppose a police officer *were* to happen upon a person about to engage in an activity that the officer considers so dangerous, foolhardy, self-destructive, etc., that the officer believed that a presumption of nonvoluntariness of choice existed. We are agreed that the officer (or anyone) may shout out a warning—indeed, it is plausible that both have an obligation to give a warning, especially when the suspected cause of the nonvoluntariness is ignorance of the foreseeable consequences of the act. And even restraining a person—while a warning is given—might be permissible, or even obligatory, in some circumstances: for example, the risk of danger is high, the degree of danger is severe, and there is no other way to effectively deliver the warning. But now we are supposing that the person has been warned, and yet has given every indication that the warning will not be heeded. According to Feinberg's proposal, the person is to be seized, and brought before the Voluntariness Tribunal.

Of course constitutionality is not the final word on matters such as this. But it is an obvious truth that there are strong moral arguments for many constitutional provisions. Constitutionality can thus serve as an indicator—if a practice is unconstitutional, we ought to investigate just why it is so, prior to countenancing it. Now as constitutional matters stand, a police officer may make an arrest only if a warrant has been issued or an indictment handed down, or if there is probable cause to believe the suspect has committed a crime. Using Feinberg's example of John Doe about to chop off his hand with an ax, we may ask: Under what authority could Officer Richard Roe arrest John Doe? Under what authority could Roe seize Doe, attempting to prevent the hand-chopping? Obviously, since Doe has not yet performed the hand-chopping, there can be no outstanding arrest warrant, or a grand jury indictment.

There are two obvious alternatives for solving this difficulty. First, it could be made a crime to do anything which might be viewed by a police officer as creating a presumption of nonvoluntary choice. Second, the Constitution could be amended to create an analog of arrest called "paternalistic seizure." Let us consider these in turn.

Actually, enacting a law making it criminal to do, or to engage in, activities which could be viewed as self-destructive, foolhardy, etc., would not accomplish the legal paternalist's goal: preventing a person from harming oneself nonvoluntarily. What would have to be made criminal is not the activity itself—by then the damage will be done—but the *attempt*! We could give the police the authority to arrest, by making it criminal to attempt to engage in conduct which, were it to be observed by the police, would lead them to believe that one's choice to engage (more precisely, one's choice to attempt to engage) was nonvoluntary.

Even casual familiarity with law-writing, and constitutional constraints on laws, is sufficient to see the impossibility of this task. I think it uncontroversial that there are at least indefinitely many (and perhaps infinitely many) activities in which a person might engage, or attempt to engage, which could lead a police officer to believe that the choice was not voluntary. Thus, indefinitely many laws would have to be enacted in order to give the police the authority to arrest. And as people discover new and different ways of risking life and limb (as they are wont to do), even more laws will be required. It is clear that this is not feasible.

Perhaps, it could be replied, a single law would do: a law making it criminal to attempt to engage in *any* activity whatsoever, were that activity to be of a sort that were one to engage in it, an observer would (could? might?) presume that the choice to engage in it was not voluntary. The constitutional difficulty with such a law, of course, is that it is *vague*—and it is not uncommon for laws to be found unconstitutional on account of vagueness. An important principle of the criminal law is that it must be clear just what actions are forbidden. It is simply wrong to arrest and punish a person for doing something there was insufficient reason to believe was legally prohibited.

Thus, it does not seem possible to give police officers the authority to arrest paternalistically by making certain actions criminal.

Could we create a new procedure called "paternalistic seizure?" The moral arguments which *underlie* various constitutional provisions now come to the forefront. To the person who is being forcibly restrained, the difference between "arrest" and "paternalistic seizure" is at best a legal nicety, at worst Kafkasque irony. The arguments which show that no precise criminal law(s) could be written also show, *mutatis mutandis*, that no precise restrictions on paternalistic seizure could be written. Thus, paternalistic seizures could be as capricious and arbitrary as would be arrests of the sort just discussed. And an analogous legal principle applies: a person ought not to be seized for doing something one had no reason to believe was legally forbidden.

We are faced, I believe, with these two alternatives: either we cannot confer upon the police the authority to arrest, or we vest in them the power to enact, spontaneously, "bills of attainder." That is, we give the police the right to make a person's conduct criminal, or in some other way legally prohibited, "on the spot": at *this* time, regarding *this* person, the conduct is forbidden. But both seizure without authority, and authority on account of bills of attainder, are morally repugnant.

Whether arrested or "paternalistically seized," the detainee would be taken into custody. Just as police officers need to be protected from arrestees, police officers would need to be protected from detainees. A person with an ax, acting in a way that leads others to believe that he is not acting voluntarily, is so unpredictable and so potentially dangerous that it would be foolish to not take extraordinary precautions—ordinary precautions, and then some. Ordinary precautions include disarming the "detainee," a pat-down search, handcuffing, transportation to some facility, and a strip search, including body cavity search. (Bear in mind that Doe also poses a danger to fellow detainees; this contributes to the justifiability of these precautions.) Thus, anyone paternalistically seized, like anyone arrested, will be subjected to the whole array of indignities of arrest, as detailed in the Introduction.

3. The Problem of Justifying the Tribunal Itself

If part of the cause and justification of there being social organization is the enhanced life prospects of the members (and this can hardly be doubted), then the responsibilities imposed upon each of the various parties to a criminal proceeding strike one as justified. A person cannot be compelled to show that one is not guilty of some offense unless the police have discovered reason to believe the person is indeed guilty, and the prosecution has made, consistent with rules of evidence, a *prima facie* case that the person is guilty. If these conditions are met, however, the accused must go forward with a defense, again consistent with the rules of evidence. The party which prevails is determined by the court according to the standard believed to be optimal in avoiding two grave evils: punishing the innocent, and freeing the guilty.

The intent of this brief excursion into criminal procedure is to call attention to the moral foundation of the criminal justice system: what justifies the state's arresting an individual, compelling the accused to appear before a tribunal, to go forward with a defense (a defense consistent with the rules of evidence), and meet a society-established burden of proof, is the belief that the society's right to be free of offenses against its members *entitles* it to make these demands. Now whether these rules of evidence, or this standard of proof are the most just, is not relevant here; I am not arguing for any specific rules or standards. I simply point out that when the state is asked to justify the criminal justice system, the appeal is to the protection of the individual members of the society from their fellow citizens.

Consider, in contrast, the person brought before Feinberg's Voluntariness Tribunal. In some respects that person is like the plaintiff in a civil suit—bearing the burden of proof, one must go forward with evidence in attempting to show that one's choice is voluntary. Such a person is *unlike* the plaintiff in a civil suit, however, in an important respect—the person did not *initiate* the legal proceedings. One's presence is compelled by the state, so in this respect one resembles the defendant in a criminal action. One further resembles the criminal defendant in that it is one's liberty that is at stake (as is detailed below). One is *unlike* the defendant in a criminal case, however, in that a person accused of a crime enjoys the presumption of innocence. It is the state which has the burden of proof. No such presumption is enjoyed by the person brought before the Voluntariness Tribunal; by virtue of one's seizure, the presumption is that one has not chosen voluntarily. In sum: the person brought before Feinberg's Voluntariness Tribunal (as designed in "Legal Paternalism") is put in the most difficult legal position: the person did not initiate the proceedings, the person is presumed to have not chosen voluntarily, the person must undertake the burden of proof, it is the person's very liberty which is a stake, and one must meet the Tribunal-established standard of proof. What justification is there for placing a citizen in this most difficult legal position? The justifications for the treatment of a criminal defendant recounted above are wholly inapplicable. No writer, so far as I can determine, has ever argued that either the prime cause of, or the prime justification for, civil society, is protection of the individual from the effects of one's own nonvoluntary choices. And it is surely doubtful that protecting individuals from the consequences of their respective involuntary actions is essential to the continued existence of social organization. In short: the reasons which justify the demands placed on a defendant in the criminal justice system do *not* justify the demands Feinberg wishes to place on the person seized in the Voluntariness Tribunal system. At least at this point, these demands are not justified.

4. The Problem of the Verdict: "Not Voluntary"

Let us suppose *arguendo* that the problems of detection and arrest, and the problems of justifying the Tribunal itself, can be resolved.

Suppose that John Doe, who has been discovered about to chop off his hand with an ax, is arrested (or detained) and brought before a Voluntariness Tribunal. Further suppose that the verdict-analog of the Tribunal is that Doe's action is nonvoluntary, and thus impermissible. What are we to do with Doe?

The tribunal could simply free Mr. Doe, having informed him of its findings (i.e., that his contemplated action would not be voluntary), and that as a consequence his chopping off his hand is not permissible. Electing this alternative would be outrageous. If the tribunal is correct—if Doe's "choice" of action would not be voluntary—it seems likely that (in that state of mind) he would leave the Tribunal and hunt for an ax. Not only would the entire voluntariness proceeding have been a waste of public funds, but the essential moral purpose—protecting citizens from the consequences of their own nonvoluntary choices—will have been wholly unfulfilled.

If the Voluntariness Tribunal procedure is to provide any moral benefits whatsoever, citizens must *in fact* be protected from their own nonvoluntary acts. In the instant case, Mr. Doe must be protected from chopping his hand off with an ax. How is this to be accomplished? Given that axes are readily available, and that it would take only an instant for Doe to do the deed, he must be under perpetual guard. Perhaps round-the-clock security guards, strong enough to overpower Doe were it to become necessary, and not susceptible to bribes, etc., could be assigned to guard him. Alternatively, he could be incarcerated—and subjected to the intended, as well as the unintended but known, consequences of incarceration (as detailed in the Introduction). Or it might be even worse: given what we know of the trafficking of weapons in prisons, solitary confinement would be required.

Something has, of course, gone badly awry here. The former "solution" would be prohibitively expensive. The latter is simply immoral; to protect Doe from the evil consequences of an involuntary action of his own—chopping his hand off—the state denies wholesale his freedoms, and subjects him to a panoply of evils. To protect Doe from living an otherwise normal life as an amputee, we incarcerate him in isolation. Surely the cure is worse than the disease.

The difficulty here is devising a way of preventing a person from doing some act, while simultaneously (i) not encroaching on the other rights of that person, and (ii) not creating or using machinery that is prohibitively expensive.

There is yet another complication. If the Voluntariness Tribunal system is to achieve its goals, it seems that not only the *intended* act of the person seized, but "similar" acts, must be prevented. (The vagueness of "similar" here constitutes a problem which is either analogous to, or a species of, the problem of constitutional arrest or seizure.) If it has been determined by the Voluntariness Tribunal that, for example, Doe's chopping off his hand with an ax would be nonvoluntary, and thus is to be prevented, then presumably his chopping off his foot with an ax, or his hand with a machete, ..., his arm with a chain saw, is to be prevented. But is he to be prevented from jumping a canyon (well, *attempting*) on a rocket motorcycle, or bungee jumping, or eating fried foods?

In sum: it is not clear just what "carrying out the sentence of the tribunal" amounts to, or whether it could be carried out at a reasonable cost, or whether it could be carried out morally, or whether it could be carried out at all.

5. *Pretrial Incarceration*

There is a problem which actually arises earlier in the Voluntariness Tribunal procedure, but which is better discussed now that the problems of a negative "verdict" have been presented. On the (safe) assumption that there will be some delay between the time that a person has been arrested or paternalistically detained, and when he or she is actually brought before the Voluntariness Tribunal, the question arises: what is to happen to the person in this interval? Again, if the system is to achieve its goal, it must *prevent* the contemplated act until the Tribunal has heard the case and issued its ruling. If the person is simply freed, it is likely that the issue will become moot—whether the action was voluntary or not, the hand will be off. Thus, all the measures taken upon a negative verdict must be employed *prior to* the proceedings—the person seized must be placed in solitary confinement, or otherwise (armed guard, etc.) prevented from completing the act. The person cannot be freed on bail, of course, since if the choice *is* in fact not voluntary, he cannot be trusted to abstain from the act prior to the proceedings. Thus, the most severe measures of the criminal justice system (short of capital punishment) are visited on the person detained, *prior to* any judgment, and based solely on the arresting officer's belief that that person's choice to engage in some activity was not voluntary. Surely this is morally odious.

6. *More Costs of the Voluntariness Tribunal*

I have argued that the benefits of the Voluntariness Tribunal will be meager—few people will actually be *prevented* from harming themselves. Yet the costs of the Tribunal are high: social resources diverted to building and operating machinery that is similar to, or identical with, the machinery of the criminal justice system. And there are the costs of placing citizens in the most awkward of legal position. But these are not the only costs; two others deserve discussion.

First, it would be particularly easy to convert the institutions of the Voluntariness Tribunal into the instruments of capricious or genuinely evil exercises of discretion. A person can be "paternalistically seized," provided only that the seizing official "believe" that the activity, or the "intended" activity, was not chosen voluntarily. A *prima facie* case of nonvoluntariness could be made for so wide a range of behavior that officers would be given carte blanche to harass and intimidate. Officers who are racist, classist, sexist, homophobic, etc. could make the lives of blacks (whites), the poor (the rich), women (men), and gays *quite* miserable by "discovering" them doing something that the officer "believed" was not voluntarily chosen. And what it is essential to remember is that, in an important respect, it just doesn't matter whether the Voluntariness Tribunal ultimately vindicates the person's choice. Great evils will already have been inflicted by the seizure and the procedure.

Second, the institution of the Voluntariness Tribunal could be used to discourage, and perhaps stifle, dissent. Suppose that some people *were* discovered about to commit some act that police officers "reason" could not be the consequence of a voluntary choice. Perhaps they are about to cut themselves (to bleed on Selective Service files), or they lie down in front of construction equipment (to protest the building of a nuclear powerplant, or a radioactive waste site, or a toxic waste dump), or to chain themselves to a giant sequoia, or steer a small raft in front of a much larger ship (in an attempt to prevent the harpooning of whales). The police, with the wide-ranging power of arrest or seizure essential to an institution of legal paternalistic intervention, could seize them, keep them incarcerated prior to appearance before the Voluntariness Tribunal, and place them in the awkward legal position detailed above: they must undertake the burden of proof of voluntariness (the presumption is that the choice was not voluntary), in a proceeding initiated by the state, with their very freedom at stake. Once again, all these costs are exacted regardless of the Tribunal's "verdict." Surely this would have a chilling effect on dissent.

I find it most unsettling to contemplate expanding the power of the police in this way—especially when the "justification" offered is *not* an attempt to reduce harm to others, *not* an attempt to reduce offense to others, but only to attempt to prevent people from harming themselves by nonvoluntary choices. I do not believe that the benefits of the Voluntariness Tribunal could exceed these costs.

Some of these criticisms of Feinberg's early, bold proposal are, I believe, telling against *any* scheme of legal paternalistic intervention. *No* scheme actually produces any benefit (as detailed above) unless persons are detected before harming themselves. Thus, every scheme faces the problem of detection—and unless this is solved, the benefits produced by the scheme will be paltry. Similarly, every scheme must employ some species of "arrest" in forcibly intervening. This use of the state's power requires justification. And any scheme, to be successful—to produce any good *at all*—must use some means to prevent the act, and "similar" acts, both prior to the person's appearance before the "tribunal" (of whatever sort), and upon a "verdict" against the person seized. Thus, the bulk of the objections I have raised apply not only to Feinberg's Voluntariness Tribunal as devised in "Legal Paternalism," but to *any* such scheme of legal paternalistic intervention.

III. THE "VOLUNTARINESS TRIBUNAL" IN HARM TO SELF

A revised version of the proposed Voluntariness Tribunal appears in *Harm to Self*.[34] While one objection I raised against the proposal found in "Legal Paternalism" is blunted, I believe that the rest are still telling. The relevant passages begin as follows:

> . . . there are actions of a kind that create a powerful presumption that any given actor, if he were in his right mind, would not choose them. The point of calling this hypothesis a "presumption" is to require that it be overridden before legal permission be given to a person who has already been interfered with to go on as before. So, for example, if a policeman (or anyone else) sees John Doe about to chop off his hand with an ax, he is perfectly justified in using force to prevent him because of the presumption that no one would voluntarily choose to do such a thing. The presumption, however, should always be taken as rebuttable in principle. If there were an

[34]Chapter 20, Section 6.

> official tribunal to investigate such matters, it would require that once the presumption against voluntariness is established (perhaps by expert witnesses, perhaps from its own records), it must be overturned by evidence from some source or other, including the voluntary testimony of the petitioner, Doe himself. [HTS 125]

Now one of my objections to the Voluntariness Tribunal as it is designed in "Legal Paternalism" is that the person seized was placed in the most awkward of legal positions: while not the initiator of the proceedings, one would have the burden of proof in seeking to overturn the presumption that one's choice was not voluntary. That objection is not so serious here; Feinberg continues

> The "presumption" implies nothing about a "burden of proof." It would be a dubious compliment to Doe's autonomy to make him *prove* that he is calm, competent and free, and still wishes to chop off his hand. The existence of the general statistical presumption requires only that an objective determination be made, either by the usual adversary procedures of law courts, or, much more likely, by a collective investigation by the tribunal into the available facts. [HTS 125-6]

Do note, however, that the person interfered with *still* will be constrained—perhaps incarcerated—prior to the "hearing," and throughout the "hearing"—indeed, until such time as one is given "legal permission" to carry on. How long might that be? And what if the "verdict" of the tribunal is that the choice is not voluntary? What becomes of the person? Feinberg does not say; it certainly *seems* that the person will be constrained, for the indeterminate future.

The new, *Harm to Self* version still suffers the problem of detection—it is unlikely that many people will be detected about to harm themselves, and successfully prevented from doing it. The HTS version suffers the problem of arrest—the proposed expansion of police power still lacks justification. It suffers the problem of the verdict of "not voluntary"—if the tribunal determines that the person's choice would not be voluntary, then it must incarcerate the person indefinitely—contrary to Feinberg's claim that it would be "temporary." [HTS 126] Pretrial incarceration (of some species) is necessary too; unless the person is prevented from carrying out the self-destructive act between the time of "arrest" and appearance before the Tribunal, the procedure will be moot (and no good will have been produced).

Will the tribunal of HTS pose a threat to rational, dangerous dissent? It might seem that it would not. Let us look to the conclusion that Feinberg draws, and then to his important qualifications.

> We are thus led to a liberal doctrine which, in its immediate effects, can be confused with paternalism, but which is essentially quite different from it, namely that the state has the right to prevent self-regarding harmful conduct when but only when it is substantially nonvoluntary, or when temporary intervention is necessary to establish whether it is voluntary or not. When there is a strong presumption that no normal person would—because few normal persons do—voluntarily choose or consent to the kind of conduct in question, that should be a proper ground for detaining the person until the voluntary character of his choice can be established. [HTS 126][35]

Immediately this is "qualified;" Feinberg limits the operation of the presumption to two categories of actions: "psychiatric categories" (the sorts of behavior generally recognized as a "symptom of psychotic impairment"), and "typical mistakes" (the sorts of things that people do only if they have made a mistake of one sort or another). [HTS 126-7] But we must ask: Is it a "simple mistake" to steer a small boat into the path of a much larger ship? Is it "crazy" to tie oneself to a tree? I am not persuaded that Feinberg's qualifications here provide much protection for dissenters. Nor do they provide much protection against officials of the system who are racist, sexist, ethnocentric, or homophobic.

It is important to note that Feinberg's "liberal doctrine" claims that a person can be detained "until the voluntary character of his choice can be established." What if it can*not* be established? What if the judgement of the tribunal is that the person's choice is essentially *not* voluntary? Precisely what action is countenanced by Feinberg's "liberal doctrine?" Does this "liberal doctrine" justify perpetual detention?

What underlies detention or release is Feinberg's philosophically perplexing concept of "legal permission." Precisely what does it mean to need, or to

---

[35]Feinberg's claim that "the state has a right to prevent self-regarding harmful conduct" is akin to, or an instance of, the "assumption of compliance." So as to not interrupt the flow of the critique, I do not discuss it here. However, this use of "prevent" is prominent in the paternalism of Derek Parfit as well; I discuss it in the following Topic.

receive, or to be denied "legal permission?" In what other contexts—if any—is "legal permission" required?[36] What are the consequences of performing an action without "legal permission?" Suppose, for example, that Doe had been denied "legal permission" to cut off his hand with an ax, and did the deed anyway. What happens *then*? If *nothing* happens, if there are no negative consequences for doing that for which one does not have "legal permission"—whatever is the *point* of denying—or even *granting*—"legal permission?

Perhaps it could be made a *crime* to do that which one has been denied "legal permission" to do. But now look where the argument has travelled. The justification offered for Doe's detainment was concern for the welfare of Doe—the intention of preventing damage to Doe as a result of Doe's own nonvoluntary course of action. But now he's gone and done it, despite being denied "legal permission" to do it. Can it *now* be in Doe's interest to be imprisoned, to be subjected to the indignities of arrest, the expense of defense, the consequences of incarceration, and the encumbrances of conviction, for having already injured himself? If Doe has gone ahead and chopped off his hand with an ax (after being denied "legal permission"), is the state entitled to imprison him? Whatever would justify that state action? And whatever would justify that state expenditure? Feinberg owes us answers to these questions, owes us an explanation of his concept of "legal permission" in this context.

The restriction of seizures to those persons whose behavior either falls into a "psychiatric category," or else is typical of a "mistake," puts *theoretical* limits on the abuse of the institution *vis-a-vis* rational but dangerous dissent. Whether these would be effective in practice, however, is open to question. But *if* effective, this restriction simultaneously narrows the scope of the potential good that might be done by the institution. That is, there will be even fewer occasions on which people are prevented from doing self-destructive acts. This makes it even less likely that the benefits of the Voluntariness Tribunal will exceed its costs.

I agree with Feinberg that substantially non-voluntary, self-regarding harmful conduct does not fall within "individual sovereignty;" the arguments which Mill offers for placing actions within the Sphere of Individual Liberty are inapplicable to such actions. It might even be the case that these actions

[36]The state will refuse to enforce a contract if the law of contracts is not followed. But that is an after-the-fact judgement, not before-the-fact "legal permission."

fall under "Society's Jurisdiction." But it has not yet been shown that society is justified in interfering with this sort of conduct, is justified in *attempting* to prevent it, in the ways specified by Feinberg. Indeed, justifying the Voluntariness Tribunal might well require subscription to an additional "liberty-limiting principle," *viz.*,

> *Benefit-Conferring Legal Paternalism*: It is always a morally relevant reason in support of a proposed prohibition that it is probably necessary to *benefit* the very person who is prohibited. [HTO 27]

And this Feinberg is loath to do.

In sum: The Voluntariness Tribunal is unlikely to produce very much benefit for society, would exact costs that are yet to be justified, and is open to serious abuse.

(So what *should* a police officer [or anyone else] do upon seeing a person about to cross an unsafe bridge? Seize and warn. And what if the person "is delirious, or in some state of excitement or absorption incompatible with the full use of the reflecting faculty"? [OL 117] I'm not sure. Perhaps existing procedures—arrest, followed by psychiatric observation—are the best that can be done. We must resign ourselves to the fact that some unfortunate events will occur in society. But in my judgement, the Voluntariness Tribunal would not prevent many, and is dangerous, and is a misallocation of scarce resources.)

If one is "captured by the picture" of Balancing, then what one sees is, upon the removal of "weighty" reasons for individual liberty, is the movement of the indicator towards Society's Jurisdiction. And since Balancing, with Feinberg's "liberty-limiting principles," does not acknowledge the possibility that an action falls in Society's Jurisdiction, but nonetheless ought not be criminalized (interfered with forcibly), one may well see the indicator pointing toward the permissibility of criminalization—or at least to state interference, with the possibility of long-term detention. As my objections to the Voluntariness Tribunal show, however, this institution is not justified. And that is the result one gets by adopting Filtering rather than Balancing. *Even if* actions not voluntarily chosen do not fall within the Sphere of Individual Liberty, even if they fall within Society's Jurisdiction, it does not immediately follow that these actions may morally be made the objects of forcible paternalistic interference, or that the state may use force against them at all. For *that* to be justified, it must be shown that the proposal—the Voluntariness Tribunal, of whatever incarnation—would produce more benefit than cost. As my arguments demonstrate, it would not. The proposed Voluntariness Tribunal ought to be rejected. And the *reasons* for its rejection bolster the case for Filtering's being the superior decision-procedure for morally justified coercion; the investigation at the Pragmatics Filter highlights the sorts of considerations that prove decisive.

Topic Four
PRESENT SELVES, FUTURE SELVES, AND OTHER SELVES: PARFIT ON PATERNALISM

In *Reasons and Persons*,[37] Derek Parfit offers a novel argument which he claims "supports paternalism." After a quick sketch of the traditional paternalist/anti-paternalist dialogue, he writes

> But we do believe that we have a general right to prevent people from acting *wrongly*. This claim may not apply to minor wrong-doing. But we believe that it cannot be wrong, and would often be our duty, to prevent others from doing what is seriously wrong. Since we ought to believe that great imprudence is seriously wrong, we ought to believe that we should prevent such imprudence, even if this involves coercion. Autonomy does not include the right to impose upon oneself, for no good reason, great harm. We ought to prevent anyone from doing to his future self what it would be wrong to do to other people. (321)[38]

In the Introduction to this work, I discussed the "assumption of compliance:" the assumption that, if a criminal statute is enacted, the citizenry will comply. But *whether* a new statute is greeted with compliance is an empirical matter. The danger of the "assumption of compliance" is that it misdirects our attention. One is inclined to ask whether society would indeed be better if the prohibited action did not occur—and if one answers "yes," one thinks one's got a justification for the prohibition. What one ought to ask is whether the enactment and enforcement of the statute will, in fact, reduce the incidence of that action—and what that enforcement will *cost*—in resources, and in liberty. To neglect those costs is to fail to justify coercion.

The "assumption of compliance" takes many forms, has many disguises. An important one employs the term "prevent." Strictly speaking, to "prevent" is

---

[37]Derek Parfit, *Reasons and Persons* (New York: Oxford University Press, 1984).

[38]Parfit concludes by acknowledging that "there remain the well-known objections. It is better if each of us learn from his own mistakes. And it is harder for others to know that these are mistakes." (321)

an *achievement*: if some action was, strictly speaking, "prevented," then it did not happen. Loosely speaking, to "prevent" can be a *task*: Smokey the Bear says "Only you can prevent forest fires." To say that someone "ought to prevent" something is to say that that person ought to take certain actions aimed at preventing, or intended to prevent. Which actions? That remains to be specified. And of course the measures one might take to prevent some action, some event, are properly subject to moral assessment. It is surely possible that some measures which might prevent, which are aimed at preventing, are morally impermissible.

In the passage from Parfit just cited, the word "prevent" is used four times. In my judgement, Parfit's position illicitly gains strength by trading on the task/achievement ambiguity of that term. (Since it is not clear whether Parfit is proposing a criminal statute, it may not be appropriate to for these to be called instances of the "assumption of compliance.")

According to Parfit, "we have a general right to prevent people from acting *wrongly*." But: can we succeed, can we secure this "achievement?" Sometimes. What we have a general right to do of course, is to take certain measures designed to prevent people from acting wrongly. We have a right to take *some* measures, but do not have a right to take *other* measures. Of all the measures we might take in attempting to prevent someone from doing something, it is likely true that some will be morally permissible, and some will be morally impermissible. It is possible to prevent a person from acting wrongly by killing that person. It is easy to imagine cases in which that would be permissible; it is easier still to imagine cases in which it would not. Thus, to say that we have a "right to prevent" is to say that we have a right to some *attempts* to prevent—to attempt in some ways, but not in every way imaginable.[39]

The second appearance of "prevent" trades more seriously on the task/achievement ambiguity. According to Parfit, we believe it cannot be wrong, and would often be our duty, to prevent others from doing what is seriously wrong." *Even if* a person is about to do something "seriously" wrong, there may well be measures we could take that would not be morally permissible, that would make the world morally worse. Far from being our duty, electing such options is morally prohibited.

---

[39]I could prevent my starting forest fires by killing myself; is that what Smokey wants?

According to Parfit, "we ought to believe that we should prevent such imprudence, even if it involves coercion." Should we use coercion to prevent great imprudence? In my judgement, this cannot be answered without a careful specification of the proposed coercion—including its prospects for success, since it is a methodological mistake to assume success. We ought *not* believe that preventing—i.e., attempting to prevent—even great imprudence justifies just *any* coercion.

Finally, the fourth—and most important—appearance. "We ought to prevent anyone from doing to his future self what it would be wrong to do to other people." Ought we? Once again, this cannot be answered without a careful specification of the action we would *attempt* to prevent, and close moral scrutiny of the attempt itself. When we reflect on the critique of Scoccia's "condition (*c*)," and the critique of Feinberg's "Voluntariness Tribunal," we may well come to the conclusion that "preventing" people from doing harmful things to themselves is exceedingly difficult to achieve, and that *attempting* to prevent it is exceedingly problematical. I offer no encore of those critiques here, merely reminding the reader that it is difficult for an interferer to be precisely located for a successful interference, and that the interference itself—whether successful or not—might well be worse than the action prevented (if it is indeed prevented).

For the sake of argument, let us accept Parfit's theory of individual identity. What follows from this is that actions of a current self which would do great harm to one's future self do not fall within that current self's "Sphere of Individual Liberty." Does this "support paternalism?" Well it does in this: actions which fall outside a person's SIL lack that "special immunity from interference" that arises from respect for autonomy—and that's a necessary condition for justified paternalistic interference. But to know that an action falls outside a person's SIL is not to know where it *does* fall—in particular, it is not sufficient to morally authorize the use of force (coercion). More—*much* more—would have to be specified, before a moral assessment of this sort of interference could be undertaken.

I readily agree that my current self might pose a serious threat to my future self. I further agree that the same might be true of other current selves. Yet I think it best that my marginal tax dollar be spent on the attempt to prevent *other current selves* from seriously harming *my current self*. As worried as I sometimes get about the effects of my current behavior on my future self—too much rich food, not enough exercise—I am far more worried about the effects, caused by other current selves, on my current self. That is why I have deadbolts on my doors, keep my car locked when driving, and don't leave home without traveller's checks. And I suspect that I am not alone in this judgement.

Topic Five
SOME HARD WORDS ABOUT SOFT PATERNALISM

Joel Feinberg devotes a section of *Harm to Self* to "Hard and soft paternalism." [HTS 12-16]

> Hard paternalism will accept as a reason for criminal legislation that it is necessary to protect competent adults, against their will, from the harmful consequences of their fully voluntary choices and undertakings. . . . Since it imposes its own values and judgments on people "for their own good," it seems well named by the label "paternalism." [HTS 12]

In contrast,

> It is not clear that "soft paternalism" is "paternalistic" at all, in any clear sense. Certainly its motivating spirit seems closer to the liberalism of Mill than to the protectiveness of hard paternalism. Soft paternalism holds that the state has the right to prevent self-regarding harmful conduct (so far it *looks* "paternalistic) when but only when that conduct is substantially nonvoluntary, or when temporary intervention is necessary to establish whether it is voluntary or not. [HTS 12]

Thus, although "soft paternalism" may have the appearance of paternalism—interference "justified" by the welfare of the interferee—it isn't really paternalism at all.

> . . . the law's concern should not be with the wisdom, prudence, or dangerousness of *B*'s choice, but rather with whether or not the choice is truly his. Its concern should be to help implement *B*'s real choice, not to protect *B* from harm as such. After all, to whatever extent *B*'s apparent choice stems from ignorance, coercion, derangement, drugs, or other voluntariness-vitiating factors, there are grounds for suspecting that it does not come from his own will, and might be as alien to him as the choices of someone else. The harm to others principle permits us to protect a person from the choices of other people; soft paternalism would permit us to protect him from

> "nonvoluntary choices," which, being the genuine choices of no one at all, are no less foreign to him. [HTS 12]

Feinberg concludes that "soft paternalism is really no kind of paternalism at all." [HTS 16] But he is unwilling to swim against the terminological tide by calling it something different.

I agree with Feinberg (and others) that actions which are "substantially nonvoluntary," which are affected by "voluntariness-vitiating factors" (Feinberg's phrases), constitute a peculiar class of actions. I further agree that such actions may be as "alien," as "foreign" to an individual as the actions of someone else. But precisely what follows from this—and more importantly—what *doesn't* follow from this?

In these passages, Feinberg uses "prevent" in the same way that Parfit used it, i.e., in a way that facilitates our forgetting that interference may fail, and facilitates our forgetting that the costs and benefits of the interference itself must be assessed. Additionally, Feinberg's use of "protect" trades on the same sort of task/achievement ambiguity. If we understand "protect" as an *achievement*, then it is misleading to claim that "criminal legislation . . . is necessary to protect competent adults." Legislation establishes actions as criminal. That may be sufficient to deter some people; it will not be sufficient to deter everyone. Strictly speaking, we cannot "protect" people; all we can do is to take various measures in an *attempt* to protect them. The measures may succeed, or they may fail. Some measures we might take are, I suspect, morally permissible. Some measures we might take are, I am confident, not morally permissible. Feinberg's claim is richly underspecified; no moral assessment is possible without fuller specification.

According to Feinberg, "Soft paternalism holds that the state has a right to prevent self-regarding harmful conduct." Presumably, soft paternalism holds that the state has a right to *attempt* to prevent such conduct. Presumably, soft paternalism does not hold that any and every attempt to prevent self-regarding harmful conduct is a right of the state. Feinberg finishes: "when but only when that conduct is substantially nonvoluntary, or when temporary intervention is necessary to establish whether it is voluntary or not." It is possible to envision the state mildly and successfully "preventing" conduct, with one of two consequences: the conduct is judged voluntary (if atypical), or the person regains the "full use of the reflecting faculty,"[40] and decides against the previously "chosen" course of action. But as we saw regarding the Voluntariness Tribunal, interferences are unlikely to be timely, and cannot be mild (for the sake of protecting the interferee, the officers, and other detainees). And we are owed a detailed specification of what the state is to do if the self-regarding harmful conduct is determined to *not* be voluntary. What then may the state morally do? for how long? at what expense? And how easy will it be for public officials to abuse this institution?[41]

It seems clear to me that Mill's arguments for actions' falling within the Sphere of Individual Liberty do not apply to self-regarding harmful actions; it isn't very plausible that a person is developing one's faculties and talents when one's actions are "substantially nonvoluntary." Furthermore, if the "substantially nonvoluntary" actions are genuinely harmful to the agent, then *ipso facto* they do not fall into one's SIL as "harm-less" self-regarding actions. Thus, these actions do not fall within an individual's Sphere of Individual Liberty.

So: where on the topography of actions *do* they fall? The hard words I have for soft paternalism are these: preoccupation with the "voluntariness-vitiating factors" of these actions makes philosophers prone to making the "assumption of compliance" (or something analogous to that), and prone to committing "topographic errors." It is so easy to become so fixated on the "voluntariness-vitiating" features of such actions, to (correctly) conclude that these actions do not fall within an individual's SIL, that one infers im-mediately—i.e,. not mediated by other moral concerns—that *interference* with such actions is therefore morally permissible. So taken are some philosophers with the fact that these actions do not fall within an individual's SIL, that they are mesmerized into thinking that that is *sufficient* for these actions' falling within "physical force," wielded by private individuals, or by the state. But this just is a topographic error. Such actions may well fall into the "interstice"—although there are no persuasive arguments for their falling into the SIL, there may be no persuasive reasons for their falling into "physical force" either. It might be the case that no effective interference is possible;

---

[40]The phrase is Mill's, *On Liberty*, p. 117.

[41]This use of "protect" is not limited to paternalism. Feinberg writes, in a passage quoted above, "The harm to others principle permits us to protect a person from the choices of other people . . . ." What it permits, of course, is some measures designed to protect; it permits some—but by no means all—attempts to protect people from the choices of others.

it might be the case that no effective interference is cost effective; it might be the case that all effective interference violates other moral constraints (on the individual or on the state). More bluntly: *even if* the action of a fellow citizen is essentially nonvoluntary, it does not follow that a "public officer or anyone else" [OL 117] is entitled to interfere in just any way which that person chooses, or perhaps in any way at all.

Individuals may or may not have a right to their neuroses, their neurotic actions, or to their false consciousness. Even if they don't, that fact alone does not authorize the forcible interference of others. Happening upon a person about to do something we think no person could voluntarily choose to do may cause in us an impulse to interfere. But acting on that impulse may or may not be morally permissible; it remains possible that exercising force would make matters morally worse than exercising restraint—despite the fact that, as a consequence, a person is injured by his or her "substantially nonvoluntary" action. It may be wrong for a current self to do to one's future self that which it would be wrong for a current self to do to other current selves. But the mechanics of preventing—of *attempting* to prevent—injuries to oneself from other current selves, are quite different from the mechanics of other people preventing—of attempting to prevent—injuries to one's future self committed by one's current self. And the former are vastly more urgent.

Do not take me to be claiming something stronger than I am. I am not claiming that interference with the "substantially nonvoluntary" actions of others is *never* justified. What I am claiming is that the suspicion of "substantially nonvoluntariness" alone is not sufficient to morally warrant interference (beyond warning); I am claiming that even the *fact* of "substantial nonvoluntariness" alone is not sufficient to warrant interference (beyond warning). Interference beyond warning—especially *forcible* interference, especially forcible interference of some duration—is *itself* in need of moral scrutiny, in need of moral assessment. Whether motivated by base meddlesomeness, or pure compassion, extended forcible interference with a person is an enterprise of great moral seriousness. That the interferee's conduct was "substantially nonvoluntary" will play a role—indeed, a large role—in any successful justification of that forcible interference. But it does not, in and of itself, *constitute* a justification.

CHAPTER FIVE

OBLIQUE ATTEMPTS TO EXPAND THE CRIMINALIZING AUTHORITY OF THE STATE

Topic One
CONCERNS ABOUT FEINBERG'S "GARRISON SITUATIONS"

I. INTRODUCTION TO THE ISSUES

As we know, in *The Moral Limits of the Criminal Law* Joel Feinberg defends "The Liberal Position (on the moral limits of the criminal law): The harm and offense principles, duly clarified and qualified, between them exhaust the class of good reasons for criminal prohibitions." [HTS xvii] Feinberg explicitly *rejects* Legal Paternalism, which (roughly) would permit the criminalization of actions to prevent harm to the actor, and Legal Moralism, which (roughly) would permit the criminalization of actions that are inherently immoral. [HTS xvii][1] *A fortiori*, Feinberg rejects variants of these principles which would permit even greater limitations on liberty. [HTS xvi-xviii] Only "other-regarding" actions can morally be criminalized, those which (roughly) harm others (or pose a clear and present danger of harm to others), and those which offend others.

It would seem, then, that numerous actions which the Legal Paternalist or the Legal Moralist (and more generally, any non-Liberal) might want to criminalize, may *not* morally be criminalized, according to Feinberg. However, in *Harm to Self* there is a discussion of the distinction between "self-regarding" actions and "other-regarding" actions which is of great significance in the dispute between Liberals and anti-Liberals—in particular, Legal Paternalists and Legal Moralists. Feinberg claims that in certain situations, "garrison situations," actions that would otherwise be self-regarding become other-regarding. While "withdrawing" from society (discussed in detail below) would in most circumstances be *self*-regarding, in a garrison situation it would be *other*-regarding. And this is sufficient, for Feinberg, to warrant the "prohibition" of such actions.

---

[1]For a precise statement of these principles, see Feinberg, *Harm to Others*, pp. 26-7. I have quoted them in Chapter Three.

I am persuaded that, in garrison situations, the act of "withdrawing" is not self-regarding, but is in fact other-regarding. I am *not* persuaded, however, that this is sufficient to justify a "prohibition." Indeed, Feinberg's inference—in the context of a military garrison itself, and in its application to society generally—are paradigm cases of the "topographic error."

Let us first take a close look at the situation of a military garrison under siege, and the act of "withdrawal" from such a siege. I shall argue that Feinberg is mistaken about prohibiting withdrawals even in this context. The prohibition is not warranted even here, not because withdrawing doesn't harm others—indeed it does—but because there is no effective way to *prevent* withdrawing. Thus the prohibition is utterly without point. I shall then look to the extension of the argument to society generally, arguing that the failure of the argument in the context of an actual garrison under siege, combined with important disanalogies between military garrisons and society generally, doom this line of argument. I shall show that arguing from garrison situations does not offer Legal Paternalists or Legal Moralists an oblique way to advance their criminalizing agenda.

II. GARRISONS UNDER SIEGE, AND "GARRISON SITUATIONS" IN SOCIETY

Feinberg's argument begins with a rather dramatic thought-experiment.

> . . . imagine a beleaguered garrison of settlers under attack from warlike Indians. Everyone is working furiously to repel the assault. The men are firing at the mounted marauders while the women load the muskets, and children pour water on fires started by flaming arrows. At the peak of the excitement, John Wayne becomes so bored and depressed, that he withdraws with the announced intention of killing himself. "After all," he says, "my life is my own and what I do with it is my own business." [HTS 22][2]

Under ordinary circumstances, one would be inclined to agree with Wayne's claim—but the circumstances are not ordinary. Feinberg continues,

---

[2]Presumably all the men are better sharpshooters than any of the women.

> Of course, he could not be more wrong. What he does is *everybody* else's business since the issue is so close that the withdrawal of one party threatens to tip the balance. There is no distinction in these circumstances between self-regarding and other-regarding . . .. Anyone who does not help inflicts serious harm on all the others. [HTS 22-3]

The profound importance of this denial of the distinction between self-regarding and other-regarding actions in a military garrison under siege is made clear in the following sentence: "Insofar as any larger, more complex, society resembles the garrison situation, the debate over legal paternalism is otiose." [HTS 23] If the Legal Paternalist can show that society is in a "garrison situation" with respect to some sort of "withdrawal," then criminalization of that withdrawal is permissible under the Harm Principle—with no need to refer to, to defend, the highly controversial principle of Legal Paternalism. Feinberg writes,

> The closer any society is to what we might call "the garrison threshold," the more the harm principle comes into play, until at a given point, any further withdrawals pose a clear and present danger, and can be emphatically prohibited by the harm principle without any help from the principle of legal paternalism. [HTS 23]

Thus the garrison situation provides Legal Paternalists (and Legal Moralists, and indeed *any* anti-Liberal) with an entirely new argument strategy for advancing their criminalizing agenda. No longer need Legal Paternalism or Legal Moralism be defended as acceptable Principles of State Authority (or for Feinberg, "liberty-limiting principles"); it is enough to accept the Harm Principle. The garrison situation is, for the anti-Liberal, a wonderful bit of philosophical alchemy. It turns the lead of self-regarding actions (which the anti-Liberal wishes to criminalize) into the gold of other-regarding actions (which can be criminalized under the Harm Principle).

Topographically, the claim is this: in ordinary circumstances, the act of "withdrawing" falls within a person's Sphere of Individual Liberty.

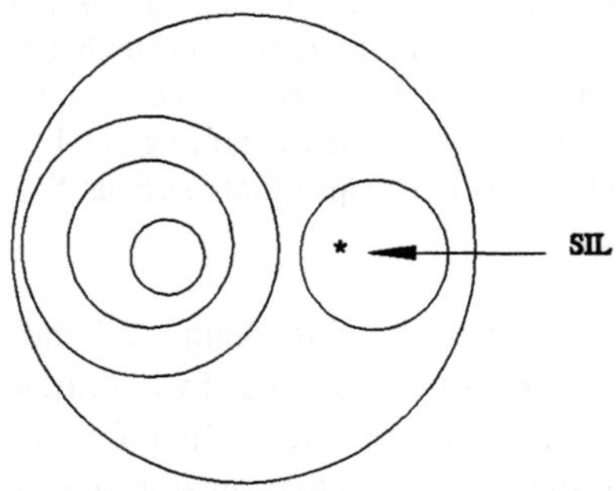

Figure 5 — 1

In *un*ordinary circumstances, however—in a "garrison situation"—withdrawing may be "emphatically prohibited." I understand this to mean that the action of withdrawing falls within the "physical force of legal penalties."

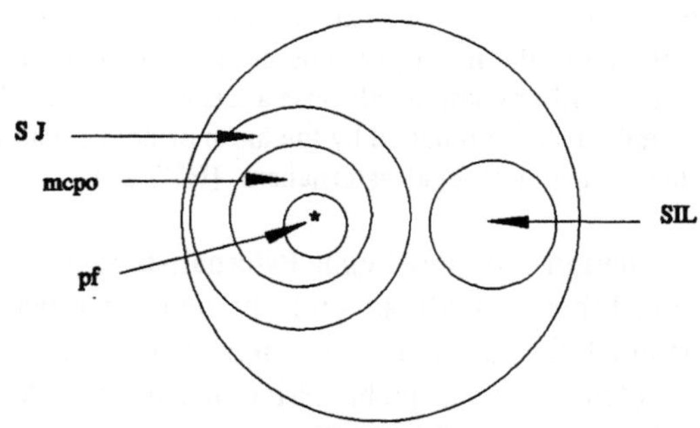

Figure 5 — 2

The Legal Paternalist or Legal Moralist can achieve the desired criminalization without defending either Legal Paternalism or Legal Moralism against the critiques of Liberals—e.g. Feinberg and me. This is why the strategy of garrison situations is worth worrying about.

III. JOHN WAYNE'S WITHDRAWAL & COERCION IN THE GARRISON UNDER SIEGE

Throughout this book I have been at pains to respect various distinctions *within* the class of actions that constitute "Society's Jurisdiction" (i.e. other-regarding actions): some may be discouraged by "physical force" (exercised by private individuals, or the "physical force of legal penalties"), others may morally be discouraged only by the "moral coercion of public opinion," yet others are best ignored. In this discussion of garrison situations, Feinberg fails to respect this topography of actions. We can agree with Feinberg that, as regards a garrison under siege, "there is no distinction in these circumstances between self-regarding and other-regarding;" we can further agree that "anyone who does not help [i.e., anyone who withdraws] inflicts serious harm on all the others." (To anticipate: we can even accept this part of the analogy with society; we can agree that, in garrison situations, withdrawing falls within Society's Jurisdiction.) However, we must *then* ask whether "withdrawing" is one of those actions to be tolerated, or discouraged by legal penalties, or discouraged only by public opinion. Feinberg does not ask; without further consideration, he concludes that withdrawing "can be emphatically prohibited."

Let us postpone for a moment our consideration of the analogy Feinberg draws between a garrison under siege and garrison situations in society. For now, consider the military garrison itself. And let us think topographically. The border between the "moral coercion of public opinion" and "physical force of legal penalties" is the Pragmatics Filter; at this Filter, we are to investigate the realities of enacting and enforcing a prohibition.

So let us continue with Feinberg's thought experiment. Imagine that you are the Commandant of the garrison, that John Wayne has announced his intention to withdraw, and that Feinberg has persuaded you that Wayne's withdrawing would be an other-regarding action, and indeed would constitute a serious harm to others. Precisely what would—what *could*—you do? Wayne has already said that he plans to kill himself; what sort of "emphatic prohibition" is likely to prevent Wayne's withdrawing? What can you, as garrison Commandant, threaten to do to Wayne, that he will find worse than his intended course of action: death? What can you do to enforce the prohibition, what can you threaten to do, so that Wayne will thereby be motivated to not withdraw? Perhaps you could threaten to torture him. But the moral issues of torture aside, that's no help; so long as Wayne is being tortured, he has *in effect* withdrawn: he is no longer helping to repel the Indians. And of course his torturers have effectively withdrawn too! Thus, you do not advance, but rather *frustrate*, your goal of repelling the attack. Perhaps you could chain Wayne to the ramparts. But if he wants to die, he can make himself an easy target. And in any event, he need not fire his rifle, or aim accurately. Perhaps you could have some strong men force him to hold his rifle, and aim for him. But again—how have you gained? Of course the Commandant could reason with Wayne, remonstrate, entreat, etc. But that requires no justification at all.

The fundamental problem here is that prohibiting a person's "withdrawing" is a prohibition of a very curious sort. It is not prohibiting the *doing* of any particular thing, so that compliance is "refraining." (There are crude but effective ways of preventing people from performing certain actions—e.g., imprisoning them, or executing them.) But this is completely different; it is prohibiting the *not* doing of something. Compliance, then, is a "specific performance." And compelling "specific performance" is notoriously difficult. At the Pragmatics Filter, we are to ask whether the enactment and enforcement of a measure would produce a net balance of benefit over cost. What are we to say of the proposal to "emphatically prohibit" Wayne's withdrawal? Well, there cannot be a balance of benefit over cost unless some benefit is produced. And unless there is some way of compelling Wayne to not only not withdraw, but to effectively participate in the defense of the garrison, then no benefit at all is produced—much less a benefit sufficient to exceed the costs of enforcement.

The upshot is this: I agree with Feinberg that Wayne's withdrawal would, in the context of a garrison under siege, be other-regarding and not self-regarding. I further agree that that withdrawal would result in significant harm to others. What I reject is the inference that *prohibiting* the withdrawal is thereby justified. For it is quite peculiar to claim that a prohibition is justified, even though that prohibition is an empty threat, a hollow ceremony. It is peculiar to maintain "Prohibiting action *a* is morally justified—though there is no way to effectively enforce the prohibition, and thus the prohibition can produce no good." Once again: what's the *point*?

This is another instance of the "topographic error." Having shown that John Wayne's withdrawal would not be self-regarding (does not fall within Wayne's Sphere of Individual Liberty), Feinberg concludes—without additional argument, without asking how that might be achieved—that it may morally be prohibited. Absent the requisite investigation and argument, the claim that Wayne's withdrawing may be "emphatically prohibited" remains unproved.

I do not wish to "psychologize" Feinberg. It is not without interest, however, that Feinberg has explicitly subscribed to "Balancing." And when using Balancing in the context of a garrison under siege, Feinberg sees some "weight" removed from the pan against coercion—his argument that withdrawing in this situation is other-regarding "lightens" the case for that action's falling within the Sphere of Individual Liberty, and the indicator of the Balance inevitably moves *towards* coercion. But does it move *to* coercion? I think not. Whether coercion is justified depends (in part) upon whether there are measures the state may morally take that adequately reduce the incidence of that action. In the terms of Filtering, justifiable "physical force" depends not merely upon the action's passing through the Principles Filter (I have agreed it does), but also the other two Filters. But John Wayne's withdrawing cannot pass through the Pragmatics Filter; there just isn't anything the state can do—at least morally do—that results in a net of benefit over cost.[3]

IV. IS SOCIETY A GARRISON UNDER SIEGE?

If my critique to this point is sound, the "prohibition" in the case of an actual garrison under siege is not justified; it is built upon a "topographic error." This alone raises serious doubts about extending the argument to "garrison situations" in society. But let us consider that proposed analogy. In what follows, I grant Feinberg that withdrawing—at some point anyway—is no longer self-regarding but other-regarding, and that it may well cause harm to others. However, I believe that Feinberg is confused about precisely what constitutes withdrawing from society, in contrast with the withdrawing from the defense of a garrison under siege. Further, when once it is clear just what withdrawing really is, it will also be clear that it may *not* justifiably be "emphatically prohibited," as Feinberg claims. Again, my arguments will be based on the considerations of the Pragmatics Filter: investigating precisely what those prohibitions would look like, and determining whether enacting and enforcing them would yield a net benefit to society. While Balancing can indeed *accommodate* the issues of the Pragmatics Filter, it is easy for those issues to get lost amongst other issues—for example, whether the action in

---

[3]Perhaps the state could threaten to torture loved ones (after the siege), or permanently besmirch his reputation. But this raises issues of "secondary moral arguments" of the Pragmatics Filter—what the state may do in seeking to achieve its goals.

question is self-regarding or other-regarding. In making these issues a distinct step in a multi-step process, Filtering insists that these issues be examined.

What must be done first, however, is to explain what is intuitively correct about Feinberg's argument about garrison situations; I have to identify that plausibility, and then dispose of it, in order to show the *im*plausibility of the garrison situation as an anti-Liberal strategy.

Feinberg (and the anti-Liberal who would commandeer his argument) is quite right in saying that some level of withdrawing is inconsistent with a maintaining a community at all. Beyond some point of people's withdrawing, the remains will not be identifiable as an ongoing social enterprise. To see that this is so, note just how silly it would be to assert its denial: that a society *could* endure as a social enterprise, no matter how many of its (former) members withdrew. So let us agree *ab initio* that there is some incidence of withdrawing that no society could endure; let us agree that there is a "garrison threshold." (Of course this rate may well vary from society to society, but there will be some such rate for every society; again, try asserting the denial of this.)

But to say that there *is* a garrison threshold is *not* to say that determining precisely where it lies will be easy, or even possible. Nor is it to say that determining just what sorts of activities are withdrawals will be easy. Nor is it to say that one will be able to specify just what sorts of withdrawals will imperil society, and which will not. Nor is it to say that criminalizing some sorts of withdrawing and not criminalizing other sorts of withdrawing can be done in accord with defensible principles of distributive justice. Nor is it to say that criminalizing various sorts of withdrawing will be effective in preventing people's withdrawals. Nor is it to say that the costs of such criminalization won't be excessive, and perhaps themselves imperil society. Let us examine why all this is so; let us look at the many ways in which society is *not* like a garrison under siege. These disanalogies limit the relevance to society of arguments arising from actual garrison situations. *Even if* one is persuaded that "emphatic prohibitions" are justified in actual garrison situations (and I am not, for I see no way for them to prove effective), the crucial differences between a military garrison and society have the consequence that those arguments are weakened, or are wholly irrelevant. I shall then look at other difficulties that confront the anti-Liberals' quest to invoke the garrison situation in criminalizing the actions on their agenda.

Society is not a garrison under siege: there are important disanalogies as regards *duration*, *size*, and *function*.

Consider first *duration*. Sieges are of (relatively) short duration; society is conceived of as continuing into the indefinite future. Part—a substantial part—of the appeal of the garrison situation as described by Feinberg is that it is a temporary emergency. And good people are willing to make sacrifices during such temporary emergencies—including acquiescing in violations of their rights (and not seeking redress for rights-violations). But the sacrifices one is willing to make *temporarily*, one may be quite *un*willing to make for one's lifetime, and the lifetimes of one's children, and one's grandchildren . . . . Yet the goal of invoking the garrison situation is to justify criminal statutes, laws that presumably would remain valid into the indefinite future. The point here: the garrison situation gets added appeal—illegitimately—from the "temporariness" of the scenario that Feinberg describes. We are misled into thinking that the sacrifices will be brief. But if the garrison situation is invoked to justify criminal statutes, they won't be. Indeed, what must be envisioned—if the criminalizing strategy of the Legal Paternalist or Moralist is to succeed—is a society under perpetual siege, or continuous siege. It is as if one were asked to fire a musket for the rest of one's life, and that one's children would have to put out fires until old enough to either fire a musket or load a musket (depending upon their gender), and precisely the same fate awaited their children, and their children's children, etc. This greatly reduces the intuitive appeal generated by Feinberg's model; that someone might want to withdraw under *these* conditions is both more understandable and more defensible.

Next consider *size*. Garrisons have (relatively) small populations; nation-states have (relatively) large populations. In Feinberg's example, the withdrawal of even a single individual could be decisive, turning the tide of the battle. ("What he does is *everybody* else's business since the issue is so close that the withdrawal of one party threatens to tip the balance." [HTS 22-3]) Were the garrison somewhat larger (more populous), John Wayne's withdrawal (and thus of course the withdrawal of anyone else) would not be decisive; were the garrison somewhat larger still, Wayne's withdrawal would not be important at all. In a nation-state of 260 million people, quite a few citizens can withdraw without significant effect, much less causing the dissolution of the society as an ongoing community (as Feinberg himself has agreed). The Liberal can agree that there is indeed a garrison threshold—but precisely how many persons can withdraw before the garrison situation is reached wants specification.

Finally, consider *function*. The garrison is under military siege; there is a readily identifiable threat, and it is to be repulsed by *military* means. It is quite clear just what constitutes withdrawing—for men, failing to aim and fire a musket accurately; for women, failing to load muskets. But society is *not* a garrison under a military siege that needs to be repulsed by military means. We must ask: precisely what actions, in the context of society, constitute withdrawing? What actions are analogous to withdrawing from the defense of a garrison? Feinberg offers an answer, but extreme care must be exercised here. We must determine precisely what it *is*—and even more importantly, what it is *not*, and indeed *can*not be.

> One way in which a society can approach the garrison model is through a steady accumulation of individual withdrawals, although each may seem in its own terms primarily self-regarding. A nonproductive life devoted entirely to lotus-eating, opium-smoking, or heroin shooting, in which all of one's waking moments are spent cultivating or enjoying dreamy euphoric states, may be "no one else's business" when one, or a hundred, or ten thousand self-supporting persons do it of their own free choice. But when ten percent of the whole population choose to live that way, they become parasitical, and the situation approaches the threshold of serious public harm. When fifty percent choose to live that way it may become impossible for the remainder to maintain a society at all. [HTS 23]

It might seem from this passage that Feinberg is claiming that lotus-eating, opium-smoking and heroin-shooting *per se* are instances of withdrawing. However, Feinberg isn't really claiming that opium-smoking etc. are instances of withdrawing—nor is that what is required by his argument. The threat to society (from people's withdrawing) is not a military threat, but an economic one: stagnation, decline, and ultimately, economic collapse. To repulse the threat, what is needed is not the firing of a musket, but people's performing some economic function: farming, making sealed bearings, assembling automobiles, serving fast food, transporting commodities, etc. What really constitutes withdrawing is not lotus-eating, heroin-shooting or opium-smoking *per se*, but rather an *economically nonproductive life*—whether devoted entirely to these activities, or to *any other* nonproductive activities. Thus, once again, we find that prohibiting withdrawal is actually mandating "specific performance"—although here the range of activities which could constitute compliance is quite large, namely, "economically productive activity." To the extent that opium-smoking, heroin-shooting etc. are compatible with a productive life (and they are not so incompatible as popular imagination would have us believe[4]), these activities generate no movement towards the garrison threshold. Furthermore, a life devoted to *any* activity that is economically *non*productive *does* move society closer to the garrison threshold, closer to becoming a garrison situation. A nonproductive life devoted to playing video games, watching MTV, sunbathing, etc., constitutes a threat to society no less than a nonproductive life devoted to heroin-shooting etc. Thus, the shock value of "opium-smoking" and "heroin-shooting" is a *distraction* here. Much more importantly: no threat to society is posed, no movement towards the garrison threshold is generated, by an economically *productive* life conjoined with the recreational use of lotus, opium, bourbon, gin or heroin. One need not be nonproductive merely for using various of these "drugs." Furthermore, there are indefinitely many ways of living a nonproductive life which *do* push society towards the garrison threshold—and thus, on Feinberg's reasoning, are eligible to be "emphatically prohibited."

A potential solution to this difficulty raises deeper, more subtle—and more important—moral issues. One might criminalize not *actions* (which may or may not be withdrawals), but withdrawing itself, i.e., becoming nonproductive or parasitical in any of the indefinitely many ways that this is possible. But this would blatantly violate a central principle of our legal system, that conduct ought not be made criminal unless citizens are given fair notice precisely what conduct is criminally prohibited. Alternatively, one could prohibit specific individuals' withdrawings, once society is approaching the garrison threshold (on the assumption that that threshold could be determined). But this too is highly objectionable on moral grounds. It would permit a certain sort of action—withdrawing—to some citizens (those who withdrew early, while society was not approaching the garrison threshold), while prohibiting it to other citizens (those who desired to withdraw as society approached the garrison threshold). To do this is to fail to treat all citizens as moral equals. Thus, it is not clear that criminal statutes prohibiting withdrawing could be justified, and it is not clear what they would even look like.

There are practical consequences of enacting criminal laws, and some of those consequences are of great moral moment. These, of course, are the arguments of the third Filter, the Pragmatics Filter. The social ills that will

---

[4]See Chapter Six, "The 'War on Drugs'."

be caused by enacting a proposed criminal statute must be factored into the decision whether to enact it. (While Feinberg acknowledges this, he does not give it the proper attention. [HTO 10]) For example, a law intended to prevent people's withdrawing via the use of narcotics creates a "crime tariff" on those drugs. As I discussed in Chapter Three, this has an array of negative consequences: as a result of the artificially exorbitant price, users are led to commit acquisitive crimes and to recruit new users; profits are generated that result in the corruption of public officials and the funding of organized crime, etc. The havoc wreaked on society by these practical consequences of criminalization may pose more of a threat to a society's continued existence than do the withdrawals that such laws were intended to prevent. Additionally, enforcing those laws guarantees that many people will be engaged in economically nonproductive careers—for example, the "extra" workers in the criminal justice system. This in itself pushes a society closer to the garrison threshold.

V. GARRISON SITUATIONS: A SUMMARY OF THE ARGUMENTS

Society is not a garrison under siege. Criminal statutes of the sort which the anti-Liberal seeks to justify by invoking the garrison situation are not temporary measures enforced for the duration of an emergency, but laws enforced into the future. Unlike a military garrison under siege, not every person's efforts are needed; some fair determination must be made as to who will be permitted to withdraw and who will not. But what counts as withdrawing is difficult to specify. Many actions that may *appear* to be withdrawals are in fact perfectly consistent with an economically productive life (i.e., are *not* withdrawals). Outlawing individually the various ways of withdrawing would require enacting indefinitely many laws; outlawing "nonproductivity" in general transgresses the principle of the criminal law that citizens must be given fair notice precisely what conduct is prohibited. Outlawing the withdrawal of some citizens but not that of others is failing to treat those citizens as moral equals. Finally, the array of social ills that arise from criminal statutes themselves—issues of resource allocation, and the "secondary" moral arguments of the Pragmatics Filter—must be factored into the decision whether to enact proposed laws.

The prospects for the anti-Liberal's justifying criminal statutes by invoking the garrison situation can be seen, upon close scrutiny, to be bleak indeed.

And, as has been shown, the arguments which demonstrate this are those of the topography of actions relevant to criminalization, and the arguments of Filtering—especially the issues raised at the Pragmatics Filter.

It would be wrong for Wayne to withdraw from the defense of the garrison. However, there just isn't much that can be done about it, if he does indeed decide to withdraw. Wayne's withdrawal does not fall within his Sphere of Individual Liberty. But it doesn't fall within the "physical force of legal penalties" either.

Even if an action falls within Society's Jurisdiction, it may well be the case that no state action is, all things considered, both effective and morally permissible. This will be a source of frustration for many.[5]

If my arguments are sound, the "moral limits of the criminal law" constrain state action more tightly than Feinberg believes.

[5]Cf. Chapter Three, Section VII., "Some Sources of Frustration."

Topic Two
DECONSTRUCTING COMMUNITY SELF-PATERNALISM

I. INTRODUCTION TO THE ISSUES

Richard J. Arneson[6] suggests, and Cass R. Sunstein[7] urges, another "oblique" justification for criminal legislation. For reasons which will become clear, I shall (initially) call this "community self-paternalism." The central thesis of this topic is that "community self-paternalism" as championed by Arneson and Sunstein is *not* an acceptable justification for criminalization; Liberals—and everyone else—ought to reject it.

In Section II, I offer an account of the positions of Arneson and Sunstein—showing that, at a point, Arneson's position collapses into Sunstein's. Additionally, I discuss just what it means to offer a "novel justification" for criminalization. In Section III, I expose Sunstein's proposal to close philosophical scrutiny; the position is revealed to be significantly different from what it appeared to be—and it begins to lose its initial appeal. I argue against Sunstein's position in Section IV; I seek to further erode its intuitive appeal, and I urge its rejection. In Section V, I summarize the argument against "community self-paternalism."

The matter of "community self-paternalism" is philosophically delectable. Initially, it has great intuitive appeal as a justification for criminalization. Careful philosophical analysis, however, shows it to be quite different from its initial appearance. That analysis, combined with powerful arguments, show that it is *not* an acceptable justification of criminal legislation. But in light of that initial appeal, and its potentially wide applicability, its careful consideration—and rejection—are important matters in the philosophy of the criminal law.

---

[6]Richard J. Arneson, "Liberalism, Freedom, and Community," *Ethics* 100 (1990): 368-385.

[7]Cass R. Sunstein, "Legal Interference with Private Preferences," *The University of Chicago Law Review* 53 (1986): 1129-1174.

II. THE NOVEL JUSTIFICATION

II. A. Richard J. Arneson

In the course of a critical review of Joel Feinberg's *Harmless Wrongdoing*, Arneson discusses Irving Kristol's well-known challenge to liberalism, the prospect of fight-to-the-death gladiatorial combat.[8] Provided that the participant gladiators are of age, and neither forced nor deceived, fight-to-the-death combat could not be criminalized under the Harm Principle; provided that spectators are of age, and neither forced nor deceived, such combat could not be criminalized under the Offense Principle. Since it *ought* to be illegal—according to Kristol and others of his ilk—and *can*not be made illegal under Liberalism (which accepts the Harm Principle and the Offense Principle only), Liberalism is defective. There must be an acceptable justification for criminalization, they hold, in addition to the Harm Principle and the Offense Principle—one that countenances the criminalization of gladiatorial combat. While this is an interesting philosophical issue in its own right, I set it aside.[9] I want to focus on Arneson's endorsement of a potential justification for the outlawing of gladiatorial combat. It is found in a self-contained paragraph; I quote it in its entirety.

> I do want to mention another plausible response to the Kristol example, also not mentioned by Feinberg and also forcing some revision in his liberalism, if accepted. Suppose that many people, faced with a proposal to extend legal toleration to fight-to-the-death combat organized as a new professional sport, are opposed to legalization not because they are confident they will continue to hate the new regime of tolerance but precisely because they fear that in time they will come to tolerate the new sport, eventually become

---

[8]See Arneson and Feinberg for the full discussion and citations.

[9]Except to disagree with Arneson's claim that "fight-to-the-death athletic spectacles should be banned in any decent society." (373) Entirely too much significance is attached to criminalization *per se*. The hallmark of the decent society is not its banning of such spectacles; in a decent society, it does not seriously occur to anyone to promote such events, it does not seriously occur to anyone to participate in such events, and it would not seriously occur to anyone to attend such events. Indeed, if a criminal statute is all that stands between a community and gladiatorial combat, it has pretty much lost its claim to decency already. And the enactment of a criminal statute prohibiting gladiatorial combat would not restore its claim to decency.

> occasional spectators at it (or even participants!), and gradually find their conception of acceptable public spectacle and acceptable sport changing in ways that they now consider repulsive. This motivation has been called "self-paternalism." I do not want to extend legal tolerance to a type of activity because I fear that in time the legal availability of the activity will alter my character and values in ways that I now regard as odious. Once again we should distinguish self-paternalistic reasons based on merely actual preferences from self-paternalistic reasons founded on preferences that would sustain themselves through full rational self-deliberation with full information. It seems to me that self-paternalism is in principle a legitimate reason for instituting criminal prohibitions or comparable government restrictions on individual liberty. (Feinberg's discussion of preserving a traditional way of life [pp. 39-80] appears to ignore self-paternalistic rationales for restriction.) [Arneson, 375; internal cite omitted]

As formulated, Arneson's argument relies upon the first-person singular: "I do not want . . .", "I fear . . . ." This gives plausibility to the term "*self*-paternalism." Yet Arneson is making an argument for "instituting criminal prohibitions." Thus Arneson must have in mind the various members of the community *each* holding that "I do not want," etc.—the first-person singular is a disguised universal. Consequently the proposed justification is not *individual* "self-paternalism," but rather "*community* self-paternalism."

To enact criminal statutes under this proposed justification is to take measures to protect one's "true self" from the temptations which appeal to one's baser desires. Surely this motivation is admirable. Yet to be determined, however, is whether employing the criminal law in such an effort is morally acceptable.

II. B. Cass R. Sunstein

As Sunstein's position relies upon a key distinction, let us begin with that. A "first-order preference" is a preference to do or to have—typically, an action or a state of affairs. A "second-order preference" is a preference about preferences. For example, I might have a first-order preference for chateaubriand with sauce bordelaise; I might have a second-order preference that I develop a discriminating palate, so that I am able to enjoy rich and complex French creations.

Now it might happen that I have a second-order preference to *not* have some first-order preference—having watched documentaries on PBS, or read articles in the semi-scientific literature, and so forth, I might decide that I would prefer to reduce my consumption of cholesterol, or nicotine, or marijuana, or alcohol. It might further happen that other citizens come to share one (or more) such second-order preferences. Opportunity knocks. How about employing the legal system in an effort to extinguish, or to keep from acquiring, specific first-order preferences? I am tempted to do some action *a*—I now have a preference for *a*-ing, or I am concerned that I might acquire such a preference. But *a*-ing, I have come to believe, ought to be avoided—I have a second-order preference that I *not* retain or acquire a first-order preference for *a*-ing. Now if *a*-ing were made a criminal offense, I wouldn't be tempted to engage in it—or at least, I wouldn't succumb to the temptation—and, over time, I wouldn't be tempted at all. (This distinction provides a more precise way of discussing Arneson's position on gladiatorial combat: I have a second-order preference to not acquire a first-order preference for watching [or participating in!] gladiatorial combat.)

Sunstein's strategy is to develop a "political analogue" of the legend of Ulysses and the Sirens. Although Ulysses wanted to hear the songs of Sirens, he knew that if he did, he would acquire the first-order preference to hear them ever better. He would order his ship steered to their island, where all would perish. Ulysses had a second-order preference to not acquire a first-order preference that, if satisfied, would result in the deaths of all hands. So Ulysses stops the ears of his crewmen with beeswax; they can hear neither the Sirens nor his commands to row to their island. And he has his crew bind him to the mast, preventing his interfering with their safe navigation of the vessel—thereby enforcing his second-order preference.[10]

Now we think of Ulysses as prudent and foresightful in having himself bound to the mast in order to enforce his second-order preference for safe passage. Might not a *community* adopt similarly foresightful and prudent measures, binding itself with criminal legislation? Sunstein believes a community—or at least a majority of the citizens—might indeed.

> Suppose . . . government is responding to efforts by a majority of the public to use state force to prevent the satisfaction of harmful desires.

---

[10]*The Odyssey of Homer*, trans. Richard Lattimore (New York: Harper & Row, 1965), pp. 186-190.

> Laws may, in short, reflect the majority's "preferences about preferences," or second-order preferences, at the expense of first-order preferences. This phenomenon—voluntary foreclosure of consumption choices—is the political analogue of the story of Ulysses and the Sirens. [Sunstein, 1140]

Sunstein lists some legal interferences which might be justified in this way:

> Numerous possible examples come readily to mind: laws requiring nonentertainment broadcasting on television, preventing the advertising of cigarettes, requiring the wearing of seatbelts, outlawing the use or possession of narcotics, protecting the environment, calling for a balanced budget, and establishing social security and welfare measures. Each of these measures may be regarded as in part an effort by the public to protect itself against its own misguided choices. [Sunstein, 1140-41]

Now Sunstein claims that, contrary to appearances, this sort of government interference is *not* the violation of individual autonomy, but rather the protection of it—provided that we think of autonomy as the "selection rather than mere implementation of ends." [Sunstein, 1141] As regards these laws, "The majority is seeking to *bind itself*, and the legal system is the best way to accomplish that task." [Sunstein, 1141; emphasis added; cites omitted]

Sunstein claims that justifying the foreclosure of options is unproblematical if the interference is supported unanimously.[11] "But more serious difficulties are produced if the law imposes on a minority what it would regard as a burden rather than a benefit." [Sunstein, 1141]

In discussing the passage from Arneson above, I noted that the first-person singular had to be understood as a universal. Genuine "community self-paternalism," however, requires *unanimity*; a "community" cannot be *self*-paternalistic unless each person agrees to the measures binding on himself or herself. Is it morally acceptable for a community to foreclose certain options, thereby enforcing second-order preferences, by enacting criminal legislation—provided that the citizens support those restrictions *unanimously*?

[11]"If the measure at issue is adopted unanimously, there should be no ground for objection." [1141] But there is this problem: the society must address the issue of whether the enforcement of the interference is, all things considered, a wise expenditure of social resources. (I develop this point in Section IV.)

Perhaps—but the issue is moot. It is not believable that unanimity can be achieved in any contemporary nation-state—that is, in any context of serious interest to philosophers of the criminal law. And even if unanimity were achieved at some particular time, citizens might change their minds. Additionally, individuals who dissent might attain their legal majority, thereby becoming new citizens of the community. So long as there is even a single dissenter, the real issue must be this: may the *majority* morally criminalize actions on account of a second-order preference to not acquire or retain a first-order preference to elect certain actions? Thus, it is not "community self-paternalism" that is at issue, but rather *majority* self-paternalism, conjoined with raw coercion of the minority by the majority. Since there's no claim that the coercion is to *benefit* the minority—indeed, concern for the minority's welfare is excluded from the justification of the statute—this *cannot* be an issue of "paternalism."[12]

Sunstein now turns to the issue of the majority's coercing itself, and also coercing the minority. In all realistic cases, Arneson's position collapses into Sunstein's position.

Sunstein's argument proceeds as follows:

> Suppose, for example, that a significant percentage of the population wants to use narcotics, but that a majority succeeds in obtaining a ban because of its desire to foreclose itself. It might be thought those who perceive a need to bind themselves should not be permitted to do so if the consequence is to deprive others of an opportunity to satisfy their consumption choices. . . . The weaknesses of a majority, it might be thought, are an insufficient reason to bar a minority from doing something that it wants to do. [Sunstein, 1141-2]

Nonetheless, Sunstein holds that

> The foreclosure of the preferences of a minority is unfortunate, but in general it is hard to see what argument there might be for creating an across-the-board rule against self-binding through politics. If the majority is prohibited from vindicating its second-order preferences through legislation, its own desires will be frustrated; the choice is between the preferences of the majority and those of the minority.

[12]Hence my critique of Arneson and Sunstein does not appear in the previous chapter, "Issues in Paternalism."

> A decision to forbid voluntary foreclosure of choices through government would be a significant intrusion on what is by hypothesis the preference of a majority. [1141-42; cites omitted]

Now Sunstein *does* urge caution in employing the legal system in this way.[13] Nonetheless, it is fair to commit him to the position that legal interference is sometimes justified by its being the enforcement of the majority's second-order preference. Given the intuitive appeal of "majority rules," and the (seeming) analogy with Ulysses's foresight and wisdom, the "majority's binding itself" (often hereafter "MBI") has substantial prereflective plausibility as an acceptable, oblique justification for criminalization.[14]

II. C. What Counts as a "Novel Justification?"

Just what does it take for the "majority's binding itself" to constitute a *novel* justification of criminal legislation? At a minimum, there's this: there must be at least one action (type) which would be justifiably criminalized were we to accept MBI, that is *not* justifiably criminalized under the Harm Principle or the Offense Principle. Put another way: if an action is justifiably criminalized under the Harm Principle or the Offense Principle, then even if one accepted MBI, it is superfluous in that case. And if there is no particular case in which it is *not* superfluous, then it is superfluous *simpliciter*. For the "majority's binding itself" to be philosophically interesting, it must be *decisive* as regards at least one action-type: the action is not justifiably criminalizable under the Harm Principle or the Offense Principle, it would be justifiably criminalizable under MBI were that an acceptable justification, and finally, that action *ought* to be a criminal offense.

What follows from this is a strategy for the Liberal wishing to *reject* MBI: for every action, show that either (i) it can be criminalized under the Harm Principle or the Offense Principle, or (ii) that it ought not be a criminal

[13]" . . . the voluntary foreclosure of choice will interfere with minority desires, and it should for that reason be permitted only when less restrictive alternatives, including private arrangements and limitations to those who wish to be bound, are impossible or ineffective." [1142; cites omitted]

[14]For the remainder of this Topic, I shall understand "legal interference" as "criminal prohibition," arguing that criminal statutes of this sort are not justified. I will not have shown, of course, that lesser sorts of legal interference are not justified. However, *many* of my objections to criminal legislation will apply, *mutatis mutandis*, to less intrusive measures.

offense.[15] (This is, of course, the same strategy I adopted in "Two Dogmas of Paternalism.)

III. CLARIFYING SCRUTINY

Upon close scrutiny, much of the prereflective plausibility of the "majority's binding itself" evaporates. Consider these disanalogies and clarifications.

III. A. Composition

The task to be achieved in *The Odyssey* was to restrict the behavior of *one* individual—Ulysses. We must not be seduced by the surface grammar of "*the* majority" in Sunstein's proposed "political analogue." At issue here is not restricting the behavior of "one" thing, but of many—in a modern nation-state, perhaps hundreds of millions of people. This task will require far more than the rope and beeswax solution of *The Odyssey*. This sort of serious social coercion will require the machinery of the criminal justice system: police, prosecutors and public defenders; judges, juries and jailers.

III. B. Metaphor

Ulysses was, quite literally, *bound* to the mast—tied with ropes. As regards legislation, "binds" is used metaphorically. No one is tied up. When the majority "binds itself" with legislation, what that means is that, with a vote, it enacts a criminal statute. That enactment does not physically fetter. Rather, it establishes the action as criminal, and authorizes police to arrest, prosecutors to prosecute, judges to try, and wardens to imprison. The intention in enacting a criminal statute is to restrict behavior through *intimidation*. Individuals are threatened with undesirable consequences if they elect certain actions. So to say that the "majority binds itself" is not to say, that some thing ties itself, or arranges to be tied. It is to say that a majority of those voting have authorized an array of measures by state officials. Of course *whether* those measures are sufficient to restrain behavior is an empirical issue, and remains to be seen.

---

[15]On the concept of "mixed justifications," cf. Gerald Dworkin, 'Paternalism', in *Paternalism* ed. Rolf Sartorius (Minneapolis: University of Minnesota Press, 1983), pp. 20-1; Joel Feinberg, *Harm to Self* (New York: Oxford University Press, 1986), pp. 16-21.

III. C. The Logic of "Bound by a Statute"

Sometimes, when we say that a person is "bound by a statute," we are making a claim about *legal validity*: there exists a duly enacted statute, and it applies to that person. As a claim about legal validity, it is correct to say that all citizens are "bound" by all valid statutes.

However, this is *not* the sense of "bound by a statute" that is relevant to Sunstein's argument; he is not making a claim about legal validity. Rather, in offering "binding" as a *justification* for criminal statutes, Sunstein means "causally sufficient to alter behavior." Ulysses could not have been "bound" by the ropes unless the ropes actually secured him to the mast, preventing his countermanding his previous order to row past the isle of the Sirens. Citizens are not "bound" by a statute—in the sense required by MBI—unless they are *in fact* coerced.

Are all citizens "bound" by all statutes in this sense? Not likely—but for two very different kinds of reasons.

As an *empirical* matter, some citizens will not be "bound by the statute"—the statute will not succeed in altering their behavior, they will elect the prohibited action despite its criminalization.

As a *conceptual* matter, some citizens will not be "bound by the statute"—the statute will have no causal role in their not electing the action in question, as they would not choose to do that action even if it were legally permissible. Strictly speaking, it is *not possible* to deter a person from some action *a* if that person has no intention whatsoever to perform that act.[16] If Person *P* has no intention of doing action *a*, wouldn't do *a* even if *a* were not a criminal offense, then it is at least misleading, and arguably just false, to say that *P* was *bound by the statute* prohibiting action *a* in the sense required by Sunstein's argument. Ulysses *was* bound by the fetters, for without them he *would* have had his crew row to the Sirens' island. In sharp contrast, Person *P* in this instance is not "bound by the statute;" it is much more accurate to say that Person *P* was merely *disinclined* to engage in action *a*. When a majority

---

[16]Various philosophers have noted this as regards *nuclear* deterrence, the threat to visit an evil on an adversary may not *deter* that adversary from some course of conduct: as a factual matter (one's adversary may not believe the threat will be carried out, or may believe that the risk is worth it, etc.)—or, as a *conceptual* matter. Nation *N* cannot be *deterred* (*per se*) from doing action *a* if *N* wasn't going to do *a* anyway. It is at least misleading, and perhaps just mistaken, to say that some threat *deterred N* if *N* had no intention whatsoever to do *a*.

votes in favor of a statute, then, the constitutive members may or may not be, strictly speaking, "binding themselves." If in fact they are disinclined to choose the action (independent of its being a crime), then that enactment is *not* accurately described as the "majority binding itself."

This has important implications. What is offered in support of MBI as an acceptable justification for criminalization is the good it will produce, in preventing some people's first-order preferences from straying from their second-order preferences. How much good is produced? Minimally, *no* good is produced by the statute in the cases of people who are merely disinclined to elect the action that is criminalized, as that criminalization is causally superfluous. If it is true of any person that that person would not elect the action in question even if were it legally permissible, would not now and would not in the future, then the statute creates no good for that person—and such a case provides no support for MBI. Indeed, benefits accrue to MBI only in those cases where the criminal statute is *decisive*: without the statute the person would elect the action; with the statute, the person would not elect the action. Thus, *all* that can be offered in support of the "majority's binding itself" as a justification for criminal legislation is its decisive role in shoring up the weak wills of some members of the majority. If MBI is to be shown an acceptable justification, the good produced in doing that will have to exceed whatever moral debits accrue to MBI. Sunstein's proposal, then, is that the individuals of the majority use the criminal justice system explicitly, inescapably, to compensate for their own weakness of character, to bolster their weak wills.

It is worth noting that if a member of the majority who is merely disinclined to choose some action [i.e. who is not, strictly speaking, *bound* by the statute] *supports* that statute [e.g. votes in favor of it], then that is not an instance of the "majority's binding itself" at all, but simply an instance of a member of the majority *imposing* one's preferences—backed by criminal sanctions—on all the individuals of the minority.

III. D. Eligible Actions

What *sorts* of actions would be justifiably criminalized, were we to accept a "majority's binding itself" as a justification? It might seem that Sunstein has already identified them: "Suppose . . . government is responding to efforts by a majority of the public to use state force *to prevent the satisfaction of harmful desires*." [Sunstein, 1140; emphasis added] But we must ask: Harmful to *whom*? Sunstein can*not* mean "harmful *to others*," for he claims to be offering a justification for criminalization *in addition to* the Harm Principle. If the satisfying of a desire harms others, then that satisfying, that action, is justifiably criminalized (if indeed it *is* justifiably criminalized) under the Harm Principle. Thus Sunstein must mean "harmful to themselves." The proposal, then, is that each individual of the majority threaten oneself with arrest, prosecution, etc., to intimidate oneself into not electing an action that one judges harmful to *oneself*. However the *mode* of intimidation is a criminal statute; criminal statutes apply to everyone. Thus, the "majority's binding itself" is the claim that it is morally permissible for the majority to enact penal legislation to intimidate themselves, but which inevitably threatens those in the minority, those who do not which to be intimidated in this way. Rendered topographically: one sufficient condition for an action's falling within the "physical force of legal penalties" is that a majority has a second order preference to not have a first-order preference for that action—regardless of the minority's preferences.

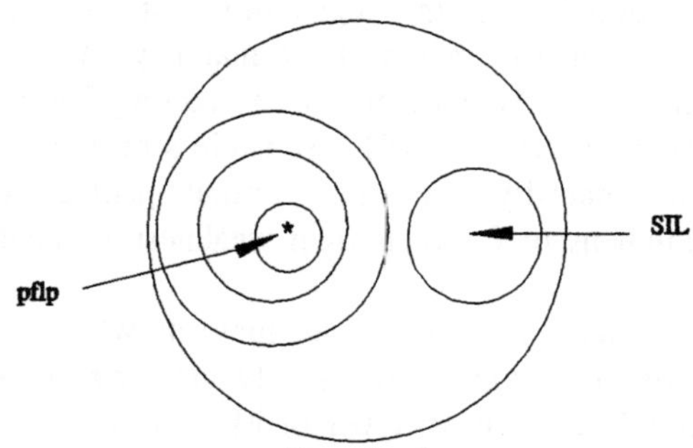

Figure 5 — 3

IV. CONTRA SUNSTEIN

I offer two sorts of arguments against Sunstein's position: "Eroding Arguments," designed to show that his supporting arguments are weaker than he thinks, and "Contravening Arguments," reasons to reject the position he advocates. I then take up the notion of a "political analogue" of Ulysses and the Sirens; this provides additional reasons for rejecting the "majority's binding itself." I conclude by discussing some morally acceptable arrangements for foreclosing one's choices; this explains the initial intuitive appeal of "community self-paternalism"—an appeal that does not extend to criminal legislation.

IV. A. The Eroding Arguments

1. Illicit Aura

Sunstein listed a number of laws—mandating the wearing of seatbelts, prohibiting the use and sale of narcotics, protecting the environment, etc.—which he said "may be regarded as in part an effort by the public to protect itself against its own misguided choices." [Sunstein, 1141] This seems intended to cast his proposal in a favorable light: many people favor such laws, and MBI countenances them too. But Sunstein's argument is fallacious. It has the form "Law *L* is a justified criminal statute; if the "majority's binding itself" were an acceptable justification, then these laws would be justified; therefore the "majority's binding itself" is an acceptable justification for criminalization." This is just the fallacy of affirming the consequent. (And it is, of course, an echo of the fallacious version of the paternalist's syllogism" exposed in Chapter Four.) It's not enough to show that some action *a* ought to be criminal, and that the majority has a second-order preference that it not acquire or retain a first-order preference to engage in *a*-ing. That does not show any role at all, in the justification of action *a*'s criminalization, of the second-order preference of the majority. If the case in favor of criminalization is sufficient *without* reference to the second-order preference of the majority—e.g., there is a compelling case for it based on the Harm Principle—then the second-order preference of the majority is wholly irrelevant. We can, for example, agree that nonexcusable, premeditated homicide ought to be a criminal offense. And it might well be true that a majority of the citizenry has a second-order preference to not have a first-order preference to commit such acts. But it does not follow that the prohibition of homicide is justified in order to enforce the majority's second-order preference; such actions are justifiably made criminal by arguments based on the Harm Principle. Indeed, to show that enforcing the second-order preference of the majority *is* grounds for justified criminalization, Sunstein must find actions that are *not* justifiably criminalized on other grounds, but that, when one factors in the majority's second-order preference, the action *is* justifiably criminalized.

He needs to show more than that the "majority's binding itself" merely *endorses* the results of e.g. the Harm Principle; he must show that it is *decisive* in some argument for criminalization. Sunstein must show that these measures are not justified without reference to the "majority's binding itself," but *are* justified when that is added to the supporting argument. This Sunstein has not done.

2. "Majority Rules"

Sunstein relies heavily on the intuitive appeal of "majority rule;" recall his claim that "the choice is between the preferences of the majority and those of the minority. A decision to forbid voluntary foreclosure of choices through government would be a significant intrusion on what is by hypothesis the preference of a majority." [Sunstein, 1142] Sunstein does note here that a *second*-order preference of the majority is in conflict with a *first*-order preference of the minority, but he does not see the crucial importance of this fact. The undeniable appeal of "majority rule" is to be found in the context of a clash of *first*-order preferences. When it is a matter of whom shall represent a congressional district, or serve as a state's governor or a nation's president, or when it is a matter of the fate of a referendum, or an initiative, then it seems clear that the majority's preference should prevail, and the minority's preference be frustrated. As regards the "majority's binding itself," however, there is a clash between a second-order preference of the majority and a first-order preference of the minority. It's *not* the case that the statute in question will permit individuals in the majority to do things that they otherwise could not legally do. The majority's preference is that there be a new criminal statute, that *every* citizen be threatened with the indignities of arrest, the expense of defense, the consequences of incarceration, and the encumbrances of criminal conviction, for engaging in an action that does not harm others, an action that the majority does not wish to elect, but the minority does. It's not an issue of "shall we be represented by the person the majority favors or the person the minority favors"—the paradigm case of "majority rules," the source of its intuitive persuasiveness. The majority is *already* perfectly free to *not* elect the action in question. What the majority wants is to *not* be legally free to elect it—but as a consequence, the members of the minority are not free to elect it *either*.

As I see it, what Sunstein claims in favor of his position—the appeal of "majority rules"—simply does not obtain. This is not a case of frustrating either the first-order preferences of the majority or frustrating the first-order preferences of the minority, and majority rules. It is a case of the majority wanting to legally forbid *everyone's* doing something—something which they are *now* free to not do, and something which neither harms nor offends others.

IV. B. The Contravening Arguments

1. The Kantian Maxim

The only "justification" that can in fact be offered, once the appeal of "majority rule" evaporates, it that the threat of arrest etc. will prove decisive in preventing persons in the majority from acquiring or keeping a first-order preference that they wish to not have. All those who do not share the majority's second-order preference are threatened with arrest, prosecution, prison, *not* because the action they wish to elect harms others, but because the statute criminalizing the activity is essential in shoring up majority members' weakness of will. This is a paradigmatic violation of the Kantian maxim that people should not be treated as means merely, but also as ends in themselves.[17] Members of the minority are threatened with the state's most severe penalties, merely as a means to compensate for the inability of members in the majority to keep from having a particular first-order preference unless their acting on that preference is made a crime. There is no need for an elaborate theory of minority rights within majority rule here. It is enough that the statute threatens *all* with criminal prosecution—including those who have no qualms about retaining the first-order preference at issue—as a *means* to prevent individuals in the majority from having a preference they prefer to not have. On the assumption that the law is in fact enforced, persons in the minority will be sent to jail *not* because the activity harms or offends others, not because they engage in activities *they* wish they didn't, but so that individuals in the majority do not acquire a preference they prefer to not have, and making that action a crime is decisive. Sunstein's proposal "justifies" the jailing of some to compensate for the weaknesses of others. From the moral point of view, this is deeply offensive.

[17]"Act in such a way that you treat humanity, whether in your own person or in the person of another, always at the same time as an end and never simply as a means." Immanuel Kant, *Grounding for the Metaphysics of Morals*, trans. James W. Ellington (Indianapolis: Hackett Publishing Co., 1981), p. 36.

2. *The Pragmatic Arguments*

(i) The "Side-Effects" of Criminal Statutes. As I have often noted before, the enactment of criminal legislation has "side-effects;" as I have argued at length, no claim that some statute is justified can be correct unless the social costs of these side-effects have been factored into the decision. The issues of the Pragmatics Filter must be addressed. Sometimes these side-effects are very serious, e.g. the creation of a "crime tariff" (as discussed in Chapter Three). When the state criminalizes commerce in a commodity for which there is an inelastic demand, it creates a "crime tariff." The price of the commodity is artificially high (i.e., much higher than the costs of production), creating exorbitant profits for those willing to risk arrest for engaging in commerce in that commodity. Both the high price and the enormous profits have serious and wide-ranging deleterious consequences for society. The high price compels many consumers to adopt a life of acquisitive crime (embezzlement, burglary, robbery) in order to obtain resources to purchase the commodity. The exorbitant profits to be made induce others to a life of smuggling, and violent measures to protect business interests: against officials attempting interdiction and seizure of the commodity, "turf wars" with competitors, bribery and corruption of state officials, etc.[18] Thus, the proponents of the "majority's binding itself" would visit these evils on their fellow citizens (and on themselves as well) in enacting criminal legislation, merely to bolster their own weak wills.

Again: before one (e.g. Sunstein) can say that some statute is justified, one must determine the side-effects of the statute, and their costs, and then argue that, nonetheless, the statute is justified.[19]

(ii) Resource Allocation Arguments. The issues of the Pragmatics Filter include issues of resource allocation. Given the demands on the public treasury—bearing in mind that there is no such thing as the "public treasury,"

---

[18]Chapter Six, "The 'War on Drugs'."

[19]We're willing to put up with the side-effects of statutes prohibiting harm to others, since that is so important to the flourishing, or even continuation, of society—e.g. the crime tariff on contract murder, importation of members of endangered species, or their body parts; the disposal of toxic wastes. But this is quite another matter. It is not the claim that "the protection of people from the violence and exploitation of others" is vital, despite the statute's side-effects; the claim must be that the shoring up of the majority's weakness justifies the imposition on society of these side-effects. And this is implausible.

but only tax revenues, an annual deficit, and a growing federal debt—how important is the effort to reduce the incidence of the conduct in question? It is stunningly difficult to believe that the efforts of police, prosecutors, etc. should be devoted *not* to reducing the incidence of the actions of some that harm *others*, but to bolster the weak wills, by threatening criminal prosecution, of those who wish they did not have, or act on, certain preferences. This is a costly indulgence. And note that, since all citizens pay taxes, members of the minority pay money to have the police detect and arrest them—not because their actions imperil others, but solely to bolster the will-power of others.

IV. C. Ulysses and the Sirens: Disanalogy and Analogy

If my analysis is essentially correct, and my arguments essentially sound, then the "majority's binding itself" is *not*, contrary to Sunstein, the "political analogue" of the legend of Ulysses and the Sirens. So let us retell the story of Ulysses so that MBI is indeed its political analogue.

Imagine that Ulysses would very much like to hear the songs of the Sirens. He takes quite seriously, however, the warning that those who hear the Sirens will steer to their island and will perish. He seeks to bolster his willpower. A couple of his crewmen are seized—despite the fact that they have neither harmed nor offended others—and imprisoned; they have some pleasant sensations, but subsequently die. (Homer is not sufficiently explicit about death on the isle of the Sirens to further detail this alternative legend.) Ulysses witnesses the fate of his innocent crewmen, and learns the lesson well. He listens to the Sirens but cruises on by, his willpower stiffened by the vivid memory of the fate of his unfortunate ex-crewmen.

Were *this* the story of Ulysses, we would not think him morally admirable. Members of his crew lost their freedom, and then their lives, *not* on account any misdeeds, but solely to strengthen Ulysses's will. Surely, from the moral point of view, they have been treated outrageously. The bolstering of Ulysses's will—or anyone else's—cannot justify their imprisonment and deaths. More generally: imprisoning Person *P*, *solely* to bolster the willpower of Person *Q*, is morally offensive.

IV. D. Morally Acceptable Arrangements

My critique of the "majority's binding itself" isn't complete without an examination of its initial appeal; I provide that explanation by sketching some "self-binding" arrangements that I believe *are* morally acceptable.

Broadly, I have urged the rejection of MBI because it necessarily treats people (the members of the minority) as means merely, and not ends in themselves; it afflicts society with the deleterious "side-effects" of criminalization; it diverts scarce social resources (including the resources of the coerced minority) to those nefarious tasks. But a person *could* establish an arrangement which would not have these moral debits. A person could, with one's own resources, contract with a private security firm to "police" one's activities, and subject one to specified penalties for various violations.[20] Under such an arrangement the only individual coerced is the individual *choosing* to be coerced—this *is* a case of "self-binding," and roughly analogous to (Homer's) Ulysses. No side-effects of criminalization are visited upon society; no social resources are devoted to the project. I think this morally unobjectionable.

Such a person might discover that some fellow citizens would also like to take measures to ensure that their first-order preferences do not stray from their second-order preferences. They might form a voluntary association, and pay dues to purchase the policing services of a security agency. Still, only those who wish to be coerced are in fact coerced; still, there are no side-effects of criminalization visited on society; still, only those who wish to be coerced pay for that coercion. The members of such an association might consider themselves members of a "community." As they are unanimous in their agreement to the terms of the coercion (and are free to resign if they come to disagree), it is perfectly appropriate to consider their association one of "community self-paternalism." Arguably, *this* is the "political analogue" of the legend of Ulysses and the Sirens. And it is the envisioning of *this* sort of arrangement, I believe, that supplies the initial intuitive appeal of "community self-paternalism."

It might happen that a *majority* of the citizenry joins the association; it might even happen that a *vast* majority joins. And still, the arrangement is morally

---

[20]Sunstein states a preference for private arrangements; cf. note 11. What I reject is going beyond private arrangements to criminal sanctions.

unobjectionable. It is, however, *quite* distinguishable from the majority's enacting a criminal statute. For it continues to be true that only those who wish to be coerced are in fact coerced.

A final note on preferences and justification. I know that some people are deeply grateful for the existence of certain criminal statutes, because those statutes prohibit actions that said persons might be tempted to elect were that not a criminal offense. Provided that the statute in question is justified (under the Harm Principle or the Offense Principle), I have no objection to a person's having this attitude (though it does not speak well of that person's character). My quarrel is with those who offer that gratitude as a *justification* for a statute that is not otherwise justifiable.[21]

V. SUMMARY

The term "community self-paternalism" is accurate only if the citizens of the community are *unanimous* in their support of self-binding criminal legislation. As it is not believable that unanimity will be found in any contemporary nation-state, "community self-paternalism" is a misnomer.

It might happen that a majority of the citizens of a community are unanimous in their support of certain criminal statutes—but those statutes apply to all citizens. While this is a case of "self-paternalism" for the individuals of the majority, it is straightforward *coercion* of the individuals in the minority. Furthermore, the "majority's binding itself" would not be the affecting of one thing, but of millions of individuals; they are not really bound, but rather deterred, intimidated. Additionally, it is not accurate to say that the citizens constituting the majority are "bound" unless they would indeed elect the prohibited action were it not criminally prohibited—otherwise, they are merely "disinclined" to elect the action.

Arneson considers this "in principle a legitimate reason for instituting criminal prohibitions" [Arneson, 375]; Sunstein claims that "in general it is hard to see what argument there might be for creating an across-the-board rule against self-binding through politics." [Sunstein, 1142]. The in-principle, across-the-board reason for rejecting the proposed justification of criminalization is that it necessarily treats people—the members of the

---

[21]In Chapter Six, I discuss this sort of "justification" as regards psychoactive substances.

minority—as means merely, and not as ends in themselves. The members of the minority would be threatened with criminal prosecution, and would be subject to criminal penalties, *not* for conduct which harms or offends others, but solely in an effort to bolster the weak wills of individuals in the majority: the criminal prosecutions of citizens in the minority are designed to intimidate members of the majority into first-order preferences that are compatible with their second-order preferences. And there are additional reasons for rejecting the proposed justification of criminalization. The relevant statutes could well have deleterious side-effects for the society; these would be suffered by the minority (as well as those who "benefit" from the statute). Adding insult to injury: the minority would share in the expense of enforcing those statutes—perhaps to the neglect of enforcing laws essential to the community, laws which prohibit harming or offending others.

Certain private arrangements could achieve the goals of weak-willed individuals, without incurring these moral debits—and thinking about such arrangements identifies them as the source of the initial intuitive appeal of "community self-paternalism." But such arrangements are *quite* distinct from the enactment of criminal legislation.

The new tack taken by Arneson and Sunstein, this oblique approach, is not a course to an acceptable new justification of criminalization.[22]

---

[22]Arneson notes that "community self-paternalism" is not discussed by Feinberg, and would necessitate a revision of his liberalism if accepted (p. 375). Accepting it would indeed require a revision—but "community self-paternalism" ought to be rejected.

Topic Three
OF SHEEP AND MEN:[23]
ON THE CRIMINALIZATION OF BESTIALITY AND THE "ASSUMPTION OF COMPLIANCE"

I. INTRODUCTION TO THE ISSUES

In the final volume of *The Moral Limits of the Criminal Law*, Joel Feinberg argues against the criminalization of "harmless wrongdoing"—roughly, "evils" which neither harm nor offend identifiable individuals. Richard J. Arneson, in "Liberalism, Freedom, and Community,"[24] argues that "Feinberg-style liberalism" ought to be rejected in favor of "utilitarian liberalism." [Arneson, p. 382] Now for Arneson to be persuasive on this, he must achieve two distinct tasks. First, he must show that "utilitarian liberalism" is in-practice different from "Feinberg-style liberalism"—and to do that, he must find an action such that one sort of liberalism would countenance its criminalization but the other sort would not. (This is more clear in the contrapositive: if there is no action justifiably criminalizable under one but not the other, then "Feinberg-style liberalism" and "utilitarian liberalism" have not been shown practically different.) Second, Arneson must show that "utilitarian liberalism" gets the matter right—that the action at issue ought (or ought not) be criminalized, despite "Feinberg-style liberalism's" argument to the contrary.

The action Arneson selects for showing this in-practice difference is bestiality—the private fornication with (non-human) animals. (*Public* fornication—with humans, with non-humans, with inanimate objects, even—is justifiably criminalized under the Offense Principle; there is no disagreement amongst Feinberg, Arneson and me on this issue.) According to Arneson, criminalizing bestiality would not be justified under Feinberg-style liberalism—on this I think he's right. However, Arneson also claims that such a criminal prohibition *is* justifiable under utilitarian liberalism, and furthermore, that bestiality *is* indeed justifiably criminalized—thus utilitarian

[23] I found the allusion to John Steinbeck irresistible. Of course the arguments of this Topic are gender neutral (regardless of species). However, research reveals that most human/animal sexual contact involves human males.

[24] Richard J. Arneson, "Liberalism, Freedom, and Community," *Ethics*, Vol. 100, No. 2, January 1990, pp. 368-85.

liberalism is both practically different from, and superior to, Feinberg-style liberalism.

Under this topic, I argue that Arneson is mistaken in claiming that bestiality is justifiably criminalized under "utilitarian liberalism." Arneson offers a set of propositions about the practice of bestiality that he calls "stylized;" on the basis of social science research, I call them "in-credible." And when one looks to the consequences of criminalizing bestiality as it is believably practiced, the assessments of utility and disutility are *quite* different than they are in Arneson's scenario. If my arguments are sound, "utilitarian liberalism" does not countenance the criminalization of bestiality. Consequently, Arneson has not shown a practical difference between the two positions, and *a fortiori* he has not shown the superiority of utilitarian liberalism.

These results, as regards bestiality, are important in the ongoing argument over justified criminalization—especially as we bear in mind just how serious it is to be arrested for, prosecuted for, and convicted of, a criminal offense. But there is here a more important, more subtle matter, one with far-reaching implications for the issue of criminalizing other sorts of "harmless wrongdoing," and of course for the issues of criminalization *generally*. Collectively, Arneson's "stylized" propositions amount to a very subtle form of the "assumption of compliance:" if an action is criminalized, the citizens will comply; the prohibited act will no longer occur. As I have argued, it is always a methodological mistake to assume compliance; whether a criminal statute will be obeyed is an empirical matter. And when an accurate account of bestiality has been provided, it will be clear that compliance with a prohibitory statute can*not* be expected.

II. ARNESON'S POSITION

Arneson seeks to distinguish "utilitarian liberalism" from "Feinberg-style liberalism" as follows:

> A better example to illustrate a likely area of practical disagreement between Feinberg-style liberalism and utilitarian liberalism would be prohibition of bestiality. Assume these stylized, but I think reasonably accurate, propositions: the vast majority of a community harbor a strong revulsion against the prospect of associating with persons who fornicate with animals even in the privacy of their homes. On the other side, a very small minority

> would welcome the legal option to practice bestiality, but this is a quite mild preference, not by any stretch of the imagination a dominant aim or important need for anybody. This particular nonstandard sexual option would not be anyone's sole feasible sexual outlet. Also, assume that the mild desire to practice bestiality is not concentrated in that portion of the population that is already below-average in welfare and so should be given special consideration in a welfare-sensitive policy. On these stylized facts, I suppose that fair welfare-maximizing might well recommend a ban on bestiality, whereas Feinberg-style liberalism must oppose any such ban on principle, whatever the distribution of preferences and preference satisfaction in society. Even if only one person has any desire at all for bestiality, and his desire ranks low on his preference ordering, and he is now best off in terms of preference satisfaction, whereas everybody else strongly desires a bestiality ban, Feinberg must still insist that the right to personal autonomy trumps any number of external preferences of any intensity. This insistence is extreme. One can allow external preferences to count in the calculation that determines acceptable state policy without forsaking a reasonable deference to personal autonomy—letting individuals live their lives as they choose so long as the interests of others are not thereby seriously adversely affected. [Arneson, 382]

According to Arneson, the criminal prohibition of bestiality produces utility in that it protects the "vast majority" of citizens from that which triggers a feeling of revulsion, namely, "the prospect of associating with persons who fornicate with animals." They are ensured of this protection because that "very small minority" who practiced bestiality before the ban had but a "mild preference" for the act—indeed, sexual contact with animals was "not by any stretch of the imagination a dominant aim or important need for anybody." Given that the inclination towards bestiality is but a "mild desire" (and no one's "sole feasible sexual outlet"), the criminal prohibition will prove sufficient to end the practice—thus creating the aforementioned utility for the "vast majority." And for those same reasons, the disutility which accrues to those who formerly engaged in bestiality will be quite small.

III. THE PRACTICE OF BESTIALITY

Arneson claims that his propositions about the practice of bestiality, although "stylized," are nonetheless "reasonably accurate." He does not, however, cite any evidence in support of this claim, and I have uncovered no evidence that gives warrant to it. As Arneson tells it, the typical, sexually aroused zoophile is roughly indifferent between a bonnie lass and a fetching ewe. But this is not an accurate account of the practice of bestiality.

Alfred C. Kinsey *et. al.*, authors of the landmark *Sexual Behavior in the Human Male*, open Chapter 22: "Animal Contacts," with these words:

> To many persons it will seem almost axiomatic that two mating animals should be individuals of the same species. . . . To those who believe, as children do, that conformance should be universal, any departure from the rule becomes an immorality. The immorality seems particularly gross to an individual who is unaware of the frequency with which exceptions to the supposed rule actually occur.[25]

After relating data on interspecific sexual contacts among non-humans, Kinsey reports that ". . . it is certain that human contacts with animals of other species have been known since the dawn of history, they are known among all races of people today, and they are not uncommon in our own culture . . . ." [Kinsey, p. 669] Not surprisingly, the incidence of "animal contacts"[26] is

---

[25]Alfred C. Kinsey, Wardell B. Pomeroy, Clyde E. Martin, *Sexual Behavior in the Human Male* (Philadelphia: W. B. Saunders, 1948), p. 667.

[26]Kinsey provides the following lists of animals and activities. "The animals that are involved in these human contacts include practically all of the species that are domesticated on the farm or kept as pets in the household. Because of their convenient size, animals like calves or, in the West, burros and sheep are most often involved. Practically every other mammal that has ever been kept on a farm enters into the record, and a few of the larger birds, like chickens, ducks and geese. Vaginal coitus is the most frequent technique in the relations, but in at least parts of the country the fellation of the boy by the calf is not uncommon, and occasionally the household pets, particularly the dog and even the cat, may be induced to so perform. There is some anal intercourse. In some cases the boy masturbates by frictation against the body of the animal. There is an occasional record of the human male fellating the male animal.

"Masturbation of the animal by the human subject is almost as frequent as vaginal coitus. Masturbation may be either on the male or female animal, but it is most common with the male animal, particularly with the male dog." [pp. 674-5]

highest amongst those males with the greatest access to animals, *viz.*, those raised on farms.

> Among boys raised on farms, about 17 per cent experience orgasm as the product of animal contacts which occur sometime after the onset of adolescence. As many more have contacts which do not result in orgasm, and there are still others who have pre-adolescent experience which is not included in the above calculations.
>
> It is, in consequence, something between 40 and 50 per cent of all farm boys who have some sort of animal contact, either with or without orgasm, in their pre-adolescent, adolescent, and/or later histories. These must be minimum data, for there has undoubtedly been some cover-up in the reports of these activities.[27]

Kinsey also notes that "There are a number of city-bred boys (4% between adolescence and age 15 alone) who have animal contacts in their histories, and the fact that most of their experiences occur when they visit on farms suggests that the entire human male population might have animal contacts as frequently as farm boys do if animals were available to all of them."[28]

The vast majority of animal contacts occur during the pre-adolescent and adolescent years; bestiality is, according to Kinsey, a "sympathetic emotional response" to "contemplating the coitus that occurs among the animals themselves." [Kinsey, p. 675] For most—but not all—it is a stage through which one passes:

> With most males, animal contacts represent a passing chapter in the sexual history. They are replaced by coitus with human females as soon as that is available. On the other hand, the male who has had any considerable amount of animal experience may become so conditioned that he still finds himself erotically aroused by contemplating such possibilities, even years after he has stopped having actual contacts. [Kinsey, p. 677]

Indeed, "There are . . . occasional individuals who have regular contacts from adolescence into their fifties, and there is one case of a male past 80 years of

---

[27]Kinsey, p. 671; figures and tables omitted.

[28]Kinsey, pp. 670-1; table omitted.

age who had had such contacts regularly throughout the whole of his life." [Kinsey, p. 673]

Thus, bestiality is practiced by individuals constituting two overlapping but distinguishable groups: a majority of farm-raised adolescent males "inspired by a quite understandable curiosity to try what [they] have discovered to be a possible sort of activity," and a few individuals for whom sexual activity with animals in an important element of their sexual lives for a significant portion of their lives. [Kinsey, p. 675]

IV. THE CONSEQUENCES OF CRIMINALIZATION

Let us consider now the consequences of the criminalization of bestiality, as bestiality is actually practiced. Let us Filter bestiality, directing our attention to the issues of the Pragmatics Filter.

IV. A. The Fall of Utility

The statute prohibiting bestiality is to generate utility by creating a society that conforms to the "settled preferences" of a majority of its members—a society in which one will not have to do that which one has a revulsion against, namely, associate with those who fornicate with animals. In light of the *non*-stylized account of the practice of bestiality by Kinsey, it is just not credible that enacting a prohibitory statute will ensure citizens that they indeed are not associating with people who consort with animals. Passing a prohibitory statute is quite some distance from preventing bestiality—and it is light years from justifying confidence that one lives in a bestiality-free society. Experimenting adolescents are unlikely to even know of the statute. Additionally, they are driven by forces far more powerful than the desire to fulfill civic duty. And as regards those who emerge from adolescence with this sort of love for animals? Well, it's just not credible that the statute will have a significant effect on what Old MacDonald does in the privacy of his own sheep pen.

Thus, the utility that is to be created by the statute—a great many people shielded against revulsion—is in fact *not* created; *despite* the ban, they will still be associating with people who fornicate with animals.

Now some people in Arneson's imaginary community might believe—especially if they subscribe to Arneson's "stylized" propositions—that the criminal prohibition *is* sufficient to "prevent" interspecific love, and are much happier about their society as a result. Ought not we count the utility of this? No. This is not Arneson's argument; the utility he envisions arising from the statute does not arise from the creation of a "fool's paradise." Additionally, it is not plausible that utility will be maximized by the creation of such delusions; cf. John Stuart Mill on the utility of attaining truth.[29]

IV. B. The Rise of Disutility

Let us suppose that which it is reasonable to suppose, namely, that many adolescents will continue to experiment with animals, and that a minority of the post-adolescent population will continue to practice bestiality, even after the enactment of a prohibitory statute. Let us investigate some of the consequences of attempting to enforce that statute.

1. Detection

As barnyard animals seldom swear out criminal complaints, it is not likely that very many individuals will be arrested—they will have to be caught *flagrante delicto*. How might this happen? A police officer might chance by—to discuss an unrelated police matter, or just to chat about the crops. Alternatively, the police might use sophisticated—and unsavory—surveillance techniques. In the former sort of case, the person arrested will feel profoundly unlucky and alienated; in the latter sort of case, the person arrested will feel violated and alienated. And *both* sorts of cases will have a corrosive effect on police-civilian relationships, thereby creating disutility.

(There will be very limited opportunity to employ another controversial police tactic, the use of decoys.)

2. Malicious Prosecution

When people are robbed or killed, or their houses burglarized or cars stolen, etc., (generally) a complaint is filed—consequently, it is public knowledge that a crime has been committed. And often the aggrieved party (or that person's survivors) *press* the matter, insisting upon investigation and prosecution. Both

---

[29]*On Liberty*, Chapter Two.

the public knowledge of the fact of the crime, and the continuing attention of the wronged, make it difficult for the police, prosecutors, and other officials of the criminal justice system to be overly selective in deciding which cases to pursue. These factors make it more difficult (though of course not impossible) for public officials to devote criminal justice time and energy in accord with their prejudices, or inclinations, or to further personal vendettas. But both these constraining factors are *absent* as regards the private practice of bestiality—*whether* it has occurred may well be known only to the police, and in all likelihood, no one will be demanding the prosecution of specific cases. This creates the perfect opportunity for the abuse of police and prosecutorial discretion; officials of the criminal justice system can select precisely whom they will prosecute and whom they will not—advancing political agenda, continuing private feuds, etc.—and no one will be the wiser. Additionally, this is a perfect opportunity for official corruption: upon payment of a bribe, the case is dropped. Once again, nobody is the wiser. Indeed, the bare *threat* of arrest would be effectively coercive—given the attitude of the hypothetical majority of the citizens—even if the charge is subsequently dropped.

3. Private Blackmail

Also as a result of the hypothetical majority's revulsion, those who persisted in the practice of bestiality would become prime targets of private blackmail. The statute prohibiting bestiality would foster, via the gathering of material for blackmail, America's kinkiest home videos.

4. Resource Allocation

In an era of persistent budget deficits, and a mushrooming public debt, one must wonder whether devoting social resources to the enforcement of the proposed statute is a wise allocation of social resources. Perhaps the money would be better spent in the effort to discourage behavior that harms others, or offends others.

Typically, the criminal justice system is funded by tax revenues.[30] In a sense, then, the prosecution of perpetrators will be paid for (in part) by the tax revenues collected from perpetrators themselves. As regards the enforcement

[30]Fines, and the sale of seized assets, provide some revenue.

of laws prohibiting harming and offending others, we think this perfectly appropriate; such actions so threaten the social order that devoting money collected from wrongdoers to the effort of preventing or punishing such conduct is satisfyingly ironic. But it is quite another matter as regards enforcing laws prohibiting bestiality—or any other instance of harmless wrongdoing. In such a case, tax dollars are collected from individuals and devoted to the effort of preventing or punishing actions which, *ex hypothesi*, neither harm nor offend others. The "justification" offered is not the essential "preservation of the social order," but rather the accommodation of people who are sickened by the mere thought of certain conduct (that is, associating with people who fornicate with animals). The propriety of the state's engaging in this activity needs to be argued.

5. *A Quandary*

There is an important tension here, essential to the utility calculation, that must be noted. If resources are *not* devoted to enforcement, there's no reason at all to believe that the incidence of bestiality will decline—and thus the statute does not create the utility of shielding people from associating with zoophiles. But if resources *are* devoted to enforcement, that enforcement will have the various unhappy consequences described above. Put another way: if not enforced, the statute fails to produce utility (except perhaps the utility of the "fool's paradise"); if enforced, that enforcement produces disutility—while *still* failing to produce the anticipated utility (anticipated, at least, by Arneson). For these reasons, it is not believable—as regards a believable community—that utility supports the criminal prohibition of bestiality.

V. CONCLUSION

If my arguments are essentially sound, then Arneson has not in fact discovered an action whose criminalization is countenanced by one view (utilitarian liberalism) and not by the other (Feinberg-style liberalism). Thus, he has not shown them in-practice different. *A fortiori*, he cannot have shown the superiority of "utilitarian liberalism," cannot have shown that "Feinberg-style liberalism" ought to be rejected in favor of "utilitarian liberalism."

VI. ARNESON'S "STYLIZED" PROPOSITIONS: THE "ASSUMPTION OF COMPLIANCE"

Suppose we *accepted* Arneson's "stylized" propositions—would he then have shown a practical difference between "utilitarian liberalism" and "Feinberg-style Liberalism?" I am willing to assent. This would, however, severely limit the relevance of Arneson's position to the wider issue he seeks to address: the criminalization of harmless wrongdoing.

The various "stylized" propositions of Arneson's account, taken together, constitute a subtle form of the "assumption of compliance." Arneson does not explicitly *claim* that there will be universal compliance with the proposed statute prohibiting bestiality. However, the assumption of compliance is imbedded in his "stylized" propositions about the practice of bestiality. Recall his reference to the "mild desire to practice bestiality," and his specification that bestiality is "not by any stretch of the imagination a dominant aim or important need for anybody," and that it is not "anyone's sole feasible sexual outlet." If all this were accurate, then compliance could be expected, as zoophiles would have very little motivation to disobey the statute. And, as I have shown, Arneson relies upon compliance in his utility calculations. *If* the practice of bestiality were as Arneson describes, then the enactment of a prohibitory statute *would* generate high utility and low disutility. If prohibiting were sufficient for preventing, then the enactment of the statute would secure a bestiality-free society: the "very small minority" *would* cease and desist without much pain, and the majority of citizens would indeed be spared the revulsion of associating with those who fornicate with animals.

The assumption of compliance has an analogous impact on the several sources of *dis*utility discussed above. First, there would be no disutility arising from detection by chance or by surveillance, as there would be no incidents of bestiality to detect. Second and third, there would be no opportunity for malicious prosecution or private blackmail, as the act would not occur. Fourth, there would be no concerns about resource allocation; no special efforts to enforce the statute would be needed.

But there simply aren't any reasons to believe that Arneson's stylized account of bestiality is veridical.

VII. GENERALIZING THE CRITIQUE

I readily agree that, as regards *any* sort of criminalization, if we assume compliance with a prohibitory statute, the utility created by that statute rises, and the disutility wilts. But *whether* the citizenry's response to the new statute will be compliance is an *empirical* matter; an investigation is required for each sort of action one proposes to criminalize. And if the response of a significant number of citizens is *not* compliance, but is resentful, furtive and alienated *non*compliance, utilitarian considerations may well show that enacting a proposed statute is *not* morally justified. Put another way: a society might well be utility-wise better if a particular action did not occur, but utility-wise *worse* if that action were made a criminal offense. When one eschews the "assumption of compliance," and accurately assesses the pragmatics of law enforcement efforts, one sees a chasm between the claim that "Society would be better if action *a* did not occur," and the claim that "Action *a* may morally be criminalized."

VIII. THE NONCONSEQUENTIALIST CASE AGAINST CRIMINALIZING BESTIALITY

To this point, I have accepted the constraints of Arneson's argument, staying within the bounds of utilitarianism. But before leaving this subject, I want to sketch a different argument, a non-utilitarian argument against the criminalization of bestiality—and, *mutatis mutandis*, against the criminalization of other sorts of harmless wrongdoing.

Ex hypothesi, harmless wrongdoings are actions which do not harm others, nor offend others. To criminalize such actions is to authorize police to arrest people, prosecutors to prosecute people, and (upon conviction) wardens to imprison people—at significant expense, with far reaching consequences (unintended, as well as intended)—for actions which neither harm nor offend others. This is to treat other people—in Feinberg's accurate term—merely as elements of one's "environment," and not as autonomous individuals [HW 67-8] It is thus another paradigmatic case—not unlike the majority's use of the criminal law discussed in the previous topic—of violating the Kantian

Maxim. For it is treating others as means merely, and not as ends in themselves.[31]

[31] "Act in such a way that you treat humanity, whether in your own person or in the person of another, always at the same time as an end and never simply as a means." Immanuel Kant, *Grounding for the Metaphysics of Morals*, trans. James W. Ellington (Indianapolis: Hackett Publishing Co., 1981), p. 36.

CHAPTER SIX

THE "WAR ON DRUGS"

In the Preface to Part One of this work, I discussed some of the methodological issues one confronts in arguing that a certain decision-procedure for morally justified criminalization is superior to a competing procedure. An important difficulty, in arguing that Filtering is superior to Balancing, concerns the selection of actions which might be prohibited, or criminal statutes (extant or proposed) as the basis for comparison. If one selects statutes about which there is little controversy, it is unlikely that the virtues and vices of the two procedures will become evident. Indeed, it might well be the case that yielding a certain result—about murder, rape, assault, etc.—is an adequacy condition on *any* decision-procedure for criminalization. Alternatively, if one selects statutes about which there is great controversy, it is unlikely that the virtues and vices of the two procedures will become evident; they are likely to remain enmeshed in the controversies that swirl around the action or statute under discussion. I have sought to evade these companion difficulties by selecting for discussion two different sorts of issues. First, I have investigated some statutes that, although controversial, are not (too) emotionally charged: seat belt laws, motorcycle helmet laws, and laws prohibiting bestiality. Second, I have investigated some specialized issues in the philosophy of the criminal law: the "Voluntariness Tribunal," "garrison situations," "Community Self- Paternalism," etc. Although the discussions of these are found in the professional literature, I have tried to make clear their great importance, their potential for having a serious impact on our ordinary, daily lives. As each of these would expand the criminalizing authority of the state, each would authorize subjecting citizens to the indignities of arrest, the expense of defense, the consequences of incarceration, and the encumbrances of criminal conviction, for a greater range of actions they might elect.

In this chapter, I take up one of the most serious public policy controversies of our time: the "war on drugs." At issue are the laws which make criminal the use (as well as the manufacture, distribution and sale) of a variety of psychoactive substances, typically called "recreational" "drugs." Typically these chemicals alter mood, cognition and behavior.

Some of the arguments of this chapter originally appeared in my article "On Various Hypocrisies of the "Drugs" in Sports Scandal," recently published in

The Philosophical Forum.[1] Despite this article's title, I spent relatively little space discussing "sports" *per se*; this is really a work in the philosophy of the criminal law. (Indeed, it contains an early version of the decision-procedure I now call "Filtering.") Understanding the reason for the word "sports" in the title, and the (albeit brief) discussion of the trials and tribulations of professional athletes, will be of help in gaining perspective on the issues of "drugs." At the time the article was written (1987-8), there wasn't much interest in the issues of "drugs." Very little ink was devoted to "drugs," in either the professional or popular press; my discussion of "sports" was a "journalistic hook." Since that time, of course, the Reagan and Bush administrations have declared war on drugs;[2] writing about "drugs" has become the preoccupation of some, and the occupation of others. No journalistic hook is needed in 1993.

In this chapter, I argue for a set of proposals, proposals which include—subject to numerous conditions—the decriminalization of many psychoactives whose use is currently illegal. In arguing for that set of proposals, I shall employ Filtering—i.e., I shall ask whether the action of using "drugs" passes through the Principles Filter, the Presumptions Filter, and the Pragmatics Filter. Ultimately, I shall argue that it passes through *none* of them; recall that failure to pass through *any* of them is sufficient to show that the prohibitory statute is not justified.

In addition to arguing for these proposals, I shall argue that Filtering is the superior decision-procedure for criminalization. Along with arguing that certain laws are not justified, I want to show that Filtering brings structure and organization to this very complex and muddled controversy.

Essential to understanding the various issues of "drugs"—and my critique of the "war on drugs"—is a grasp of three related, but distinguishable phenomena: mystification, false consciousness, and hypocrisy.

Mystification. A substantial portion of the population suffers from *mystification*. They have a set of beliefs about "drugs" themselves, and about the "business" of illegal drugs. Some of these beliefs are veridical, but most are inchoate, or confused, or exaggerations, or demonstrably wrong. What distinguishes them from ordinary sorts of garbled or false beliefs is that they

---

[1]Jonathan Schonsheck, "On Various Hypocrisies of the 'Drugs' in Sports Scandal," *The Philosophical Forum*, Vol. XX, No. 4, Summer 1989.

[2]As of this writing, the Clinton administration has not made clear its "drug" policy.

form a web, they are interconnected, and they are mutually reinforced by a variety of people, and by the cultural generally. This web of beliefs is promoted by politicians, public officials, news readers, activists, entertainment executives, and other ordinary citizens. The issues of the "war on drugs" are discussed in town meetings, displayed on the editorial pages of newspapers, and featured in television shows, movies and novels. In all these contexts, people hear others say what they themselves believe; they themselves say the same sorts of things. In this way, the public conversation reinforces the confusion, the exaggeration, and the falsity.

The central subjects of this mystification are the precise characteristics of the various psychoactive substances called "drugs" (and in particular, the health consequences of their use), and the dynamics of the illegal "drug" business.

One symptom of this mystification is the widespread public perplexity about what substances *are* "drugs." When speaking of the recreational "drug problem," most people include in the extension of "drugs" those psychoactive substances whose use is illegal in nearly all jurisdictions—e.g. cocaine, marijuana and the opiates. But there is no similar consensus as regards those psychoactives whose use is legal (by persons who have reached their majority) in nearly all jurisdictions—e.g. alcohol and nicotine. The list of regulations at a playground near our favorite vacation site in Michigan includes "NO DRUGS OR ALCOHOL"—thereby distinguishing them. A popular bumper sticker proclaims "Alcohol is a Drug" and then asks, "Do You Abuse Drugs?"—thereby denying the dichotomy between "drugs" and alcohol. We shall encounter this ambivalence often, for example in several of the direct quotations provided in support of the chapter's arguments. I shall make no attempt to "resolve" the matter here; I will continue to use "scare quotes" around the term "drugs" whenever it appears, as a continuous reminder of the fact of society's ambivalence—for this will play an important role in my arguments about the mystification that cloaks this public policy issue.

The most powerful instrument of mystification is the military metaphor itself: "the *war* on drugs." It makes no literal sense to declare war on inanimate chemicals, to do battle with psychoactive substances. When we fight, we fight with other living beings; typically, it is other people we engage in combat. And when we look for people to be the enemies in the "war on drugs," we do not have to look far: the people who grow, process, transport, sell, buy and use "drugs." (But only certain "drugs;" those who grow, distill, cure, transport, sell, buy and use *other* drugs are fine, upstanding citizens—they are probably us.) Unreflectively, without any analysis of the complex economic relationships that constitute the business of "drugs," we vilify and demonize "drug" users.

Since we are engaged in a *war*, we have to fight, and have to fight to *win*. Any outcome other than total victory is a retreat, defeat, surrender. To even consider an alternative other than all-out warfare is to commit an act of treason.

I think the most pernicious effect of the mystifying military metaphor is that it precludes reflection on these issues, thwarts the serious consideration of alternative public policies. The mutually reinforcing rhetoric combines with the richness of the metaphor: it is politically catastrophic to be perceived as "soft on drugs," to "propose surrender," to not be solidly committed to the "war on drugs."[3]

But after all, the "war on drugs" is just a public policy. It is not a Divine mandate. And it might not be the optimal policy.[4]

False Consciousness. A related phenomenon is *false consciousness*. As I shall use the term, a person is afflicted with false consciousness when attempting to lie to oneself. At a superficial level, the person subscribes to the various beliefs of the mystification; at a deeper level, the person feels that something is amiss. As matters stand, the use of some psychoactive substances (alcohol, nicotine) is perfectly legal; the use of other psychoactives (marijuana, cocaine) is seriously felonious. Attaining one sort of altered consciousness is perfectly acceptable; attaining another sort is so wrong that the state is justified in imprisoning a person for years. *Is* there a consistent criterion of criminalization that yields this result, one wonders?

There are myriad incongruities which might give rise to misgivings of this sort. An obvious one: adults are legally free to become nicotine addicts by

---

[3]Douglas N. Husak offers a list of the chilling things that public figures have said about "drugs," and speculates: "Perhaps no politician has ever lost a vote by promising to take a harder stance on drugs than an opponent." *Drugs and Rights* (New York: Cambridge University Press, 1992), p. 13.

[4]Again, Douglas N. Husak: "Perhaps we should not be talking about a drug *war* at all, but rather about a drug *policy*. A rational policy might well include massive efforts by our criminal justice system, but other components of a sensible policy—treatment, education, and the option of simply leaving people alone—are not easily expressed within a war mentality." *Drugs and Rights*, p. 16.

inhalation, but may not (legally) free themselves of that addiction by transdermal absorption ("the patch") without a doctor's prescription.[5]

But then one flees from the question of legal consistency, soothing oneself with the beliefs of the mystification. "There *must* be a reason for the difference," one tells oneself.

Hypocrisy. The third phenomenon is *hypocrisy*. Some people do indeed know the pharmacological facts about the various psychoactives, and understand the complex causal networks of the illegal drug business. However, they stand to gain financially from existing arrangements. There are profits to be made from the manufacture, distribution and sale of (currently) legal psychoactive substances, and vastly greater profits to be made from the manufacture, distribution and sale of (currently) illegal psychoactives. Many people have a vested interest in preserving the status quo; they keep their jobs and reap their gains. Their motivation for championing "drug" laws, and (attempts at) their strict enforcement, has little to do with drug use *per se*, little to do with saving lives, but much to do with saving markets and market share—i.e., with the protection of profits. Avarice explains their promoting the mystification.

The phenomena of false consciousness and hypocrisy are, I believe, reasonably familiar, and reasonably well understood. Mystification may be more obscure. It will, I believe, become clearer and clearer with example upon example.

I believe that existing legal arrangements, which make the use of certain psychoactives perfectly legal, and the use of other psychoactives seriously felonious, are preserved by the interplay of mystification, false consciousness and hypocrisy. The central public policy thesis of this chapter is that existing legal arrangements are not morally justifiable. People are wrongly subjected to the indignities of arrest, the expenses of defense, the consequences of incarceration, and the encumbrances of criminal conviction. Extant legal arrangements are inflicting serious injustices on individuals.

There is indeed a "drug problem" in American society—and, indeed, in the world. But it has been, and is systematically being, *misidentified*. This misidentification arises from mystification, false consciousness, and hypocrisy. It is aided and abetted by the inapt military metaphor, the "war on drugs."

---

[5]I first raised this issue in my review of *Drug Legalization: For and Against*, ed. Rod L. Evans and Irwin M. Berent (LaSalle: Open Court Press, 1992), in *Canadian Philosophical Reviews/Revue Canadienne de Comptes rendus en Philosophie*, April 1993, p. 26.

This chapter is divided into three Topics. The first, and longest, is a general philosophical critique of the "war on drugs." In the second, under the title "More Internecine Warfare," I criticize a recent philosophical work that argues for (some) "drug" decriminalization. I argue that the article sacrifices rhetorical power by accepting the military metaphor, and that it contains confusions of the sort that Filtering can help us avoid. The third Topic has the title "On the Alleged Racism of 'Drug' Decriminalization." I reject the argument against "drug" decriminalization according to which decriminalization is "racist," that is would be particularly deleterious to impoverished African-Americans. I argue that quite the opposite is true, that impoverished African-Americans would be specially benefitted by my proposals of decriminalization—in part because they are especially burdened by the social costs of current arrangements. Indeed—to finish this work with a burst of controversy—I shall argue that the optimal political strategy for a committed but covert racist would be to declare a "war on drugs."

A final preliminary. What I argue against here is the legal inconsistency based upon mystification, false consciousness, and hypocrisy. I do not argue for the use of "drugs;" nothing I say should be taken as generally advocating the use of psychoactive substances. I do not argue that society would be better, all things considered, were more people to use more such substances. Nor do I argue that society would be better, all things considered, were fewer people to use fewer such substances.

Topic One
A GENERAL PHILOSOPHICAL CRITIQUE OF THE "WAR ON DRUGS"

I. INTRODUCTION TO THE ISSUES

The essence of my general philosophical critique of the "war on drugs" will be the use of Filtering to organize and structure the controversy. But before Filtering the action of using psychoactives, we need to gain perspective on "drugs:" the characteristics of the chemicals and the dimensions of the social problems to which they give rise. This I do in Section II. In Sections III, IV, and V, I take up the issues of the Principles, Presumptions and Pragmatics Filters. At the Principles Filter, I consider Legal Paternalism and the Harm Principle—the Principles of State Authority which could most plausibly be invoked in arguing that "drug" use passes through the Principles Filter. I shall argue that Legal Paternalism ought to be rejected. I shall also argue, however, that *even if* Legal Paternalism were an acceptable Principle of State Authority, the current legal distinction between alcohol and nicotine on the one side, and marijuana and cocaine and heroin on the other, is unjustified. I shall, of course, accept the Harm Principle as a Principle of State Authority. However, I shall go on to argue that most of the harm "associated with" the use of "drugs" comes not from "drug" use *per se*, but from the *criminalization* of the use of certain psychoactive substances. Thus, there is this curiosity: These harms are not reasons in favor of prohibitory statutes at the Principles Filter, but rather "debits" of the statute at the Pragmatics Filter. These debits, I shall argue, far exceed any credits that accrue to these statutes. I offer a set of proposals for reform in Section VI, and discuss the obstacles to their implementation—mystification, false consciousness, and hypocrisy—in Section VII. In Section VIII, I argue that the so-called "scourge" of drugs is not a single (purported) malady, but (at least) two quite different ones. And there is good reason to believe that the most effective remedy for one malady will exacerbate the other, and conversely. Filtering reveals mutually exclusive social goals; Balancing disguises this fact. I consider a final, desperate argument for criminalization in Section IX, an argument which accepts the foregoing critique; I argue that it too fails. Finally, in Section X, I argue that the use of psychoactive substances falls within the competent adult's Sphere of Individual Liberty.

II. GAINING PERSPECTIVE ON "DRUGS"

There may well be a reluctance on the part of some to the lumping together, under the name "psychoactive substances," of cocaine and marijuana and alcohol and nicotine. In light of our long association with the latter "drugs," and recent media hysteria concerning the former, this would not be surprising. Yet vague impressions and intuitions are not always supported by research, and (as is so often the case) gaining perspective on these issues is absolutely essential.

Let us look at the characteristics of the chemicals themselves, focusing on their potential to create dependency, the health consequences of their use, and the difficulty of ending one's addiction. Let us also look at the magnitude of the "social costs" attributable to each of these psychoactive substances. Finally, let us pose the question: Why is there such a wide divergence between popular opinion about "drugs," and the pharmacological facts? The answer I shall offer is, of course, the mystification that has enveloped the issue of drugs. In this instance, it is the tendency to confuse the characteristics of the chemicals with the consequences of their criminalization. This confusion, merely parroted by some, is created and nurtured by others. Defending this answer will require the work of the remainder of this Topic; I offer it in this Section to show the overall direction of my critique.

"As I have said many times, drugs are not bad because they are illegal, they are illegal because they are bad," proclaims John C. Lawn, former Administrator of the U.S. Drug Enforcement Agency.[6] Lawn claims that currently illegal psychoactives are "bad," and at least implies that currently legal psychoactives are *not* bad—or at least, not *as* "bad." Lawn's position seems to be endorsed by James Q. Wilson, who writes in comparing nicotine and cocaine:

> . . . we treat the two drugs differently, not simply because nicotine is so widely used as to be beyond the reach of effective prohibition, but because its use does not destroy the user's essential humanity. Tobacco shortens one's life, cocaine debases it. Nicotine alters one's habits, cocaine alters one's soul. The heavy use of crack, unlike the heavy use of tobacco, corrodes those natural sentiments of sympathy

---

[6]John C. Lawn, "The Issue of Legalizing Illicit Drugs," *Hofstra Law Review*, Vol. 18, No. 3, Spring 1990, p. 703.

> and duty that constitute our human nature and make possible our social life.[7]

Does cocaine debase one's life and alter one's soul in ways that nicotine does not? Or has Wilson failed to distinguish the characteristics of the two chemicals from the consequences of the criminalization of but one of them?

The empirical evidence does not support Lawn and Wilson. Prohibitionists are fond of citing animal studies in which monkeys press a lever to get cocaine, and will continue to press it, to the exclusion of food, water and sex, unto death. Consider this passage for the Bureau of Justice Statistics's *Drugs, Crime and the Justice System*:

> Animal studies provide compelling evidence of cocaine's power to stimulate compulsive and excessive use. Every species tested—rats, dogs, and several varieties of monkeys—learned to self-administer cocaine with no reward but the effects of the drug. They preferred higher to lower doses. The animals ate almost nothing and suffered serious health effects when they had unlimited access to cocaine. Experiments showed that most monkeys died a few days after having cocaine-induced convulsions.[8]

But consider this review of the literature—in particular, its final sentence:

> Research, surveyed by Dr. Louis Harris of the Medical College of Virginia, shows, for example, that monkeys can be easily addicted to crack and that the addiction could hardly be more severe.
>
> The monkeys were taught to press a lever to receive a cocaine injection. Once they learned how, they repeatedly pressed the lever until they died, stopping neither to eat nor to sleep. Monkeys also did this for nicotine. . . .[9]

So: animal studies do *not* support the "drug" distinction which Lawn and Wilson seek to draw.

---

[7]James Q. Wilson, "Against the Legalization of Drugs," *Commentary*, February 1990, p. 26.

[8]*Drugs, Crime, and the Justice System: A National Report* (U.S. Department of Justice, Office of Justice Programs, Bureau of Justice Statistics, December 1992, NCJ-133652), p. 21.

[9]"Experts Finding New Hope On Treating Crack Addicts," by Gina Kolata, *The New York Times*, August 24, 1989, p. A1, B7.

What is revealed by studies of human beings? According to Ethan Nadelmann,

> . . . evidence . . . suggests that only a small percentage of people who snort cocaine end up having a problem with it. In this respect, most people differ from captive monkeys, who have demonstrated in tests that they will starve themselves to death if provided with unlimited cocaine.[10]

So: *human* studies do not support the "drug" distinction which Lawn and Wilson seek to draw.

No illegal psychoactive has seized the American consciousness like the smokable form of cocaine, popularly known as "crack." And this is due, I suspect, to the widespread belief that crack seizes lives, by seizing brains. One often hears the claim that crack is "instantly addictive." One puff, one addict—an addict for life. A life destined to be "solitary, poore, nasty, brutish and short."[11] The facts belie—though have yet to dispel—crack hysteria. Research has begun to reveal the unusual neurological activities of crack. A report on that research shows, however, that the best way to gain perspective on one psychoactive is by comparing it with other psychoactives. "Yes, [crack] has a rare biochemistry that seems to addict people faster than any other known substance, with the exception of cigarettes."[12]

> Dr. Jack Henningfield, chief of the clinical pharmacology branch at the Addiction Research Center of Baltimore, said 9 out of 10 people who tried cigarettes in real life went on to become addicted; 1 in 6 who tried crack became addicted, and 1 in 10 who tried alcohol did so.[13]

---

[10]Ethan A. Nadelmann, "Drug Prohibition in the United States: Costs, Consequences, and Alternatives, *Science*, 1 September 1989, p. 944.

[11]Of course this is Hobbes' description of life in the state of nature. *Levithan*, ed. C. B. MacPherson, Pelican Classics, p. 186.

[12]"Experts Finding New Hope On Treating Crack Addicts," p. B7.

[13]*Ibid.*, p. B7.

If only one person in six becomes addicted, crack can hardly be "instantly addictive." Indeed, the psychoactive most worthy of that appellation is a currently legal "drug," nicotine.

According to a Report from the Center for Health Communication of Harvard School of Public Health, "More people are dependent upon tobacco than on any other drug, and cigarette smoking is the leading preventable cause of disease and premature death."[14] (Note the classification of tobacco as a "drug.") The bulk of the report contains a comparison of tobacco and opium, "to highlight the parallels between their constituent drugs, nicotine and heroin."[15] Studies are cited which show those parallels as regards physiological dependence, withdrawal, tolerance, relapse, identification of neuroreceptors, and psychoactivity. The Report concludes that

> . . . nicotine has a profile of behavioral and physiologic effects typical of other drugs of abuse and, like the heroin derived from opium, meets rigorous experimental criteria as a drug with considerable potential to cause dependence. There is now no question that tobacco use leads to a state of dependence in most regular users.[16]

Sometimes people addicted to illegal substances seek treatment. In a major study, people addicted to nicotine and some other drug were asked to compare the difficulty of quitting cigarettes with the difficulty of quitting the substance for which they sought treatment. "Seventy-four percent reported that cigarettes would be at least as hard to give up as their problem substance; 57% said that cigarettes would be harder to give up."[17]

> In other research, addicts were asked to compare cocaine to heroin and they said that they found heroin more difficult to quit. Dr. Charles A. Haertzen of the Addiction Research Center asked former

---

[14]"Research Status Report: Nicotine Dependency and Compulsive Tobacco Use," Center for Health Communication, Harvard School of Public Health, June 19, 1986, p. 1.

[15]*Ibid.*, p. 2.

[16]*Ibid.*, p. 10. Due to vagueness as regards "addiction," "dependence" is the accepted scientific criterion. Cf. the Report, p. 1, footnote.

[17]Lynn Kozlowski *et.al.*, "Comparing Tobacco Cigarette Dependence With Other Drug Dependencies," *Journal of the American Medical Association*, February 10, 1989, p. 899.

> addicts how difficult it was to stop using various drugs that they had tried. The addicts consistently said heroin was the most difficult to stop, followed very closely by cigarettes. Next came alcohol and finally cocaine, either injected, sniffed or smoked.[18]

To experience the seriousness of nicotine addiction firsthand, one need merely tour any major hospital: patients dying of emphysema, still clutching a cigarette; patients who have had surgery for cancer of the larynx, smoking a cigarette through a tracheostomy tube.

Although cocaine's illegality makes more difficult the gathering of solid statistics, the evidence indicates that nicotine (inhaled in the smoking of cigarettes) poses far greater health hazards than cocaine—provided that the cocaine is of known potency, and is uncontaminated.

> Cocaine is associated with a series of psychiatric problems which can become severe in certain cases. However, there is no present evidence that long-term cocaine use is a risk factor for any major physical diseases.[19]

In contrast, cigarette smoking

> . . . is a major cause of coronary artery disease, peripheral vascular disease, cerebrovascular disease, lung, laryngeal, oral, esophageal, bladder, pancreatic, and kidney cancers, and of chronic obstructive pulmonary disease. If it were not for cigarette smoking, there would be little lung cancer or chronic obstructive pulmonary disease in this country.[20]

Thus, when we focus on the pharmacological facts, we discover that it is easier to become addicted to nicotine than to cocaine, it is more unhealthy to be addicted to nicotine, and it is more difficult to end the addiction to nicotine than cocaine. In light of these facts, it is most implausible to hold that cocaine debases one's life and alters one's soul, while nicotine does not.

---

[18]"Experts Finding New Hope . . .," B7.

[19]Steven Jonas, *ibid.*, p. 768. Internal cites omitted.

[20]Steven Jonas, "Solving the Drug Problem: A Public Health Approach to the Reduction of the Use and Abuse of Both Legal and Illegal Recreational Drugs," *Hofstra Law Review*, Vol. 18, No. 3, Spring 1990, p. 765. Internal cites omitted.

Let us consider now the social costs, in contrast with the individual costs, of the use of nicotine and cocaine. In 1986, *Time* reported that ". . . more people (570) died from appendicitis last year than from cocaine abuse (563). The death toll from cocaine is minute compared with the number of fatalities attributed in 1980 to alcohol (98,186) and tobacco (some 300,000 annually).[21] And more recently, this from the Harvard School of Public Health's *Report*:

> . . . tobacco is . . . the cause of more than 350,000 deaths/year—*more than ten times* the number of deaths caused by all hard drugs, including opiates, barbiturates, cocaine and hallucinogens, taken together.[22]

We have all heard the exclamation, "God, I'm dying for a cigarette!" However, we do not hear the exclamation, "God, I'd rob, mug, burglarize or kill for a cigarette." Although there is good reason to believe that the media are hysterical as well as misleading about it,[23] there surely is a connection between acquisitive crime and cocaine—but no such connection with cigarettes. Perhaps it is this *predation* that warrants Wilson's claim that cocaine, unlike nicotine, "destroys the user's essential humanity," and "corrodes . . . natural sentiments of sympathy and duty." Or, perhaps not. Perhaps Wilson has once again confused the consequences of criminalization with the characteristics of the chemical.

A more thorough investigation of the consequences of the criminalization of various psychoactives will be offered in subsequent sections. However, it is appropriate to sketch some of those consequences; only then can the difference between facts and mystification be shown.

The "street price" of cocaine is wildly disproportionate to the costs of production.[24] This is due, of course, to its criminalization—only those willing

---

[21] *Time*, September 15, 1986, p. 64.

[22] "Research Status Report. . . ." *op. cit.* Emphasis added; internal cites omitted.

[23] Douglas N. Husak, *Drugs and Rights* (New York: Cambridge University Press, 1992), p. 127, and citations.

[24] Ethan Nadelmann, *Science*.

to run the risks of illegal commerce enter the "business,"[25] and these entrepreneurs expect exorbitant profits for that risk-taking. A direct result of the artificially high cost of the chemical: users can be led to squander their savings, spend the rent, neglect the home and children. It can drive users to a life of acquisitive crime, or prostitution, etc., to secure the resources for the substance. This surely constitutes a corrosion of one's natural sentiments of sympathy and duty. Just as surely, however, these are consequences of criminalization.

This sort of "inapt comparison" permeates the mystification of "drugs." Two psychoactive substances are selected for comparison—one currently legal, the other currently illegal. Something quite bad is attributed to the illegal "drug," accompanied by the claim—often true—that this bad thing cannot be attributed to the legal "drug." What's gone profoundly wrong in the thinking is that the person arguing believes that this comparison shows something about the two drugs themselves—that one is bad in a way that the other is not. However, no such thing is shown. The "bad" that is cited can be shown to *not* be a characteristic of the illegal chemical, but a consequence of the criminal statute prohibiting the use of that chemical. Typically, two theses are true. First, if the illegal "drug" were legal, it would not give rise to the "bad" that was cited. Second, if the legal "drug" were criminalized, then it too would give rise to that "bad" thing.

Thus, no one would deny that it is worse—for oneself, and for others—to be addicted to cocaine than to nicotine, in 1993 America. But this is the "inapt comparison." To make an *apt* comparison, one must imagine a world in which cocaine and nicotine have the same legal status. Imagine that cocaine can be purchased like cigarettes—close to the cost of production, known to be uncontaminated, available at respectable retail outlets. Or—more vividly—imagine that cigarettes have been criminalized, that they are exorbitantly expensive, of unknown composition, and available only from criminals in dangerous surroundings. Would we not witness Wilson's "corrosion of the natural sentiments of sympathy and duty" of nicotine addicts?

Let us now direct our attention to another popular and legal "drug," alcohol. The *Fifth Special Report to the U.S. Congress on Alcohol and Health from the*

---

[25]And it is a business; see Louis Kraar, "The Drug Trade: Think of it as a huge, multinational commodity business with a fast-moving management, a widespread distribution network, and price-insensitive customers," *Fortune*, June 20, 1988. The Bureau of Justice Statistics's *Drugs, Crime, and the Justice System* has a chapter entitled "Dynamics of the Illegal Drug Business" (*op. cit.*).

Secretary of Health and Human Services opens with this assessment: "Alcohol is undoubtedly the most widely used—and abused—drug in America."[26] (Note the "drug"/alcohol conflation.) That same source catalogues some of the negative health consequences of alcohol use: "Alcohol affects every level of the nervous system—from the neurochemicals within single cells to the macrofunctions governing thought processes and behavior. . ."[27] The Report also cites the well-documented, deleterious effects of alcohol consumption on the brain's processing of stimuli, on memory, and on various organs—especially the liver. Other chapters of the Report document the *addictiveness* of alcohol.

> While the health cost of drug abuse was estimated by one National Center for Health Statistics study at $59.7 billion in 1983, the medical bill for alcohol abuse was $116.7 billion. "There is no question that alcoholism in terms of social costs remains our No. 1 problem. We can't lose sight of that because of our emphasis on drugs," says the NIDA's Schuster.[28]

(Note here the distinction drawn between alcohol and "drugs".) And as Nadelmann dryly notes, "No illicit drug, however, is as strongly associated with violent behavior as is alcohol."[29]

Thus, while no one would deny the serious health consequences of (currently) illegal psychoactives, both in terms of dependence and health care costs, they constitute but a fraction of the total U.S. "drug" problem. Indeed, one pharmacologist has constructed a chart ranking various "drugs" as regards hazard to both society and to the individual user. According to this research, alcohol (distilled spirits) is the most hazardous "drug," ranking even higher than cocaine; heroin was deemed of only "intermediate" hazard, only slightly outranking cigarettes—which were judged more hazardous than opium.

---

[26]*Fifth Special Report to the U.S. Congress on Alcohol and Health from the Secretary of Health and Human Services*, U.S. Department of Health and Human Services; Public Health Service; Alcohol, Drug Abuse, and Mental Health Administration, December 1983, p. xiii.

[27]*Ibid.*, p. 39.

[28]*Time*, September 15, 1986, p. 64.

[29]Nadelmann, *op. cit.*, p. 941.

Slightly less hazardous than opium was beer, and beer was ranked more hazardous than marijuana.[30]

It is thus *quite* mistaken to think that "drug" criminalization is a function of the seriousness of the health consequences of the various "drugs": that legal "drugs" are less hazardous than illegal "drugs," or that the greater legal penalty for using a particular "drug," the more dangerous it is.

Two facts about the use of currently illegal drugs—gleaned from the government's own statistics—are particularly noteworthy. First, "More than 75 million persons in the U.S. household population have used illicit drugs."[31] Thus, a substantial portion of the United States's population could be imprisoned for "drug" use. Second, only a small fraction of the people surveyed report having used "drugs" in the recent past—thus the vast majority could hardly be "addicted."[32]

To summarize: the health consequences of cocaine use for the individual are not as deleterious as are those of nicotine. The "social costs" of illicit "drug" use pale in comparison with the social costs of licit "drug" use. While a significant portion of the population has experimented with illicit "drugs," only a minute fraction have genuine "problems" with that use. Thus, John C. Lawn's claim that "drugs are illegal because they are bad" is not supported by the facts; it is not true that the less dangerous psychoactives are legal, while the more dangerous psychoactives are criminalized.

There could hardly be a wider chasm between the pharmacological facts and popular opinion. Douglas N. Husak opens his book by noting that

> For a period of sixteen months from 1989-1990, a majority of Americans identified drugs as our nation's greatest concern, surpassing crime, the environment, taxes, the homeless, education and the deficit.[33]

The "war on drugs" is a paradigm case of the phenomenon for mystification. Its hot rhetoric is at great variance with the cold facts. The complexities of the

---

[30]Samuel Irwin, "A Rational Approach to Drug Abuse Prevention," 2 Contemporary Drug Problems 3 (1973), p. 21.

[31]*Drugs, Crime, and the Justice System*, p. 26.

[32]*Ibid.*, p. 27.

[33]Douglas N. Husak, *Drugs and Rights* (New York: Cambridge University Press, 1992), p. 9.

causal networks facilitate it; the dynamics of the military metaphor, and the making of inapt comparisons, are its powerful instruments. And vested interests in the status quo make it incredibly profitable.

Bearing in mind these facts about "drug" use—and not the political rhetoric of the "war on drugs"—let us "Filter" the use of psychoactives, in order to determine whether laws prohibiting the use of (currently illegal) "drugs" are justified. For ease of exposition, I shall focus on marijuana, cocaine and heroin. However, also to be kept in mind is the broader issue of consistency: are extant arrangements, taken together, in fact justified? Can a persuasive case be made that all currently legal psychoactives should be legal, and that all currently illegal psychoactives should be illegal?

III. FILTERING: THE PRINCIPLES FILTER

Beginning with Part Two of this book, I have declared my allegiance to Liberalism: only the Harm Principle and the Offense Principle are acceptable Principles of State Authority. As a Liberal, "drug" use passes through the Principles Filter only if it falls under the Harm Principle or the Offense Principle. However, some who support the criminalization of various "drugs" are Legal Paternalists. So I begin by arguing for the rejection of Legal Paternalism.

III. A. The Principle of Legal Paternalism and "Drug" Laws

Should one desire to prohibit "drugs" on the basis of Legal Paternalism, one must argue both that Legal Paternalism is an acceptable Principle of State Authority, and that the use of (currently illegal) psychoactives falls under its purview. I argue that Legal Paternalism ought to be rejected. But even if it *is* accepted, that is not enough to justify criminalization; one then confronts the issues of the Presumptions Filter and the Pragmatics Filter. Finally, I argue that one cannot find a justification for the existing legal disparity as regards psychoactive substances. To defend existing arrangements, one must show telling differences between currently legal psychoactives and currently illegal psychoactives, differences that justify the legal disparity.

The acceptability of Legal Paternalism has been disputed by many philosophers—among them, of course, John Stuart Mill.

In Chapter Two, I reconstructed the two central arguments offered by Mill for creating and respecting a Sphere of Individual Liberty for every competent adult. My concern in that chapter was to develop a topography of actions. Since I was anxious that that topography be perfectly general among various substantive positions in the philosophy of the criminal law, I made very limited use of those arguments. All I claimed, at that point, was that a Sphere of Individual Liberty, of unspecified size and contents, ought to be respected; to deny this is to subscribe to an untenable totalitarianism. I made greater use of these two arguments in Chapter Four. These arguments' bearing on an action provide powerful reason for believing that that action does indeed fall within an individual's Sphere of Individual Liberty (though an action may fall within an individual's SIL even if Mill's arguments do not apply to it). In this chapter, I endorse Mill's arguments; they provide solid grounds for rejecting Legal Paternalism.

Very briefly, the first argument focuses on the development of individual faculties and talents. Faculties and talents are developed by being used; when not used, they atrophy. In developing and living out one's own plan of life, one uses one's faculties and talents. People who have developed their talents are better able to achieve happy lives (more sources of pleasure are available to them), and are better able to contribute to the overall happiness of society (contributions to culture—construed very broadly—are typically made by those individuals who have developed their talents). As a consequence, a large Sphere of Individual Liberty ought to be respected, a sphere bounded only by the rights of others to not be harmed or unavoidably offended. The second argument focuses on the differences among people. Different people have different sources of pleasure, and different susceptibilities to pain. If individuals' respective Spheres of Individual Liberty are too restrictive—actions which neither harm others nor offend others are prohibited—then people will enjoy less pleasure, and endure more pain. Once again, a Sphere of Individual Liberty bounded only by the Harm and Offense Principles ought to be respected. Actions which imperil no one, or only an individual oneself, fall within the Sphere of Individual Liberty, ought not be prohibited. And thus Legal Paternalism ought to be rejected; it is not an acceptable Principle of State Authority.

All very elegant, all very grandiose, one might reply; surely society ought to allow for individuality, for individual growth and development; society ought not fetter its citizens. But "*drugs*?" How can psychoactive substances play a role in developing faculties and talents? How can these be elements of a plan of life that makes individuals more valuable to themselves, more valuable to others, human life more rich, diversified, animating. . .the human race better worth belonging to? To this there is both a general, and a more specific, Millean reply.

The general reply focuses on the value to society of originality, and the social environment necessary for originality. Mill writes,

> . . . there are but few persons, in comparison with the whole of mankind, whose experiments, if adopted by others, would be likely to be any improvement on established practice. But these few are the salt of the earth; without them, human life would become a stagnant pool. [OL 78]

And these few, these whose experiments of living prevent stagnation, must be nurtured. "Persons of genius, it is true, are, and are always likely to be, a small minority; but in order to have them, it is necessary to preserve the soil in which they grow." [OL 78-9] It can be granted that maximizing freedom in society, while providing the opportunity for some to flourish, will provide the opportunity for others to make a shambles of their lives. Not everyone is capable of using freedom to good ends; some will be adrift through life. But Mill (and I) believe that society ought to pay that price, given that it is necessary if society is to progress.

There is a more specific Millean response, one that answers the objection both directly and forcefully. Psychoactive substances *do* in fact play a significant role in the lives of many individuals who are creative, in the lives of many whom all could agree contribute to society by making it more rich, diversified, animating, etc. Many writers—novelists, playwrights and poets, as well as academics—would not (attempt to) write, could not write, without a cup of coffee or tea (caffeine) and/or a cigarette. (This is no less true for its being largely anecdotal.) Many an athlete relies upon the "nicotine rush" of chewing tobacco or snuff.

Examples abound of creative thinking, or novel insights gained, when under the influence of various other psychoactive substances. In a direct comparison of two of the psychoactive substances under discussion, Thomas De Quincey writes, in *Confessions of an English Opium Eater*, that "whereas wine disorders the mental faculties, opium, on the contrary, if taken in a proper manner, introduces . . . the most exquisite order, legislation, and harmony;" although "wine robs a man of his self-possession: opium greatly invigorates it." Finally, "Wine unsettles and clouds the judgement, and gives a preternatural brightness and a vivid exaltation to the contempts and the admirations, the loves and the hatreds, of the drinker: opium on the contrary communicates serenity and equipoise to all the faculties . . . ."[34]

Perhaps the best-known example of creativity while "under the influence" is Samuel Taylor Coleridge's writing of "Kubla Khan," the opening lines of which are familiar to everyone:

In Xanadu did Kubla Khan
A stately pleasure-dome decree:
Where Alph, the sacred river, ran
Through caverns measureless to man
  Down to a sunless sea.[35]

In the preface, Coleridge remarks that he had fallen asleep as a result of taking "an anodyne" for "a slight indisposition;" speaking of himself in the third person, he writes, "The Author continued for about three hours in a profound sleep, at least of the external senses, during which time he has the most vivid confidence, that he could not have composed less than from two to three hundred lines . . . .[36] Upon awakening, Coleridge wrote the extant poem. In a footnote to the phrase "profound sleep, at least of the external senses," the editor dryly comments, "In a manuscript note Coleridge explains that the sleep was actually a reverie brought on by opium."[37]

Now it has been commented that not very much good poetry has been written under the influence of psychoactives. I agree. It is also true, however, that not very much good poetry is written by people who are *not* under the influence of psychoactives.

The use of laudanum by the Romantics was not an unmixed blessing. De Quincy complained of tormented dreams in *The Pain of Opium*.[38] And Coleridge, in a letter to Joseph Cottle, wrote that " . . . for years the anguish

---

[34]Thomas De Quincy, "The Pleasures of Opium," from *Confessions of an English Opium-Eater*, excerpted in *English Romantic Writers*, ed. David Perkins (New York: Harcourt, Brace & World, 1967), p. 727.

[35]*English Romantic Writers*, p. 431.

[36]*Ibid.*, pp. 430-31.

[37]*Ibid.*, p. 432, note 3.

[38]"The Pain of Opium," *ibid.*, pp. 728-731.

of my spirit has been indescribable, the sense of my danger *staring*, but the conscience of my GUILT worse, far far worse than all!" He acknowledged that the cause was Laudanum, and reports that " . . . in two instances I have warned young men, mere acquaintances who had spoken of having taken Laudanum, of the direful consequences, by an ample exposition of it's [sic] tremendous effects on myself . . . "[39] However, in this same letter Coleridge himself writes of the initial *benefits* of the opium. "I had been almost bed-ridden for many months with swellings in my knees . . . . It acted like a charm, like a miracle! I recovered the use of my Limbs, of my appetite, of my Spirits . . . . "[40]

Laudanum's analgesic effects surely were of benefit to Coleridge, and its euphoric effects made possible at least a portion of his contribution to English literature. Laudanum's addictiveness caused Coleridge much torment and guilt. It is thus difficult to offer any conclusive assessment of Coleridge's experience with opium. It is unclear whether Coleridge would have written poetry of higher quality, or created a larger body of work, had he never taken laudanum; however, it is not implausible to maintain that his physical ailments would have proved so debilitating without the use of laudanum that his essays—to say nothing of his poetry—would have suffered, or would not have been possible at all.

Another feature of Coleridge's experience with laudanum is quite relevant to this discussion. Also in his letter to Cottle, Coleridge complains that his involvement with laudanum was due to ignorance of its effects.[41] Suppose Coleridge had known then what we know now about laudanum. Would he have pursued that "cure?" Once again, it is difficult to say. What I do claim, however, in urging the rejection of Legal Paternalism, is that that decision ought to be left to Coleridge (and, respectively, to you and to me). It is regrettable that Coleridge did not know more about the consequences of laudanum's use (more precisely: that so little was known at that time). In general, autonomy is enhanced by increased knowledge;[42] those of us opposed

---

[39]*Ibid.*, p. 529.

[40]*Ibid.*

[41]*Ibid.*

[42]I am not unaware of the argument that, for a few people, receiving additional information leads to a kind of mental paralysis rather than enhanced freedom—hence the qualification "in general."

to Legal Paternalism favor the wide dissemination of information, so that fully informed choices can be made. But we also argue that choices such as these ought to be left to the *individual*; the Legal Paternalist would arrogate that to the state. As much as we may admire, learn from, and even love Coleridge's writings, it remains the case that he did not *owe* these to us. What is owed to Coleridge is the legal right to design and live out his own plan of life. This includes the right to make his own assessment as to the costs and benefits of using laudanum, and the right to live according to that assessment.

(An irony of the criminalization of "drugs" is that it has inhibited research.[43] The less that is known about the consequences of "drug" use, the more likely it is that people—like Coleridge—will make uninformed choices.)

A very common use of psychoactive substances, of "recreational drugs," is for "winding down" from performances (athletes, actors and musicians), or from periods of intense mental activity (e.g. writing) by all manner of creative people. Performing at one's peak, in many endeavors, requires extraordinary concentration: the marshalling of all of one's powers, and the focusing of them on a single project. Upon the completion of the project, or completion of a particular stint of work, *dis*-engaging can prove nearly impossible. One wants to move on to other activities in life, but cannot: the poem, the essay, the proof, the play (athletic or thespian) continues to occupy the stage of consciousness. Like a playground bully it pushes away all others seeking attention—family and friends, relaxation and other projects. This sort of mental disruption—indeed, the commandeering of one's own consciousness—can become truly debilitating. Ingesting a psychoactive substance is, for some, the most efficient way to regain control of one's own mental life.

Finally, David A.J. Richards lists yet other functions of the use of "drugs":

> Drug use serves many disparate purposes: therapeutic care and cure, the relief of pain or anxiety, the stimulation or depression of mood or levels of arousal, the exploration of imaginative experience for creative, aesthetic, religious, therapeutic, recreational, or other purposes, and sheer recreative pleasure.[44]

---

[43]Herbert Packer, *The Limits of the Criminal Sanction*, p. 333.

[44]David A. J. Richards, *Sex, Drugs, Death, and the Law: An Essay on Human Rights and Overcriminalization* (Totowa, New Jersey: Rowman and Littlefield, 1982), p. 183; cites omitted.

(A final proposed justification for "drug" laws, based on Legal Paternalism, is the reduction of accidental deaths associated with "drug" use. I consider this proposal below, having discussed variability in potency and purity—the root causes of such deaths.)

Ultimately, arguments based on Legal Paternalism depend upon just what choices ought to be left to competent adults. Currently, we allow adults to choose whether to engage in many sorts of risky or self-destructive activities: smoking, drinking, eating high-cholesterol foods, boxing and skydiving. And it's just no good to say that the deleterious consequences of some of these activities are slow to accumulate. The effects of skydiving accidents generally aren't slow to accumulate. There are many recorded instances of immediate death from excessive alcohol consumption. And many a gourmand risks paralysis and death from dining on a Japanese specialty, *fugu*, made from the puffer fish.

Now no one claims that every adult will choose wisely—by our standards, or by his or her own. But some surely will; and none may unless permitted a Sphere of Individual Liberty. As Mill writes, concerning activities that put oneself at risk, ". . . . no one but the person himself can judge of the sufficiency of the motive which may prompt him to incur the risk . . . ." [OL 117] And, as we have seen, there are indeed many such "motives." Finally, we must recall that justifications for criminal legislation under Legal Paternalism are designed to promote the welfare of the person coerced, the person whose contemplated activities are prohibited. To make self-regarding behavior felonious may deter some individuals from the prohibited activity. But whether it is indeed in that person's interest to be deterred in this way, via specific deterrence, is doubtful. Knowing what we know about the U.S. prison system today (recall the descriptions and accounts provided in the Introduction), I think it safe to say that there are very few things a person could choose to do, that pose a danger to him alone, that are worse than serving a prison term. Jailing a person to prevent him from choosing a risky activity, to protect him from himself, is most unlikely to genuinely advance his interests.

The goal of these arguments in the rejection of Legal Paternalism; all provide reasons for believing that it is not appropriate to cite the perceived welfare of a competent adult, contrary to his or her expressed preferences, in seeking to justify the legal coercion of that competent adult. If these arguments are persuasive, then "drug" use does not pass through the Principles Filter on account of Legal Paternalism. Indeed, we have encountered numerous reasons for believing that the use of psychoactive substances—whether alcohol and nicotine, or marijuana and cocaine—falls within each competent adult's Sphere of Individual Liberty. Put more starkly: every competent adult has a *right* to an array of altered mental states.[45]

Legal Paternalism ought to be rejected. However, even if it is *not* rejected, the devastating health consequences of the use of currently legal psychoactives recounted above proves that Legal Paternalism provides no grounds for the existing legal disparity among psychoactive substances.

*III. B. The **Harm Principle** and "Drug" Laws*

I suspect that the concern of many, as regards my arguments rejecting Legal Paternalism, will have been tempered by the belief that sufficient justification for "drug" laws can be found under the Harm Principle: what really justifies the criminalization of cocaine etc. is the harm caused to others, and not the attempt to prevent competent adults from harming themselves. So now we must determine whether the use of various psychoactive substances passes through the Principles Filter by coming under the purview of the Harm Principle.

So: what *are* the harms to others of the use of "drugs"? It is here that the political rhetoric of the "drug warriors," and the hysteria of the media—the creation and preservation of mystification—have had the most pernicious consequences on clarity and sound thinking.

Unquestionably, a great deal of evil is "associated with" "drugs." But these "associations" are many, and diverse, and complex. Determining precisely what harms to others are caused by "drug" use requires a significant amount of disentanglement.

If it is the case that mere ingestion of some particular "drug" is causally sufficient for anti-social behavior—at least in a significant percentage of cases—then the use of that "drug" passes through the Principles Filter by falling under the purview of the Harm Principle. (Of course that does not yet mean that a prohibitory statute is justified—it isn't, unless the action of using said psychoactive also passes through the Presumptions Filter and the Pragmatics Filter.) The drug known variously as PCP, "Angel Dust," or "crystal," is a plausible candidate for this classification. But as we have noted,

---

[45]Douglas N. Husak offers a powerful argument for this in *Drugs and Rights, op. cit.*

"No illicit drug . . . is as strongly associated with violent behavior as is alcohol."[46]

However—despite the representations of the movie "Refer Madness"—the same can*not* be said of marijuana, cocaine or the opiates. As regards these, the preponderance of the evil "associated with" their use is *not* a causal consequence of that use, but rather a causal consequence of the criminal statutes which prohibit their use. The impact of this mistake on arguments about decriminalization can hardly be overstated.

An analogy might be of some help. There are many sorts of mistakes one might make in one's checkbook. Arithmetic errors are a constant concern. One might forget to enter a deposit, or forget to enter a withdrawal. The worst *sort* of error one can make, the sort that, generally, is likely to have the worst consequences, is to enter a debit as if it were a credit. In making this mistake, one not only fails to deduct the debit from one's balance, misleading one into thinking that one has on deposit more than one in fact has—but one doubles the delusion, for having "added" that amount to one's balance.

Similar though more subtle mistakes of this worst sort permeate the argument over "drug" criminalization and decriminalization. Genuine evils, genuine harms are identified—but then treated as if they "weigh" in favor of criminalization ("Balancing" being the dominant metaphor), when in fact they "weigh" against criminalization, for they are the effects of the prohibitory criminal statutes, and not the effects of "drug" use itself. In the vocabulary of Filtering: various harms are cited, with the intention of showing that "drug" use passes through the Principles Filter under the purview of the Harm Principle. What tracing the causal ancestry of these evils reveals, in stark contrast, is that they arise from the enforcement of the prohibitory statutes themselves. Thus, far from *justifying* those statutes, these evils militate powerfully against them *at the Pragmatics Filter*. One evil after another turns out, upon investigation, to be a social cost of the criminal statute, a reason against the action's passing through the Pragmatics Filter, a reason against the justifiability of the statute.

So let us consider the main evils "associated with" "drugs." Each has been offered as a justification for "drug" laws; each will be shown to undermine the purported justification. Or in the vocabulary of "Filtering:" each has been offered as a reason that "drug" use passes the Principles Filter; each will be

---

[46]Nadelmann, *Science*, p. 941.

shown to be a reason that "drug" use does not pass through the Pragmatics Filter.

Now it must be borne in mind that what is at issue is the *use* of psychoactive substances *per se*, and not the doing of various things while under the influence of such a substance. To defend the legality of alcohol consumption is not to be committed to the permissibility of driving while intoxicated, or flying an airplane while intoxicated, or performing brain surgery while intoxicated, etc. Mill himself draws the distinction very nicely: "No person ought to be punished simply for being drunk; but a soldier or a policeman should be punished for being drunk on duty." [OL 99-100] Thus, it is simply mistaken to claim that, since persons using cocaine or marijuana pose a harm to others if they operate an automobile or fly a plane or perform brain surgery etc., there is, on these grounds, a Harm Principle justification for laws prohibiting the use of these psychoactives. The dangers of drunk driving provide a Harm Principle justification for laws prohibiting drunk driving, but not for making the drinking of alcohol itself illegal. The same is true of the other psychoactives; even if a law prohibiting some activities while under the influence of psychoactives can be justified under the Harm Principle, it just does not follow that a prohibition of the use of psychoactives itself is thereby justified.

I have discussed precisely this issue on numerous occasions, in numerous contexts, both informal and professional. It is disheartening and discouraging that my dialogue with the audience—pretty much without exception—begins in this way. No one wants to return to Prohibition. Virtually everyone thinks that driving a car, flying an airplane, performing surgery, etc., etc. while under the influence of alcohol poses so serious a threat of harm to others that these activities are properly criminalized. Virtually everyone thinks that driving a car, flying an airplane, performing surgery, etc., etc. while under the influence of marijuana, or cocaine, or heroin, poses a serious threat of harm to others. Virtually everyone concludes that the very use of marijuana, cocaine and heroin ought therefore be criminalized. The solution to drunk driving, flying and operating is the criminal prohibition of those activities, though not the criminalization of the use of alcohol. The solution to stoned driving, flying and operating *is* the criminalization of the use of those psychoactives *simpliciter*. (I am mildly pleased to report that, though virtually all discussions begin this way, not all discussions end this way.)

It is undeniable that a vast amount of criminality is "associated with" drug use. Secretary of Education William Bennett has claimed, "When you get caught up with cocaine, you get involved in a web of criminality," and mentions specifically international terrorism and the assassination of drug enforcement agents.[47] And Nancy Reagan has charged, "The casual user may think when he takes a line of cocaine or smokes a joint in the privacy of his nice condo . . . that he's somehow not bothering anyone. But there is a trail of death and destruction that leads directly to his door."[48] More mystification. We must ask: just what *is* this "web of criminality," this "trail of death and destruction"? Precisely what is the "association" between this vast array of criminality and illegal psychoactives? The panoply of evils "associated with" the use/distribution/sale of "drugs" arises *not* from the use itself, but from the *criminalization* of these psychoactive substances. In other words, the criminal statutes prohibiting the use/sale etc. of these "drugs," far from being a solution to the "drug" problem, are the very *cause* of the "drug" problem.

"Crime Tariff" Arguments

Essential to understanding why so much of the harm "associated with" "drugs" is due to their criminalization is gaining an understanding of what Herbert Packer calls the "crime tariff."[49] And to understand that one needs to understand the economic concept of "inelastic demand"—best understood through its contrastive, "elastic demand." The demand for a commodity is said to be elastic just in case increases in the price of the commodity result in decreases in the demand for it. The demand for a commodity is said to be *in*elastic if increases in price do not result in a decrease in demand.

Now when a commodity for which there is a relatively inelastic demand is made criminal, a "crime tariff" is established; this consequence is no less certain for its being unintentional. Packer writes,

> Commerce involves transactions between willing buyers and willing sellers, each of whom gets what he wants from the deal. By making conduct that answers to this description criminal, what we

---

[47]MacNeil/Lehrer News Hour, July 14, 1986, transcript, p. 7. (WNET/Thirteen: 356 West 58th Street, New York, New York, 10019).

[48]Associated Press Newswire, March 1, 1988.

[49]Herbert Packer, *The Limits of the Criminal Sanction* (Stanford: Stanford University Press, 1968), pp. 277-282.

> are in effect doing is limiting the supply of the commodity in question by increasing the risk to the seller, thereby driving up the price of what he sells. It may be suggested that driving up the price is just what we want to do: make it so expensive to buy narcotics, for example, that people will stop buying them. As we know from current experience, it doesn't work that way.[50]

The primary consequence of establishing a crime tariff is the generation of exorbitant profits for those willing to run the risk of arrest. As Packer notes,

> Regardless of what we think we are trying to do, when we make it illegal to traffic in commodities for which there is an inelastic demand, the effect is to secure a kind of monopoly profit for the entrepreneur who is willing to break the law.[51]

Elasticity and inelasticity are endpoints on a continuum, of course; it is perfectly sensible to speak of the demand for a commodity as being "relatively" elastic or inelastic, of being "nearly" inelastic or "fairly" elastic. *Ceteris paribus*, we will find a correlation between the elasticity of the demand and the amount of the tariff: the less elastic the demand, the higher the crime tariff.

So: is the demand for "drugs" inelastic? Yes and no. For some people, during some portions of their lives, the demand will be inelastic. (We generally speak of these people as "addicted.") For those same people, during *other* portions of their lives, the demand will be relatively elastic. For other people—whom we generally speak of as "recreational" users—the demand may well be more elastic. People of substantial means, however, who particularly enjoy certain altered mental states, may well be willing to pay the higher price.

Despite the intricacies and subtleties of individual appetites, a safe generalization can be made. There is in the United States in 1993, a continuous and significant demand for currently illegal substances, and this demand is sufficient to establish a substantial crime tariff on these "drugs."

We know that the actual production costs of cocaine and marijuana are quite low, and that the street price is many times higher than those production costs. The incredible profitability of "drug" trafficking is explained by the crime

---

[50]Packer, *The Limits of the Criminal Sanction*, pp. 278-9.

[51]Packer, *Limits*, p. 279.

tariff. And it is this *profitability*—which is the direct result of the criminalization of these psychoactive substances—that is the cause of the vast majority of the social evils "associated with" "drugs."

Let us survey some of these social evils, all of which must be attributed not to "drug" *use*, but rather to the criminalization of these "drugs."

1. Acquisitive Crimes

A very high percentage of all acquisitive crime (crimes of acquisition like burglary and robbery) are committed by individuals seeking to acquire the money necessary to buy "drugs." (This is perhaps the most visible of the criminality "associated with" "drugs"—and "involves" harm to others.) This is a justification for criminal statutes against "drugs," in the minds of many. But we must inquire: why is it that drug users steal in order to acquire money? Perhaps because they are too lazy, or too spaced out, to hold a job.[52] And of course not many legitimate jobs (other than as a professional entertainer or a professional athlete) pay well enough to underwrite a "drug" habit; drugs are very expensive. But why, when the cost of production is so low? Because of the crime tariff, of course. People are driven to acquisitive crime by economic realities; for most, it is the only way to secure the money to pay the artificially high price of "drugs."

Police know that if there is a "major bust"—a significant interruption of the supply of drugs—the price will go up, and (given inelastic demand), acquisitive crime will increase. So just at the time when it might seem we should feel safer—immediately following a host of arrests, the seizure of a large quantity of drugs—we are in fact the least safe.

Mugging is dangerous; even on the assumption that users would persist in the criminal acquisition of money for drugs, and even if there were more drug users, the elimination of the crime tariff—lowering the price of drugs through competition—would dramatically reduce the incidence of acquisitive crime "associated with" drug use.

---

[52]Despite the difficulties posed by current criminalization, the majority of even heroin addicts can live reasonably normal lives. See Steven Jonas, "Solving the Drug Problem: A Public Health Approach to the Reduction of the Use and Abuse of Both Legal and Illegal Recreational Drugs," *Hofstra Law Review* 18 (1990), pp. 768-9.

2. *Recruitment—Especially of Children*

Given that the street cost of "drugs" is much higher than the cost of production, how (besides acquisitive crime) might a "drug" user obtain the funds to purchase them? It is common knowledge that many users are also dealers; a rudimentary knowledge of the principles of capitalism is sufficient to see why this is so. Given that every "middleman" "cuts" the drugs that he handles, and adds a "mark-up" to the price, there is a profit to be made in dealing—a profit which can be spent on the "drugs" that the dealer himself needs. Like any successful salesman, the drug dealer is continuously anxious to meet new clients, to expand his sales territory, etc. So it is not surprising that "drug" salespeople, just like those who sell other pharmaceuticals, or computers, or life insurance, view the youth of the nation as potential customers. In other words, the way to understand "drug" dealers' recruitment of new users is *not* to conceive of them as iniquitous individuals anxious to corrupt children as an end in itself. (I know of no evidence that that is the goal of "drug" dealers.) Rather, that activity is to be understood as an economic decision, a perfectly rational solution to an economic problem: the high cost of "drugs." And that high cost is the consequence of the criminal statutes which make its sale illegal—i.e., of the crime tariff.[53]

In addition to being recruited to be users, children are recruited as "drug" couriers. Street-wise youths—and the adults who use them—know that the criminal justice system must treat children as children; criminal statutes have little deterrent effect on them—especially when one considers the money that can be earned as a courier, and the designer clothing and jewelry that that will buy.[54]

In addition to being recruited as users, and as couriers, children are recruited to be dealers. Once again, criminal statutes have little deterrent effect, given the tremendous amounts of money that can be "earned" by selling "drugs." This too is made possible by the crime tariff on psychoactives. The essential recruitment tool: the tremendous amounts of money that can be

---

[53]Cf. Louis Kraar, "The Drug Trade: Think of it as a huge, multinational commodity business with a fast-moving management, a widespread distribution network, and price-insensitive customers," *Fortune*, June 20, 1988; Isabel Wilkerson, "Detroit Drug Empire Showed All the Traits of Big Business," *The New York Times*, December 12, 1988, pp. 1, 42.

[54]Nadelmann, p. 942.

"earned" by selling "drugs." That too is possible only because of the crime tariff.

3. *Funding of Criminal Organizations*

Organized crime flourished as a direct consequence of the first major crime tariff established in the United States, the Prohibition of alcohol. Packer comments,

> Prohibition was a classic example of the operation of the crime tariff. Traffic in liquor became the monopoly of the lawbreakers, who proceeded to earn enormous monopoly profits and, behind the protective wall of the crime tariff on liquor, to build criminal organizations that could rapidly take advantage of any other crime tariffs with which we were willing to oblige them. *With the disappearance of the crime tariff on liquor, a similarly profitable traffic in narcotics developed.*[55]

And according to Ethan A. Nadelmann,

> The greatest beneficiaries of the drug laws are organized and unorganized drug traffickers. The Criminalization of the drug market effectively imposes a de facto value-added tax that is enforced and occasionally augmented by the law enforcement establishment and collected by the drug traffickers. More than half of all organized crime revenues are believed to derive from the illicit drug business; estimates of the dollar value range between $10 and $50 billion per year.[56]

At least as worrisome as the simple unjust enrichment of organized crime figures is the funding of organized crime encroachment into legitimate businesses.[57]

---

[55]Packer, *Limits*, p. 279. Italics added.

[56]Nadelmann, *Science*, 1 September 1989, p. 941.

[57]Cf. Humbert S. Nelli, *The Business of Crime* (New York: Oxford University Press, 1976), pp. 262ff.; *An Economic Analysis of Crime: Selected Readings*, ed. Lawrence J. Kaplan and Dennis Kessler (Springfield, Illinois: Charles C. Thomas, 1976), especially Chapters 8 and 9.

4. *Corruption of Public Officials*

We are all familiar with the sordid news stories about various public officials being "corrupted" by the traffic in "drugs." Police officers (i) take bribes in exchange for not arresting "drug" dealers, or (ii) turn in only a fraction of the drugs that they seize, keeping the remainder for use or sale. (Note how this *de facto* conspiracy works to the "advantage" of both parties, thereby reducing the prospects of anyone's complaining. The corrupt officer gets "drugs" for sale or use, the arrested individual is charged with possessing or dealing less than he or she actually possessed—generally, a less serious offense, carrying a less serious punishment [if convicted].) "Evidence"—"drugs"—disappear from evidence rooms with amazing—although predictable—regularity.[58] Prosecutors are bribed to not bring charges, or to plea bargain, or—perhaps most subtly, and insidiously, to commit a "reversible error;" the prosecutor obtains a conviction (for his record and reputation), the defendant is freed upon appeal. Judges are offered the same sorts of temptations: throwing cases out on so-called "legal technicalities" (consider the latitude of judicial discretion, especially as regards matters such as search-and-seizure, valid arrest, entrapment, etc.), reversible error, and so forth. These corrupting activities depend crucially upon enormous sums of money—the exorbitant profits of the "drug" business—profits due solely to the crime tariff imposed by "drug" laws.

Not only public officials, but other officials are subject to corruption by "drug" profits. Bank tellers, for example—or bank vice-presidents—can be induced to circumvent the currency laws governing cash transactions (laws designed to identify "drug" dealers). Again, the funding is made possible by the crime tariff.

5. *Gang Violence*

The above-cited social evils coalesce and culminate in gang violence. "Turf" must be protected; in so doing, one protects one's market. Competition must be "eliminated." Public officials must be intimidated, corrupted or killed. Civilization itself is caught in the crossfire. Only the profits of "drug"

---

[58]Accounts of these are legion; as an example, cf. "Can Miami Save Itself?: A City Beset by Drugs and Violence," *The New York Times Magazine*, July 19, 1987, p. 24.

trafficking—made possible only by the crime tariff—can explain this phenomenon.[59]

6. Nation-State Corruption, Violence, Instability

No new explanatory devices are needed to account for the paroxysms of violence which threaten to destroy certain nation-states, for example, Columbia.[60] The crime-tariff-generated profits of "drug" commerce constitute the final cause. As James Ostrowski writes,

> The main problem with producing countries, such as Columbia, is that drug money derived mainly from sales in the United States and Europe creates a huge illegal slush fund that is used to corrupt democratic governments and courts and fund terrorist and revolutionary movements.[61]

7. Pollution of Soil and Water

The production of illegal "drugs" (like the production of legal "drugs") is a complex process that requires the use of dangerous—carcinogenic, poisonous, explosive—chemicals. And the manufacturing processes produces similarly dangerous waste products. The operators of these illegal laboratories are generally not conscientious about the proper handling of solvents and waste products. The consequence: serious pollution of soil and water. And what makes this particularly worrisome: in contrast with the manufacturers of legal "drugs," the Environmental Protection Agency does not monitor, does not even know of, these polluters. There are toxic waste sites scattered over the countryside, often in isolated, rural areas, that will need to be cleaned up—once they have been discovered. A joint task force of the Environmental Protection Agency, the Drug Enforcement Agency and the United States Coast Guard has produced a forty-three page booklet, "Guidelines for the Cleanup

---

[59]See the series of articles in *Time*, March 14, 1988.

[60]See *Time*'s cover story, March 7, 1988; Nadelmann, *Science*, op. cit.; *"Cocaine Inc.: The New Drug Kings*: Cold-blooded and efficient, Columbia's Cali cartel has cornered the market," *Time*, July 1, 1991.

[61]James Ostrowski, "The Moral and Practical Case for Drug Legalization," *Hofstra Law Review* 18, Spring 1990, p. 668.

of Clandestine Drug Laboratories."[62] Unquestionably, this pollution poses a clear and present danger of harm to others. The proximate cause of the pollution: those individuals engaged in the production of illegal "drugs." However, the economic incentive to produce these "drugs" is supplied by the statutes which make their manufacture criminal, their price artificially high, the profit potential so great.

8. Bizarre Causal Consequences

New rules and regulations can have unintended and unforeseen consequences. A very popular bar in Columbus, Ohio raised the price of draft beer ten cents, and within a week, all of the bartenders quit. (The beers had been $.90; the price was raised to $1.00. Nearly everyone had paid for the ninety-cent beer with a dollar bill, and left the dime as a tip for the bartender. Since the bar was popular, these tips added up to a hefty sum. After the price increase, few customers went to the trouble of finding a tip for the bartender. Deprived of a substantial portion of their (untaxed) income, the bartenders left in search of better terms of employment.)

A bizarre—but perfectly intelligible—causal chain explains how it is that "drug" laws make it more likely that a person will drown, following a boating accident off the coast of Florida. There are some straightforward reasons: the U.S. Coast Guard is so busy pursuing "drug" traffickers that they might be unable to respond as quickly; the increase in traffic makes collisions themselves more likely. But the bizarre causal chain consists of these links. Drug smugglers need fast boats to smuggle drugs. And they need to steal those boats. Why? Well, given the surveillance of U.S. Customs and the U.S. Coast Guard, a boat that is noted at times and places appropriate to smuggling will come to the attention of authorities. So a boat can be used for only a limited number of "runs." Now the profits of the drug trade are sufficient to purchase new boats at frequent intervals—but of course a pattern of purchases such as that will not go unnoticed by the authorities. So stealing boats is the solution. But marinas are guarded, have burglar alarms, etc.—that's dangerous. Far better to pirate boats on the open seas. But the ocean is so large, and the boats so small. To find them, send out a fake distress signal; if it is answered by a suitable boat, board it, kill the crew and

[62]As reported in *The Post-Standard*, Syracuse, New York December 10, 1990, p. A-1.

passengers, use it until it becomes suspected, then sink it and pirate another. Hundreds of boats, and thousands of people, are missing in the waters off Florida; it is widely believed that this has been their fate. So now the captains of boats are reluctant to answer distress signals, fearing a trap. So now if one is in a genuine boating accident in that part of the Atlantic Ocean or the Gulf of Mexico, one is more likely to drown. (And it is important to remember that this piracy is profitable only because of the exorbitant profits of drug traffic—made possible by the laws prohibiting drug use.)

Non-"Crime Tariff" Arguments

Consider now some other "harms" to others, those not immediately arising from the crime tariff.

9. Problems of Purity and Potency

It is uncontroversial that the "drugs" available on the street vary considerably as regards both potency and purity. They vary in potency in that the percentage of a psychoactive substance (versus inert "filler") can vary from extremely high potency to extremely low potency. They vary in purity in that drugs are sometimes "cut"—reduced in concentration—by the addition of noxious or even lethal chemicals. Since neither the potency nor the purity of currently illegal psychoactives can be known with certainty, the health of users of such "drugs" is in perpetual jeopardy. If the substance purchased is impure, the user ingests poison with psychoactive; in not knowing the potency, one risks death through an overdose. This fact has often been cited by proponents of "drug" laws as a justification of said laws; (then) Secretary of Education William Bennett claimed, contrasting one illegal psychoactive (cocaine) with a legal psychoactive (alcohol): "Say what you want about beer drinking or drinking scotch, the Anheuser-Busch Company and the Seagrams Company exercise quality control. They don't put strychnine in their stuff, benzine in their stuff. Drug dealers do."[63] (This is, of course, a justification that depends upon the acceptance of "Legal Paternalism" as a liberty-limiting principle.) Now I agree that the issue of accidental deaths is a serious one. But this "justification" is deeply inconsistent. One must ask just why it is that

---

[63]William Bennett, *op. cit.*, p. 7.

the potency and purity of these "drugs" does indeed vary so widely. The immediate answer is the lack of quality control in manufacture and distribution. But the reason for that, of course, is the fact that the "drugs" are illegal—there are no regulations (like those binding on the prescription "drug" industry, or the beer and liquor industry) governing their manufacture and sale. Thus these deaths, far from constituting a *justification* for "drug" laws, are the direct *consequence* of those laws. They cannot be cited in support of enforcement of laws, if it is those laws themselves that are the ultimate cause of the evil that wants a remedy. This is yet another example of mystification.[64]

10. Undesirable Police Practices

Even police officers who are not directly corrupted by the money generated by the drug business are led to engage in undesirable practices; surveillance needed not to apprehend merely, but even to detect that a crime has been committed.[65] These routine invasions of privacy are an additional undesirable consequence of "drug" laws; information about all manner of legal but confidential activities could be secured during this sort of surveillance, and put to various nefarious purposes (e.g., blackmail).

11. The Threat to Civil Liberties

Perhaps the most serious social cost of the "war on drugs" is extracted from civil liberties. James Ostrowski lists these threats.

> Drug war hysteria has created an atmosphere in which long-cherished rights are discarded wherever drugs are concerned, Suspected drug users are subject to urine testing, roadblocks, routine strip searches, school locker searches without probable cause, abuses of the good faith exception to the exclusionary rule, preventive detention and nonjudicial forfeiture.

---

[64]Bennett holds the Ph.D. in philosophy. It is difficult to believe that this sort of pronouncement isn't at least false consciousness, and perhaps hypocrisy.

[65]Packer, *The Limits of the Criminal Sanction*, p. 322.

> These governmental intrusions into our most personal activities are the natural and necessary consequence of drug prohibition.[66]

According to the mystification, the use of "drugs" is so bad that only genuinely evil people partake; it is only the rights of these people that are imperiled. But that is not the case; the rights of all are imperiled.

12. The Genuine "Drug" Disparity Argument

It could be argued, in response to all that I have said thus far, that the existing legal disparity among psychoactives is justified by a genuine disparity amongst psychoactives themselves. The argument grants that alcohol and nicotine are powerfully addictive, and acknowledges the enormous social costs exacted by the widespread use of these "drugs." Nonetheless, the argument continues, there is a qualitative difference between currently legal psychoactives and at least some currently illegal psychoactives—the one most frequently cited is cocaine. The particular euphoria produced by cocaine, conjoined with its addictiveness, make it unique. While many people can use alcohol and nicotine without becoming addicted, the same cannot be said for cocaine use; one becomes enslaved more easily, and more thoroughly, by cocaine use than by alcohol or nicotine. Differences among *psychoactives* justify the existing legal disparity.

In order to confront the argument in its strongest formulation, I shall consider cocaine unique in euphoria and addictiveness—despite the contrary data related in Section II, "Gaining Perspective on Drugs," above.

As it stands, it is unclear whether this argument invokes Legal Paternalism or the Harm Principle; let us consider each possibility.

If based upon Legal Paternalism, the argument's essence is that even though people do not need to be protected from the consequences of their choices as regards alcohol and nicotine, they do need to be coerced as regards cocaine. Because of its uniquenesses *vis-a-vis* euphoria and addictiveness, even competent adults ought not be legally permitted to choose whether to use cocaine.

A series of objections can be raised against this. First and foremost, of course, is the acceptability of Legal Paternalism as a Principle of State

---

[66]James Ostrowski, "The Moral and Practical Case for Drug Legalization," *Hofstra Law Review* 18, Spring 1990, pp. 664-5. Internal cites omitted.

Authority. Proponents of this position must, before anything else, defend the legitimacy of state coercion of competent adults that cites the purported welfare of those adults, contrary to their own professed desires. And even if one accepts Legal Paternalism, the *magnitude* of the legal disparity must be acknowledged, and justified. A person who has reached one's majority may, without legal impediment, purchase, possess and consume as much alcohol, as much nicotine, as one pleases; mere possession of even a few ounces of cocaine can result in a prison sentence of a decade or more. Even if we stipulate cocaine's uniqueness, can *this* differential be justified? And can we take seriously the Legal Paternalist's claim that there ought to be no legal consequences should a person devote his or her life to cigarettes and muscatel, but that it is better *for that person* (since it is Legal Paternalism that we are considering) to spend a decade or more in a penitentiary than to use cocaine even once? Credulity would have to be phenomenally elastic to stretch this far.

In lists of the ills of a cocaine-dissolute life, one frequently encounters such items as financial ruin, the risk of damage or death due to unusually high potency or the presence of contaminants, the inconveniences of evading detection—and of course the profound dangers of a life of acquisitive crime. All these entries on such a list are quite illegitimate; once again, the consequences of criminalization have been substituted for the characteristics of the chemicals. These are "negatives" no doubt, but all are consequences not of cocaine use *per se*, but of the *criminalization* of cocaine. No one contests the claim that there are risks "associated with" conduct that is in fact felonious—but these cannot rightly be cited as justifications for the law that makes that conduct felonious. One cannot legitimately point to difficulties of this sort in the lives of cocaine users one knows, in the attempt to justify (under Legal Paternalism) laws against cocaine use; that is another "inapt comparison." What *is* relevant, is precisely what difficulties they would experience were there no threat of arrest and imprisonment, were purchases themselves not risky, were potency and purity assured, were there no need to be evasive, were there no need to resort to a life of acquisitive crime, and so forth.

Consider now the version of the Genuine "Drug" Disparity argument that invokes the Harm Principle. Here the claim is that the pleasure of cocaine is so alluring and the addictiveness of cocaine so powerful that so many people will use it, and become so enslaved by it, that the social consequences will be catastrophic. So many people will be so stoned, for example, that economic activity will decline steeply—to the detriment (harm) of all.

Recall, however, the burden of proof that the argument must bear. The U.S. economy can survive the losses suffered due to the widespread use of alcohol and nicotine (recall the statistics cited earlier); indeed, those "drugs" pose so negligible a threat that there need be no legal impediment to an adult's drinking as much alcohol, or smoking as much tobacco, as consciousness allows. However, cocaine use poses so serious a threat that possession of even a small amount warrants a prison term of years, or tens of years.

For the sake of argument, I supposed that there is some disparity between cocaine and other psychoactives. That there is *this* great a disparity will have to be proved.

13. The Argument from Weakness of the Will

One of the Topics I addressed in Chapter Five was "Community Self-Paternalism." Proponents of Community Self-Paternalism argue that a community's desire to foreclose certain options (generally in an effort to advance their own "second-order" preferences) constitutes an acceptable justification for criminal legislation. In that chapter, I argued that it does not constitute an acceptable justification. Unless the community is unanimous in the desire to foreclose options, this is not *self*-paternalism at all, but coercion of a minority by the majority. Furthermore, when the argument is purified—elements of harms-to-others removed—this is the position that some individuals may morally be subjected to the indignities of arrest, the expense of defense, the consequences of incarceration, and the consequences of a criminal conviction, merely to bolster the weak wills of other people. This, I argued, is morally outrageous.

My concern in Chapter Five was to reject Community Self-Paternalism as a general justification for criminal statutes. In this chapter, I want to consider it—and of course reject it—in a very specific context: as a proposed justification for the criminalization of the use of "drugs."

Some people are grateful for existing criminal statutes as regards cocaine, and many other "drugs," precisely because that illegality insures an artificially high price, and the continuous threat of prosecution for purchase, possession, and use. Such people have sampled the euphoric delights of cocaine, for example, have affirmed its addictiveness, and have come to the conclusion that were it not exorbitantly expensive and criminally risky, they would soon succumb to the temptation to live a life of cocaine use—to the neglect of family, career and the pleasures of hard-won achievements. For such people, the laws that criminalize the use of cocaine function to bolster a weak will; the law makes it extremely difficult to choose a way of life they couldn't help but choose, couldn't keep themselves from choosing, were it not for the existence of that law (and its causal consequences).

As I noted in Chapter Five, we generally think of people as perceptive when they acknowledge their individual shortcomings (like weakness of the will), and as admirable if they take measures to compensate for those shortcomings. Criminal statutes, however, do not coerce only those who wish to be coerced; they are applicable to, and enforced against, all citizens. Thus, even if one rejoices in the criminal statute for the reason that one feels oneself coerced by it, it is not a case of *self*-coercion merely. Were there "individualized" criminal statutes, making certain conduct criminal for only the one person (or specified others, at their voluntary request), the analogy with Ulysses and the Sirens (as discussed in Chapter Five) would be more plausible. But to support a criminal statute that coerces everyone (whether they wish to be coerced or not) as a measure to compensate for one's own weakness of will, is a paradigm case of treating other persons as means merely, and not also as ends in themselves. It is, in a most offensive way, to *use* people. For Person *P* to hold this position is for *P* to claim it morally acceptable for Persons *Q*, *R*, *S*, etc. to be threatened with imprisonment, or to be actually imprisoned, in order to help Person *P* resist a temptation to which he or she might otherwise succumb.

And there is more to be said against this proposed justification for the criminalization of "drugs." Part of that which enables the weak-willed person to resist temptation is the artificially high price of psychoactives, as a consequence of the crime tariff. (Indeed, the weak-willed person hopes that the price will become, quite literally, "prohibitive.") As I have detailed above, the crime tariff on "drugs" has far-reaching and deleterious consequences. It accounts for a large percentage of acquisitive crime, and makes rational the recruitment of new "users." The profits it creates corrupts police, prosecutors and judges, and finances other criminality. Thus, the person who seeks to justify criminal statutes prohibiting the use of "drugs" by citing their role in bolstering his or her weak will not only treats other persons as means merely, but also would visit upon society the vast array of evils that arise from those statutes. According to this position, what justifies the social insecurity that results from the crime tariff on "drugs," and the other social costs of criminalization, is one's own weakness of will. This is philosophically untenable.

In the final analysis, I do not mind very much a person's being grateful that prohibitory statutes make a tempting psychoactive prohibitively expensive—though that does say something very unflattering about the person's character. What is morally objectionable is to consider that gratitude in any way a *justification* for the statute.

These are the "harms to others" most often "associated with" the use of "drugs." We have seen that, in every case (at least as regards cocaine, the opiates and marijuana), it is not the use of those "drugs" that is the cause of the harm to others, but that the harm arises from the criminalization of those "drugs," e.g., from the crime tariff. As David Richards concludes, "Arguments of criminogenesis are generally circular and question-begging; they argue for criminalization of drug use on the basis of the evils that criminalization, not drug use, fosters;" indeed, these criminal statutes "actually encourage what they purport to combat."[67]

If the arguments of this section are persuasive, then although the Harm Principle is an acceptable Principle of State Authority, the harms "associated with" currently illegal psychoactives are not caused by the use of those "drugs," but rather by the statutes that criminalize that use. Thus the "harms to others" so often cited in support of "drug" laws, quite to the contrary, constitute powerful objections to them. As regards each harm, I began by asking whether that harm supports the claim that the use of "drugs" passes through the Principles Filter. I ended by showing that each harm, at the Pragmatics Filter, is a social cost of the statutes which criminalize "drugs."

Although intended primarily as a discussion of the issues of the Principles Filter, this has been—quite unavoidably—a discussion of some issues of the Presumptions Filter, and a great many issues of the Pragmatics Filter. I needed to address some issues of the Presumptions Filter to counter the claim that, were psychoactives like marijuana, cocaine and heroin decriminalized, their use would skyrocket. Educational campaigns, and the living examples of the consequences of abuse, would have a salutary effect. I was forced to discuss many issues of the Pragmatics Filter because many of the harms to others "associated with" the use of "drugs" just *are* issues of the Pragmatics

---

[67]David A.J. Richards, p. 167.

Filter—despite the fact that they are so often offered as issues of the Principles Filter.

IV. FILTERING: THE PRESUMPTIONS FILTER

At the Presumptions Filter, we are to ask whether any state action less coercive than a criminal statute would be sufficient to adequately reduce the incidence of the action, or alternatively, to adequately reduce the baneful consequences of the action. Immediately we are confronted with the difficulty of specifying the baneful consequences which need to be reduced. Of course many evils "associated with" the manufacture, distribution, sale and use of "drugs" have been discussed above. As we have seen, however, these evils are not the consequence of the use of "drugs," but of their criminalization; to reduce (or perhaps even eliminate) these evils, some program of "drug" decriminalization is necessary. That these evils *seem* to many people the very evils of "drugs" that we should try to reduce, is compelling evidence of the mystification that shrouds the "war on drugs."

Just what are the "baneful consequences" that need to be reduced? It is not accurate to hold that the goal is simply to reduce the incidence of "drug" use. As we have seen, "drugs"—both those which are currently legal, and those which are currently illegal—are a very mixed blessing. They can enhance creativity, self-control, religious practice and enjoyment; they can detract from lives, increase pain and suffering, and cause death.

Because the use of psychoactive substances has the potential for both great good and great evil, what is to be discouraged is the *ignorant* use of "drugs." It is the incidence of unknowledgable ingestion that needs to be reduced. As a consequence, the state ought to support unbiased research, and unbiased dissemination of the results of that research. (In making my proposals below, I say somewhat more about information and education.)

V. FILTERING: THE PRAGMATICS FILTER

At the Pragmatics Filter, one is to investigate the operation of a prohibition—actual or hypothetical. For the most part, this has already been done. At the Principles Filter, we looked for reasons to believe that "drugs" cause harm to others (and thus will pass through that Filter in virtue of the

Harm Principle). What we discovered is that the vast array of harms to others "associated with" "drugs" are consequences of their criminalization, and not characteristics of the chemicals themselves. As such, they are "costs" of the prohibition, to be tallied at the Pragmatics Filter. Thus, the features of the issue itself have compelled us to look ahead, to catalogue the costs of criminalization. These costs include the inducement to acquisitive crime, the recruitment of children as dealers and users, the funding of organized crime, the corruption of police and prosecutors and judges and jailers, creating the profitability of gang warfare, causing the political destabilization of "drug" growing countries, the pollution of soil and water, generating a host of bizarre causal consequences, increasing the dangers of overdose and poisoning, fostering undesirable police practices, and encouraging the violation of civil liberties.

Though these costs are extraordinarily high, they are but a partial accounting. We must factor in the costs of actually *waging* the "war on drugs." The U.S. Department of Justice offers the following figures.[68]

Type of cost	*Millions*
Federal drug expenditures (1991)	$10,841
All law enforcement	7,157
Interdiction	2,028
Investigations	1,288
International	640
Prosecution	584
Corrections	1,265
Intelligence	104
State and local assistance	1,016
State and local drug crime expenditures (1988)	5,240
Enforcement of drug laws	2,007
Adjudication of drug law violators	123
Correction of drug law violators	3,072
State prisons	1,158
Local jails	890

[68]*Drugs, Crime, and the Justice System*, U.S. Department of Justice, Office of Justice Programs, Bureau of Justice Statistics, December 1992, NCJ-133652, p. 126.

We must consider: are these wise expenditures of the marginal tax dollar? (Is it worth worsening the federal deficit for these activities?)

It must be borne in mind that the resources used to wage the "war on drugs" are not available for other social needs: health care, deficit reduction, tax relief. What's also unavailable for other use are existing prison cells. According to James Ostrowski,

> Currently, there are not enough judges and prosecutors to try cases or enough prison cells to house convicts. In 1987, the federal prison system had 44,000 inmates. 16,000 were drug offenders. Official capacity in federal prisons was only 28,000. In addition, many prisons are operating under court orders due to overcrowding or poor conditions. Because of the lack of prison space, violent criminals frequently are given deals, probation, or shorter terms than they deserve. Then they are back on the streets, and often back to serious crime.[69]

Husak, citing government statistics, reports that "More than three-quarters of those arrested are eventually charged with possession, typically of marijuana."[70] Even if we ignore the criminality that is caused by prohibitory statutes, the diversion of resources to waging the "war on drugs" is making us less safe, less secure.

Let us consider now the social *benefits* of these statutes; we need to determine whether the benefits exceed these costs.

First and foremost, of course, is that the prohibitory statutes prevent the use of "drugs."

But do they *really*? To what extent? We must proceed with great caution here, for as we learned in Chapter Five, the following inference is fallacious:

Law *L* prohibits action *a*
Person P does not elect action a
Law *L* "prevents" Person *P* from doing action *a*

---

[69]James Ostrowski, "The Moral and Practical Case . . .," *Hofstra Law Review* 18 (1990), pp. 662-3. Internal cites omitted.

[70]Husak, *Drugs and Rights*, p. 12. Internal cites omitted.

Determining precisely why Person *P* does not elect action *a* is an empirical matter; the fact that action *a* is a crime may well—but may well *not*—play a role in person *P*'s decision against *a*-ing. Person *P*'s reasons for not electing action *a* may be based wholly on the fact that action *a* is a crime, or only partially, or may not be based on that fact at all. The first would be proved if, were action *a* decriminalized, Person *P* would immediately elect it. The second would be proved if, were action *a* decriminalized, Person *P* would seriously consider electing it. The third would be proved if, were action *a* decriminalized, Person *P* *still* would not do it. In such a case, it is not accurate to say that Law *L* "deters" Person *P* from doing action *a*; it is accurate to say that Person *P* is merely *disinclined* to do action *a*. Thus, when assessing the social benefits of a statute, it is legitimate to include only those who are in fact deterred—assuming, of course, that the action in question is an action better left unelected. However, it is quite illegitimate to include the *entirety* of those who do not elect the action, for that includes some people who are in fact merely disinclined to elect the action. As the statute has no causal relevance to their lives, their (in)action cannot be considered a social benefit of the statute.

The use of many psychoactives is illegal; many people do not use illegal psychoactives. How many people do not use them *because* they are illegal, and would use them if only their use were legal? I don't know. Neither my Mom nor my Dad snorts coke. Were it decriminalized, they still wouldn't. I think they're not unique in being disinclined to snort coke. I know some other people who don't snort coke. Were it decriminalized, they might. And I know some people who do snort coke.

The point is this. In assessing the social benefits of statutes which criminalize various psychoactives, it is legitimate to include *only* the benefits which are causally attributable to the statutes. Only instances in which the criminal statute is causally decisive is there a "social benefit" that counts in favor of the statute. The abstinence of individuals who are merely disinclined to use psychoactives cannot correctly be counted in favor of the prohibitory statute. Proponents of "drug" criminalization must offer evidence of this causal relationship; "drug-free" lives do not, in and of themselves, count as a benefit of "drug" criminalization.[71]

---

[71]And one of the costs of criminalization is the elimination of the benefits to some individuals of the use of psychoactives.

VI. PROPOSALS & PROSPECTION

I want to summarize my arguments at the three Filters, and then offer a set of proposals supported by these arguments. Finally, I look forward: what would society be like, were (something like) my proposals accepted?

VI. A. A Summary of the Arguments

At the Principles Filter, I have rejected Legal Paternalism. I have endorsed Mill's arguments against the acceptability of Legal Paternalism; I have argued that the use of various psychoactives falls within the Sphere of Individual Liberty. There's no denying, I believe, that the use of "drugs"—those currently legal, as well as those currently illegal—is indeed a mixed blessing; "drug" use has the potential to enrich lives and to destroy lives. The decision whether to use "drugs," and which "drugs" to use (other than those known to themselves cause behavior harmful to others) is a decision which ought to be left to each competent adult.[72] I have accepted the Harm Principle. However—contrary to the beliefs of many, and virtually all of the portrayals in the media—the genuine harms "associated with" the use of "drugs" are attributable to the criminalization of "drugs" and not to the use of "drugs" itself. This is even clearer when one imagines currently illegal "drugs" available under conditions similar to those applicable, for example, to alcohol. Thus, "drug" use does not pass through the Principles Filter.

When we assume *arguendo* that "drug" use does pass through the Principles Filter, and arrives at the Presumptions Filter, we find the action whose incidence ought to be reduced is not the use of psychoactives *simpliciter*, but use while ignorant of the consequences of that use. And of course it makes sense to promote "responsible" "drug" use—not flying, driving, etc. while under the influence of psychoactives—but that's an umproblemmatical Harm Principle position. But "drug" use does not pass through the Presumptions Filter.

When we assume *arguendo* that "drug" use does pass through the Presumptions Filter, and arrives at the Pragmatics Filter, we find that the "social benefits" of "drug" laws are not so great as many assume: the criminal

---

[72]For a sustained and powerful argument that competent adults have a *right* to use recreational drugs, see Douglas N. Husak, *Drugs and Rights* (New York: Cambridge University Press, 1992).

statutes produce a benefit only in those cases where the statute is causally decisive in altering behavior. More importantly, we find the vast array of social costs—genuine harms to others—so often cited by the proponents of "drug" laws. But we find them as powerful arguments for a program of "drug" decriminalization.

Mine is not a pro-"drug"-use position. A person could claim that there are no significant costs—either to the individual or to society—of "drug" use: but that is not my claim. A person could hold that, although there are significant costs of "drug" use—to both the society and the individual—these costs are generally outweighed by the greater benefits: but that is not what I hold. My position is that the use of "drugs" has the potential for great utility and great disutility, for both the individual and for society. The use of cocaine, marijuana and opium is not without risk, nor is it without reward (as has been detailed above). Precisely the same can—and indeed *must*—be said about the use of alcohol and nicotine. My position is that to distinguish among these as is currently done in most jurisdictions, making the use of latter set perfectly permissible and the use of the former set seriously felonious, is without justification. Yet, on the basis of that legal disparity, thousands of lives have been, are being, irreparably damaged. This injustice cries out for remedy.

As I remarked at the outset, the lineaments of my proposals will have come quite naturally to mind in the detailing of various aspects of these issues. And the strongest support for these proposals arises from their ending, or at least ameliorating, so many of the evils generated by existing arrangements.

VI. B. Proposals for Reform

The first proposal is that the whole range of psychoactive substances—except those which have been scientifically proved to be the proximate cause of antisocial behavior—be readily available to competent adults. This proposal is perfectly consistent, however, with all of the following.

(a) Psychoactives should be readily available to competent adults *only*. Mill says that his anti-paternalist position " . . . is meant to apply only to human beings in the maturity of their faculties. We are not speaking of children or of young persons below the age which the law may fix as that of manhood or womanhood." [OL 13] The same is true of these proposals; nothing I have said runs contrary to the claim that decisions regarding the use of various psychoactives—nicotine and alcohol, as well as cocaine and marijuana—are important, indeed momentous decisions. As such they are to be made by competent adults and not children. (There is good reason to believe that the state's adopting these proposals will assist greatly in restricting these decisions to competent adults; I argue this below.)

(b) It is not contrary to the specification that psychoactives be "readily available" to competent adults, that they be available only at state-operated, or state-licensed, outlets. This would be of help in restricting sales to competent adults, and would make easier the monitoring of social "drug" use, the compiling of statistics for research, etc. Nor is it contrary to the specification that they be "readily available" to competent adults, that advertising be prohibited.

(c) The state should supervise the production of all psychoactives, inspecting and testing them (as it does with many "drugs" today), to assure purity and determinate potency. This would eliminate, or at least reduce the incidence of, a number of the evils "associated with" "drug" use—especially accidental overdose, and injury due to contamination. State supervision would also eliminate the problems of pollution by clandestine "drug" laboratories (or more accurately: it would become a component of the pollution problems posed by legal "drug" manufacturers.) The availability of a wide spectrum of psychoactives whose production was quality-controlled would sharply reduce the appeal of dangerous, amateur-produced "designer drugs."

(d) All sales of psychoactives must be accompanied by the best available information on the health consequences of the use of that particular psychoactive. In deciding just what to imbibe with dinner, information about cirrhosis of the liver ought to be as readily available as information about the merits of the '82 Bordeaux. In selecting one's after-dinner delights, one should be able to easily learn of the effects of the nicotine in cigars, the alcohol in port wine and brandy, and the addictiveness of opium (as well as the cholesterol in Dove Bars).

(e) The various psychoactives must be priced so as to not create a crime tariff on "drugs." (Given the costs of production, this will be easy to achieve.) With the elimination of the crime tariff, society would realize a wide spectrum of substantial benefits. There would be a dramatic reduction in acquisitive crime. Without the enormous profits created by the crime tariff, we could expect a sharp reduction in the corruption of police officers, prosecutors, judges, jurors, jailers, bankers, etc. Most of the funding of organized crime's foray into legitimate business would be eliminated. The incidence of undesirable police practices would be reduced; the bizarre causal consequences of "drug" law enforcement recounted above would be eliminated. A particularly happy consequence of ending the crime tariff on "drugs" is ending the economic incentive that "drug" users *currently* have to recruit new users—including children. The social resources currently devoted to (attempts at) enforcement of "drug" laws prohibiting adult use would be released for other social purposes—including "drug" education and counseling—and the enforcement of laws prohibiting the sale of "drugs" to minors. These proposals would eliminate the incentive to sell to minors, enhance education and enforcement efforts, and eliminate the profits which make "drug" dealing so attractive a profession. It is doubtful that more could be done to protect children than this sort of regulated decriminalization for adults.

(f) Taxation of psychoactives to raise revenues (e.g. to fund research and education programs) would certainly be permissible (and need not significantly raise the price of the commodity). Taxation to discourage use, however, would not be permissible. As Mill eloquently argues, "To tax stimulants for the sole purpose of making them more difficult to be obtained is a measure differing only in degree from their entire prohibition, and would be justifiable only if that were justifiable." [OL 122] And as I have argued, such a prohibition is *not* justifiable. However, "taxation for fiscal purposes is absolutely inevitable," and thus "[i]t is hence the duty of the State to consider, in the imposition of taxes, what commodities it can best spare. . . ." [OL 122] As regards this, I am in disagreement with those who believe that a system of differential taxation should be used to steer "drug" users away from more dangerous "drugs" and towards less dangerous "drugs."[73]

(g) The enforcement of laws prohibiting various activities while "under the influence" of psychoactives is also perfectly consistent with these proposals. Pilots and podiatrists, as well as pitchers and punters, ought to be legally free to use psychoactives—but not while piloting or doctoring.

The second proposal is that this regulated decriminalization be accompanied by serious programs of research, education and counseling. Consider these in reverse order.

(a) No one pretends that all competent adults will be able to design and live out a plan of life without assistance. Thus, a network of "drug" counselling facilities, featuring a variety of treatment approaches and techniques, ought to be funded by the state. (I suspect that the savings realized from ending the

[73]See Irwin, "A Rational Approach. . . ." *op. cit.*, p. 35.

[adult] "war on drugs" would more than pay for such a network, even without being supplemented by the revenues of taxing psychoactives.)

(b) Research will be needed to determine which psychoactives' use causes antisocial behavior, to determine precisely the health consequences of using the various psychoactives, and so forth.

(c) A significant educational program should be sponsored, one which avoids silly and false stereotypes (like "Reefer Madness"), avoids simplistic responses to complex issues (like Nancy Reagan's "Just say NO!"), and avoids unjust selectivity (cf. the disparity between current warnings and media accounts of the dangers of smoking cigarettes, and the virtual silence about the dangers of alcohol).

"Drug" education is needed not only about the consequences of "drug" use, but, just as importantly and urgently, about the consequences of "drug" *laws*. If my arguments are essentially sound, mystification about the consequences of drug laws contributes substantially to the existing legal disparity among psychoactives. Just as individual decisions about "drug" use cannot intelligently be made without accurate information about the consequences of such use, social decisions about "drug" laws cannot intelligently be made without accurate information about the consequences of "drug" laws.

VI. C. Prospection

So: what *would* society be like, were my proposals, or similar proposals for decriminalization, be enacted?

According to John J. DiIulio Jr.,

> Ideological bents aside, there are really just two kinds of drug policy experts: those who know they're skating on empirically thin ice, and those who don't (or who probably do but won't admit it).[74]

Ruefully, I agree. Nonetheless, some claims about the consequences of decriminalization are more plausible than others, some less plausible. That we cannot *know* the future is no justification for policy paralysis.

The greatest fear of prohibitionists is that, upon decriminalization, the use of psychoactives will "skyrocket," and the attendant individual and social problems will be devastating. As legalization proponent Ethan Nadelmann

---

[74]John J. DiIulio Jr., "Cracking Down," *The New Republic*, May 10, 1993.

cautions, "All the benefits of legalization would be for naught, however, if millions more people were to become drug abusers."[75]

Of course I agree that there is *some* level of psychoactive use that would make continuing social life impossible—there is some degree of "withdrawals" from society, that would precipitate economic collapse.[76] At issue is whether that is a likely scenario. Would we witness so many people electing to "turn on, tune in, and drop out?"[77]

There are many good reasons for thinking that we would not.

First, there is the U.S. experience with the prohibition of alcohol: there was a fear, which proved unfounded, that the country itself would begin to lead a dissolute life. It did not. And there is the experience of other countries, which have pursued various policies of decriminalization, without catastrophe.[78]

Why is this? The best explanation, I believe, is based on my earlier analysis of "deterrence," and the issue of precisely which people are, strictly speaking, *deterred* by prohibitory statutes. It is a serious mistake to believe that everyone who does not do some action that is proscribed by the criminal law refrains because of the criminal law. There are lots of things that lots of people wouldn't do, even if those actions were not crimes. Significantly many people do not partake of currently *legal* psychoactives; it is most implausible to hold that these people aren't using *il*legal psychoactives just because they are illegal: and would, upon decriminalization begin using them, to the point of economic collapse. Many people decline to smoke cigarettes, or drink alcohol, even though both are legally permissible. Different people abstain for different reasons: knowledge of health consequences, religious convictions, psychological inhibitions, etc. Having chosen to not use these, how plausible is it that such people, upon the revocation of criminal sanctions, would begin to use currently illegal "drugs?" Ostrowski observes,

---

[75]Nadelmann, *Science*, p. 943.

[76]I speak here of withdrawals from economic productivity, for whatever reason: "drugs," sunbathing, television watching, simple indolence, etc. Cf. Chapter Five, Topic One: "Concerns about Feinberg's 'Garrison Situations'."

[77]Timothy Leary, in a lecture of June 1966. *The Oxford Dictionary of Modern Quotations*, ed. Tony Augarde (New York: Oxford University Press, 1991), p. 133.

[78]See Ostrowski, "The Moral and Practical Case for Drug Legalization," pp. 672-5.

> As our society grows increasingly health and fitness conscious, heavy drug use will lose its appeal. Many are trading in the tavern for the health club and choosing vitamins over martinis.[79]

Second, the power of education ought not be underestimated. The more that is known about the health consequences of cocaine addiction, and the more widely that that information is publicized, the more likely it is that people will choose to not live that sort of life. Indeed, "drug" education is being credited as the major factor in the recent decline in cocaine use in the United States.[80] Recall too that there would no longer be a financial motive for current users to recruit new users. And were more people to use currently illegal "drugs" after decriminalization—and their effects as deleterious as the prohibitionists claim—there would be in society many examples of the consequences of a life of such "drug" use to serve as deterrent examples. As Mill writes concerning self-regarding, destructive conduct, " . . . the example, on the whole, must be more salutary than hurtful, since, if it displays the misconduct, it displays also the painful or degrading consequences which, if the conduct is justly censured, must be supposed to be in all or most cases attendant on it." [OL 101]

Envision a society in which the use of marijuana, cocaine and heroin is not criminally proscribed, and in which (as a consequence) the use of these drugs escalates. This means that more people are "enslaved" by "drug" addiction, and their economic productivity declines. Health care costs too would escalate. But we must also envision the elimination of the crime tariff on these "drugs." As a consequence of ending the black market, the cost to the addict of the addiction will be greatly reduced. Acquisitive crime would decline dramatically, even if all the users of these "drugs" resorted to crime to finance their habits. (No one now has a $400-a-day muscatel habit; it is the crime tariff that makes possible that expensive a cocaine habit.) No longer would

---

[79]The passage continues: "This process of bringing legal drug use under the influence of positive social values such as health and moderation has less influence on the illegal drug scene. There, hard-core drug users form subcultures that reinforce the values of heavy, reckless drug use." "The Moral and Practical Case for Drug Legalization," p. 673. That prohibitory laws create such subcultures is yet another cost that accrues to those statutes at the Pragmatics Filter.

[80]"Trend data from the National Household Survey on Drug Abuse indicate that current use of most drugs rose from the early to late 1970s, peaked between 1979 and 1982, and has since declined. The increase in cocaine use was especially sharp in the late 1970s. Between 1988 and 1991, the current use of most drugs declined or remained stable for all age groups." *Drugs, Crime, and the Justice System, op. cit.*, p. 30.

there be an economic incentive to "deal," or to recruit new users. Thus, it would be much easier to enforce laws prohibiting sales to minors. Eliminated too would be the crime-tariff-generated profits used to corrupt police officers, prosecutors, and other public officials.

It is not easy to say whether society would be better off, all things considered, with relatively more people under the influence of psychoactives (but with a drastic reduction in acquisitive crime, recruitment of children, corruption of public officials, etc.), or relatively fewer persons under the influence of psychoactives (accompanied by a continuation of the social ills attributable not to drug use *per se*, but to drug laws). But one can say with reasonable confidence that the increase in incidence of "drug" use, and the increase in the total negative consequences of that use, would have to be *quite* high, in order to exceed the social benefits realized from bringing to an end the array of deleterious consequences of criminalization.[81]

Finally, let us take seriously the possibility that "drug" use would increase sharply. Suppose that, as it happens, more people become "drug" users. Suppose that, after decriminalization, more people used "drugs" (of both sorts), more people became abusers (rather than recreational users), more people ruin their lives with psychoactives. But we are supposing also that the crime tariff on "drugs" has been eliminated. Consequently, there is substantially less acquisitive crime in society; there is no funding (from "drugs") of the corruption of police, prosecutors, judges and jailers; there are few attempts to recruit new users (either adult or children), there are no wealthy "drug" dealers in ghettos functioning as role models, there is an end to gang warfare over "drug" sales territory (though of course there are conflicts of other sorts). Police are freed to devote attention to other sorts of criminality; fewer people are imprisoned (saving substantial social resources).

Let us define "evil" in a non-theological sense, and mean by it "regrettable events or states of affairs." So what we are supposing is that, upon decriminalization, the "evils" of degradation will increase, for more people will ruin their lives through the abuse of "drugs." Put another way: there will be

---

[81]Some people have claimed that, even after decriminalization, there would continue to be an illicit "drug" business (with many of the problems already discussed). I think this scenario not credible. It is doubtful that independent producers could grow, harvest, refine,. transport and distribute "drugs" more efficiently than pharmaceutical corporations, and thus undersell the government. Add the quality control measures employed in the manufacture of officially sanctioned "drugs," and it is difficult to see much of a market for nonsanctioned producers.

an increase in the evils that people inflict upon themselves. But we are also supposing that the evils of predation will decrease: there will be a decrease in the evils that some people inflict on other people. Now even if we suppose that the sum total of "evil" is unchanged after decriminalization, the society is, all things considered, morally superior. It is unfortunate that people sometimes do things destructive to themselves. Nonetheless, for any given amount of "evil" (however quantified), it is worse for a person to inflict it on another, than to inflict it on oneself. Indeed, even if the sum total of evil increased (within some limits), since relatively more was self-inflicted, and relatively less was other-inflicted, that society would be morally superior for the change.

VII. MYSTIFICATION, FALSE CONSCIOUSNESS AND HYPOCRISY

I am not very optimistic that my proposals will be adopted very soon. The mystification that enshrouds the issues of "drugs" is pervasive, and has a tenacious grip on popular consciousness. In this Section, I want to discuss a few instances of this mystification. I make no claims about the mystifiers—whether they are merely parroting the falsities of others, or whether they harbor misgivings about extant legal arrangements (suffer from false consciousness), or whether they are simply hypocritical.

VII. A. Criminogenesis

David A. J. Richards, writing before the current "war on drugs" was declared, rejects one explanation of prohibition, and offers another.

> It is disingenuous to suppose that the American criminal prohibition of drug use is based on the secular concerns of criminogenesis and control of drug-related injuries. Neither argument can justify such prohibition; indeed serious concerns with the evils adduced by both arguments would require the opposite conclusion. These arguments are, at best, post hoc empirical

> makeweights for justifications of a different order, namely, moralistic and paternalistic arguments of a peculiarly American provenance.[82]

Of course I concur fully with Richards' claim that, upon careful scrutiny, the phenomena of criminogenesis and drug-related injuries militate powerfully against criminalization. But have these phenomena received the needed scrutiny—so that they can be dismissed as not being relevant, as not being a force for continued criminalization? No; quite the opposite is true. A central element of the mystification of "drugs" is criminogenesis: that drug use *causes* crime. Although it is true that the facts of criminogenesis count against criminalization, the popular perception is that they count in favor of criminalization. Consider the accounts and descriptions of "drug" sale, distribution and use in the media, from movies to commercial advertisements to local and national news telecasts. "Drug" users are portrayed as depraved and enslaved sociopaths continuously engaged in acquisitive crime. Precisely *why* they are engaged in such activities, and the relationship to "drug" laws, are not addressed. (And it is only the users of *some* "drugs" that are so portrayed; the users of other "drugs" are portrayed as people who are successful, sophisticated, sexually attractive, etc.) "Drug" dealers are portrayed as vicious and exploitative, continuously looking for innocents to seduce into a life of degradation. The principles of capitalistic salesmanship that explain this behavior are not addressed. (And it is only the dealers of *some* "drugs" that are so portrayed; the suppliers of other "drugs" are shown as upstanding businessmen engaged in the happy enterprise of supplying the entertainment needs of their successful, sophisticated, sexually attractive clientele—i.e., "drug" users.) The various constituents of the criminal justice system—police officers, prosecutors, judges—are portrayed in a ceaseless and valiant struggle to protect innocents from the violence of "drug" users and the rapaciousness of "drug" dealers—and seeking respite from fighting the good fight by ingesting their own psychoactive of choice. Upon occasion a valiant "drug" warrior falls; through weakness of will or bad character, a police officer, a prosecutor, a judge, is corrupted by "drugs." But upon no occasion

---

[82]Richards, p. 168. Indeed, Richards sees the Principle of Perfectionism as *the* "principle of criminal legislation" invoked in the attempt to justify "drug" laws. Richards argues powerfully against its acceptability (p. 172); accepting Perfectionism as a principle of criminalization is *so* inconsistent with pluralistic democracy that I have declined devoting textual space to its rejection.

do we receive an explanation of the economics of the drug business, the workings of the crime tariff, and so on.

Richards' claim that criminogenesis cannot be the energizing force of continued criminalization presupposes that these complex phenomena are correctly and widely understood. But that just isn't true. The American consciousness is fed a steady diet of misinformation about "drugs" and criminality; the result is a pervasive false consciousness. One rarely encounters the claim, "I know that criminal statutes prohibiting the use of various psychoactives creates a crime tariff, which explains acquisitive crime, recruitment, corruption, etc.; but nonetheless I support drug laws because I think people should conform to a certain conception of the ideal character." Rather, one continuously encounters claims about "drug" use, users, dealers, etc. that are demonstrably false but nonetheless held to be true.

First, consider a recent article in *Time*'s "American Notes" section. The category is "Drugs," the headline is "Criminals Just Say Yes," the entire text is as follows:

> Police have long contended that drug abusers are likely to commit street crimes. A Justice Department study last week revealed the extent of the problem: half to three-fourths of the men arrested for serious crimes in a dozen U.S. cities had recently used drugs. In New York City, 79% of those tested had used cocaine, marijuana or some other illegal substance. In Washington the proportion was 77%, in San Diego, 75%. Those figures were 'much higher than anyone had anticipated,' said James Stewart, the study's director. "If we are going to do something about the crime rate, we are going to have to confront the drug problem."[83]

This is a textbook example of the *post hoc* fallacy; *Time*'s readers are led to believe that ingesting illegal psychoactives causes people to commit crimes. We know that that is, in most cases, just false. The article makes no mention of the role of the crime tariff, due to *criminalization*, in explaining the observed phenomena.

On some occasions, law enforcement officials are candid. Ostrowski reports that the Deputy Chief of the New York City Police Department, commenting on the claim that 38 percent of the murders in 1987 were "drug related,"

---

[83]*Time*, February 1, 1988, p. 25.

explained that these were "territorial disputes" or "disputes over possession," and not the result of the psychoactive properties of the substances.[84] In other words, they were caused by criminalization, not by the use of the chemical.

More generally: a main element of the mystification is that "drugs" cause crime.

VII. B. A Subtle Instance of the "Inapt Comparison"

Another element of the mystification is the inapt comparison: looking at one legal "drug," and one illegal "drug," "showing" that the illegal "drug" is worse by citing some "evil" that arises from its criminalization, and not its inherent characteristics. Typically, these inapt comparisons are blatant. But a subtle instance can be found in Joel Feinberg's *Harm to Self*. The context is not criminalization, but various issues of voluntariness. Feinberg says he will, for the purposes of his argument, assume that "heroin is legal, so that there are no risks of the sort that stem from law enforcement." [HTS 121] A person contemplating the use of heroin could show that his choice was fully voluntary, claims Feinberg, by showing that he understood the consequences of his choice—e.g., by talking to "advanced addicts in their squalid hovels." [HTS 121] But wait: if heroin *really were* decriminalized, really were available under conditions similar to the conditions under which currently legal psychoactives are available, why would even advanced heroin addicts be living in "squalid hovels?" There is persuasive evidence that heroin use—under these conditions—is compatible with gainful employment and an essentially normal life.[85] Of course heroin addicts *might* be living in squalid hovels—just like advanced muscatel addicts. But perhaps they could be visited in their knotty-pine paneled dens, dens just like those of some advanced bourbon addicts, and some advanced scotch whiskey addicts.

---

[84]James Ostrowski, "The Moral and Practical Case for Drug Legalization," *Hofstra Law Review* 18, Spring 1990, p. 651.

[85]Steven Jonas, "Solving the Drug Problem: A Public Health Approach to the Reduction of the Use and Abuse of Both Legal and Illegal Recreational Drugs," *Hofstra Law Review* 18, Spring 1990, pp. 768-9.

VII. C. The Fallacy of Ignoratio Elenchi

A television ad sponsored by the "Coalition for a Drug-Free America" features the husband of a woman killed in the infamous Amtrack crash of January 1987; the train's engineer, Ricky L. Gates, tested positive for marijuana.[86] The husband claims to have a counterexample to the claim that "marijuana doesn't hurt anyone." But of course he does not. No proponent of decriminalization holds that it ought to be permissible to drive a train under the influence of marijuana (or alcohol, for that matter). No one (seriously) holds that "marijuana doesn't hurt anyone" entails that it ought to be legally permissible to drive a train under its influence. And of course—as I have been at great pains to show—that it ought to be illegal to drive a train under the influence of marijuana (or a supertanker under the influence of alcohol) is not sufficient to show that the *use* of marijuana (or alcohol) ought to be illegal.

VII. D. Vested Interests in the Status Quo

It is in the financial interests of many people that currently legal psychoactives remain legal, and that currently illegal psychoactives remain illegal. The strong forces opposed to self-consistent social and legal policy as regards psychoactives is a bizarre alliance of growers (of marijuana, tobacco, fermentable grains, opium poppies, coca plants, etc.), "drug" dealers (including both distillers and dope pushers), and public officials, the economic interests of all of whom converge on maintaining the status quo.

Consider first the purveyors of currently legal psychoactive substances. Existing arrangements create a quasi-monopoly for their products. So long as marijuana and cocaine are illegal, those people desiring an altered state of consciousness are far more likely to turn to the products of Seagrams and Stroh's, Phillip Morris and R. J. Reynolds. (This is not to say that these corporations could not develop new products were the laws to change. It would be quite easy, for example, for cigarette manufacturers to substitute one psychoactive—the THC of marijuana—for another—the nicotine in tobacco—in the manufacturing process.)

---

[86]"Engineer Is Indicted on 16 Counts of Manslaughter in Amtrack Crash," *The New York Times*, May 5, 1987, p. 1, p. D 30.

These suppliers of "drugs" invest substantial sums of money to insure that shoppers for psychoactives are aware of their substances. Year after year, the leading tobacco companies, and the leading companies in the wine, beer and liquor industry, are among the leaders in revenue spent on advertising.[87]

Several professional teams—e.g. the St. Louis Cardinals, the Montreal Expos and the Toronto Blue Jays—are owned by "drug" dealers (i.e., the purveyors of currently legal psychoactives). Professional athletes promote "smokeless tobacco" on television. Worse—since actions speak louder than words—the telltale short cylinder in the hip pocket as athletes take the field.[88] And ex-athletes pitch alcohol; throughout the entire championship season of 1987, New York Mets fans were induced to drink: Baseball Hall of Famer Ralph Kiner "pushing" "Mets fans, this Bud's for you!" Particularly galling are those who decry the use of "drugs," who champion severe penalties for "drug" use—while smoking, pinching, quaffing or sipping—and *profiting* from it, and profiting from inducing others to do likewise.

Consider now the purveyors of currently illegal psychoactive substances. As we have seen, incredible profits are generated by the "crime tariff" on such "drugs." Anyone in a "profit-sharing plan" associated with these substances has a monetary interest in preserving the existing arrangements. This set includes (but is not limited to): growers (for whom marijuana or opium poppies, or coca plants constitute a cash crop more profitable than anything else they could grow), smugglers (whose "markup" of the commodity assures a substantial income), dealers (whose life-style of conspicuous consumption is funded by the profitability of the "drug" traffic), and governments (for some of which psychoactives constitute the leading export). It also includes corrupt police officers, corrupt prosecutors, corrupt judges, corrupt jailers, etc., all of whom receive a substantial portion of their respective incomes from said profits. And it even includes many members of the "anti-drug" bureaucracies who would be unemployed were the use of these substances not illegal (though of course some of these are sincere and high-minded). When one sums the economic motives of those who profit from currently legal "drugs" and the motives of those who profit from currently illegal "drugs," one finds the solution to the puzzle of a social policy that seemingly has no rational basis:

---

[87]For the most recent statistics available, see *Advertising Age*, September 29, 1993.

[88]"St. Louis Cardinals infielder Luis Alicea, on smokeless tobacco and baseball: 'Being in baseball and not dipping or chewing is like being in a bar and not drinking a beer'." *The Syracuse Post-Standard*, August 13, 1993, p. D-1. Enough said.

the existing arrangements as regards the criminalization of only *some* psychoactive substances. Indeed, the motivation for maintaining the mystification is captured by the aphorism, "It's only money."

VIII. MUTUALLY EXCLUSIVE GOALS

More than a few people believe that there are two distinct justifications for the laws which prohibit "drug" use. For ease of exposition, we can use two terms I invoked earlier: degradation and predation.

Consider first *degradation*. Although I have argued that prohibitionists are apt to exaggerate the number, I do indeed believe that drug laws deter some citizens, that for some people, all that stands between abstention and degradation is the criminal law.

Consider second *predation*. More than a few people believe that it is primarily, or exclusively, the *use* of drugs that causes some people to prey upon other people: to rob, to burglarize, to murder.

Thus, more than a few people believe that "drug" laws are justified in that they reduce degradation, and reduce predation.

For the moment, set aside all the arguments which conclude that the vast majority of "drug" predation is the consequence of prohibitory statutes and not the psychopharmacological properties of the chemicals. Set aside as well my critique of Balancing; recall its ubiquity as a common-sense decision-procedure. What all this gives rise to is the "two scoops" solution to the problem of arguments arising from different Principles of State Authority. It will seem that the case in favor of criminalization gets two scoops of weight: a scoop of degradation (Legal Paternalism), and a scoop of predation (Harm Principle). The combined weight may well be believed to tip the balance.

Figure 6 — 1

Reflect now on my critique of Balancing, and the arguments tracing the causal ancestry of the predation "associated with" psychoactives. As I have argued, the social goal of dramatically reducing predation can be achieved *not* by more strict enforcement of "drug" laws—for they are the ultimate *cause* of predation—but by the decriminalization of "drugs." The social goal of deterring (this certain set of) people from ruining their lives by abusing "drugs" can be achieved only through continuing criminalization of "drugs." Thus, combining the reduction of degradation with the reduction of predation does *not* constitute a "weighty" case for criminalization. Far from being compatible social goals, they are mutually exclusive social goals. The most efficient way to reduce predation—criminalization—will exacerbate degradation. The most efficient way to reduce degradation—continued criminalization—will exacerbate predation. This phenomenon is revealed by Filtering, since one is directed to look to the consequences of criminalization (at the Pragmatics Filter) as regards the (alleged) malady cited at the Principles Filter. When Balancing, in contrast, it is easy to miss the fact that reducing predation and reducing degradation are mutually exclusive social goals; when Balancing, they may well seem perfectly compatible. And given the naturalness of the "two scoops" solution within the metaphor of Balancing, it may well seem that adding their weights is perfectly appropriate, But these are not compatible social goals, and adding their "weights" isn't the appropriate procedure.

Near the end of Chapter Three, I discussed in the abstract this infirmity of Balancing; I promised to make the abstract critique concrete when discussing "drugs." I have now kept that promise.

IX. THE "NO MORE (LEGAL) DRUGS" ARGUMENT

Let us consider a final, desperate attempt to justify existing arrangements, an argument which concedes all I have argued regarding the comparative health consequences, for both individuals and society, and which grasps the complex causal networks of the illegal "drug" business.

It could be argued that, when one considers the array of psychoactive substances legally on the market today, and their associated social costs, simply adding *more* psychoactives to those already legally available will have unacceptable consequences. It's not that there's any philosophically acceptable basis for the legal distinction between alcohol etc. on the one hand, and cocaine etc. on the other. It's just that some psychoactives happen to be legal, and others illegal. Let's leave it at that. Read my lips: "No More (Legal) Drugs."

Two replies can be made to the "No More (Legal) Drugs" Argument. First, it should be noted that the argument is a complete capitulation to the charge of hypocrisy. No attempt is made to distinguish one set of psychoactives from the other in a way which would justify their different legal statuses, i.e., that one set is legally permissible while the other is felonious. Second, it raises a significant issue of fairness. Those who prefer one sort of altered mental state may do so with impunity; those who prefer another sort of altered mental state risk the indignities of arrest, the expenses of defense, the consequences of incarceration, and the encumbrances of conviction. In the absence of a reason for different treatment, this criminalization inflicts a serious injustice.

X. "DRUGS" AND THE SPHERE OF INDIVIDUAL LIBERTY

In my judgement, the use of psychoactive substances falls within the Sphere of Individual Liberty of (competent) adults. People have a right to the recreational use of alcohol, marijuana, cocaine, heroin and nicotine.[89] In light of the psychopharmacology of these "drugs," the most prominent candidate for criminalization; given the health consequences of these "drugs," the most prominent candidates for criminalization are alcohol and nicotine.

---

[89]The use of PCP is problematical; I set aside that issue. Husak, in *Drugs and Rights*, describes the properties a hypothetical drugs would have to have, for the state to have the authority to prohibit its recreational use.

Had I argued a persuasive case for this thesis at the Principles Filter, the consideration of the Presumptions and Pragmatics Filters would have been unnecessary—at least, for the determination of morally justified criminalization. If the use of psychoactive substances does indeed fall within the Sphere of Individual Liberty, then (by definition) it does not pass through the Principles Filter; it may not be morally criminalized. But as I have argued, the issue of "drugs" is mystified; I believed it impossible to argue persuasively that people have a right to recreational "drug" use unless I worked at de-mystification. So long as people are persuaded (or confused, or deluded) into thinking that current legal arrangements are justified, they cannot believe that "drug" use is a right—that current legal arrangements *violate* rights.

Writing as a philosopher of the criminal law, my main concern is to be persuasive that Filtering is the superior decision-procedure for morally justified criminalization, and that the use of psychoactive substances does not pass through all three Filters (i.e., that it fails to pass through at least one Filter). I am less concerned to be persuasive that we actually have a *right* to use psychoactives.

If one accepts the presumption in favor of liberty, and if my arguments (and those of other anti-prohibitionists) show that the state lacks the "special justification"[90] for criminalization, then taking "drugs" falls within the Sphere of Individual Liberty (or at worst, in the "interstice" between the SIL and Society's Jurisdiction). If one sees the value of the use of psychoactives—for creativity, for religious experience, just for fun—then one will see that use as a right. For more sustained an argument, I refer the reader to the work of others: Thomas Szasz,[91] James Ostrowski,[92] and especially Douglas N. Husak's *Drugs and Rights*.

---

[90]The phrase is Feinberg's, *Harm to Others*, p. 9.

[91]Thomas Szasz, *Our Right to Drugs: The Case for a Free Market* (Praeger, 1992).

[92]"The Moral and Practical Case for Drug Legalization," *Hofstra Law Review* 18, Spring 1990, pp. 625-641.

Topic Two
MORE INTERNECINE WARFARE

The author[93] of a recent article in *QQ*[94] argues in favor of some "drug" decriminalization. Despite this (partial) convergence in practical recommendations, I am critical of much in this work. Various portions of it are unfortunate, confused, or wrong. It does, however, provide an excellent opportunity for demonstrating some of the virtues of Filtering.

1. What is *unfortunate* about the article is its title, and consequently the rhetorical tack it takes. The title: "The War on Drugs: Is it Time to Surrender?" In accepting the inapt military metaphor, this title presupposes that there is a war, that we ought to win that war, but we are *unable* to win that war, so we ought to surrender. Rallying the troops for surrender is oxymoronic as well as rhetorically moronic; this is not a good tactic, if one wishes to win the hearts and minds of the citizenry. This is not an effective way to persuade people to decriminalize "drugs." Calling the social policy of criminally proscribing psychoactives a "war," as I have argued, is most misleading, and obscures rather than clarifies the complex economic relationships of the business of illegal "drugs." Since it's not a war, *ipso facto* it's not a war that ought to be won.

It will prove more effective, I think, to expose the "war on drugs" as a failing and destructive social policy, a policy founded on mystification, and "advanced" with purple prose and hyperbole. "Drug" decriminalization, far from a shameful surrender, is the adoption of a morally superior public policy.

2. What is *confused* in the article is the argument over "anti-paternalism" (which I shall understand as Liberalism).

In the opening paragraphs, anti-paternalism is accepted as regards some psychoactives—but not for "crack," the smokable form of cocaine:

> But it hardly takes a set of stuffy "middle-class values" to argue that involvement with a highly addictive drug such as crack counts as a form of slavery. The insatiable craving for crack leads people to neglect and abuse their children, to live in unspeakable filth and

[93]The article is unsigned; as needed, I will simply refer to "the author."

[94]*QQ: Report from the Center, op. cit.*

> foulness, to commit any crime to service one all-encompassing obsession. [*QQ* 3]

The point of painting this portrait of crime and degradation is to motivate the rejection of anti-paternalism:

> The anti-paternalistic argument for legalization of drugs is the most persuasive for benign and non-addictive drugs like marijuana—but marijuana is the least of our drug problems today. When the drugs to be legalized are dangerous and highly addictive drugs like crack, the argument fails. If paternalism is justifiable anywhere, it is justifiable here. Paternalistic prohibitions against highly addictive drugs are legitimate in principle; the central issue, as we shall see shortly, is how they work in practice. [*QQ* 3]

Now I agree that *a* "central issue" is "how they work in practice." However, I reject the claim that "[p]aternalistic prohibitions against highly addictive drugs are legitimate in principle." Certainly the argument of this section does not show it so.

Reflect on the relationships among Principles of State Authority, to see how they bear on this (attempted) rejection of anti-paternalism. One invokes the "Harm Principle" if one claims that "harm to others" allows an action to pass through the Principles Filter. One invokes "Legal Paternalism" if one claims that "harm to oneself" allows an action to pass through the Principles Filter. The "anti-paternalist" rejects Legal Paternalism, holds that it is not an acceptable Principle of State Authority. The purported benefits to the individual coerced do not constitute a reason for criminalization, according to the anti-paternalist; an action's being "harmful" to the agent is not sufficient for the action's passing through the Principles Filter.

Consider now the proposed criminalization of some action *a*. If the engaging in action *a* causes harm to others, then those who accept the Harm Principle (and virtually everyone does) hold that that counts in favor of criminalizing *a*. Of course that is not enough—it might be the case that less coercive measures would suffice (it does not pass through the Presumptions Filter); it might be the case that the consequences of criminalizing action *a* are so deleterious that, all things considered, the society would be better off if action *a* is *not* criminalized (it does not pass through the Pragmatics Filter). Suppose that action *a* also results in (what some would judge) "harm" to the agent oneself. For the Legal Paternalist, this too counts in favor of the criminalizing of action *a*; for the anti-paternalist, it does not. But note: the quarrel between the Legal Paternalist and the anti-paternalist concerns the relevance of harm to *self* in justifying criminal statutes. An action's harming *others*—while of course relevant in the ultimate decision as regards the statute—has no bearing on the debate between the Legal Paternalist and the anti-paternalist, whose dispute is whether harm to *self* is properly a factor in determining whether a statute is justifiable. More particularly: showing that some action harms *others* is wholly irrelevant to the Legal Paternalism/anti-paternalism debate, and thus cannot be used in the rejection of anti-paternalism. Showing that action *a* passes through the Principles Filter because it harms others has no bearing whatsoever on the issue of whether it would also pass through the Principles Filter because it harms the agent oneself—i.e., it has no bearing whatsoever on the issue of the acceptability of Legal Paternalism.

Return now to the relevant passage from the Article. A consequence of "crack" use, it is claimed, is the "neglect and abuse of one's children." If this is so, it provides some reason (though not necessarily *conclusive* reason), under the Harm Principle, for the criminalization of crack. It leaves wholly unscathed, however, the anti-paternalist's position. It is perfectly consistent for the anti-paternalist to hold that the effects of crack use *on the user* are irrelevant to the issue of a statute's justification, though the harm to *others* (for example, one's children) does indeed count in favor of criminalization. In sum, it is wholly illicit to cite "abuse and neglect of children" in arguing against the anti-paternalist; one cannot legitimately derive support for Legal Paternalism by citing harm to others.

So let us delete, from the rejection of anti-paternalism, the neglect and abuse of children. Let us focus on what remains: ". . .to live in unspeakable filth and foulness, to commit any crime to service an all-encompassing obsession." [*QQ 3*]

Early in the Article, we find good sensitivity to the fact that most of the social evils "associated with" "drugs" are properly attributed not to drug use itself, but to the criminalization of said substances: "The greatest costs are incurred, it can be claimed, not by drugs per se, but as a direct or indirect by-product of their criminalization." [*QQ* 2] In the overall argument about decriminalization, mistaking the costs of criminalization for the costs of use are doubly damaging. Considerations are offered in support of criminal legislation which in fact weigh in favor of *de*criminalization; the argument for criminalization appears stronger than in fact it is, while the argument for decriminalization appears weaker than in fact it is. (Recall the "checkbook" analogy drawn earlier in this chapter.) Given the declared sensitivity to this sort of error, it is ironic to find that the argument against anti-paternalism is mistaken in precisely this way.

The final substantive section of the Article discusses (some of) the consequences of "drug" criminalization. Featured are the "hyper-inflated profits" of the drug business, and some of the consequences of those profits, e.g. that there will always be individuals willing to take risks in order to "earn" that money. Some other important consequences are not mentioned: the corruption of police, prosecutors and judges (just another "business expense"); the murder of police, prosecutors and judges who are uncooperative (also another "business expense"). One neglected consequence is of central concern. "Hyper-inflated profits" can be realized because, due to criminalization, the "street price" of illegal psychoactives is wildly disproportionate to the costs of production, transportation and distribution. It is this "hyper-inflated" street price of illegal "drugs" that drives many users to a life of acquisitive crime, to obtain the resources to purchase "drugs." Thus, that the users of currently illegal psychoactives are motivated to commit crimes, and neglect housework, is a causal consequence not of use *per se*, but of criminalization.

We are offered acquisitive crime and personal degradation as considerations weighing for paternalistic intervention in the form of a criminal prohibition (at the Principles Filter). Quite to the contrary, these are consequences of that prohibition itself, counting against the criminal prohibition at the Pragmatics Filter. As such, far from supporting the in-principle legitimacy of a paternalistic prohibition, they support anti-paternalism.

The portrait painted of the crack addict is not a pretty picture—but neither is the picture of, for example, the muscatel addict. And in comparing them, we must envision the two addictions in themselves, and not compare lives while one "drug" is legal and the other illegal. We must envision the crack addict able to purchase her psychoactive of choice at nearly the cost of production, and of known purity and potency—that is, under conditions analogous to the purchases made by the muscatel addict. Under such conditions, would the personal degradation be worse for the crack addict than the for the alcohol addict? I do not see it that way; at a minimum, that must be argued. As the anti-paternalist prevails in the latter case, it prevails in the former.

Topic Three
ON THE ALLEGED RACISM OF "DRUG" DECRIMINALIZATION

Arguments against "drug" decriminalization arise from a variety of sources. As a consequence of mystification, some arguments are based on ignorance of the causal relationships of the illegal "drug" business. Some arguments are based on vested interests in current arrangements; careful philosophical scrutiny exposes these for what they are.

The final topic I consider in this chapter is the most emotionally-charged objection to programs of "drug" decriminalization: that such programs are *racist*, and would be particularly deleterious to impoverished African-Americans.

After reviewing some aspects of this objection, I reject it with three sorts of arguments. First, it is the African-American community that currently suffers the worst effects of the war on "drugs." Second, a program of decriminalization (such as I outlined above) would specially benefit African-Americans. Third: the mystification that has enveloped the war on "drugs" is uniquely suited to be an instrument of racism. Indeed—as I shall conclude—a committed but covert racist could not conceive a more effective strategy for advancing his nefarious ends than declaring "war on drugs."

Recently, The Washington Post published an article entitled "Legalize Drugs? Two Views."[95] Arguing against legalization is John Ray, a lawyer, a District of Columbia City Councilman, a candidate for mayor of the District—and an African American. Of the war on "drugs" Ray writes

> Now that we have finally begun to fight, it is all the more disturbing to see the legalization advocates attempt to raise the white flag of surrender.
>
> I will not sacrifice the poor for an immoral and impractical quick fix. There's a better way to take the crime and violence out of the drug trade. [Ray, 13]

Alas, Ray too accepts the mystifying military metaphor; in its terms decriminalization is a species of (presumably dishonorable) surrender. As I

[95]*Washington Post Health*/January 2, 1990.

have argued, we need to free ourselves of the mystification, and dispassionately assess "drug" decriminalization as a public policy alternative.

How is it that the poor would be *sacrificed*? We receive no answer. Nor does Ray defend his claim that decriminalization would be "immoral" and "impractical."

What is Ray's proposal, his "better way?" Ray offers three suggestions; consider the third proposal first:

> Third, increase the resources for medical research to find better ways of treating addiction and for more facilities to make treatment a real possibility for the many who want it. [Ray, 13]

Of course this is something with which I agree; indeed, its one of the proposals I made a few years ago. However, there is no reason to believe that this will "take the crime and violence out of the drug trade." So long as the "crime tariff" remains in effect, and the demand for "drugs" persists, so will the "crime and violence of the drug trade."

Consider now John Ray's first suggestion:

> First, let's commit our enormous human and monetary resources to raising a generation of drug-free children. [Ray, 13]

Sure, let's. But this isn't, strictly speaking, a suggestion, a proposal—it's a *goal*. And as I have argued at length, the main obstacles to achieving this goal arise from the crime tariff: economic inducement to sell "drugs" to children, and to involve children in the drug business; "drug" dealers as role models, etc.

So Ray has one suggestion left, one way to achieve the goal of raising a "generation of drug-free children," to "take the crime and violence out of the drug trade."

> Second, prosecute the dealers, and send them to prison for a long time and allocate funds for more police officers, courts and prisons to make punishment a real threat and a real deterrent. [Ray, 13]

Suppose that, magically (and it would take magic), all the dealers were captured all at once, and were incarcerated. Would that end the enterprise, end the "drug" business? Surely not; despite the deterrent, the economic incentives of the "drug" business are too powerful. But don't take my word for it—take Ray's:

> In the ghettos, neither the marijuana of the '60's nor the crack of today is a toy of fleeting interest. It's a way of life. A baby who grows up watching adults—even teenagers—smoke, shoot and snort all kinds of drugs almost inevitably repeat the cycle. It's as ordinary as soda pop, and the only real avenue of escape from poverty that grinds hope into dust . . . .
>
> For the poor, there is no beach vacation to escape the daily struggle for work to pay for food, clothing and shelter. The only jobs to be had rarely pay more than the minimum wage, and the earnings are never enough to sustain the hope of raising one's children in safe and well-maintained housing. Under these conditions smoking crack becomes the only way to escape from the daily horror. Selling it becomes the only road to the real world of nice houses and the possessions the wealthy take for granted. [Ray, 13]

If the *use* of "drugs" is that central to life in the ghetto, and if the *sale* of "drugs" really is the only road to the real world of nice houses and other material possessions, then the dealers who have been "magically" jailed will quickly be replaced by *other* individuals seeking prosperity. And of course if those dealers are "magically" jailed, they too will quickly be replaced. And if *those* dealers are "magically" jailed . . . .

John Ray evidences no understanding of the complex causal and economic relationships of the "drug" business. Even if in-credibly successful, the "war on drugs" is waged, and can be waged, only against particular individuals—e.g., those people who are dealers at a given time. But the arrest of particular individuals isn't really relevant. Only in a trivial sense is it true that particular dealers bring "drugs" into the ghetto—and that is why the magical, instantaneous arrest of all extant "drug" dealers would itself be trivial. Ray is quite right that it is hopelessness, and the desire for escape, and the willingness to pay for an escape from hopelessness, that really brings "drugs" into the ghettos. It goes without saying that the problems of poverty and hopelessness must be addressed. But "drug" law enforcement efforts, far from being an element of the solution, work against it. And so long as the demand for "escape" remains relatively inelastic, the principal effects of enhanced enforcement efforts will be an increase in the cost of the "drugs," and an increase in the social costs of criminalization—a cost paid largely by African Americans.

Columnist George Will has addressed these issues; one of Will's columns ends with these words:

> Today, interest in legalization is increasing as drug abuse becomes increasingly concentrated among poor minorities. This is proof that many privileged people are failing to measure up to minimal standards of responsibility and empathy.[96]

What Will fails to explain, however, is precisely how the criminalization of psychoactive substances *does* satisfy "minimal standards of responsibility and empathy." How is it that creating a crime tariff on "drugs," and inflicting on African Americans all the evils that arise from the crime tariff, *is* responsible and empathetic? It isn't.

Scattered throughout this chapter are accounts of the pernicious consequences of the statutes that criminalize "drugs." Let us gather together those which are particularly relevant to poor African-Americans, developing some in finer detail.

A number of these have already been collected by Ethan Nadelmann:

> Perhaps the most unfortunate victims of the drug prohibition policies have been the poor and law-abiding residents of urban ghettos. Those policies have proven largely futile in deterring large numbers of ghetto dwellers from becoming drug abusers but they do account for much of what ghetto residents identify as the drug problem. In many neighborhoods, it often seems to be the aggressive gun-toting drug dealers who upset law-abiding residents far more than the addicts nodding out in doorways. Other residents, however, perceive the drug dealers as heroes and successful role models. In impoverished neighborhoods from Medellin and Rio de Janeiro to many leading U.S. cities, they often stand out as symbols of success to children who see no other options. At the same time, the increasingly harsh criminal penalties imposed on adult drug dealers have led to the widespread recruiting of juveniles by drug traffickers. Where once children started dealing drugs only after they had been using them for a few years, today the sequence is often reversed.

[96]George Will, column of December 12, 1989.

> Many children start to use illegal drugs now only after they have worked for older drug dealers for a while.[97]

As I have argued,

1. Extant laws have not stemmed the flow of illegal "drugs" into urban ghettos. It is not believable that decriminalization would make "drugs" more readily available; only a person skilled in the use of a shoehorn could wedge even more "drugs" into many areas—despite the criminal prohibition.

2. It is African-Americans who are most often victimized by the violence of sales territory warfare, and unintended but inevitable side-effects of that violence, e.g., the accidental shooting of children.

3. "Drug" dealers function as role models for children.

4. Children are drawn into the "drug" business as traffickers.

Adding to the list from other portions of the chapter:

5. Extant arrangements include economic incentives to recruit new "drug" users; children constitute an especially appealing market.

6. Because of their proximity, African-Americans in urban ghettos are especially likely to become victims of acquisitive crime.

7. Because of the presence of "drugs," African-Americans are especially vulnerable to violations of their Constitutional rights—in particular, rights against unwarranted search and seizure.

8. To the extent that criminal justice resources are devoted to the war on "drugs," they are not available for other law-enforcement missions in urban ghettos—thereby making life more dangerous for all residents.

The program of "drug" decriminalization I have offered addresses each of these evils.

1. The economies of scale, conjoined with assurances of purity and known potency, will make decriminalized but regulated drugs the psychoactives of choice. Competition with illegal "drugs" will provide better control over the flow of illegal "drugs" than criminal statutes.

2. No doubt gangs will find other reasons for conflicts. But ending the incredibly lucrative trade in "drugs" should result in a precipitous decline of the most dangerous sort of violence.

3. By eliminating the profits of the crime tariff on "drugs," one eliminates the profiteers—and thus eliminates them as role models.

---

[97]Nadelmann, *op. cit.*, p. 942.

4. Incentives to enlist children will be replaced by disincentives. The state has no interest in recruiting new users; regulation of the pharmaceutical companies involved in the manufacture of "drugs" can assure that they have no such interest either.

6. Even if "drug" users continued to engage in acquisitive crime to obtain "drugs," significantly less crime would suffice—given the sharply reduced price of decriminalized "drugs."

7. No longer combatants in the war on "drugs," police officers would have less official pressure to engage in rights-violating practices.

8. Significant social resources would be released for other law-enforcement efforts—including enforcement of laws prohibiting the sale of "drugs" to children.

Imagine now a committed but covert racist, an individual who wishes for very bad things to happen to African-Americans, but who doesn't wish to be identified as a racist. In declaring a "war on drugs," such an individual visits on African-Americans the array of serious evils enumerated above. These evils can be perpetuated by nurturing the mystification of the illegal "drug" business. The racist could, for example, scream that "drug" decriminalization is racist, and accuse the proponents of decriminalization of "racism," and of being "soft on drugs." And, in the loveliest and most vicious irony of all, the racist can place the *blame* on African-Americans. If only they had the will, if only they would stop using "drugs," the "drug" problem would end. *They* are at fault.

Of course this fails to factor in the non-African-American market for illegal psychoactives, the source of so much of the capital that makes the "drug" business so profitable, and gives so many people such strong economic incentives to preserve the status quo—including all the evils inflicted on the African-American community.

I am not accusing either John Ray or George Will of being racist. It is important to realize, however, that by declaring war on "drugs," the committed but covert racist inflicts a vast array of substantial evils on African-Americans, prevents the amelioration of those evils, and blames African-Americans themselves for their suffering. What better strategy could be adopted by a racist?

OVERVIEW AND REVIEW

I want to review the work of the entirety, providing an overview of the theses I have advanced, and the arguments and evidence I have offered. Of necessity, some intricacies, some details, some qualifications, etc. will be omitted. In the final analysis, my arguments are the arguments as they appear in the individual chapters. My goal here is to provide an accessible narrative of the flow of my work.

The Introduction emphasized the importance of the issues of this work. I showed their philosophical importance by displaying their centrality in the philosophy of the criminal law; I showed their life importance by displaying the seriousness of a citizen's encounter with the criminal justice system. An individual who is suspected of committing a crime is subjected to the indignities of arrest—apprehension, searching, rights-reading, handcuffing, transport, strip-searching, and lock-up with other arrestees. Subsequently, the individual must bear the expenses of defense—the notoriety of arrest, and the fiscal costs of attorneys, investigators, expert witnesses. (Alternatively, one must bear the many "costs" of being represented by a public defender.) If convicted, the individual is subjected to the consequences of incarceration. Some of these, like the loss of freedom are intended; other consequences—like assault, battery, rape and murder—are not intended (but nonetheless known to occur). Finally, the encumbrances of a criminal conviction will constitute obstacles throughout the remainder of one's life. It is precisely *because* the machinery of the criminal justice system is so powerful, can have so profound an impact on the life of an individual, that the *operation* of that machinery is of the greatest moral moment. To say of some action, "That ought to be a crime!" is to make a claim that requires especially thorough and persuasive justification.

We might think, we might all agree, that some particular action is "bad." We might further agree that society would be better if no one elected it. But making that action *criminal* does not entail that no one will elect it, that it won't happen in our society. It means merely that those who continue to elect it—if discovered and apprehended—will be subjected to great unpleasantness. We are not entitled to assume compliance with criminal statutes (new or existing). When thinking about criminalization, we must not simply ask "Would society be better were this action not elected?" We must ask "Precisely what are we willing to do in attempting to reduce the incidence of this action—and is that effort morally permissible, and is it worth what it will cost?"

Philosophers of the criminal law—among others—tend to underestimate the burden of proof for justifying criminalization, for two distinct reasons. The first is this (illegitimate) "assumption of compliance." The second reason is reliance on "Balancing" as a decision-procedure. When Balancing, one is to "weigh" all the reasons in favor of criminalization, and "weigh" all the reasons opposed to criminalization; the "weightier" set of reasons is to prevail. Absent from the metaphor is a specification of the weights to be placed on the two pans of the balance; this facilitates the omission of crucial "weights." Additionally, Balancing does not direct one to consider alternatives to criminalization, state actions which might be just as effective, or even more effective—but less costly.

Although these are two of the prominent defects of Balancing identified in the Introduction, and in Chapter One, there are others. Balancing requires that "weights" be assigned to an array of incommensurable considerations, yet it is difficult to see how this is to be done. And to be helpful when most needed—as regards highly controversial criminal laws—the assignment of weights must be *very* precise; a small error could "tip the balance." Additionally, movement of the balance's indicator can be deceptive. Discovering a new reason for (or against) criminalization—weight gets put on one pan or the other—moves the indicator. Upon seeing this indicator move towards criminalization, for example, one might be deceived into thinking that it has moved *to* criminalization—even in cases where it has not. And though everyone agrees that the difficulties of enforcing a statute (including the deleterious "side-effects" of a statute) somehow "weigh against" it, the converse is not true: that a statute would be easy to enforce does not, in and of itself, "weigh" in favor of it. This asymmetry wants explanation.

Despite its ubiquitousness, Balancing is a deeply flawed decision-procedure. In Chapter Two, I developed "A Topography of Actions Relevant to Criminalization." Although I began with the work of John Stuart Mill's classic *On Liberty*, the final topography of actions that emerged is perfectly neutral among the various substantive positions in the philosophy of the criminal law (except for anarchy and totalitarianism). Each competent adult ought to have a Sphere of Individual Liberty, a set of actions over which one is sovereign. But some actions fall under Society's Jurisdiction. Between these two mutually exclusive sets lies an "interstice;" as regards some actions, there may be no compelling argument that it falls within the SIL and no compelling argument that it falls within SJ. Society's Jurisdiction is itself made up of three sets: Society's Jurisdiction merely, the "moral coercion of public opinion," and "physical force." Some actions that fall within Society's Jurisdiction ought to be ignored, some ought to be discouraged, but only by "moral coercion." (My discussion of the "social sanction" did show that the "moral coercion of public opinion" could be quite powerful.) Yet other actions are properly discouraged by the use of "physical force," whether wielded by private individuals, or by the state as the "physical force of legal penalties."

On the basis of this topography of actions, I defined "topographic errors." A topographic error is committed whenever one infers, from the fact that an action does *not* fall within an individual's Sphere of Individual Liberty, that it *does* fall in some other particular region: in Society's Jurisdiction (when it might in fact fall within the interstice), or more egregiously, that it falls within "physical force," when it might fall within the interstice, or in the "moral coercion of public opinion." A conclusive argument that an action does not fall within the SIL does nothing to show where on the topography it does fall; in order to show that it falls within "physical force," *more* argument is needed: in particular, argument that assesses the morality of that very use of force.

In Chapter Three, I defended "Filtering" as a decision-procedure for morally justified criminalization." When it is proposed that some action be made criminal, we ought to determine whether it will pass through three distinct Filters. If it passes through all three, its criminalization is morally justified; if it fails to pass through any one, its criminalization is not justified.

At the Principles Filter, one inquires whether the action is of a *sort* with which a state is appropriately concerned. At this Filter, we find the dispute among Liberals, Legal Paternalists, Legal Moralists, etc. as regards the moral authority of the state. These competing positions were reformulated as Principles of State Authority, since Feinberg's formulations of them as "liberty-limiting principles" induce the use of Balancing as one's decision-procedure. One possible result of this investigation is a determination that the action in question falls within individuals' Spheres of Individual Liberty—and thus of course is not justifiably criminalized. If the action passes through the Principles Filter, it arrives at the Presumptions Filter. At this Filter—operating on the presumption that less coercive measures are, *ceteris paribus*, to be preferred over more coercive—one inquires whether means less coercive than a criminal statute would sufficiently reduce the incidence of the action (or alternatively, sufficiently reduce the negative consequences of the action). If that question is answered in the affirmative, then the action does not pass through the Filter, and thus may not morally be criminalized. However, less coercive state action—the "moral coercion of public opinion"—may well have been shown justified. If the action passes through the Presumptions Filter, it arrives at the Pragmatics Filter. At this Filter, one inquires into the social costs and social benefits of enacting and enforcing a statute prohibiting that action. Included in the social costs are various moral debits, e.g. the morality of creating a "crime tariff," and the morality of various allocations of scarce social resources. Only if the benefits of a proposed prohibitory statute exceed its costs, does the action pass through the Pragmatics Filter. An action's passing through all three Filters means that the action may morally be criminally prohibited.

As a decision-procedure for criminalization, Filtering is superior to Balancing. This is shown first of all in that Filtering respects the topography of actions developed in Chapter Two, while Balancing encourages various "topographical errors." It is further shown by comparing the two procedures as regards the misgivings about Balancing discussed in Chapter One. Filtering directs attention to three distinct clusters of issues: the moral authority of the state, the possibility of less coercive remedies, and the practicalities (and impracticalities) of enforcement. Although it cannot *guarantee* that essential considerations won't be neglected (and *no* decision procedure can), it does make more difficult the neglect of these essential considerations. No assignment of "weights" is necessary—much less the very precise assignment of weights. There is no "indicator," and thus no deceptive movement of the indicator. And the "curious asymmetry" is explained by identifying a genuine symmetry: enforcement difficulties count against criminalization, ease of enforcement does count in favor of criminalization—but only at the Pragmatics Filter, when it has already been determined that the action in question falls within Society's Jurisdiction, and that less coercive measures will not satisfactorily reduce its incidence.

I claim that Filtering brings structure and organization to disputes about criminalization, facilitating philosophical progress. This can be shown only by putting the decision-procedure to work—and that is the activity of Part Two.

In the chapters of Part Two—"Failures to Justify Coercion"—I simultaneously undertook a number of different tasks. I constructed the Liberal position on a variety of recalcitrant issues in the philosophy of the criminal law, and defended that position: against anti-Liberals, and also against wayward Liberals (generally Joel Feinberg). In doing this, I relied upon the topography of actions developed in the second chapter, thereby demonstrating its usefulness. And in assessing purported justifications of coercion, I employed Filtering, thereby demonstrating its superiority to Balancing.

The actions put to the test of the competing decision-procedures had to be selected with particular care. If I had selected actions we all agree ought to be crimes—homicide, rape, arson, battery, etc.—it is not likely that the distinctive features of the two procedures would have become apparent. ("According to Balancing," I can hear a critic say, "the criminalization of homicide is justified; according to Filtering, the criminalization of homicide is justified. So what's the difference, why abandon Balancing and embrace Filtering?") Alternatively, if I had selected issues of emotionally-charged controversy, it is not likely that the distinctive features of the two decision-procedures could have been separated from their respective outcomes. ("If Filtering says that that ought to be criminalized—to hell with it; I'll stick with Balancing.") In consequence, I began with issues of controversy that aren't too emotionally charged—seat belt and motorcycle helmet laws—and an array of specialized issues in the professional literature. But to say that the second set of issues is "specialized" is *not* to say that they are divorced from ordinary life. In each case, the claim is made that *additional* coercion is justified; if left unchallenged, these would subject even more of the actions of individuals to private forcible interference, or the indignities of arrest, the expense of defense, the consequences of incarceration, and the encumbrances of criminal conviction.

I addressed a number of "Issues in Paternalism" in Chapter Four. While I found it difficult to get very concerned about seatbelt and motorcycle helmet requirements, so long as transgressions are merely "violations" and not crimes, the possibility of criminalization makes these restrictions worth worrying about. Furthermore, the fact that seatbelt and helmet laws are so often used by Legal Paternalists as a "wedge," to make way for additional "paternalistic" legislation, piqued my interest.

Filtering was of particular help here, keeping Legal Paternalism pure—i.e., precluding surreptitious reliance on harm-to-others. The pure Legal Paternalistic argument—that the state is justified in arresting, prosecuting and imprisoning people for beltless driving, solely for their own good, is most implausible. Nor, I concluded, was the state justified in criminalizing the failure to wear a seatbelt on Harm Principle grounds. The state *might* be justified in requiring the purchase of special insurance by those who do not wear seat belts—but alternatively, the state might choose to accommodate the special fears some citizens have about being trapped in a burning or submerged car. On that alternative, the "extra" expenses of preventable injuries would be indemnified by mandatory standard insurance policies, which would include "uninsured beltless motorist" provisions. Some might claim that requiring motorists to carry insurance, and requiring insurance policies to include a provision for uninsured beltless motorists, is an unjustified encroachment on liberty. But even if these requirements are encroachments on liberty, they are so minor as to not merit serious philosophical concern.

The issue of motorcycle helmet laws is more complex and more interesting. The use of a helmet can protect its wearer against some injuries to the head. However, the use of a helmet, by distorting sounds, makes more probable one's involvement in collisions. The choice between these two bundles of risks ought to be left to the individual cyclist. And even if research reveals that the bundle of risks associated with helmetlessness is far greater than the bundle of risks associated with the use of a helmet, this would justify only a special insurance program, not a criminal statute mandating use.

Next I turned attention to a number of individual "paternalistic" proposals. Danny Scoccia claims that private, forcible interference with actions arising from nonautonomous values is permissible. I claim that it is not. Scoccia commits a topographic error; *even if* such actions are themselves not autonomous, nothing immediately follows about forcible interference. The restrictions on this use of force provided by Scoccia center on detailed, personal, counterfactual knowledge of the interferee. If applied strictly, it is doubtful that there will be many—if any—interferences which meet them. If applied loosely, they countenance seriously immoral actions. Additionally, they would provide little guidance to potential interferers (even if well-intentioned)—yet it is the prospect of helpful interference that makes paternalistic interference of practical and philosophical interest.

Joel Feinberg proposes a new state institution for paternalistic interference. He claims that the Voluntariness Tribunal will engage in "temporary" interference only, and this merely to determine the voluntariness of the detainee's action. However, the Pragmatics Filter directs us to investigate the actual operation of the institution—and this investigation reveals much that is morally suspect, or morally objectionable, in this proposal. First, it is most unlikely that state officials will happen upon about-to-be-inflicted self injuries, and be able to intervene in a way that prevents it. Second, the protection of those state officials necessitates that the "processing" of the detainee will include virtually all of the indignities of a criminal arrest. The detainee will have to be continuously incarcerated—perhaps in solitary confinement—prior to the meeting of the Tribunal (lest the self-injury be completed). If the detainee's action is judged "not voluntary" by the Tribunal—then what? To merely set the person free would make the entire proceeding a farce; if the Tribunal is correct (the person is not acting voluntarily), the injury to self will be inflicted. Thus the institution will have prevented *no* evil. If the institution is to prevent evil, the incarceration will have to continue—indefinitely. Can this *really* be in the interests of the detainee? And is this a justifiable allocation of scarce social resources? The motivation behind the Voluntariness Tribunal is admirable; no one wants to see another damaged as a consequence of an action that is not really that person's "choice." But an operating Voluntariness Tribunal would pose a serious threat to individual rights.

Derek Parfit believes it morally wrong for a present self to harm one's own future self; it would be wrong to do to one's future self anything that it would be wrong for one's present self to do to another present self. I guess I agree. But I don't agree that this is a new justification for "paternalism." Given the failure of Feinberg's Voluntariness Tribunal—which would attempt to prevent present selves from harming very near future selves—however could the state (or anyone else) successfully intervene on behalf of distant future selves? Once again, we find a topographic error; once again, the Pragmatics Filter directs our attention to the vital issues. And once again, I am far more worried about my present self being injured by other present selves; protection of present selves from other present selves is the wiser resource allocation.

I am concerned about "soft paternalism" generally, because it induces people to commit topographic errors. Having granted that self-destructive, nonvoluntary actions do not fall within an individual's Sphere of Individual Liberty, soft paternalists are inclined to find that forcible interference is justified. But it isn't—at least, it isn't unless one morally assesses the proposed interference *itself*. That an individual's action is essentially nonvoluntary does not give others permission to interfere in any way whatever—or perhaps in any way at all.

In Chapter Five, I considered some "Oblique Attempts to Expand the Criminalizing Authority of the State." I call them "oblique," because they are not arguments that Liberals ought to accept Principles of State Authority in addition to the Harm and Offense Principles; they are arguments of a different *sort*. Nonetheless, they do attempt to justify additional criminalization, or private coercion.

Feinberg is right in claiming that, in a military garrison under siege, an action that otherwise would be self-regarding—"withdrawing"—becomes other-regarding. Feinberg is wrong in claiming that, in a garrison situation, withdrawing may be "emphatically prohibited." Even though other-regarding, even though harmful to others, a prohibition is not morally justified if it would be wholly pointless, completely ineffective. To prohibit withdrawing is to require specific performance. Feinberg has not discussed, and I have not discovered, any way to *compel* non-withdrawal, to compel effective defense of the garrison.

The extension of the argument of society generally is even more dubious. Society is unlike a garrison in crucial respects: it is *larger* (so that more withdrawals can be accommodated without peril), and it is of significant *duration* (not a temporary crisis calling for temporary sacrifices). Most importantly, it differs in *function*: "non-withdrawal" is economic productivity. Declaring that a society is in a garrison situation would permit the state to compel people to be economically productive. Although the range of actions that could be economically productive is far wider than the range of actions that could be the effective defense of a garrison, the proposal *still* amounts to requiring specific performance. Feinberg has not shown that this could be morally achieved, or even achieved at all. Society's becoming a garrison situation may turn self-regarding actions into other-regarding actions, but that is not sufficient to justify coercion. To think that it is, is to commit a topographic error.

Richard J. Arneson and Cass R. Sunstein argue that a community may morally use the criminal law to foreclose its own options, i.e., to keep its first-order preferences (preferences about actions) consistent with its second-order preferences (preferences about preferences). But we must not be fooled by the singular here; unless the community is unanimous in its desire to foreclose options, it is not accurate to claim that "the community binds itself." Nor is it accurate to claim that this is a political analogue of Ulysses and the Sirens. If there is even a single dissenter—as unquestionably there would be, in any modern nation-state—then this is really a case of the political majority binding (coercing) the political minority. Undeniably, "majority rules" has intuitive appeal. But it gets that appeal from clashes of first order preferences, e.g. which candidate will be sent to Congress. It does not get its appeal from clashes between the majority's second-order preferences and the minority's first-order preferences. In such cases, the majority is *already* free to decline, free to not elect a particular action. The point of the proposed statute is to bolster that decision; the effect of the statute is to criminalize the action for everyone in society—including those in the minority who wish to be free to choose it. Philosophical scrutiny reveals that this proposed justification of criminal sanctions is not really "community self-paternalism" at all, but rather the coercion of the minority by the majority. And when offered *as* a justification, all that can be said on its behalf is that the statutes it countenances would help bolster the weak wills of those in the majority. This is a clear case of the individuals in the minority being treated as means merely, and not as ends in themselves. Exacerbating this evil: the minority too would suffer the negative "side effects" of the new statutes, and would also be contributing resources, through taxation, for the enforcement of these statutes against themselves. This is morally unacceptable.

I have no objection to an individual's privately contracting with other people to wield force in order to keep that individual's first-order preferences consistent with second-order preferences. Nor do I have any objections to groups of individuals doing this—provided that all are members of the group voluntarily. Given that the members are unanimous in their desire for coercion, this is in fact "community self-paternalism." But such an arrangement is *far* from the enacting and enforcing of a criminal statute. Arneson and Sunstein have failed to create, in this oblique argument, a new justification for criminalization; they have failed to justify coercion.

Arneson has urged the rejection of Feinberg's Liberalism in favor of a more "utilitarian liberalism." He claims that "utilitarian liberalism" is in-practice different from, and also superior to, Feinberg's Liberalism—and that bestiality shows it so. He argues that bestiality is justifiably criminalized, and that its criminalization is justified under utilitarian liberalism, but not under Feinberg's.

I rise to Feinberg's defense. Arneson's account of bestiality is not believable. Worse, it hides the "assumption of compliance." If the practice of bestiality really were as Arneson describes, then the enactment of a prohibitory statute would indeed end the practice, and produce utility: the joy of knowing that one lives in a bestiality-free society. An accurate understanding of the practice of bestiality discharges the assumption of compliance; enactment alone would not end the practice. The statute would have to be *enforced.* An inquiry into the difficulties of enforcement—directed by the Pragmatics Filter—reveals significant disutility. Thus "utilitarian liberalism" would *not* justify the criminalization of bestiality. Thus Arneson has not shown an in-practice difference between Feinberg's liberalism and his species of liberalism—and thus cannot have shown the superiority of the latter. He has failed to justify the (additional) coercion of "utilitarian liberalism."

As I showed in Chapter Six, the public policy debate about "drugs" is a mess. Thinking is misdirected by the inapt military metaphor. The entire discussion is mystified, and is permeated with hypocrisy. False consciousness abounds.

The methodology of Filtering brings structure to the controversy. By distinguishing the issues of the Principles Filter from those of the Pragmatics Filter, it is more difficult to do that which has been done by so many: confusing the characteristics of the chemical with the consequences of criminalization. It became clear that, in case after case, oft-cited "drug-related" evils are caused by criminalization, and not by use itself.

At the Principles Filter, I argued the plausibility of the claim that competent adults have a right to the recreational use of "drugs." But even if they don't, the existing legal disparity between nicotine and marijuana, between alcohol and cocaine, cannot be justified. And this is true even if one accepts Legal Paternalism.

Reflections at the Presumptions Filter gave rise to hope for non-statute measures. The investigation of the consequences of criminalization, the issues of the Pragmatics Filter, revealed just how heavy a burden must be borne by "drug" prohibitionists—and the implausibility of the claim that they can indeed bear it. It is time—indeed, long past time—to begin various trial programs of decriminalization. The argument that decriminalization is racist is misguided. It is African Americans who bear the brunt of the evil consequences of criminalization; it is African Americans who can benefit most by a change in policy.

I began this essay by discussing the seriousness of criminalization, dramatizing the disruptiveness of arrest, prosecution, and incarceration, and the difficulties of life as an ex-con. Before doing this to fellow citizens, I argued, we must be very sure of ourselves. It is by Filtering actions that are, or might be made criminal offenses, that we will best be able to meet that most serious moral obligation.

INDEX

Arneson, Richard, on bestiality, 215-226; community self-paternalism, 196-214

Assumption of compliance, 18, 20, 87, 96, 101, 105, 117, 129, 171, 175-6, 181, 215, 216, 224, 225, 302, 309; defined, 8-11

Balancing, 7, 11, 15, 16, 25, 27, 29, 30, 32-38, 40, 61, 62, 63, 65, 67, 80-93, 96, 97, 99, 101, 110, 112-114, 117-119, 125-127, 140, 160, 173, 189, 227, 233, 251, 286, 287, 302, 303, 304, 305; as a decision-procedure, Ch. One 29-38; inferior to Filtering, 80-97

Bennett, William, 252, 261

Bestiality, 19, 20, 51, 105, 106, 215-225, 227, 309

Coleridge, Samuel Taylor, 246, 247, 248

Consequences of incarceration, 2, 4, 11, 36, 69, 80, 99, 102, 117, 118, 139, 140, 166, 172, 208, 227, 231, 265, 288, 301, 305

Crime tariff, 11, 70, 72-74, 78, 194, 210, 253-61, 266, 267, 274, 275, 278, 279, 282, 285, 295, 297, 298, 304

De Quincy, Thomas, 246

Drugs, 20, 27, 70, 73, 94, 102, 106, 179, 193, 194, 210, 227-310

Dworkin, Gerald, 20, 109, 114, 142, 203; on motorcycle helmet laws, 121-127

Encumbrances of criminal conviction, 5-6, 11, 36, 69, 80, 99, 102, 117, 139, 140, 172, 208, 227, 231, 288, 303-05

Expense of defense, 2, 4, 6, 11, 36, 69, 80, 99, 102, 117, 118, 139, 172, 208, 227, 231, 265, 288, 305

Feinberg, Joel, 6, 18-20, 31, 35, 49, 50, 58, 63, 77, 101, 103, 104, 111, 120, 142, 150, 155, 179, 183, 197, 203, 215, 283, 304, 306; regarding bestiality, 215-226; regarding "garrison situations, 184-195; regarding motorcycle helmet laws, 120-138; regarding "soft paternalism", 179-182; regarding "Voluntariness Tribunal", 155-174

Filtering, 16-21, 25-27, 29, 33, 38, 101-103, 106, 110, 113, 114, 117, 119, 125, 126, 140, 149, 158, 160, 173, 174, 189, 190, 195, 227, 228, 232, 233, 243, 251, 268, 287, 289, 290, 303, 304, 305, 310; as a decision-procedure, Ch. Three,

63-99; superior to Balancing, 80-97

Husak, Douglas, 24, 242, 271, 290

Indignities of arrest, 1-3, 6, 11, 36, 69, 80, 99, 102, 117, 118, 139, 140, 164, 172, 208, 227, 231, 265, 288, 301, 305

Mill, John Stuart, 12, 15, 23, 24, 31, 39, 104, 133, 145, 152, 155, 156, 157, 159, 173, 179, 181, 221, 243, 244, 249, 252, 274, 275, 279, 302; topography of actions, 34-49

Motorcycle helmet laws, 20, 110, 114, 120-140, 227, 305, 306

Nadelmann, Ethan A., 236, 239, 276, 297

Ostrowski, James, 259, 263, 270, 278, 283, 290

Packer, Herbert, 1, 11, 71, 73, 76, 248, 253

Parfit, Derek, 18, 20, 104, 171, 175, 307; on paternalism, 175-78

Ray, John, 294, 295, 296, 299

Richards, David A. J., 248, 267, 280

Scoccia, Danny, 17, 20, 103, 142-54, 306

Seat belt laws, 107-120, 139-141

Sunstein, Cass R., 19, 21, 103, 105, 196-214, 308

Topographic error, 16-18, 53-55, 61, 86, 104, 105, 122, 152, 181, 184, 188, 189, 303, 306, 307, 308; and "Balancing", 83-86; defined, 53-55

Topography of actions, 39-62

Two scoops solution, 90-93, 96, 112, 119, 140, 286, 287

Will, George, 297, 299

Wilson, James Q., 234, 235, 236, 239, 240

Law and Philosophy Library

1. E. Bulygin, J.-L. Gardies and I. Niiniluoto (eds.): *Man, Law and Modern Forms of Life.* With an Introduction by M.D. Bayles. 1985 ISBN 90-277-1869-5
2. W. Sadurski: *Giving Desert Its Due.* Social Justice and Legal Theory. 1985 ISBN 90-277-1941-1
3. N. MacCormick and O. Weinberger: *An Institutional Theory of Law.* New Approaches to Legal Positivism. 1986 ISBN 90-277-2079-7
4. A. Aarnio: *The Rational as Reasonable.* A Treatise on Legal Justification. 1987 ISBN 90-277-2276-5
5. M.D. Bayles: *Principles of Law.* A Normative Analysis. 1987 ISBN 90-277-2412-1; Pb: 90-277-2413-X
6. A. Soeteman: *Logic in Law.* Remarks on Logic and Rationality in Normative Reasoning, Especially in Law. 1989 ISBN 0-7923-0042-4
7. C.T. Sistare: *Responsibility and Criminal Liability.* 1989 ISBN 0-7923-0396-2
8. A. Peczenik: *On Law and Reason.* 1989 ISBN 0-7923-0444-6
9. W. Sadurski: *Moral Pluralism and Legal Neutrality.* 1990 ISBN 0-7923-0565-5
10. M.D. Bayles: *Procedural Justice.* Allocating to Individuals. 1990 ISBN 0-7923-0567-1
11. P. Nerhot (ed.): *Law, Interpretation and Reality.* Essays in Epistemology, Hermeneutics and Jurisprudence. 1990 ISBN 0-7923-0593-0
12. A.W. Norrie: *Law, Ideology and Punishment.* Retrieval and Critique of the Liberal Ideal of Criminal Justice. 1991 ISBN 0-7923-1013-6
13. P. Nerhot (ed.): *Legal Knowledge and Analogy.* Fragments of Legal Epistemology, Hermeneutics and Linguistics. 1991 ISBN 0-7923-1065-9
14. O. Weinberger: *Law, Institution and Legal Politics.* Fundamental Problems of Legal Theory and Social Philosophy. 1991 ISBN 0-7923-1143-4
15. J. Wróblewski: *The Judicial Application of Law.* Edited by Z. Bańkowski and N. MacCormick. 1992 ISBN 0-7923-1569-3
16. T. Wilhelmsson: *Critical Studies in Private Law.* A Treatise on Need-Rational Principles in Modern Law. 1992 ISBN 0-7923-1659-2
17. M.D. Bayles: *Hart's Legal Philosophy.* An Examination. 1992 ISBN 0-7923-1981-8

KLUWER ACADEMIC PUBLISHERS – DORDRECHT / BOSTON / LONDON

Law and Philosophy Library

18. D.W.P. Ruiter: *Institutional Legal Facts.* Legal Powers and their Effects. 1993 ISBN 0-7923-2441-2
19. J. Schonsheck: *On Criminalization.* An Essay in the Philosophy of the Criminal Law. 1994 ISBN 0-7923-2663-6

KLUWER ACADEMIC PUBLISHERS – DORDRECHT / BOSTON / LONDON

MIX
Papier aus verantwortungsvollen Quellen
Paper from responsible sources
FSC® C105338

If you have any concerns about our products,
you can contact us on
ProductSafety@springernature.com

In case Publisher is established outside the EU,
the EU authorized representative is:
Springer Nature Customer Service Center GmbH
Europaplatz 3, 69115 Heidelberg, Germany

Printed by Libri Plureos GmbH
in Hamburg, Germany